T4-ALI-959

The Preservation and Transmission of Anglo-Saxon Culture

The Preservation and Transmission of Anglo-Saxon Culture

Selected Papers
from the 1991 Meeting of
the International Society of Anglo-Saxonists

Edited by
Paul E. Szarmach
and
Joel T. Rosenthal

Studies in Medieval Culture XL
Medieval Institute Publications

WESTERN MICHIGAN UNIVERSITY

Kalamazoo, Michigan, USA—1997

Library of Congress Cataloging-in-Publication Data

The preservation and transmission of Anglo-Saxon culture: selected papers from the 1991 Meeting of the International Society of Anglo-Saxonists / edited by Paul E. Szarmach and Joel T. Rosenthal.
p. cm. -- (Studies in medieval culture ; 40)
Includes bibliographical references and index.
ISBN 1-879288-90-7 (casebound : alk. paper). -- ISBN 1-879288-91-5 (softbound : alk. paper)
1. Civilization, Anglo-Saxon--Historiography--Congresses. 2. Great Britain--History--Anglo-Saxon period, 449-1066--Historiography--Congresses. 3. Great Britain--Antiquities--Collection and preservation--Congresses. 4. English literature--Old English, ca. 450-1100--Criticism, Textual--Congresses. 5. Learning and scholarship--History--Medieval, 500-1500--Congresses. 6. Manuscripts, Medieval--England--Congresses. 7. Anglo Saxons--Historiography--Congresses. 8. Manuscripts, English (Old)--Congresses. 9. Transmission of texts--Congresses. I. Szarmach, Paul E. II. Rosenthal, Joel Thomas, 1934- . III. International Society of Anglo-Saxonists. Meeting (5th : 1991 : State University of New York at Stony Brook) IV. Series.
IN PROCESS
942.01--dc21 97-34096
CIP

Printed in the United States of America

Cover Design by Linda K. Judy

CONTENTS

Preface

The papers in this collection represent the majority of those delivered on the conference theme of the Fifth Meeting of the International Society of Anglo-Saxonists, 22–26 July 1991, at the State University of New York (SUNY) Stony Brook. These papers look at the general theme "The Preservation and Transmission of Anglo-Saxon Culture," with special reference to North America. This theme seemed appropriate, for the 1991 conference was the first ISAS Conference held in the United States, jointly sponsored by the sister campuses of SUNY at Binghamton and at Stony Brook. Coming to the United States entailed some real differences for the ISAS conference, with the "spirit of place" as, perhaps, the most significant. Unlike previous venues (and others to come), the conference could not offer its participants an ambiance full of Anglo-Saxon antiquities, or even of medieval ones, for that matter. Rather, the location reflected the story of how Anglo-Saxon Studies are conducted in the United States (and in this case in a newish public university, at that). There was a heavy emphasis—perhaps almost an overbalance—on literature and related topics. This theme bespeaks the relative lack of other-than-literary sources and of easy access to Anglo-Saxon material culture that is typical of "new world" universities and the relative ease with which we can turn to the literary texts.

Because we knew of these problems and special constraints, we worried that the response to the call for papers would compound the chances of the overbalance. Therefore a special effort was made in arranging the program to incorporate papers outside of literature, along with others that would help expand the chosen theme into other disciplines and towards issues beyond "internal" literary criticism. The conference plan, capitalizing on the renewed interest in the foundations of historical disciplines, was to accommodate both established and younger scholars; they would be invited to describe and assess the various sub-fields and the present and likely future state of the question. In addition they would be encouraged to comment on new directions and to add their own views, as based on new data and on new disciplinary and methodological insights.

The nature of the conference plan and theme was in some measure a response to current disciplinary concerns. Since the late 1970's and throughout the 1980's the academic pursuit of the humanities has been called upon to face numerous challenges from within as well as without the academy. The challenges from without, e.g., questions of "relevance" lingering from the 1960's and fundamental American cultural concerns regarding the usefulness of education in the historical disciplines, are significant, general issues that may attach themselves to any discipline and are challenges worth addressing. The challenges from within the academy are certainly no less pressing, and one may make the case that these challenges are even more fundamental because they go to the root of the enterprise itself by questioning assumptions and hidden values as well as goals and directions, ends and means. In the last half generation such theoretical concerns as the application of Marxist criticism to the humanities, post-structural analysis, gender-based re-evaluation of texts and of accepted readings of texts, and New Historicism, among others, have appeared. While some disciplines within the academy are engaged in a full debate on these and similar theoretical concerns, others have only recently begun to hear these new voices.

The study of Anglo-Saxon England is a relative late-comer to such debates and their call for re-evaluation and reassessment. However, in the last decade the Annual Bibliography in the *Old English Newsletter* has shown the importance—marked by both the quantity and quality of new work—of the rising interest in the new agenda. A quick review of scholarship that argues for the use of critical theory in Old English might perhaps begin its search for work in the French mode with Colin Chase's 1986 discussion of intertextuality and source work (presented at Kalamazoo in 1983), which he turned to a statement on editing scribal (not authorial) texts. Another 1986 publication, *Style* 20.2, featured two essays in Anglo-Saxon Studies, one by Allen J. Frantzen and Charles L. Venegoni and the other by Martin Irvine, on the volume's theme, *Medieval Semiotics*. Women's Studies and Anglo-Saxon Studies also came together in the 1980's, as in books by Christine Fell et al. (1984), Helen Damico (1984), and Jane Chance (1986). This kind of work has been extremely stimulating, and as the decade turned more works were forthcoming; Helen Damico and Alexandra Hennessey Olson, for example, brought forth a collection of "readings" on women in Anglo-Saxon literature by various hands (1990). It is in this collection and in some recent articles that one can see traditional scholarly interests in women in Old English life and literature becoming focused on issues of gender and power *per se*. Anglo-Saxon studies have always had a special relationship to the questions of orality and literacy, and here too we are witnessing a sea change. Traditional concerns of style, deriving their views ultimately from Magoun, are becoming broadened to consider culture, literacy, and power. Long-accepted assumptions in the editing of texts are being questioned and revisited, as in the work of Katherine O'Brien O'Keeffe and A. N. Doane. This very selective and allusive bibliography that we offer here treats only three areas and does not survey the many papers, in numerous sub-fields, that have been offered recently at different conferences, where non-traditional views are being presented, particularly by younger scholars.

In addition to the changing currents of literary analysis and theories of texts and textual criticisms, the field of Anglo-Saxon Studies faces several problems unique to it. These reflect the effects of "secular currents" in the world of education and culture rather than of academic fashion within the ranks. If one begins at the beginning, so to speak, the first problem the field must face concerns the set of language barriers that looms not only for beginners but, at increasing levels of complexity, for advanced researchers. Old English and Anglo-Latin are no longer easy to acquire in many graduate programs, not to mention the helpful collateral Celtic and Norse languages. This problem is not a teaching problem solely; it becomes a research problem when historians move toward a reliance on translations of the *Anglo-Saxon Chronicle*, literary scholars upon ponies to help them work through the Latin sources. At the 1989 meeting of the Medieval Academy of America, John Leyerle, former Director of the Centre for Mediaeval Studies at Toronto, suggested that in another decade Old (and Middle) English might cease to be known as they had been, becoming available perhaps at only a very select number of advanced programs. A subject restrained and informed by the translations of a previous generation will hardly prove to be a flourishing one. Do the remedies lie in the direction of intensive post-doctoral summer seminars in the dead, and now disappearing, languages, perhaps focused on specific problems in cultural history? Of course, this may be an overly gloomy prognosis; we all have moments when we feel beleaguered, and the narratives below that cover the creation of Anglo-Saxon Studies in North America show that much struggle, much dedication, was always needed to give the field legitimacy and security. From another viewpoint, we can too easily take earlier advances for granted and accept their fruits as a given.

As arguably the oldest of the sub-fields of Medieval Studies, given its origins in the religious controversies of the sixteenth century, Anglo-Saxon Studies carries the burden of a lost past entwined in its current scholarship. The removal of layers of previous knowledge and interpretation—the advice and prescription being suggested by some working in contemporary theory and criticism—requires a scholarly archaeology that is sensitive to the Victorian rage for things Teutonic, to Romanticism and primitivism, to seventeenth-century antiquarianism, to Stuart claims for absolute monarchy, and to the Protestant Reformation, among other pitfalls and turns in the road. And this assumes that twentieth-century intellectual biases of all stripes can be identified and de-layered before we go on to our older traditions or burdens. Nor should we shrink from asking, in the face of current sensitivity to epistemology, whether the older agendas of scholarship are necessarily or invariably less valid or less significant.

Is it the case that all the "interesting" texts have been edited and translated, the manuscript illustrations described, the stone crosses numbered and catalogued, thereby rendering all further "neo-positivist" research repetitive and mechanical? Are only ever more ingenious interpretations of the same information the likely future of the field? Or is there scholarly merit in establishing the as yet unestablished corpus of Anglo-Latin literature, in cataloguing "Books Written or Owned to 1100," and in studying the Anglo-Saxon knowledge of Greek? We ask what we hope are provocative or perhaps merely traditional questions, though we have no confidence regarding which answers, if any, will eventually achieve scholarly consensus.

Reflecting in a unique way the intersection of newer theories and older agendas is the matter of interdisciplinary study. Anglo-Saxon Studies has had a tradition that anyone seeking to do research in the field must come equipped with the methodologies and knowledge of several sub-fields well under control. The effective beginnings of this perspective may lie in H. M. Chadwick's teaching, where one may find the idea of "know the culture, know the literature" espoused, though there are likely to be many other sources contributing to this view. It is a view that assumes a concrete reality when the International Society of Anglo-Saxonists meets in its accustomed unitary sessions—by conscious program decision—rather than in concurrent interest sessions. This policy was adopted, after due deliberation, so as to require all the Anglo-Saxonists present to be interested (or at least to profess an interest) in all fields, be they unitary sessions on sigillography, sound shifts, or marginalia. Today, practically speaking, few scholars can be truly interdisciplinary in their research, though many may follow and even teach and research an adjacent area. Can the newer ways of looking at knowledge assist an interdisciplinary orientation that is or might become more practically effective than that proceeding from the older agendas? Is sign theory and its special language, as one example, a potentially mediating perspective that will link the disciplines? To what useful extent can we expect North American scholars to bring archaeology to bear on literature, when North American Anglo-Saxon archaeologists are so few in number and, relative to literature, when archaeology is steadily moving towards the technical and scientific? In short, is *interdisciplinary* a word in search of a context in the 1990's, as it seems to have been in Anglo-Saxon Studies in the 1980's?

In these conflicts between old and new agendas, traditional models and theoretical advances, and promising but possibly ill-adapted technologies, some voices suggest that Medieval Studies (not to mention Anglo-Saxon Studies) must build bridges to the contemporary scene lest historical studies become marginal and peripheral, if not merely an amateurish antiquarianism. It is not always clear whether these voices are themselves committed to the value of the historical enterprise and can see it as filling a role other than a secondary one in humanistic studies. Still, as the best scholarship has always taught, mere defensiveness in the face of the new and explicitly challenging is less convincing than a constructive engagement with it. Anglo-Saxon Studies has much to offer contemporary humanities. Those reading Walter Ong's celebrated *Orality and Literacy* with care realize that a good part of his seminal argument comes from the research in oral literature and oral culture that such Anglo-Saxonists as Magoun, Creed, Foley, and others have done. Anglo-Saxon Studies likewise can contribute insights into the fast-moving field of women's studies and feminist criticism. Damico, Fell, and Chance, among others, have suggested that Anglo-Saxon women had a measure of freedom and independence that their later medieval counterparts did not—intriguing if not-uncontested views about sex, gender, and the whole spectrum of social relations and social change. Locating the moment, the causes, and the weight of negative epiphany, after the Anglo-Saxon moment, is in itself a reverse challenge to the reigning notion of the Dark Ages. Anglo-Saxon Studies, when guided by insights like these, can thus have a positive effect when turned towards the arena of contemporary ideas. The studies may support or adjust or even refute contemporary attitudes, especially those that casually read back into the past the concerns of the present.

Anglo-Saxon Studies, like the humanities generally, is at a cross-roads. Will the future be the best of times or the worst of times? The basic twin dynamic of the field has been its dual relationship to cultural studies at large: it has followed the larger subject in many things, while in other respects it has been insular and insulated, segregated from the literary bibliography because "literature" never occurred before Chaucer and from the canonical curriculum because of its special demands. Its scholars need to engage the other disciplines as equals, neither as appellants nor as inferiors, nor as the privileged trail blazers without whom all others are lost in the dark wood of error. Valid scholarship, historical and traditional, can be merged with new perspectives to give the common subject the fullest meaning that its cultural artifacts and our interpretive skills and methods permit.

The papers assembled for this collection take up special, focused issues within the originally broad call for papers. Fred C. Robinson's introduction is an exception, for it is an "op-ed" piece, deliberately printed to catch the lively and informal after-banquet talk he gave at the conference. Robinson intended his comments as a general overview of the current state of the art, especially with reference to its status and prospects in North American academia. The other essays on this conference theme of transmission and preservation naturally group themselves under several rubrics: Historiography, Medieval Reception, Present State and Future Directions in Art and Archaeology, Literary Approaches, and Manuscript Studies. The first two sections could even be retitled "some versions of reception," because of their explication of how things Anglo-Saxon made their way to America, where just about the last receptors were to be found, and through medieval Europe, where the first receptors were encountered; the second two rubrics could arguably be retitled "what's new?" in three major fields. The last section, perhaps the most obvious answer by philologists to the call for papers, shows that the art of manuscript study is alive and well at the end of the second millennium of this era.

* * *

Both co-ordinator-editors would like to thank some of the many individuals who assisted with the conference and the collection. The Stony Brook Office of Conferences was the *sine qua non*: Ann Forkin, Ann Brody, Arlene Skala, Lucy Scuria, and Arlene Hinkson. Andy Policano, Dean of Social and Behavioral Sciences, was extremely generous, and we also received valuable support from Eli Seifman of the Social Science Interdisciplinary Program. The Department of History shared space and facilities, and the Department Staff lent a hand in numerous ways. The Stony Brook Foundation was a helpful and sympathetic banker, and various officers of the academic administration went out of their way to welcome the Conference. At Binghamton, Mrs. Ann DiStefano, the CEMERS Secretary, did much of the day-to-day administration of the conference planning and mailing, ably assisted by Ms. Sandra Sammartano. At Western Michigan University this book project came to completion thanks to the staff of Medieval Institute Publications, most notably Candace Porath, Deborah A. Oosterhouse, and Kevin Glick. They approached their work with their usual efficiency and good humor. Ms. Dana-Linn Whiteside and Ms. Helene Scheck, doctoral students at Binghamton with special interests in Old English studies, did much of the word-processing and book manuscript sub-editing and styling. The co-editors owe special thanks to the editors of *Anglo-Saxon England*, messrs. Michael Lapidge, Simon D. Keynes, and Malcolm Godden, who graciously waived their prerogative of first refusal on papers delivered at ISAS meetings; without their generosity the conference plan could not have been formulated. Of course, without co-operative and patient contributors, some of whom had to accept the notion that "the first shall be last" when computers or the schedule of others held sway, there would have been neither a hare nor a tortoise to offer in print. We owe all of these people our appreciation.

Postscript: a six-year total, elapsed time from conference to publication requires some *apologia*. Since the editors never intended a collection that was a mere record of the proceedings, contributors met the requirement to revise for publication, present the needed apparatus of scholarship, and secure photographs and permissions. Not all delivered papers met these requirements. Submitted to Medieval and Renaissance Texts and Studies (MRTS), which was the monographic publishing arm of CEMERS at SUNY-Binghamton, the volume waited for about a year for the process of external review and acceptance. In February of 1995 the volume was ready to move forward to final revisions and production, but then lost time as Paul E. Szarmach had accepted a new position at Western Michigan University and the future of MRTS and CEMERS at SUNY-Binghamton became very uncertain. After nearly a year in limbo MRTS ceased all operations at Binghamton and re-organized and re-located; happily, Medieval Institute Publications was able in mid-1996 to initiate the production process of this collection.

Paul E. Szarmach
Western Michigan University

Joel T. Rosenthal
State University of New York at Stony Brook

Abbreviations and Short Titles

ASE *Anglo-Saxon England* (cited as a periodical by volume and year)

ASPR *Anglo-Saxon Poetic Records*, in 6 vols., ed. G. P. Krapp and E. V. K. Dobbie (New York, 1931–42; 2nd printing 1958–65)

BHL *Bibliotheca Hagiographica Latina*, 2 vols. (Brussels, 1898–1901)

BL British Library, London (in citations of manuscripts)

BN Bibliothèque Nationale, Paris (in citations of manuscripts)

CCCC Cambridge, Corpus Christi College (in citations of manuscripts)

CCSL *Corpus Christianorum Series Latina*, cited by volume

CSEL *Corpus Scriptorum Ecclesiasticorum Latinorum*, cited by volume

CUL Cambridge, University Library (in citations of manuscripts)

DNB *Dictionary of National Biography*, ed. Leslie Stephen and Sidney Lee, 66 vols. (London, 1885–1901)

EEMF *Early English Manuscripts in Facsimile*

EETS Early English Texts Society (cited in the various series: OS, Original Series; ES, Extra Series; SS, Supplementary Series)

Ker, *Catalogue*
N(eil) R. Ker, *Catalogue of Manuscripts Containing Anglo-Saxon* (Oxford, 1957)

MGH *Monumenta Germaniae Historica*, cited by subseries and volume

OEN *Old English Newsletter*, cited by volume and year

PL *Patrologia Latina*, ed. J. P. Migne (Paris, 1844–91), cited by volume and column

STC A. W. Pollard and G. R. Redgrave, *A Short-Title Catalogue of Books Printed in England, Scotland, & Ireland and of English Books Printed Abroad, 1475–1640*, 2nd ed. by W. A. Jackson, F. S. Ferguson, and Katharine F. Pantzer (London, 1976–91).

Introduction: Transmitting What Is Preserved: How Are We Doing?

Fred C. Robinson

It would seem appropriate at a meeting whose theme is The Preservation and Transmission of Anglo-Saxon Culture that we should pause for a moment to take stock of how well we are transmitting what is preserved today. Transmission of knowledge in our field takes place in two ways: by our classroom teaching and by our publications. First, how are we doing on the publications front? Anyone who heard the reports presented at this conference on the *Fontes*, the *Sources of Anglo-Saxon Literary Culture* project, the Leeds Thesaurus, and the Toronto *Dictionary of Old English* can hardly doubt that ours is one of the most flourishing eras in the long history of Anglo-Saxon Studies. For this is a period not only of signal contributions by individual scholars (such as Bruce Mitchell's masterly work on Old English syntax) but also of large group projects designed as launching pads for explorations that future generations will undertake in the 21st century. Nor are these projects the only grandiose undertakings now under way. I think of Helmut Gneuss's ever-growing handlist of extant manuscripts written or used in England up to the year 1100, of the *Corpus of Anglo-Saxon Stone Sculpture*, of the important monographs growing out of the computerized historical corpus for the study of English at the University of Helsinki, of the major projects of high quality going on in Japan, the most recent being a collaborative variorum edition of *Beowulf*, a trial version of which is scheduled to appear by the end of this century. And let us not forget those indispensable enterprises *The Old English Newsletter* and the *Year's Work in Old English Studies* on which we all rely so heavily. It is hard to imagine what scholarship in Old English would be like if we were not blessed with the ongoing contributions of superb scholars like Paul Szarmach, Joseph Trahern, Carl Berkhout, and their *OEN* and *YWOES* colleagues.

In order to put the progress of our scholarly transmission in an even larger context, let us survey for a moment the state of our field in various parts of the world. Scandinavia is a disappointment, for Sweden, Norway, and Denmark, whose universities once enriched Old English studies generously, have become virtually inactive—with the noble exception of the publishing house of Rosenkilde and Bagger, which remains loyally committed to the invaluable series Early English Manuscripts in Facsimile. So far as academic work is concerned, only Finland stands as a beacon in the northern darkness. Japan is a remarkable example of progress. There are some 126 national, state, and private universities there with departments of English, and since history of the English language is usually central in the English degree, many Japanese are made familiar with Old English. Most remarkable, however, is the high quality of the scholarship being produced there. The new generation of scholars represented by Michiko Ogura, Tadao Kubouchi, and Hiroshi Ogawa is maintaining the high standards set by Yoshio Terasawa, Tamotsu Matsunami, and their peers.

For another striking case, let me turn to Spain. When I was in Spain over two decades ago working with manuscripts in Madrid and the Escorial, I was asked by a Spanish acquaintance what the subject of my research was. I said, "Germanic culture, including Anglo-Saxon." He looked puzzled for a moment and then said, "Culture was invented by the Greeks and disseminated by the Romans; they only got as far as Paris. What do you mean by 'Germanic culture'?" Spain, I decided, was not likely to become a growth area for Anglo-Saxon Studies. But how wrong I was! Virtually non-existent on the Iberian peninsula at the time I was there, Anglo-Saxon Studies are burgeoning there now. Professor Antonio Bravo García informs me that three thousand university students every year are now introduced to Old English in Spanish universities, and he has sent me a list of more than one hundred books and articles published on Old English by Spanish scholars in the past twenty years. Two articles on this phenomenon have now appeared in the indispensable *Medieval English Studies Newsletter* published in Tokyo: Fernando Galván's "Medieval English Studies in Spain," *MESN*, 24 (June 1991), 3–5, and Antonio Bravo García, "Old English Studies in Spain," *MESN*, 25 (December 1991), 4–7.

I shall not belabor matters long familiar, such as the brisk production of Italian Anglo-Saxonists in Rome, Palermo, Naples, and Messina; the fine scholars publishing on Anglo-Saxon in Switzerland, Austria, and the Lowlands; André Crépin in France; and of course a multitude of distinguished Anglo-Saxon scholars in England. The two Anglo-Saxon chairs at Oxford and Cambridge have been filled with dynamic younger scholars who not only do exemplary work themselves but who are gifted impresarios of scholarship as well. Michael Lapidge at Cambridge and our Society's esteemed President for 1992–93, Malcolm Godden, at Oxford give assurance that Anglo-Saxon studies will be cultivated and protected in their universities well into the 21st century, and by protecting Anglo-Saxon studies there they help protect them everywhere.

In Germany the quality of scholarship at places like Munich and Göttingen could hardly be higher, and Freiburg now boasts a dynamic and exciting group of scholars focused on pre-Conquest Britain. One suspects, moreover, that we shall see some expansion of Anglo-Saxon studies in Germany since reunification. With Russian no longer the first foreign language in the former East German universities and their curricula adapting to the West German model, the long twilight of Old English studies in the great German universities to the east may well end. And who knows, even the former Soviet Union may begin playing a significant role in our field now that the scholars there have been liberated from the obligation to prove that every poem, potsherd, and middens-pile from Anglo-Saxon England confirms the tenets of dialectal materialism.

As I describe this golden age of Anglo-Saxon Studies in which we are living, I can imagine that some of my readers might be wondering whether Fred Robinson is not a contemporary version of Pollyanna in Hell. When Anglo-Saxonists describe the state of their profession these days, the terms they commonly use are *crisis*, *decline*, and *threat of extinction*, and desperate remedies for our predicament are being proposed. But allow me to remind you that what I have been surveying is only one of the two means of transmitting what is preserved from Anglo-Saxon England—scholarship. It is when we turn to the teaching of Anglo-Saxon culture and the question of its survival in the curriculum that voices tremble and professors of Old English speak with new anguish. The sources of our anxiety can be seen even in some of the places I have been extolling for their scholarship. At Oxford the current Wharton Professor of English Literature began his tenure of that chair by telling the press that on the one hand he is opposed to the traditional weekly essay required of undergraduates there and on the other he thinks that students specializing in English should be responsible for knowing something about only some of the periods of English rather than the entire subject. Somehow I doubt that his Marxist ideal of Oxford students who know less and write poorly has much room for Anglo-Saxon Studies in it. At about the same time the *Times Literary Supplement*, moreover, chronicled a new assault on compulsory Old English at Oxford, testing the leadership there (which, apparently, has prevailed). In Germany some of the newer universities show troubling signs of the times. An issue of the German report on English studies called *Informationen* (WS 1989–90) indicates that at Bremen there is room in the curriculum for Literary Theory, Black Women's Literature, Radical Feminist Thought, and Noam Chomsky, but none for Old English. The small curriculum at Bayreuth can accommodate courses in Oscar Wilde, recent Nigerian poetry, African novels of the 1980's, and Micro-Sociolinguistics, but not in Old English. And in Japan, where scholarly production is so impressive, the teaching of Old English presents problems, as William Schipper explained at a CARA meeting some time ago.

Anxiety runs high in North America, where many Anglo-Saxonists fear that college curricula crammed increasingly with Theory, Cultural Studies, Canon-Busting, Radical Feminism, Anti-Colonialism, Political Correctness, and New Historicism will soon have no room for Old English, while the pressure on history departments to de-emphasize Western Culture is distinctly ominous. Some of our most concerned and thoughtful colleagues are counselling that teachers of Anglo-Saxon culture should adapt themselves to the fashions that are now so conspicuously in vogue in order to survive. Only a deconstructive, post-contemporary, radical feminist, new historicist, politically correct approach to Old English, they say, has any prospect of saving us from a slow glissade into irrelevance and extinction. Now I should be the last person to turn a differently abled ear to Political Correctness, and coming from Yale I shall hardly be believed if I express a lack of sympathy with voguish theories and chic ideologies. But I believe we should reflect rather carefully on our predicament before we embrace this particular remedy. Let us consider some of the special problems in Anglo-Saxon Studies and various possible remedies for them before we resolve to adapt Anglo-Saxon Studies to the theoretical approaches newly in vogue.

Old English language and literature pose some peculiar disadvantages to those who would teach them. Old Spanish, Old French, and Old High German are closer linguistically to Modern Spanish, Modern French, and Modern German than Old English is to Modern English. Therefore we have to teach harder to get students to learn the language and see the connections. It is also a fact that *The Song of Roland*, *El Cid*, and *The Nibelungenlied* are more familiar to the average educated Frenchman, Spaniard, and German than *Beowulf* is to English-speaking people, especially English-speaking people outside of England. In part this is, I think, because while *Roland* is very much about *dolce France* and *El Cid* about crusading Spain and *The Nibelungenlied*, with its capacious geographic sweep, about German-speaking folk, *Beowulf* is not about the English. As Kemp Malone long ago observed, its patriotism is directed toward that more arcane entity, Mother Germania ("*Beowulf*," *English Studies*, 29 [1948], 161–72). The average Canadian, American, Australian, and South African have powerful myths of origin about their own individual countries, and these distract them from any sense of obligation to connect with the ancient Germanic motherland. For this reason teachers of Anglo-Saxon Studies would be well advised to welcome popularization of *Beowulf*, since this will enhance its visibility in mainstream culture. Translations, children's books, popular novels like Michael Crichton's *Eaters of the Dead*, and even comic books about *Beowulf* are all to the good, and I would myself be delighted to see Kevin Costner put out a movie or video on Beowulf, or perhaps a film called *Dances with Wulfstan*. *Beowulf*'s disadvantaged status as the primary epic of a nation which is nowhere mentioned in that epic requires that we promote the poem among our countrymen wherever we can. It was with this in mind that Randolph Swearer, Marijane Osborn, and I collaborated on a book called *Beowulf: A Likeness*, which Yale University Press published in 1990. The book seeks to use modern photography and the poetic gifts of Raymond Oliver to give people unfamiliar with Old English a sense of the power and beauty and mystery of this work that constitutes the epic beginnings of all English-speaking people.

We need to be on the alert for other means of positioning our subject advantageously in the minds and hearts of people, especially of people earning university degrees. To me what seems most distinctive about students in universities today is their total adaptation to modern technology. Most undergraduates I know are on better terms with their computer work-stations than they are with their parents or their significant others. If we want to win them over to Anglo-Saxon culture, we have to speak their language, and they speak the languages of Apple, IBM, and inexpensive clones thereof. For this reason I believe we all must follow the lead of Patrick Conner, who has done more than anyone else I know to adapt Old English to the medium that seems to have the student body in thrall. His experimental hypertext of *Beowulf* may well be the academic wave of the future. He and Peter

Baker and others who are devising ways of teaching elementary Old English through computers are pioneers of a strategy which gives our subject a competitive edge in dealing with the many new subjects claiming a place in the curriculum today. And Conner's electronic-mail group ANSAXNET is providing a major bonding experience for Anglo-Saxonists of all varieties—historians, Anglo-Latinists, linguists, literary scholars, art historians, and others in that group that Seth Lerer has called "the generous community of professional Anglo-Saxonists." Even an incorrigible technophobe like me has felt compelled to confront a computer screen in order not to be left out of this fascinating international conversation.

And finally we come back to the question of how Anglo-Saxonists should respond to New Historicism, Deconstruction, Political Correctness, and the like. Should we abandon our traditional devotion to analyzing texts and artifacts from the Anglo-Saxon period and adopt the terminologies and preoccupations of current fashions in academia?

In his excellent book *Desire for Origins: New Language, Old English, and Teaching the Tradition* (New Brunswick, 1990), Allen Frantzen has served his profession well by placing the study of Old English in its historical context and also in the context of contemporary theories and ideologies. He has read widely in the publications of contemporary theorists (now that is a *real* penance for Frantzen) and indicated perceptively how their concerns engage with what Anglo-Saxon scholars are doing. More recently Seth Lerer's *Literacy and Power in Anglo-Saxon Literature* (Lincoln, NE, 1991) has also drawn some connections between the interests of the cognoscenti of theory and those of Anglo-Saxon Studies. In a way, the most important audience for these books are the theorists themselves, who need to know that the discoveries with which they have been amazing themselves—such as the contingency of texts, the problematics of natural language, and semantic indeterminacy—are matters with which we have been dealing ever since the beginning of Anglo-Saxon Studies. The difference is that Anglo-Saxonists remain determined to attack the problems posed by textual uncertainty and linguistic slippage and pursue the philological ideal (it was never claimed that it was more than an ideal, or a governing aim) of understanding the texts on their own terms. The modern theorists, or at least the ones I have read and talked with, seem obsessed and immobilized by the uncertainties they have identified and turn away from the texts to make despairing claims that language is incapable of referring to anything outside of itself, that communication is an illusion, or that all is a darkness. Their insistence on the incapacity of language to communicate always reminds me of the comedian Tom Lehrer's observation that if a person genuinely believes that he is incapable of communicating, then the least he can do is Shut Up.

The major weakness of post-modern literary theorists is that they are so absorbed with the *problematics* of literary study that they never get around to dealing with the *problem*, which is the text and how it can best be read. They are so concerned to explore what it is we are doing when we read texts that they forget about the texts themselves. Theories of reading replace reading. Or, as one deconstructionist said to me not so long ago, "We need passages from literary texts only to illustrate our theories." Political Correctness fosters a similar flight from the text. If we spend all our time interrogating ourselves about the social, sexual, political, and other biases that we bring to our reading, we lose sight of reading itself. The greatest strength of Anglo-Saxon and Medieval Studies in general, I believe, is that by and large we have never lost our devotion to the text and to interpreting texts. We have not let theory estrange us from the life's blood of our enterprise, the texts and artifacts at the center of our study. Goethe (in *Studier-zimmer*) spoke for our age when he said, "Grau, teurer Freund, ist alle Theorie, / Und grün des Lebens goldner Baum" ('All theory, dear friend, is colored grey, and green is the golden tree of life'). There is an alarming peril in the wake of post-modern abandonment of texts for theories, a peril from which I think Anglo-Saxonists should distance themselves rather than embrace with the fashionable ideologies. Historians and literary scholars who adopt the current vogues are dangerously self-marginalizing. Literary scholars who keep proclaiming that accurate close-reading is an impossible goal, that texts read us rather than we them, that the idea of a canon of great works is a dirty political game—these critics are deconstructing the very rationale for their having a place in the curriculum. Politically correct historians who say that viewing our history departments as important vehicles for transmitting the core of western culture to future generations is racist and imperialistic are proclaiming to the people and the governments who support them that they have renounced the very principle on which much of that support is based. In short, if we want to survive by jumping on a bandwagon, we do not want to jump on one that is about to self-destruct.

I have resisted the temptation to ridicule the pretentious and sometimes barbarous terminology of much modern theory, but I do think we should remind ourselves that jargonizing familiar truths does not advance knowledge. To say that oral-formulaic poetry is "a form of intertextuality," while it may open up interesting avenues for discussion, does not tell us anything about oral-formulaic poetry that we did not already know. And we should be wary of verbal freakishness masking as originality.

In spite of all I have said, I would be the first to admit that the matters about which post-modern theorists theorize and sometimes jargonize are not unimportant. Skeptical questions about the integrity of texts, alertness to the complexities of just what reading and interpretation are, or even the politically correct scrutiny of ourselves and our cultural predispositions are all important parts of responsible reading so long as they do not pre-empt the act of reading itself. Indeed, these activities are all part of the traditional approach to literary study called philology, the ideal of reading texts on their own terms. I am troubled by some recent misuses of the term *philology* which imply that it is little more than sound changes and textual variants—the mindless accumulation of discrete data toward no particular purpose. I was disturbed to see the *Fontes* and *Sources of Anglo-Saxon Literary Culture* projects cited as examples of philology in this negative, limited sense. Nothing I have read by scholars participating in these source-projects suggests that they see their activity as an end in itself. Certainly Thomas D. Hill's informed and sophisticated exposition of the rationale of the *Sources of Anglo-Saxon Literary Culture* does not suggest this. Rather, the source projects, like the ongoing effort to question our intellectual motives and biases as we interpret the past, are a part of that philological ideal of reading a past culture on its own terms, of defining ourselves against the otherness of people who lived and thought in different times and different circumstances from our own. If we pursue this ideal while simultaneously keeping the texts at the center of our activity, we may find that students who are weary of the exchanges among professors of theory and who long to read the great works from the past will turn to those of us who still read the great works. As an undergraduate complained to me once, "I don't want to read a lot of stuff that professors write; I want to read something really good, something timeless and great." I believe that many of the students want us to transmit to them what has been preserved from the great cultures of the past. Let us continue to do so.

YALE UNIVERSITY

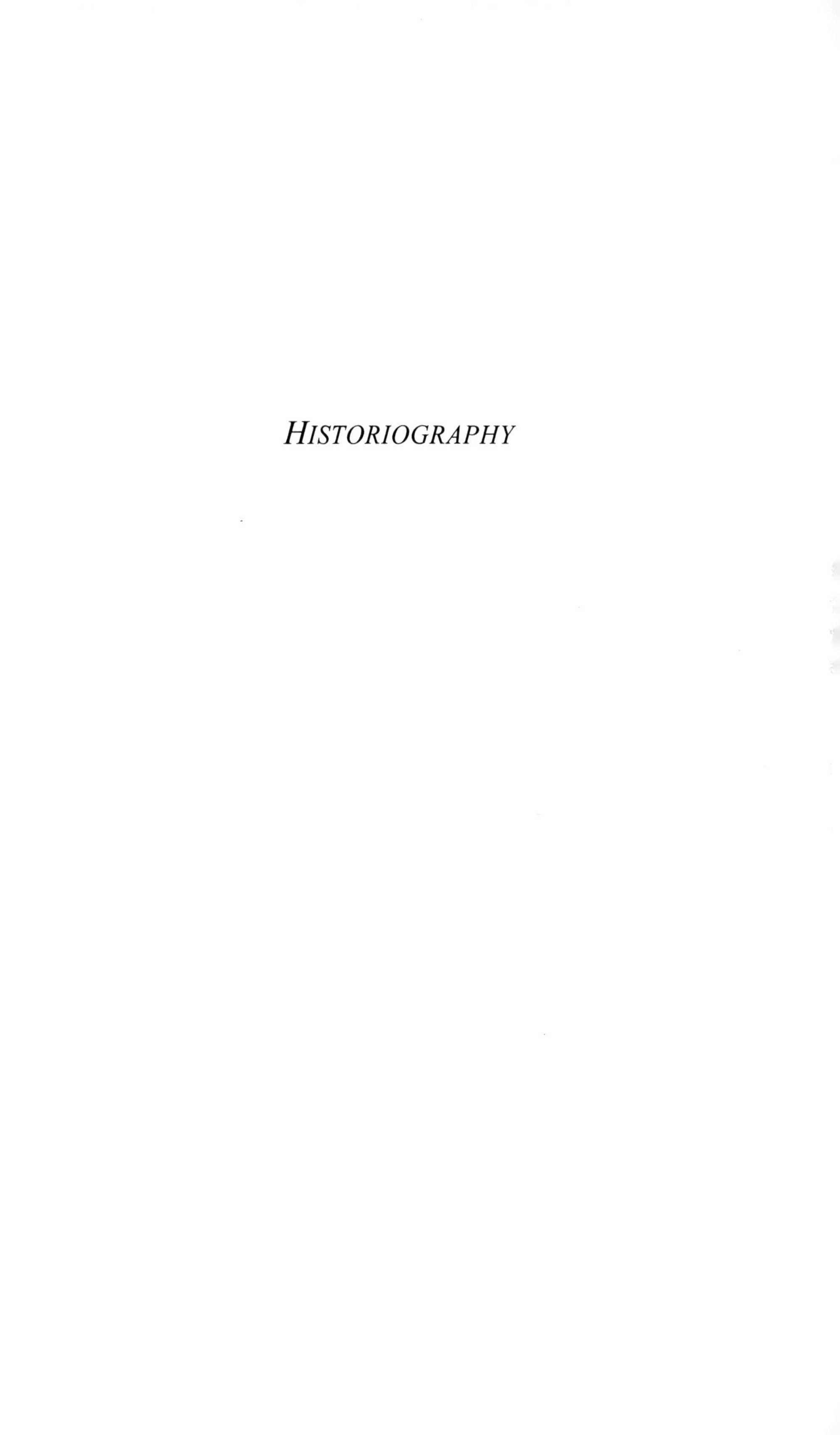

Historiography

Henry Adams and the Anglo-Saxons

Robin Fleming

By my own reckoning there are eight historians working today in this country on Anglo-Saxon England. At the same time, according to the Modern Language Association, there are 869 Anglo-Saxonists laboring in departments of literature and linguistics across the country. This is about 110 specialists of Old English poetry and prose for every reader of chronicles and charters. This is a stunning imbalance, and it is an explanation of these strange statistics that Paul Szarmach assigned to me. Why, he quite reasonably asked, are there so few historians of pre-Conquest England in America when it is clear that the period's literature can command such a large flock of admirers and specialists? Explanations for things that have not happened are not something most historians are willing to attempt, at least in print. But when pondering this very interesting question I did come across a puzzle—part irony, part mystery—that is related to the sad state of pre-Conquest history in America. The irony is this: in the 1870's Anglo-Saxon history flourished in America, and it looked as if it would take root and establish itself permanently here. The mystery is that by 1880 Anglo-Saxon history as a discipline had disappeared. The collapse of pre-Conquest history in the United States is puzzling. The field itself was growing in importance both in England and in Germany during the late nineteenth century. But more important, Anglo-Saxon history was the first historical field in America to be professionalized. Indeed, in the 1870's the first three history doctorates in this country were awarded, and they were awarded for theses written on Anglo-Saxon history. The Ph.D.s—Henry Cabot Lodge, Ernest Young, and

J. Lawrence Laughlin—were students of one of America's greatest and most beloved medievalists, Henry Adams, future author of the classic work *Mont-Saint-Michel and Chartres.* The students and teacher together wrote the first scholarly book published in America on medieval history, *Essays in Anglo-Saxon Law.*[1] They were the first historians in the country to be trained in the methods of the German seminar. They were the first U.S. historians to grasp the centrality of primary research, anthropology, and comparative legal history for historical studies. Yet, in spite of their precocity, the work of Henry Adams and his students in the field represents a dead end. Reasons for the promise-filled birth and strange death of Anglo-Saxon history in America have much to do with Henry Adams himself, and so it is to Henry Adams and the Anglo-Saxons that I would like to turn.

Henry Adams was a young man in a hurry when he graduated from Harvard in 1858. He was the son of Charles Francis Adams, a national figure, important statesman, and perennial presidential hopeful. Both Adams' grandfather and great-grandfather had been presidents of the United States, so it was only a matter of time before Adams' father, too, became President and Henry and his brothers launched political careers of their own. In the meantime, however, Adams had difficulty knowing what to do with himself. Law seemed the obvious answer.[2] His father and his two older brothers were lawyers, and law was considered an appropriate training for men interested in public service.[3] Logical as this course might have been, it was one that Adams found extremely uncongenial. His first attempt was made in Berlin, where he began, the autumn after his graduation, to study civil law. The university lectures, delivered in German and Latin, were incomprehensible to the young American.[4] He dropped out almost as soon as he had started[5] and enrolled instead in a gymnasium, to study Latin and German with the fourteen-year-old sons of "trades-people," "beerhall waiters," and "Jews."[6] Adams' mother was horrified. In January she wrote, "we hate to think of you . . . associating with third class persons. It is not good for you and lowers your standard of refinement and taste and habits."[7] Adams fled the gymnasium after three months and spent his remaining year-and-a-half in Germany reading a little German and law privately, and more regularly engaging in tri-weekly riding and fencing lessons.[8] When he returned home in the fall of 1860 not much the wiser for his two years abroad, Adams tried law once more, but by winter he had moved on. Again in the summer of 1868, after a seven-year stint in London working as his father's private secretary, Adams returned to law. But he found himself spending more time in Newport than diligent study required and soon abandoned the enterprise for a third and final time.[9]

During this same first decade of Adams' adulthood he also attempted to make a name for himself as a journalist. His father had established himself in politics with a series of articles, and his brother Charles was rapidly making a name for himself with his Grub Street journalism.[10] Henry, accordingly, planned to become known in political circles through his writings.[11] Charles suggested that Henry, while living in Germany, write for the newpapers, and he helped his brother place some "letters" from abroad in *The Boston Courier*, a paper considered by Adams' family and circle as an "unprincipled" rag.[12] Later, first in Washington and then in London, Adams began to write anonymous articles for *The New York Times*.[13] In December a signed piece of his appeared in *The Times* on the effects of the cotton shortage, caused by the American Civil War, on the city of Manchester. The piece went unnoticed in America, where it was intended to make a splash. It became infamous, however, in England, not because of its account of the problems arising from the Union's stand on cotton but because of the author's complaints about bad British manners, bad British hospitality, and bad British food. The article, because it had been authored by the son of the American minister to the court of St. James during a period of tense Anglo-American relations, was reprinted in the London papers, and *The Times* ran an editorial ridiculing the piece and its author.[14] The article was deeply embarrassing to Adams senior, and the public humiliation silenced Adams junior for half a decade.

It was not until 1866 that Adams began to write again, and in the next four years he published several articles in the *North American Review* and another in *The Edinburgh Review*. A Republican like all the Adamses, and like them a great hater of the Republican president Grant, much of his writing was leveled against Grant and his administration. One of his pieces against Grant was so nasty that the Democratic National Committee reprinted the article and used it as propaganda for its own presidential campaign. An angry Republican pamphlet was printed in response, leveling scathing criticism against Henry Adams, not as a serious backbencher but as a silly and ineffectual young man—as "a begonia," because "the begonia was remarkable for curious and showy foliage; it was conspicuous; it seemed to have no useful purpose; and it insisted in standing always in the most prominent positions."[15] Once again, Adams had embarrassed himself and his father. In journalism as in law, success eluded Henry Adams.

It is against this background that we should see Henry Adams' appointment as assistant professor of medieval history at Harvard. He was 33 years old. He had some newspaper articles, a few longer journal pieces, and a reputation as one of the "three best dancers in Washington."[16] These were slim accomplishments for a man of his family and unimpressive training for a practitioner of Anglo-Saxon history. In the fall of 1870, Adams informed his friend Charles Milnes Gaskell of his new career as a medievalist:

> The President [of Harvard] College [Charles Eliot] and the Dean [Ephraim Gurney] made a very strong personal appeal to me. . . . I hesitated a week, and then I yielded. Now I am, I believe assistant professor of history at Harvard College. . . . I am to teach mediaeval history, of which, as you are aware, I am utterly and grossly ignorant. . . . I gave the college fair warning of my ignorance, and the answer was that I knew just as much as anyone else in America knew on the subject.[17]

Adams' biographers have taken Henry's own version of events to heart and used this appointment as evidence of President Eliot's and Dean Gurney's foresight and Adams' own early and extraordinary promise.[18]

Eliot and Gurney may, indeed, have liked Adams' handful of articles in the *North American Review*, but there can be no question that the appointment was made because of Henry's powerful family. Certainly Henry had not been offered a job based on any intellectual promise he had shown as an undergraduate: Adams himself confessed on the day of his graduation, "I have not gained high rank; nor often stood below the first half of my class."[19] His lack of bookish distinction was not held against him. Adams' father, at the time of his son's remarkable appointment, was a member of the Harvard Board of Overseers, and indeed he had been offered the presidency of the college two years earlier.[20] Taking advantage of his position, and attempting to find Henry some honorable employment that would keep him out of trouble, Charles Adams set his sights on a professorship for his son. Adams senior was careful in his lobbying. In his personal diary for 18 June 1870 he wrote,

> Mr. W. Gray spoke to me about persuading my son John to speak at Commencement [during a meeting of the Harvard Board of Overseers] and President Eliot about Henry and the Professorship of history. I said I left the sons always to decide such matters for themselves, but I had no objection to mention the matter. . . . For a long period political prejudices contributed a great deal to chill all interest in [Harvard] on my part. But it is getting over this some, and beginning to realize the fact that it has no family on its record that had . . . shown so much proof of its usefulness [as] an institution of education.[21]

The diarist was not being candid with himself, however. Five days earlier, although he failed to mention the fact in his diary, Charles Francis Adams had written his son that during a picnic outing Eliot had discussed with him the difficulties he was having in hiring a professor of history. Charles took advantage of the opportunity and "casually expressed an opinion if *you* inclined to apply yourself to the task of full preparations, the general structure of your mind and education seemed to me as well adapted to the piece as that of any one I knew." Charles then went on to urge his son to take the offer if it were made, as a way of gaining a national reputation.[22] The job, offered earlier to another candidate, was duly offered to Henry and then declined by him; because he was in Europe at the time he could not be bullied by his father into the job.[23] Eliot and Gurney turned, perhaps with some relief, to another, more distinguished candidate, to whom they promptly offered twice the salary.[24] Nonetheless, Adams senior continued to press both Henry's candidacy and a five-year contract for him throughout the summer.[25] When Eliot's choice turned the position down just two weeks before term, the president offered Henry the job once more. Family pressure was intense, and Henry, whose career as a Washington journalist was floundering, accepted the job, but only after the editorship of the *North American Review* was thrown in alongside the professorship.[26]

Adams, lacking accomplishment and training though he may have been, was unprepared for the post, but not scandalously so, since there were no special qualifications demanded of an assistant professor in the late nineteenth century. Eliot himself had taught chemistry at Harvard, although he had no formal training in the subject.[27] History, moreover, was not yet a professional discipline. A full decade after Adams' appointment to Harvard, there were only eleven professors of history in America, and of these only four had published a piece of historical writing.[28] Even Oxford and Cambridge were only just beginning to feel the need to appoint historians to history chairs. The Regius Professor of History at Cambridge, for example, the decade before Adams' appointment, had been the churchman and popular novelist Charles Kingsley, and Oxford's Regius Professor of Ecclesiastical History was the mathematician W. W. Shirley.[29]

So, when Adams began to teach in September of 1870, he knew as little about his subject as any other man teaching in America. He began that autumn to lecture juniors and seniors broadly on medieval history, cribbing his lectures from the English translation of Jules Michelet's *History of France* and lecturing on the sights he knew, such as Wenlock Abbey, the location of his closest friend's country estate.[30] By 1873 he was familiar enough with the material to have acquired a special interest—the legal and political institutions of the Anglo-Saxons. He began to offer both an honors course on medieval institutions to juniors and seniors and a seminar for doctoral students on the same subject. Nonetheless, his real interest in these years was not Anglo-Saxon law but modern politics, which he found much more compelling than the Middle Ages.[31] Indeed, writing during his first semester at Harvard to one of his political acquaintances about his new career, Adams' professorship was the last thing on his mind:

> In the universal departure of our friends from Washington, I have come to the conclusion to follow the leaders, and have sought the protection of this hospitable shop [Harvard] which kindly offered me a place at its counter. . . . In order not to break entirely from old connections I have become editor of the *North American Review*, and propose to make it a regular organ of our opinions.[32]

This, according to Henry Adams in his first semester of teaching, was his new purpose in life, not the instruction of boys on the merits of the Middle Ages. Adams' correspondence during his Harvard years, especially when compared with that of contemporary English medievalists such as J. R. Green, William Stubbs, and E. A. Freeman, is noteworthy for its infrequent inclusion of talk of the college or medieval history. Except for his droll descriptions of Harvard life, written for the amusement of his English friend Charles Milnes Gaskell, the business of the medievalist and the professor rarely intrude into Adams' epistles. Instead, the letters of these years are full of *North American Review* business and politics—two topics that can hardly be separated.

Adams' obsessive interest in American politics led him to believe that the past's only value was its utility for the present. This utilitarianism is clearly exhibited in his ideas about post-graduate education. For Adams, the point was not to train a cadre of specialists who would then devote their lives to the study of medieval history. Instead he considered post-graduate work a fruitful apprenticeship for well-heeled young men who sought a public reputation. When Henry Cabot Lodge first contemplated post-graduate study in Anglo-Saxon history, Adams lectured him that "the question is whether the historico-literary line is practically worth following; not whether it will amuse or improve you. Can you make it pay? either in money, reputation, or any other solid value."[33] Churning down the Nile on his honeymoon, Adams wrote his would-be student that the subject and the speciality to which Lodge devoted himself while earning his doctorate were immaterial:

> It makes little difference what one teaches; the great thing is to train scholars for work. . . . men like you . . . can win a reputation by following up any one line of investigation. . . . It matters very little what line you take provided you can catch the tail of an idea to develop with solid reasoning and thorough knowledge. America or Europe, our own century or prehistoric times, are all alike to the historian. . . .[34]

The fruits of such training, Adams assured Lodge, were "social dignity," a "European reputation," and an excuse to travel abroad.[35] Practically speaking, Adams' pedagogic views meant that none of his students became intellectually wedded to Anglo-Saxon history during their course of studies, nor were they trained in a sufficiently rigorous and narrow manner to sustain themselves very long in the field. As soon as they had finished their dissertations, members of Adams' seminar abandoned Anglo-Saxon England to a man, to write American history, enter politics, teach law, or study economics.

Adams' attitude towards his Harvard professorship was similarly pragmatic. For Adams the position was a step, as he had thought law and journalism would be, towards political acclaim and public office. Indeed his father, trying to persuade him to take the post, had told his son that he himself would have jumped at the job, had it been offered him 30 years earlier: "At that time I had been eleven or twelve years working hard for a little reputation, and it had been granted to me by the public rather grudgingly." Henry's father intimated that had he held a professorship, his merits would have been recognized earlier and more widely.[36] When held in conjunction with the editorship of the *North American Review*, the professorship would allow Henry two different avenues for success, as a political journalist and opinion maker and as a leading man of letters.

From the beginning of his life as an Anglo-Saxonist, Adams spent the bulk of his time forging the *North American Review* into an organ for the Independent (or Liberal Republican) movement, the political faction that his father helped lead. Much of Adams' first autumn at Harvard, despite his protests that he read "nothing this side of . . . 1400," was taken up in correspondence with defectors from Grant's administration and other like-minded Republicans.[37] He attended political meetings in New York and plotted both to organize a convention of Independents and to overthrow Republican incumbents. He also spent a massive amount of time trying to commission articles for the *North American Review* that would criticize Grant and publicize the Independents' platform. He tried very hard, for example, to fashion a tendentious and controversial *Review* for January 1871, his debut issue as editor, but most of those he tried to recruit for it were too busy to accommodate him. The results, according to a review of the issue in *The Nation,* were "rather below than above average."[38] The purpose of most of Adams' editorial energies during his years at Harvard was to assure his father's nomination by the Republican Party as President. His labors, however, were for naught. The convention, so carefully and laboriously planned by Adams, his brother Charles, and their allies, met at the end of his second year at Harvard. There, his father's nomination was defeated, and in the election President Grant won a second term. Wounded but not defeated, Adams continued to publish anti-Grant pieces. His letters as editor show his determination to continue to fight for the Independent cause and his father's presidential candidacy. They also suggest that Adams believed that political power would soon come his way and that political appointments would soon be in his gift. In a letter written in April 1875 he told a fellow Independent:

> Our state commission on taxation has made a bad mull of it and the matter stands worse than it ever did before. I have thought of taking up the subject in The North American. . . . I want an article on the evils and absurdities of our local tax-system. Won't you do it for me? . . . I don't want any general policy to be advocated just yet, because I hope that by making the grievance

> notorious, so much discontent may be generated as to compel a subsequent and more intelligent discussion of reform. Perhaps we can get a new commission and put you on it if the article is a success. At present we are only at the starting point and want to have the Massachusetts tax-system ripped without mercy.[39]

Throughout his career at Harvard, Adams spent huge amounts of time attending political meetings, writing letters, and even negotiating to buy a newspaper in the hopes of transforming it into a weapon for the Independent cause. He had little real passion for the teaching of early medieval institutions. "Between ourselves," he wrote to a Yale professor, "the instruction of boys is mean work. It is distinctly weakening to both parties. I have reduced my pedagogic work to the narrowest dimensions and am working more and more back into active life."[40] To his student Henry Cabot Lodge he wrote, "I yearn, at every instant, to get out of Massachusetts and come into contact with the wider life I always have found so much more to my taste."[41] Despite all his work "to force [his] father on the parties," neither Adams' father nor any other candidate of his liking succeeded in the party. In disgust, Adams decided to break publicly with the Republicans with an article published in the autumn 1876 issue of the *North American Review*, which urged Republicans to vote for the Democratic presidential candidate.[42] The publishers of the staunchly Republican *Review* were horrified, and they printed a disclaimer of the article in the same issue. Adams resigned as editor as soon as the article appeared, but it is likely that he would have been sacked had he not. In the next year, the *Review's* new editor proclaimed that

> the objection had been made, and not without reason, that its pages were addressed to a limited class, and failed to deal with topics of immediate interest to the public at large. That objection it has been sought to remove during the past year. . . . The subjects with which the *Review* will deal will be limited by no programme laid down in advance. . . . The *Review* will not only welcome, but will take active steps to procure, the contributions of representative men of all opinions.[43]

The *Review*, which had struggled financially under Adams' regime and had few subscribers, turned around both financially and editorially under Adams' replacement and became a much more interesting and influential journal.[44] Without the editorship, Adams found little to keep him in Boston—certainly not his work as a professor of medieval history. He finished the year at Harvard, but not his contract, and ended his career as an academic historian and medievalist.

Adams during his time at Harvard used the *Review* not only as a showcase for his family's political opinions but also as a way of cultivating an international reputation for himself as a working historian. He perhaps envisioned himelf as an American von Gneist. Von Gneist was a constitutional historian and author of *Das Englische Verwaltungsrecht*. He was a famous teacher and university lecturer as well. More important, he was one of Prussia's great liberal statesmen and, therefore, exactly the kind of figure Adams so wanted to be.[45] During his years as editor Henry wrote and published some 25 book reviews, many of which concerned the work of English and German medievalists. His reviews of English authors were sharp and critical, those of German authors enthusiastic to the point of incoherence.[46] His chief criticism of English historians was that they, unlike their German contemporaries, cared nothing for theory.[47] He chided Sir Henry Maine, for example, for his insufficient acquaintance with German historiography[48] and his lack of enthusiasm for a scientific approach.[49] William Stubbs, the greatest constitutional historian of them all, according to Adams, had "no theories to advance, no principle to demonstrate," and should have abandoned the writing of history, for which he had no talent, and confined himself instead to the compilation of glossaries.[50] Adams saved the bulk of his venom, however, for E. A. Freeman, who provided an easier target, and who, it appears, had long been an object of scorn among Adams' English circle.[51] Adams criticized Freeman's *Historical Essays* for its dearth of theory and its English chauvinism:

> when there is neither a French Emperor to abuse nor an Anglo-Saxon king or earl to worship, [Freeman is] a hard student and an honest workman. That he is or ever can be a great historian, in any high sense of the word, is

> difficult to believe. . . . He shows only a limited capacity for critical combinations, and he has a true English contempt for novel theories.[52]

Adams was proud of this review and crowed to one of his friends, "glance at my notice of Freeman's Historical Essays in my next number. . . . I think I have caught him out very cleverly."[53] Freeman did not agree and wrote a furious letter to Adams as editor of the *North American Review* (because the review itself had been written anonymously). In his letter Freeman sputtered, "It is said . . . that I 'show only a limited capacity for critical combinations.' I am far from having any clear notion of what 'critical combinations' may mean, but in this imperfect world I certainly never heard of any one who had an unlimited capacity for anything."[54]

In the January 1874 issue of the *North American Review* Adams contributed a signed essay on Freeman's *History of the Norman Conquest*. In this mean-spirited review Adams suggested that Freeman's greatest work was his children's history of England.[55] Freeman is, of course, a notoriously easy target, but his Teutonism and his fervent belief in early democratic institutions, the things that tend to worry modern readers, bothered Adams not at all. Instead he chose to criticize Freeman for his portraits of Alfred the Great and Earl Godwine. Freeman's weakness for Godwine and Alfred were well known, and Adams' own copy of *The History of the Norman Conquest* still contains his markers for the main sections dealing with these two men.[56] Adams' choice of targets, however, was not derived from a careful reading of Freeman's work. Despite the printed thrashing Adams gave the *History*, he had not read it cover-to-cover. A number of pages of Adams' own copy of the work, which relate directly to Alfred or Godwine, are still uncut.[57] Adams trumpeted his attacks on Freeman whenever he could. He bragged of his merciless reviews in a letter to Henry Maine and abused Freeman thoroughly in letters to students and friends,[58] and even criticized him in reviews of other peoples' books. In his review of G. W. Kitchin's *A History of France down to the Year 1453*, for example, Adams complained that Kitchin was "infected with the pedantry which Mr. Freeman has made fashionable."[59]

Adams was also in the habit of abusing Freeman in the margins of his own books. In Volume 5 of the *Norman Conquest*, for example, Adams, in his neat, rounded hand left a trail of insults. "Untrue," "Stuff," and "What *does* the man mean?" pepper the margins of this volume, along with more philosophical complaints such as "how tedious all this petty idealism becomes in the absence of any strong lines of thought."[60] And when Freeman called Stubbs "the greatest scholar of our times," Adams nastily, if unoriginally, versified, "Thus ladling butter from their mutual tubs / Stubbs butters Freeman, Freeman butters Stubbs."[61] Freeman is even abused in Adams' copy of Edmund Burke's *Abridgment of English History*. In the margin next to Burke's silly description of the powers of King Alfred ("In a word, he comprehended in the greatness of his mind the whole of government and all its parts at once, and, what is most difficult to human frailty, was at the same time sublime and minute") Adams wrote quite unfairly, "this is better than Freeman's estimate, which is not saying much."[62]

Adams, despite his criticisms of Stubbs and Freeman, was enormously indebted to both of them. Although Adams thought of himself as an intellectual child of German academics, his whole conception of pre-Conquest England and the questions he posed were the result of his reading of Stubbs. Adams, moreover, co-opted the vocabulary of Stubbs and used it in his own writings and in his seminar. It was Stubbs who formulated the language with which historians of politics and institutions—including Adams—constructed the past. In writing about constitutional history, Stubbs combined organic, Darwinian terms (like *growth*, *development*, *life*) with the mechanical idiom of the Industrial Age (*mechanism*, *process*) and the occult vocabulary of nineteenth-century Anglicanism (*spirit*, *consciousness*). Even today the institutions of Anglo-Saxon England are understood and described through this language of Victorian metaphysics which Stubbs himself cobbled together.[63] Stubbs' metaphors and metonymy are everywhere in Adams' and his students' writing on Anglo-Saxon law and are indications that Stubbs' work, although Adams failed to recognize it, was crucial to the young professor's views on early institutions.

Adams owed less to Freeman, but shared more with him. Like Freeman, Adams used the past to illuminate present political developments.[64] Henry Adams' work on Anglo-Saxon history centered on the hundred and its court. For Adams, the hundred was "among the first, if not the first, political creation of man."[65] This institution was transported by the Saxons, "the purest of Germanic stock," to England. This transplanted institution was the popular assembly of freemen, in whose hand rested political administration and law. These hundreds flourished in England until Edward the Confessor's day because of the innate conservatism of the Anglo-Saxon soul. In France the hundred had been suppressed because Frankish kings, innovative to a man, spread their power through conquest and consolidation. These conquests gave Frankish kings enormous authority but destroyed the native democratic institution of the hundred in the process. English monarchs, however, did not extend their power through conquest but rather through confederation. The result was that Anglo-Saxon England developed a federal system. Primitive though it was, this Anglo-Saxon federation was nonetheless the ancestor of the American system of government advocated and implemented by Adams' own two presidential ancestors. This kind of analysis, although differing in detail from Freeman's reconstruction of the Anglo-Saxon past, was written in very much the same spirit.[66]

Adams' pattern of work also mimicked Freeman's. Despite the legendary pessimism of his later years, he never outgrew that particularly Victorian optimism, shared by Freeman, that all human knowledge could be related and that science could be made out of every aspect of human life. In his later years Adams wrote a series of bulky articles and books through which he attempted to reconcile history with the laws of thermodynamics.[67] He never abandoned the Victorian habit of writing interminable, multi-volume histories published over the course of a decade or more, or of interspersing his more serious works with pieces of fiction, political pamphleteering, and criticism. His pattern of publication, therefore, had much in common with Freeman's, and it indicates that Adams never lost the air of a nineteenth-century enthusiast, the committed man of letters who shunned narrow specialization in favor of a broad eclecticism. As such, Adams was one of the last of a dying breed of historical writers, rather than a harbinger of historians to come.

Adams left Harvard for Washington and a life of politics in 1877, but his dreams of power and public reputation came to naught: he was never called to office. He took solace in history, not in the history of Anglo-Saxon England but that of his own country. Over the next three decades he wrote and edited an astonishing number of volumes on the America of his more successful ancestors. Adams turned to the Middle Ages again only as an old man, when he wrote his greatest work, *Mont-Saint-Michel and Chartres*. This book, *tour de force* though it is, is not academic history. It is a piece of medievalism. Adams himself wrote that his masterwork had nothing whatsoever to do with his "dreary Anglo-Saxon Law." Instead it was inspired by his friend, the artist John La Farge:

> Between Bishop Stubbs and John La Farge the chasm has required lively gymnastics. The text of Edward the Confessor was uncommonly remote from a twelfth-century window. To clamber across the gap has needed many years of La Farge's closest instruction. . . .[68]

Mont-Saint-Michel and Chartres was also a product of Adams' growing sense of bitter estrangement from an industrialized and immigrant-ridden America. His early work on Anglo-Saxon history, although it flirted with the myths of Teutonic prowess, had never indulged in notions of Aryan racial superiority, but in his later years Adams descended into a brutish and vehement anti-semitism. He blamed Jews for everything—America's squalid industrialism, its descent into materialism, his own family's loss of power. In his autobiography he railed that even "a furtive Yacoob or Ysaac still reeking of the Ghetto, snarling a weird Yiddish . . . had a freer hand than [me]—American of Americans."[69] *Mont-Saint-Michel and Chartres* is an invective against the present, and it is about a properly ordered world in which those in power are aristocrats rather than *nouveau riche* Jews (the two terms are used interchangeably by Adams).[70] Finance and materialism had not yet reared their ugly heads in this world of Gothic and Romanesque, and the industrialized democracy of the 1880's and 1890's was nowhere in evidence.

American Brahmin intellectuals of the late-nineteenth century—men such as Edward Bemis and Herbert Baxter Adams of Johns Hopkins, Francis Amasa Walker of M.I.T., and Richard Mayo Smith of Columbia—took Adams' academic theories of Teutonic democracy and fashioned them into a nasty political and social ideology of racial superiority.[71] So, the work of Henry Adams and his students, never much read by English medievalists,[72] came to be used to prop up the racist and elitist ideology of America's Anglo-Saxon saving remnant.[73] This is certainly no fault of the young Adams, although the old Adams approved of such a reading of his work; but this misuse of the past contributed, like Henry Adams' own temperament and ambitions, to the strange death of Anglo-Saxon history in America.

BOSTON COLLEGE

NOTES

The following abbreviations have been used: *AP*: Adams Papers, Massachusetts Historical Society: Boston. (Quotations from the Adams Papers are from the microfilm edition, by permission of the Massachusetts Historical Society.) *EP*: Eliot Papers: Harvard Univ. Archives: Cambridge, MA. (Quotations from the Eliot Papers are printed with permission of Harvard Univ. Archives.) CFA1: Charles Francis Adams I. CFA2: Charles Francis Adams, Jr. *Education*: Henry Adams, *Novels, Mont Saint Michel, The Education* (New York, 1983). *Letters*: *The Letters of Henry Adams*, 3 vols. (Cambridge, MA, 1982). All of Adams' reviews from the *North American Review* are printed in *Sketches for the North American Review*, ed. Edward Chalfant (Hamden, CT, 1986), hereafter cited as *Sketches*.

1. Henry Adams, *Essays in Anglo-Saxon Law* (Boston, 1876).

2. In "The Life-Book of the Class of 1858" Adams wrote that his immediate plan after graduation was to learn languages and to study and practice law. (This piece is reprinted

in George M. Elsey, "First Education of Henry Adams," *New England Quarterly*, 14 [1941], 684.) Even after Adams fled law school in Berlin, he continued to think that the law was his future (*Letters*, 3 November 1858, to CFA2).

3. *Letters*, November 1858, to CFA2.

4. *Letters*, 17–18 December 1858, to CFA2.

5. "His first lecture was his last" (*Education*, p. 788). As early as 3 November 1858 Adams began hinting to his family that his plan would fail (*Letters*, 3 November 1858, to CFA2), and he was frantic, that first winter in Germany, to find an honorable way out of his legal studies. The level of his desperation can be gauged by the extraordinary plan he concocted to escape from law school. He begged his father's friend the statesman Charles Sumner, then recovering in France from a beating delivered by one of his political rivals, to accompany him on a foreign adventure. Adams volunteered to "leave German, Law, Latin, and all" if Sumner would journey with him to Siberia (*Letters*, 22 December 1858, to Charles Sumner). Sumner did not take Adams up on his strange offer.

6. Adams' own contemporary description of his time at the Freidrichs-Wilhelm Werdersches Gymnasium, which he wrote in hopes of publication, is printed in Harold Dean Carter, "Henry Adams Reports on a German Gymnasium," *American Historical Review*, 53 (1947), 59–74, at p. 72.

7. *AP*, Abigail Brooks Adams to Henry Adams, 16 January 1859.

8. *Education*, p. 795; Edward Chalfant, *Both Sides of the Ocean: A Biography of Henry Adams: His First Life: 1838–1862* (Hamden, CT, 1982), pp. 130–31; Ernest Samuels, *The Young Henry Adams* (Cambridge, MA, 1965), p. 65.

9. *Letters*, 25 September 1868, to Charles Milnes Gaskell.

10. Samuels, p. 153.

11. Chalfant, pp. 141–42, 197.

12. *AP*, CFA1 to Henry Adams 19–23 December 1858. Charles wrote to Henry from Boston, requesting a series of articles, which Charles could help place in Boston and New

York newspapers (Carter, p. 60; *Education*, p. 801). On the family's dislike of the paper see *AP*, Abigail Brooks Adams to Henry Adams, 28 May 1860.

13. These anonymous pieces apparently worried his father a great deal (Chalfant, pp. 224–25).

14. The article is reprinted in Arthur W. Silver, "Henry Adams' 'Diary of a Visit to Manchester,'" *American Historical Review*, 51 (1945), 74–89. The *Times* commentary appeared on 9 January 1862.

15. *Education*, p. 986.

16. Adams' articles for these years are listed in James Truslow Adams, *Henry Adams* (New York, 1933), pp. 214–17. For his reputation as a dancer see *Letters*, 17 May 1869, to Charles Milnes Gaskell.

17. *Letters*, 29 September 1870, to Charles Milnes Gaskell.

18. Samuels, pp. 203–04.

19. Elsey, p. 684.

20. Samuel Eliot Morrison, *Three Centuries of Harvard 1636–1936* (Cambridge, MA, 1946), p. 340; Donald Fleming, "Eliot's New Broom," in Bernard Bailyn, Donald Fleming, Donald Handlin and Stephen Thernstrom, *Glimpses of the Harvard Past* (Cambridge, MA, 1986), p. 65. His father was made president of the board in 1874, so he must have been an influential and dominant member in 1870 (Martin Duberman, *Charles Francis Adams* [Stanford, 1961], p. 389).

21. *AP*, Diary of CFA1, 18 June 1870. Charles Adams was editing his own father's journals for publication when he wrote this entry, so he doubtless was aware of the public nature of private documents.

22. *AP*, Letter of CFA1 to Henry Adams, 13 June 1870.

23. His father, however, did express his disappointment in a letter to Henry (*AP*, Letter of CFA1 to Henry Adams, 11 July 1870).

24. This candidate was E. L. Godkin, editor of *The Nation*. Eliot had offered him $4,000 a year for the professorship (*The Gilded Age Letters of E.L. Godkin*, ed. William M. Armstrong [Albany, NY, 1974], in a letter to Frederick Law Olmsted, 25 July 1870, p. 148). Adams was offered £400 (*Letters*, 29 September 1870, to Charles Milnes Gaskell).

25. "I saw Charles Adams yesterday, who wishes very much that Henry should take the place for five years. Rather [than] go to Washington again. Henry will be back the first week in September. I told him it had been offered to another person who had it under consideration . . . but would let him know . . ." (*EP*, Letter of Gurney to Eliot, 20 August 1870).

26. Godkin turned down the job in a letter to Eliot dated 25 August 1870 (*EP*). Gurney, who had just been made dean, was too busy to edit the *Review* and was looking for a replacement at the time.

27. Donald Fleming, "Eliot's New Broom," p. 64.

28. A. M. Schlesinger, *Historical Scholarship in America* (New York, 1932), p. 4.

29. Philippa Levine, *The Amateur and the Professional: Antiquarians, Historians, and Archaeologists in Victorian England, 1838–1886* (Cambridge, 1986), p. 146.

30. For Adams' use of Michelet see Max I. Baym, *The French Education of Henry Adams* (New York, 1951), p. 247, nn. 19, 20, 23. For his lecture on Wenlock see *Letters*, 19 November 1870, to Charles Milnes Gaskell.

31. An indication of Adams' general disinterest in anything in the period except law is evident in the approach he took to learning Old English. Adams first entertained the notion of studying Anglo-Saxon as he sailed down the Nile on his honeymoon in January 1873 (*Letters*, 2 January 1873, to Henry Cabot Lodge). By June of that year he was working his way through Old English grammar, which he found "amusing" but not something for which he had any particular facility (*Letters*, 11 June 1873, to Henry Cabot Lodge). His library contains two books that he probably used for this purpose, Hiram Corson's *Handbook on Anglo-Saxon* and Francis March's *A Comparative Grammar of the Anglo-Saxon Language* (Card Catalogue of Henry Adams' Library, Massachusetts Historical Society). In January of 1874 he began to crawl through Benjamin Thorpe's edition and parallel translation of *Beowulf*, at the rate of about 35 lines a day. By early

May, as the blood of Grendel's mother was boiling in the mere, Adams tired of the poem and gave it up. Adams' copy of Benjamin Thorpe's *Beowulf* (Oxford, 1855) is at the Massachusetts Historical Society: Henry Adams Library. In the margins of the book, beginning on p. 3, dates written in Henry Adams' own hand appear, indicating the place he had reached in the poem. The first date, 11 January 1874, appears on p. 3. The last date, 15 May 1874, appears on p. 144 at half-line 4294. Adams seems to have gone no further, since some of the pages after p. 144 are uncut (e.g., pp. 169–72). This abandonment of the poem, particularly at this point in the story, suggests that Adams had no overwhelming interest in Old English culture or society but only in a narrow piece of the Anglo-Saxon past.

32. John Eliot Alden, "Henry Adams as Editor: A Group of Unpublished Letters Written to David A. Wells," *The New England Quarterly*, 11 (1938), 148: *Letters*, 25 October 1870, to David A. Wells.

33. *Letters*, 2 June 1872, to Henry Cabot Lodge.

34. *Letters*, 2 January 1873, to Henry Cabot Lodge.

35. *Letters*, 2 June 1873, to Henry Cabot Lodge.

36. *AP*, Letter of CFA1 to Henry Adams, 13 June 1870.

37. "As yet I have seen no society. I am too busy and have to read every evening as my young men are disgustingly clever at upsetting me with questions" (*Letters*, 19 November 1870, to Charles Milnes Gaskell); " . . . [I] read nothing this side of the year 1400" (*Letters*, 12 April 1871, to Charles Milnes Gaskell). "Fearful German books are my daily bread . . ." (*Letters*, 13 November 1871, to Charles Milnes Gaskell).

38. Samuels, pp. 220–21.

39. Alden, "Henry Adams as Editor," p. 150.

40. *Letters*, 29 February 1876, to Francis Amasa Walker.

41. *Letters*, 26 May 1875, to Henry Cabot Lodge.

42. "The Independents and the Political Canvass," *North American Review*, 124 (1876), printed in *The Great Secession Winter of 1860–61 and Other Essays*, ed. George Hochfield (New York, 1958), pp. 291–92.

43. "Prospectus," published at the end of the *North American Review*, 125 (1877).

44. Frank Luther Mott, *A History of American Magazines*, 5 vols. (Cambridge, MA, 1930–68), pp. iii, 18, 23, 31.

45. Samuels, pp. 238–39.

46. See, e.g., his review of the French translation of Rudolf Sohm's book on Salic Law (*Procédure de la lex Salica*), printed in *Sketches*, pp. 102–12. Proofs of this review, heavily corrected in Adams' own hand, have been bound in Henry Cabot Lodge's copy of Sohm's book, preserved at the Massachusetts Historical Society.

47. *Sketches*, pp. 42, 46–47.

48. *Sketches*, p. 47. This accusation was unfounded. In one letter of Maine to Adams, the Englishman discussed Sohm's work (*AP*, Letter of Henry Maine to Henry Adams, 26 December 1876). In another letter, Maine points out the work of Wackernagel to Adams (Letter of Henry Maine to Henry Adams, dated 10 June, and preserved inside Henry Maine, *Early History of Institutions*, Massachusetts Historical Society: Henry Adams Library).

49. *North American Review* review of Fustel de Coulanges, *The Ancient City*, printed in *Sketches*, p. 94.

50. *Sketches*, pp. 115–16.

51. Oscar Cargill, "The Mediaevalism of Henry Adams," in *Essays and Studies in Honor of Carleton Brown*, ed. H. Milford (New York, 1940), p. 311.

52. *Sketches*, p. 42.

53. *Letters*, 14 December 1871, to Charles Milnes Gaskell.

54. *AP*, Letter of E. A. Freeman to Henry Adams, 17 February 1872.

55. *Sketches*, p. 78.

56. E. A. Freeman, *History of the Norman Conquest*, vol. 1, pp. 32–33, 344–45, Massachusetts Historical Society: Henry Adams Library.

57. See Adams' copy of Freeman, *History of the Norman Conquest*, vol. 2, Massachusetts Historical Society: Henry Adams Library. There are a number of uncut pages in this volume. See, e.g., "On the Early Norman Church," pp. 15–36; "Val-es-dunes," pp. 169–72; "English and Norman Estimates of Godwine and Harold," pp. 361– 64; and "The Alleged Spoliation of the Church by Godwine and Harold."

58. *Letters*, 22 February 1875, to Sir Henry Maine; 2 January 1873, to Henry Cabot Lodge; 31 October 1874, to Charles Milnes Gaskell.

59. *Sketches*, p. 127.

60. Adams' copy of Freeman's *History of the Norman Conquest*, Massachusetts Historical Society: Henry Adams Library. The comments quoted in the text can be found in vol. 5, pp. 309, 271, 311, 215.

61. Ibid., p. 214.

62. Edmund Burke, *Abridgement of English History*, Massachusetts Historical Society: Henry Adams Library, p. 267.

63. On Stubbs' language see J. W. Burrow, *A Liberal Descent: Victorian Historians and the English Past* (Cambridge, 1981), pp. 146–47.

64. For a description and discussion of Adams' English contemporaries' Anglo-Saxonism, see Reginald Horsman, *Race and Manifest Destiny: The Origins of American Racial Anglo-Saxonism* (Cambridge, MA, 1981), pp. 75–77.

65. *Essays*, p. 10.

66. Adams believed that his idea about the hundred was the most important historical principle to have been discovered by modern historians, and he shamelessly promoted his

view in his reviews of other historians' works published in the *North American Review*. In criticizing Henry Maine, Adams lectured that "scientific legal history" was not possible without tracing all institutions back through the hundred (*Sketches*, p. 94). In his review of Stubbs he gave a detailed exposition of his views on the hundred (*Sketches*, pp. 116–20), and reviewing J. R. Green, he praised the author for writing "constitutional theory of the best kind" but continued, "perhaps, however, this Review is no fair judge of the merits of Mr. Green's idea, which is one that supports opinions as to the origins of Parliament [that is, in the hundred] which have been heretofore pressed with some eagerness in these pages. . . . This historical principle is on the whole the most valuable of all those which modern investigation has discovered" (*Sketches*, pp. 177–79).

67. Adams' longest and most serious attempt at this enterprise can be found in Henry Adams, *The Tendency of History* (New York, 1928).

68. *Letters*, 4 May 1901, to Henry Osborn Taylor.

69. *Education*, p. 938.

70. Barbara Miller Solomon, *Ancestors and Immigrants: A Changing New England Tradition* (Cambridge, MA, 1956), pp. 39–42.

71. Solomon, pp. 68–81; Peter Novick, *That Noble Dream: The "Objectivity Question" and the American Historical Profession* (Cambridge, 1988), pp. 80–85.

72. J. R. Green, for instance, was aware of *Essays in Anglo-Saxon Law*. Nonetheless, his *History of the English People*, vol. 1 (London, 1879), and *Conquest of England* (London, 1883) ignore Adams completely and never show the least interest in his theories about the hundred. Indeed, *History of the English People* begins with a bibliographical essay in which no mention is made of Adams' book. Green is the first of a long line of English historians to overlook Adams' and his students' efforts.

73. Allen J. Frantzen has recently argued that Anglo-Saxon Studies have lost their place in departments of literature because they have been dissociated from contemporary political and intellectual issues: "The separation of instruction in grammar from socially significant issues . . . is a fatal error" (*Desire for Origins*, p. 3). This statement may be true for literary studies, but it is problematic for history. While no historical interpretation and reconstruction of the past is free from intellectual and political trends operating in the world of the historian, a monolithic and programmatic interpretation of the past, driven

by contemporary ideological demons, makes for bad history. The close association of Anglo-Saxon England with the "germ theory" and the history of the "Aryan Race" served to make a study of the Anglo-Saxon period irrelevant and suspect decades after such theories had been discredited.

Since this article was written in 1991 two important books on Henry Adams have appeared—Edward Chalfant's *Better in Darkness: A Biography of Henry Adams. His Second Life 1862–1891* (Hamden, CT, 1994) and Brooks D. Simpson's *The Political Education of Henry Adams* (Columbia, SC, 1996).

Nineteenth-Century America and the Study of the Anglo-Saxon Language: An Introduction

J. R. Hall

Anglo-Saxonism ran so strong in nineteenth-century America that the period might with reason be called the Anglo-Saxon Century. Anglo-Saxonism encompasses much more than the study of Anglo-Saxon.[1] "As the background for the markedly increased attention paid to Anglo-Saxon literature in the decade before 1855," John E. Bernbrock remarks,

> it is necessary to realize that it was part of a widespread intellectual trend in America and England whose scope far exceeded philology and literature, and whose numerous divergent manifestations can only be grouped under some such tag as "Gothicism" or the interchangeable term "Anglo-Saxonism." The motive forces behind this movement are a strange mixture of patriotism, blatant racial pride, romantic antiquarianism, militant Protestantism, and some purely scientific interest in ethnology, history, and linguistics, as well as law. The totality of these interests (and no doubt many others) acted and reacted upon each other with a cumulative effect to produce a concerted and discernible trend called even at that time "Anglo-Saxonism," and recognized as a popular and widespread phenomenon.[2]

The most famous early proponent of American Anglo-Saxonism was Thomas Jefferson, whose study of Anglo-Saxon history, culture, and language began in the early 1760's and continued for more than 60 years. As Reginald Horsman has stressed in *Race and Manifest Destiny*, Jefferson understood Anglo-Saxon not simply as the basis of modern English but as the language spoken by a people living in the Golden Age of English civilization, a people whose government was based on natural rights, on free institutions, on popular sovereignty—in short, a government that should serve as an inspiration for the United States.[3] This understanding of the Anglo-Saxon age did not wane with Jefferson's passing. As the nineteenth century progressed, so did romantic Anglo-Saxonism, and—irony of ironies, in view of today's dominant academic ideology—it became Politically Correct to exult in the specifically Anglo-Saxon roots of American culture. Some enthusiasts, like Jefferson, thought it important to learn, or try to learn, Anglo-Saxon itself. Thanks to Stanley R. Hauer, we have a precise sense of Jefferson's knowledge of the language and his contribution to furthering its study: he collected Anglo-Saxon books, wrote an essay (posthumously published in 1851) on how to understand and teach it, and made sure that upon its opening in 1825 the University of Virginia included Anglo-Saxon in its curriculum.[4]

Who else promoted study of the language in nineteenth-century America? The full story (which I hope to write) has yet to be written.[5] Here I briefly survey the most notable among those who promoted knowledge of Anglo-Saxon in America, a group that may be divided into four categories: (1) Americans who learned the language on their own; (2) Europeans who came to America knowing (or equipped to learn) the language; (3) Americans who first learned the language in Germany; and (4) Americans who first studied the language in America and later went to Germany for more advanced work. Thanks to all four groups, by the last decade of the nineteenth century a strong American tradition had been established for the study of Anglo-Saxon.

The category of Americans who sought to learn the language on their own includes, in addition to Jefferson, some prominent names, the first of whom, chronologically, is Noah Webster (1758–1843). In an illuminating essay on Webster and Anglo-Saxon, Charlton Laird points out that Webster undertook the language when he was perhaps 50 years old (which would have been about 1808) and that his annotations in four Anglo-Saxon books, which he later bequeathed to Yale and which evidently were the only Anglo-Saxon books he owned, attest his efforts. Unlike Jefferson, who used the grammars of George

Hickes and Elizabeth Elstob, Webster possessed no grammar. To judge, however, by his notes in two books—Gibson's edition of the Anglo-Saxon Chronicle, with a Latin translation, and Barrington's edition of Orosius, with a modern English rendering—Webster, like sixteenth-century English antiquaries, used the comparative method to learn the language. Not surprisingly, Webster did not become adept at Anglo-Saxon. The etymologies in his pioneering *An American Dictionary of the English Language* (New York, 1828), however, are the better for his Anglo-Saxon efforts.[6]

Webster's interest in the language had consequences beyond his dictionary; it led to lectures on the subject at Amherst College in 1840–43 by William C. Fowler (1793–1881), Noah Webster's son-in-law.[7] Nineteenth-century America's greatest Anglo-Saxon philologist, Francis A. March, in 1892 recalled Fowler's classes at the school half a century earlier:

> He had imported Anglo-Saxon books, then curiosities. He held them up and exhibited them to us, as he lectured, exactly as the natural history men did precious shells, or minerals. He said there were only two or three men living who knew anything about the language. He was working on one of the Webster dictionaries, and I became interested in the philological side of English.[8]

Fowler's reported belief in the paucity of Anglo-Saxon scholarship suggests that he had little knowledge of what was then being done in the field in Denmark, Germany, or England.[9]

Not so Henry Wheaton (1785–1848), who had close European connections. Wheaton graduated from Rhode Island College (now Brown University) in 1802 at the age of sixteen and went on to win wide fame as a jurist. Appointed *chargé d'affaires* to Denmark by President John Quincy Adams in 1827, he learned Danish and soon became friends with Erasmus Rask in Copenhagen.[10] Wheaton evinces a sound understanding of Anglo-Saxon and of European scholarship in two articles published during the 1830's: one, a review of John Josias Conybeare's *Illustrations of Anglo-Saxon Poetry* (London, 1826), together with a review of Benjamin Thorpe's translation of Rask's *A*

Grammar of the Anglo-Saxon Tongue, with a Praxis (Copenhagen, 1830);[11] the other, a review of Joseph Bosworth's *A Dictionary of the Anglo-Saxon Language* (London, 1838).[12] In his review of Bosworth, for example, Wheaton prints Northumbrian and West-Saxon versions of *Cædmon's Hymn* in parallel for the purpose of dialectal comparison.

Another scholar with strong European connections was Henry Wadsworth Longfellow (1807–82), whose Anglo-Saxon learning is the subject of a fine essay by Henry Bosley Woolf.[13] Longfellow became acquainted with Joseph Bosworth at Rotterdam in October 1835, and the two met often to discuss Anglo-Saxon, to which Longfellow had devoted some previous study. When Bosworth's *Dictionary* was published, Longfellow (at Bosworth's request), like Wheaton, reviewed it in 1838, along with four other works he deemed most important for understanding Anglo-Saxon literature: J. S. Cardale, ed., *King Alfred's Anglo-Saxon Version of Boethius De Consolatione Philosophiæ with an English Translation, and Notes* (London, 1829); Benjamin Thorpe, ed., *Analecta Anglo-Saxonica: A Selection, in Prose and Verse, from Anglo-Saxon Authors of Various Ages, with a Glossary* (London, 1834); Conybeare, *Illustrations*; and John M. Kemble, ed., *The Anglo-Saxon Poems of Beowulf, the Travellers Song, and the Battle of Finnes–burh* (London, 1833). In 45 pages Longfellow provides an enlightening—and lighthearted—survey of verse and prose. Repeatedly reprinted throughout Longfellow's life, the essay enjoyed wide readership.[14]

Another public man who promoted knowledge of Anglo-Saxon was George P. Marsh (1801–82), a non-academic of wide philological learning.[15] While a student at Dartmouth, he taught himself French, Spanish, Portuguese, Italian, and German "in his spare time" (DAB). After graduating, he pursued a successful career in law and politics and—again presumably in his spare time—the study of Scandinavian languages, publishing *A Compendious Grammar of the Old-Northern or Icelandic Language: Compiled and Translated from the Grammars of Rask* (Burlington, VT, 1838), "the first Icelandic Grammar in the English language" (p. iv). In 1849–54, Marsh served as American minister to Turkey; in 1861–82, as minister to Italy. In between he wrote, among other things, *Lectures on the English Language* (New York, 1860) and *The Origin and History of the English Language, and of the Early Literature It Embodies* (New York, 1862), each showing a sophisticated understanding of Anglo-Saxon. For all his erudition, some of Marsh's views were as naive as Jefferson's. He divided the peoples of Western Europe and of America into "Goths," who were Germanic, freedom-loving, pure, and Protestant, and "Romans," who were Latinate, tyrannical, decadent, and Catholic.[16]

During the course of his life Marsh accumulated a scholar's library of some twelve thousand books, more than a hundred of them concerned with Anglo-Saxon history, literature, or language.[17] A greater book collector and collector of Anglo-Saxonica, however, was William G. Medlicott (1816–83), who, unlike Marsh, had no formal schooling beyond his sixteenth year. Born in Bristol, England, Medlicott came to America in 1835 to seek his fortune—and found it. A decade later he was in charge of a firm manufacturing woolen goods, a position that enabled him to collect books in earnest. During the next 30 years he amassed a library of twenty thousand volumes, of which Anglo-Saxon titles were a prominent feature. By my count his Anglo-Saxon holdings totaled nearly 450 books, two-thirds of them on literature, including a hundred published before 1800. Medlicott was very generous in lending his Anglo-Saxon holdings. March, for example, thanked Medlicott for letting him borrow "Anglo-Saxon texts not elsewhere to be had for love or money."[18] Business reversals in the 1870's obliged Medlicott to sell most of his library practically lot by lot, and the collection is no longer intact.[19]

More unfortunate still was Louis F. Klipstein (1813–78).[20] After graduating from Hampden-Sydney College in 1832, Klipstein taught school in Charlottesville, where he seems to have contracted a bad case of Anglo-Saxonism from Georg Blaettermann, the University of Virginia's Anglo-Saxonist. In 1846–49, Klipstein published the first Anglo-Saxon books to be produced in America: an edition of the West-Saxon Gospels, a grammar, an edition of a homily by Ælfric, and an anthology of prose and verse.[21] Klipstein drew heavily on European scholars—his edition of the Gospels is, in fact, an acknowledged reprint of Benjamin Thorpe's—but showed flashes of independent thought.[22] Perhaps Klipstein's boldest stroke was to style himself on his title pages as "Ph.D. of the University of Giessen." It would be reasonable to suppose he had studied there.[23] Half a century after Klipstein's death, however, Walther Fischer demonstrated that Klipstein had no training whatever at Giessen, his Ph.D. being akin to the mail-order variety, secured by a cousin, August von Klipstein, a professor of mineralogy at the school, on the basis of Louis F. Klipstein's future publications in Anglo-Saxon.[24] But that is not the sad part of the Klipstein story. The sad part is that the cost of publishing the four Anglo-Saxon books severely depleted Klipstein's wife's inheritance; they quarreled; he left home, took to drink, and in 1878, the year of his death, was seen begging for food on the streets of Charleston, South Carolina.

There were other Americans self-taught in Anglo-Saxon, some famous in their own right, each deserving more than the mere mention space permits. There was Henry David Thoreau (1817–62), who, prompted by Longfellow's lectures at Harvard in 1837, spent part of the summer translating Anglo-Saxon poetry and prose.[25] There was Walt Whitman (1819–92), who clipped every newspaper and journal article on Anglo-Saxon literature he could lay hands on and drew up long lists of Anglo-Saxon words.[26] There was John S. Hart (1810–77), who taught himself the language and, as principal of Central High School of Philadelphia, required all students to take three years of Anglo-Saxon, the program being canceled in 1854 after only four years because of "Know-Nothing agitation."[27] Then there were six self-taught men who were the first to teach Anglo-Saxon at their schools: William D. Moore (1824–96), University of Mississippi, 1858;[28] Samuel M. Shute (1823–1902), Columbian College (Washington, D.C.), 1867 (or earlier);[29] Hiram Corson (1828–1911), St. John's (Annapolis), 1868, and Cornell, 1871;[30] Thomas R. Lounsbury (1838–1915), Yale, 1870;[31] Stephen H. Carpenter (1831–78),

University of Wisconsin, 1871;[32] and Morgan Callaway (1831–99), Emory, 1876.[33]

My second category concerns Europeans who came to America and taught or at least promoted the study of Anglo-Saxon. The first three Anglo-Saxonists at the University of Virginia fall into this group. The first, Georg Blaettermann (d. 1842), began teaching there in 1825, when the school opened its doors. We know little about the gentleman, but—apart from knowing that he held a doctorate from Leipzig and was capable of teaching nine different languages—we know perhaps more than we should like. More than once the students rebelled against his "Prussian personality," and he was fired in 1840 for horsewhipping his wife (an accomplished Englishwoman).[34] Virginia's next Anglo-Saxonist, Charles Kraitsir (1804–60), a native of Hungary, fared little better: he was let go after only a few years because, it was said, his wife beat *him*.[35] But perhaps the real reason is that Kraitsir was an inveterate eccentric. Although a wonderfully learned man—he earned an M.D. at the age of 24 and apparently knew some twenty languages—his book, *Glossology: Being a Treatise on the Nature of Language and on the Language of Nature* (New York, 1852), shows him to be so opinionated, arrogant, and desultory it is easy to see why students must have found him exasperating. Quite different from Blaettermann and Kraitsir was Virginia's third Anglo-Saxonist, Maximilian Schele De Vere (1820–98), son of a Swedish father and French mother, who was affable, urbane, and cosmopolitan.[36] Equipped with a Ph.D. from Berlin and a J.U.D. from Greifswald, and recommended to Virginia by Longfellow and other luminaries, he came to the university in 1844 and stayed for half a century. It is said that during the first 30 years alone he taught Anglo-Saxon to some five hundred students[37]—not always, one suspects, with complete accuracy of detail. In his *Outlines of Comparative Philology* (New York, 1853), for example, he exclaims that the early Anglican reformers "found . . . in Paschal's homily, their own views of the Eucharist" (p. 82), thus confounding Ælfric's Paschal homily, *Sermo de Sacrificio in Die Pascae*, with Ælfric himself.

At least three other Europeans can be said to have promoted Anglo-Saxon in nineteenth-century America. The earliest was John Petheram (1808–58). Born at Oldmixon, near Weston-super-Mare, Somerset, Petheram came to London as a young man and found employment as an office clerk. Unable to afford a university education, Petheram set about educating himself, which included learning Anglo-Saxon.[38] In 1834 he emigrated to America, worked in bookstores in New York and New Orleans, annoyed his employers by reading Bede under the counter, sold his private library in New York, then returned to England to set up his own bookstore and to write his wonderful treatise, *An Historical Sketch of the Progress and Present State of Anglo-Saxon Literature in England* (London, 1840).[39] It is difficult to say how much "promoting" of Anglo-Saxon Petheram undertook while he was in America. Certainly a few bookstore owners must have been made aware of the subject. It is also tempting to believe that some of the Anglo-Saxon books acquired by William G. Medlicott, who lived in New York in the 1830's and maintained contact with New York booksellers after leaving, might have come from Petheram's sale.[40]

Two other Europeans who promoted the study of Anglo-Saxon in America were highly trained German philologists who arrived in the century's last decade.[41] Ewald Flügel (1863–1914) was born in Leipzig and earned a doctorate from the university at the age of 22.[42] An associate editor of *Anglia* and the founder of *Beiblatt zur Anglia* (1890), Flügel accepted, against the advice of American friends, the professorship of English philology at Stanford in 1892. He did not introduce Anglo-Saxon to Stanford—in 1891–92, the school's first academic year, classes in Anglo-Saxon were conducted by Melville B. Anderson—but taught it thereafter until 1900.[43] Although known primarily for his work on Chaucer's lexicon, Flügel was in easy command of Anglo-Saxon scholarship, as is demonstrated in a posthumously published article (1916).[44]

The other German philologist who taught Anglo-Saxon in nineteenth-century America—and continued to teach it through his classic edition of *Beowulf*—was Frederick Klaeber (1863–1954), who in 1893 came to the University of Minnesota (of which he had not heard before being offered a position there),[45] fresh from a doctorate at the University of Berlin. A scholar whose capacity for philological labor surpassed even his natural genius, Klaeber brought renown to the school before retiring to his native land after 38 years of service in America.[46] Most of Klaeber's story belongs, of course, to the twentieth century, and he seems not to have directed an Anglo-Saxon doctoral dissertation to completion until 1900.[47]

My third category consists of Americans who, without prior formal introduction to the language, studied Anglo-Saxon abroad.[48] Edward D. Sims (1805–45) graduated A.B. from the University of North Carolina in 1824 and A.M. in 1827, then taught at La Grange College before accepting a chair in 1832 at the newly opened Randolph-Macon College.[49] Feeling the need to learn more Anglo-Saxon, Gothic, and other languages than he was able to pick up on his own, Sims secured a leave of absence, which permitted him to study at Halle in 1836–38.[50] Back home, he taught Anglo-Saxon at Randolph-Macon through the spring of 1842, when he was obliged to resign, as he wished to marry his deceased wife's sister, an act then proscribed by the laws of Virginia.[51] Evidently the state of Alabama was more broad-minded, and Sims accepted a position at the University of Alabama, where he also taught Anglo-Saxon. To judge by his notebooks—discovered in a secondhand bookstore in St. Louis in 1890—at the time of his death Sims was working on an Anglo-Saxon grammar.[52]

Francis James Child (1825–96) graduated from Harvard in 1846 and remained there as a tutor until 1849, when he left to study at Göttingen and Berlin.[53] Returning to Harvard in 1851, he introduced the study of Anglo-Saxon. The course, first taught as an elective to an interested few, came to be required of all sophomores, then reverted to the status of an elective.[54] Famed for his brilliant work on Chaucer and on ballads, Child seems not to have published scholarship directly on Anglo-Saxon; probably hundreds of students, however, learned the language from Child during his long career.

Thomas Chase (1827–92) matriculated at Harvard in 1844, a member of the last class required to read "the entire Greek Testament as an entrance requirement," and graduated four years later with high honors.[55] After serving for two years as master of Cambridge High School, he taught Latin, history, and chemistry at Harvard until early 1853, when he left for Europe to attend lectures at universities in England, France, Greece, Italy, and Germany. Evidently he was most impressed by the University of Berlin, at which he spent nearly a year. Returning to the United States in 1855, he accepted the chair of philology and classical literature at Haverford College (of which he later became president), introducing the study of Anglo-Saxon there in 1867.[56] Primarily a classics scholar, Chase, like Child, published nothing on Anglo-Saxon.

Theodore W. Hunt (1844–1930) graduated from Princeton (then called the College of New Jersey) in 1865.[57] After studying for the ministry and tutoring at Princeton, he pursued philology at the University of Berlin (1871–73), then returned to Princeton, where in 1878 he inaugurated the study of Anglo-Saxon at Princeton's new graduate school. A year later Princeton acquired 105 (58 percent) of the main entry lots in Medlicott's book catalogue under the heading "Anglo-Saxon." Hunt is the person most likely responsible for the purchase.[58] In any case, he put Princeton's Anglo-Saxon holdings to good use, in the next fifteen years publishing two books in the field, *Cædmon's Exodus and Daniel, Edited from Grein* (Boston, 1883) and *Ethical Teachings in Old English Literature* (London, 1892).[59]

Albert S. Cook (1853–1927) graduated from Rutgers in 1872.[60] After teaching in New Jersey, he studied at Göttingen and Leipzig in 1877–78, then returned to introduce Anglo-Saxon to Johns Hopkins in 1879. In 1881–82 Cook was back in Europe, studying first with Henry Sweet in London and then with Eduard Sievers in Jena, where he received the doctorate. Back home, he introduced Anglo-Saxon to the University of California at Berkeley, leaving in 1889 for Yale.[61] As Fred C. Robinson observes, Cook "brought to Yale and to America the principles and standards of medieval English studies as they were practiced by the best scholars in Europe."[62] Cook's *Judith, An Old English Epic Fragment* (Boston, 1888) and *The Christ of Cynewulf, A Poem in Three Parts* (Boston, 1900) are among the first great American editions of Anglo-Saxon verse.

Francis A. Blackburn (1845–1923) graduated A.B. from the University of Michigan in 1868 and A.M. in 1871. After teaching the classics at Albion College and the University of Michigan, he studied at Leipzig in 1875–76 and, upon returning to America, taught or served as principal at various high schools in Michigan and California. In 1889 he returned to Leipzig and in 1892, Ph.D. in hand, introduced Anglo-Saxon to the newly founded University of Chicago, where he taught until his retirement in 1913.[63] At Leipzig he worked under Richard P. Wülker, considered the head of editorial conservatism by Kenneth Sisam.[64] It comes as no surprise to learn that Blackburn used to impart to his students at Chicago "the necessity in editions of early English texts of keeping the manuscript reading if it were in any way possible to do so."[65]

My fourth and final category consists of Americans who first studied the language at home, then went abroad for advanced work. Thomas R. Price (1839–1903), James M. Garnett (1840–1916), James A. Harrison (1848–1911), Charles W. Kent (1860–1917), and J. Douglas Bruce (1862–1923) were taught by Maximilian Schele De Vere at Virginia, and each went to Germany: Price to Berlin and Kiel, 1859–62; Garnett to Berlin and Leipzig, 1869–70; Harrison to Bonn and Munich, 1868–70; Kent to Göttingen, Berlin, and Leipzig, 1884–87; and Bruce to Berlin and Strassburg, 1886–88.[66] A word on each scholar.

Thomas R. Price taught at Randolph-Macon (professor of Latin and Greek, then professor of Greek and English), Virginia (professor of Greek), and Columbia (professor of English), always holding the conviction—for which he quoted King Alfred's preface to his translation of Gregory's *Pastoral Care*—that students should first learn well their native language before attempting Latin or Greek.[67] Although Price published relatively little, he was devoted to scholarship and sent various Randolph-Macon students to Leipzig for further philological training, of whom the two most notable for the present purpose are Robert Sharp (1851–1931) and William M. Baskervill (1850–99), each of whom published Anglo-Saxon scholarship.[68] Back in America, Sharp introduced Anglo-Saxon to Tulane, of which he later became president (1913–18). Baskervill introduced it to Wofford and later taught Anglo-Saxon at Vanderbilt, sending at least two of his own students, James H. Kirkland (from Wofford) and C. C. Ferrell (from Vanderbilt),[69] to Leipzig as well: so that, as Scripture might put it, Kirkland and Ferrell were the sons of Baskervill, who was the son of Price, who was the son of Schele, who was the son of the University of Berlin.

On returning from Germany in 1870, James M. Garnett became principal of St. John's College (Annapolis), along with serving as professor of history and English language and literature.[70] In 1882 he assumed the professorship of English language and literature at Virginia and held it until 1893, when it was divided into two chairs, Garnett occupying the chair of English language. Always active in Anglo-Saxon scholarship—the Greenfield-Robinson *Bibliography* lists him as the author of more than 40 reviews—Garnett was devoted especially to translation theory and practice. His *Beowulf: An Anglo-Saxon Poem, and the Fight at Finnsburg* (Boston, 1882), the first American rendering of *Beowulf*, was well received, and his *Elene; Judith; Aethelstan, or the Fight at Brunanburh; and Bryhtnoth, or the Fight at Maldon* (Boston, 1889) went into three editions.

Although James A. Harrison's "invincible distaste for mathematics prevented his applying for any academic degree" (DAB), after returning from Germany he nonetheless taught at Randolph-Macon, then at Washington and Lee and the University of Virginia.[71] Best known as the editor of the collected works of Edgar Allan Poe, Harrison was also an accomplished Anglo-Saxonist and founded the Library of Anglo-Saxon Poetry, of which his and Sharp's *Beowulf* (Boston, 1883), the first large-scale American edition of the poem, inaugurated the series.[72] Later, in co-operation with Baskervill, he published *A Handy Poetical Anglo-Saxon Dictionary: Based on Groschopp's Grein* (New York, 1885) as well as an *Anglo-Saxon Prose Reader* (New York, 1898).

Charles W. Kent returned to America in 1887. After teaching a year at the University of Virginia, he served as Professor of English and Modern Languages at the University of Tennessee until he was summoned back to Virginia in 1893, where he taught until his death in 1917.[73] In 1887 Kent published his Leipzig dissertation, *Teutonic Antiquities in 'Andreas' and 'Elene'* (Halle). In 1889 he published an edition of *Elene* (Boston), Volume 4 in Harrison's Library of Anglo-Saxon Poetry, acknowledging his professors—Arthur S. Napier, Julius Zupitza, and Richard P. Wülker—but dedicating the book, more largely, "to those scholars to whom America owes the revival of the study of Old English."

J. Douglas Bruce returned to America in 1888 and the next year did something that would have been strange as little as a decade earlier: he enrolled at an American institution, Johns Hopkins, to work on a doctorate.[74] After serving as professor of modern languages at Centre College in 1890–91, he taught Anglo-Saxon and Middle English at Bryn Mawr in 1891–97, then departed for the University of Tennessee, where he remained until his death in 1923.[75] Bruce's dissertation, *The Anglo-Saxon Version of the Book of Psalms commonly known as the Paris Psalter* (Baltimore, 1894), was a credit both to the author and to the American school sponsoring him.

So much for the South and those who studied under Schele at the University of Virginia. Some Northerners, also introduced to Anglo-Saxon in America, sought Germany for advanced training as well. James M. Hart (1839–1916) was exposed to the language at Central High School of Philadelphia, of which his father (mentioned above) was principal.[76] After graduating from Princeton in 1860, the younger Hart studied in Geneva, Berlin, and Göttingen in 1861–64. His field was not philology, however, but jurisprudence, in which he was awarded a J.U.D. *vera cum laude* from Göttingen. After practicing law in New York City for four years, he was appointed assistant professor of modern languages at Cornell. In 1872–74 he was back in Germany studying philology at Leipzig, Marburg, and Berlin. After teaching at the University of Cincinnati in 1876–90, he returned to Cornell, where he remained until his retirement in 1907. Hart's most significant philological publication is *A Syllabus of Anglo-Saxon Literature* (Cincinnati, 1881), an adaptation of part of Bernhard ten Brink's *Geschichte der Englischen Literatur* (Berlin, 1877). His most significant publication, however, is not in the realm of philology but is a four-hundred-page volume, *German Universities: A Narrative of Personal Experience* (New York, 1874), which told American students everything they might need to know about studying in Germany, from student duels to an enterprise fraught with still more peril, examinations.[77] "For more than a generation it was the standard work on the subject in America. . . . Its appearance was timely, its influence inestimable" (DAB).

Another Northerner, Francis B. Gummere (1855–1919), graduated from Haverford College (of which his father was president) in 1872 at the age of seventeen and two years later went to study under Child at Harvard, taking a second A.B.[78] Child may have impressed upon Gummere the advantages of German education, as in 1878 he embarked on studies at Leipzig, Berlin, Strassburg, and Freiburg, from the last of which he earned a Ph.D. in 1881. After teaching in Massachusetts, he accepted a position back at Haverford, where he taught from 1887 until his death. Gummere is perhaps best remembered for his work on ballads—in *The Popular Ballad* (Boston, 1907) he argues strenuously in favor of communal origins—but he published significant work on Anglo-Saxon as well. His Freiburg dissertation, *The Anglo-Saxon Metaphor* (Halle, 1881), remains required reading for anyone at work in the area.

James W. Bright (1852–1926) worked under March at Lafayette College and graduated in 1877. He proceeded to Johns Hopkins, where he studied under Cook and other philologists and was granted a Ph.D. in 1882, his dissertation being the third earliest in the field of Anglo-Saxon in America.[79] In 1883–84 he went abroad to study under Eduard

Sievers, at Jena; Hermann Paul, at Freiburg; and Bernhard ten Brink, at Strassburg. Hired as an instructor by Johns Hopkins in 1885, Bright set about raising the standards of American scholarship and establishing a system of graduate training in philology similar to what he had experienced in German universities. He succeeded. By the time he retired in 1925, he had trained 55 Ph.D.s in English,[80] had helped establish *Modern Language Notes* (founded in 1886) as a leading journal of philology, and had founded the Albion Series of Anglo-Saxon and Middle English Poetry.[81] He also published a large number of reviews, articles, and books, among them individual editions of the West-Saxon Gospels. His most influential book, however, was *An Anglo-Saxon Reader* (New York, 1891), which, subsequently combined with a grammar (1894), lives on in Frederic G. Cassidy and Richard N. Ringler, eds., *Bright's Old English Grammar and Reader*, 3rd ed. (New York, 1971).

Halle, Berlin, Göttingen, Leipzig, Jena, Kiel, Bonn, Munich, Strassburg, Marburg, Freiburg: Did any Americans seeking advanced instruction in Anglo-Saxon stay home? Many did. Thanks to Phillip Pulsiano's *An Annotated Bibliography of North American Doctoral Dissertations on Old English Language and Literature,* it is now possible to say that at least 39 students specializing in Anglo-Saxon (ten of them women) received doctorates in America from 1880, when the first dissertation was accepted, through 1899.[82] In most instances, however, the dissertations were directed by scholars who had studied in Germany, and, as we have seen, two holders of American doctorates, Bruce and Bright, received advanced training in Germany as well. Certainly the best published work was done by Americans who studied in Germany.

There is one striking exception: the work of Francis Andrew March (1825–1911).[83] Introduced to the language by Fowler at Amherst in 1841, March (after spending some time as an instructor and in the study and practice of law) began teaching Anglo-Saxon at Lafayette College in 1855. Two years later he was appointed professor of the English language and comparative philology, "the first [chair] of the kind to be established in any institution of learning in America or Europe" (DAB). Despite being called upon to teach Latin, Greek, French, German, botany, law, political economy, political science, and philosophy as well as English and Germanic philology, March somehow managed to write *Introduction to Anglo-Saxon: An Anglo-Saxon Reader, with Philological Notes, a Brief Grammar, and a Vocabulary* (New York, 1870)[84] and, much more important, *A Comparative Grammar of the Anglo-Saxon Language; in which its forms are illustrated by those of the Sanskrit, Greek, Latin, Gothic, Old Saxon, Old Friesic, Old Norse, and Old High German* (New York, 1870). Bright, one of March's students, justly called the grammar an "extraordinary book into which one can never look without amazement," "one of the most notable monuments of industry bestowed on the study of the earliest state of our language," a book that won the "bountiful praise" of foreign scholars, who "placed his name on the list of their most eminent colleagues."[85] Germanic philologists of Germany were best positioned to appreciate March's *Grammar*. March had spent a decade studying their books, of which his own was a crowning synthesis. "He had laid the foundation on which all future historical grammarians in the field of English were destined to build," says Kemp Malone, "and his fame will ever rest secure as in a very real sense the founder of a science" (DAB).

March represents two factors crucial to the transmission of Anglo-Saxon to nineteenth-century America: German scholarship and American initiative. In 1825 Anglo-Saxon could be studied in America at only one school, Jefferson's own University of Virginia. By 1899 it could be studied at some three dozen, in every region of the country. By 1899 thousands of Americans had taken at least one course in Anglo-Saxon—more students, I should think, than in England and Germany combined—and at least 39 had doctorates in the field from American universities. By 1899 Americans had written their own Anglo-Saxon grammars and readers and linguistic or literary studies and had founded their own philological journals and societies.[86] By 1899 America had Klaeber at Minnesota, Cook at Yale, and Bright at Johns Hopkins, the three as a group a match for any three Anglo-Saxonists in England or in Germany itself. And throughout the nineteenth century the force sustaining most American Anglo-Saxonism was the pride—sometimes sinful pride—that many Americans took in what they saw as their true heritage. Thomas Jefferson is supposed to have died on 4 July 1826: he was still alive on 31 December 1899.

UNIVERSITY OF MISSISSIPPI

APPENDIX:

ANGLO-SAXON DOCTORAL DISSERTATIONS WRITTEN IN NINETEENTH-CENTURY AMERICA

The following citations, arranged chronologically, are from Phillip Pulsiano, *An Annotated Bibliography of North American Doctoral Dissertations on Old English Language and Literature* (East Lansing, and Woodbridge, 1988). (Nineteenth-century dissertations on related subjects in Pulsiano, e.g., Old Frisian, are here omitted.) Directors are given only when listed in the bibliography.

no. 134, Benjamin Willis Wells, 1880, Harvard
no. 787, James Wilson Bright, 1882, Johns Hopkins
no. 881, Harry F. Barrell, 1885, Columbia
no. 261, Charles Grandison Gill, 1887, Tulane
no. 770, Frank Gaylord Hubbard, 1887, Johns Hopkins
no. 135, Edmund Atwill Wasson, 1888, Columbia
no. 439, Mary Gwinn, 1888, Bryn Mawr
no. 136, Morgan Callaway, Jr., 1889, Johns Hopkins
no. 440, John Heddaeus, 1890, New York University
no. 137, Thomas Perrin Harrison, 1891, Johns Hopkins
no. 793, John William Pearce, 1891, Tulane
no. 138, Marguerite Sweet, 1892, Bryn Mawr
no. 139, Charles Hunter Ross, 1892, Johns Hopkins
no. 140, Frank Jewett Mather, Jr., 1892, Johns Hopkins
no. 141, Edwin W. Bowen, 1892, Johns Hopkins
no. 436, J. Lesslie Hall, 1892, Johns Hopkins
no. 67, Frederick Tupper, Jr., 1893, Johns Hopkins
no. 694, Charles Alphonso Smith, 1893, Johns Hopkins
no. 142, Joseph Hendren Gorrell, 1894, Johns Hopkins
no. 654, Edward Fulton, 1894, Harvard
no. 695, Constance Pessels, 1894, Johns Hopkins
no. 817, Allison Drake, 1894, Columbia
no. 829, J. Douglas Bruce, 1894, Johns Hopkins
no. 143, Clarence Griffin Child, 1895, Johns Hopkins

no. 696, James Waddell Tupper, 1895, Johns Hopkins
no. 697, Henry Marvin Belden, 1895, Johns Hopkins
no. 441, Kathryne Janette Wilson, 1896, Stanford
no. 649, Helen Bartlett, 1896, Bryn Mawr (James Douglas Bruce, Dir.)
no. 698, Frank H. Chase, 1896, Yale (Albert S. Cook, Dir.)
no. 810, Martha Anstice Harris, 1896, Yale
no. 896, James Pinckney Kinard, 1896, Johns Hopkins
no. 366, George Shipley, 1897, Johns Hopkins
no. 144, Clark Sutherland Northup, 1898, Cornell (James Morgan Hart, Dir.)
no. 724, Caroline Louisa White, 1898, Yale
no. 811, Lancelot Minor Harris, 1898, Johns Hopkins
no. 101, Frederick Morgan Padelford, 1899, Yale
no. 442, Alice B. Dudek, 1899, New York University
no. 679, Ida Wood, 1899, Bryn Mawr

Not listed in Pulsiano's bibliography is Charles P. G. Scott's doctoral dissertation, "Ælfrêdes Dômas: The Laws of Alfred the Great," Lafayette College, 1881. On Scott see n. 67.

NOTES

I am pleased to dedicate this to Prof. Fred C. Robinson, American Anglo-Saxonist par excellence, who has contributed so much in so many ways to the field during the last 35 years. In particular I would like to acknowledge his and the late Stanley B. Greenfield's *A Bibliography of Publications on Old English Literature to the End of 1972* (n. 14 below), invaluable to the present essay.

1. I prefer "Old English" to "Anglo-Saxon" in reference to the language spoken by the Anglo-Saxons. Here, however, I use "Anglo-Saxon" because that is the term overwhelmingly used by 19th-century American scholars and, more important, because the term directly links the study of the language to the larger subject of Anglo-Saxonism. The question of terminology was discussed early by George P. Marsh (who prefers "Anglo-Saxon" to "English"), *Lectures on the English Language*, 4th ed. (New York, 1867), pp. 47–48. On the strong preference for "Anglo-Saxon" over "Old English" in 19th-century America, see Arthur G. Kennedy, "Progress in the Teaching of Early English," in *Studies in English Philology: A Miscellany in Honor of Frederick Klaeber*, ed. Kemp Malone and Martin B. Ruud (Minneapolis, 1929), pp. 473–76.

2. John E. Bernbrock, "'Anglo-Saxonism' in Mid-Nineteenth Century America," ch. 2 of "Walt Whitman and 'Anglo-Saxonism,'" Diss. University of North Carolina, Chapel Hill, 1961, p. 57.

3. Reginald Horsman, *Race and Manifest Destiny: The Origins of American Racial Anglo-Saxonism* (Cambridge, MA, 1981), pp. 18–24. Horsman's study focuses largely on leading intellectuals or prominent public figures. For an illuminating review of Anglo-Saxonism as it appeared among lesser-known authors and in the popular press, see Bernbrock, pp. 54–108. On Jefferson's Anglo-Saxonism see also Allen J. Frantzen, *Desire for Origins: New Language, Old English, and Teaching the Tradition* (New Brunswick, NJ, 1990), pp. 15–19, 203–07.

4. Stanley R. Hauer, "Thomas Jefferson and the Anglo-Saxon Language," *PMLA*, 98 (1983), 879–98. See also J. B. Henneman, "Two Pioneers in the Historical Study of English,—Thomas Jefferson and Louis F. Klipstein: A Contribution to the History of the Study of English in America," *PMLA*, 8 (1893), xliii–xlix; and C. R. Thompson, "The Study of Anglo-Saxon in America," *English Studies*, 18 (1936), 241–46.

5. The most important sources of information to date are Thompson's article (above); Francis A. March, "The Study of Anglo-Saxon," *Report of the Commissioner of Education*

for the Year 1876 (Washington, DC, 1878), pp. 475–79; March, "Recollections of Language Teaching," *PMLA*, 8 (1893), xviii–xxii; and Morgan Callaway, Jr., "The Historic Study of the Mother-Tongue in the United States: A Survey of the Past," *University of Texas Bulletin*, No. 2538, October 8, 1925 / *Studies in English*, 5 (1925), 5–38.

6. Charlton Laird, "Etymology, Anglo-Saxon, and Noah Webster," *American Speech*, 21 (1946), 3–15.

7. On William C. Fowler see *Appletons' Cyclopædia of American Biography* (hereafter ACAB), vol. 2, p. 518; *The National Cyclopædia of American Biography* (hereafter NCAB), vol. 5, p. 311; and Callaway, p. 27. Fowler retired from teaching at Amherst to write *English Grammar* (New York, 1850). See James Wilson Bright, "An Address in Commemoration of Francis Andrew March, 1825–1911," *PMLA*, 29 (1914), cxix.

8. March, "Recollections," p. xx.

9. On the study of Anglo-Saxon in England and/or on the Continent in the early 19th century, see John M. Kemble, "Letter to M. Francisque Michel," *Bibliothèque anglo-saxonne*, ed. Francisque Michel, vol. 2 of *Anglo-Saxonica*, ed. P. de Larenaudière and Francisque Michel (Paris, 1837), pp. 1–63; John Petheram, *An Historical Sketch of the Progress and Present State of Anglo-Saxon Literature in England* (London, 1840); E. Müller, "Das Studium angelsächsischer Sprache und Literatur in Deutschland," *Archiv für das Studium der neueren Sprachen und Literaturen*, 24 (1858), 249–66; Richard Wülker, *Grundriss zur Geschichte der angelsächsischen Litteratur* (Leipzig, 1885); David J. Savage, "Old English Scholarship in England 1800–1840," Diss. Johns Hopkins 1935; Savage, "Grundtvig: A Stimulus to Old English Scholarship," *Philologica: The Malone Anniversary Studies*, ed. Thomas A. Kirby and Henry Bosley Woolf (Baltimore, 1949), pp. 275–80; Hans Aarsleff, *The Study of Language in England, 1780–1860* (Princeton, 1967; 2nd ed. Minneapolis, 1983); Marijane Louise Allen Osborn, "Foreign Studies of *Beowulf*: A Critical Survey of *Beowulf* Scholarship Outside English-Speaking Countries and Germany, with Bibliographies," Diss. Stanford 1969; Andreas Haarder, *Beowulf: The Appeal of a Poem* (Copenhagen, 1975); Birte Kelly, "The Formative Stages of Modern *Beowulf* Scholarship, Textual, Historical and Literary, Seen in the Work of Scholars of the Earlier Nineteenth Century," Ph.D. Thesis Univ. of London 1979; and Eric Stanley, "The Continental Contribution to the Study of Anglo-Saxon Writings Up To and Including That of the Grimms," *Towards a History of English Studies in Europe*, ed. Thomas Finkenstaedt and Gertrud Scholtes (Augsburg, 1983), pp. 9–39.

10. On Henry Wheaton see the DAB, vol. 10, pp. 39–42; and Adolph B. Benson, "Henry Wheaton's Writings on Scandinavia," *Journal of English and Germanic Philology*, 29 (1930), 546–61.

11. H. Wheaton, in *North American Review*, 33 (1831), 325–50.

12. H. Wheaton, in *New York Review*, 3 (1838), 362–77. It is curious that the date of Bosworth's *Dictionary* in Wheaton's review, as in Longfellow's, is given as 1837; presumably the date was changed to 1838 on the title page upon actual publication. On Wheaton's philological learning, Benson, p. 549, says: "Wheaton never became a philologist—he was a historian of culture—and it is not clear in his writings just how much he knew about linguistic relations." This is just. It is also just to note that anyone who knew Rask's *Grammar* well and who had carefully reviewed Conybeare and Bosworth must be accounted reasonably conversant with Anglo-Saxon literature and language.

13. Henry Bosley Woolf, "Longfellow's Interest in Old English," in *Philologica*, ed. Kirby and Woolf, pp. 281 89.

14. Henry Wadsworth Longfellow, "Anglo-Saxon Literature," *North American Review*, 47 (1838), 90–134. For the reprinting see Stanley B. Greenfield and Fred C. Robinson, *A Bibliography of Publications on Old English Literature to the End of 1972* (Toronto, 1980), no. 535.

15. On George P. Marsh see ACAB, vol. 4, pp. 216–17; NCAB, vol. 2, p. 439; DAB, vol. 6, pp. 297–98; and Callaway, pp. 19–20.

16. See Samuel Kliger, "George Perkins Marsh and the Gothic Tradition in America," *New England Quarterly*, 19 (1946), 524–31.

17. Upon his death Marsh's library was purchased for $15,000 by Frederick Billings and donated to the Univ. of Vermont. See *University of Vermont, Catalogue of the Library of George Perkins Marsh* (Burlington, VT, 1892). Although strong in Anglo-Saxon holdings, the most impressive single feature of the collection is the Scandinavian. In the preface to the catalogue, the (unnamed) editor quotes a letter from Marsh to Charles Lanman in which Marsh estimates his Scandinavian holdings as "more complete than any collection out of the northern kingdoms" (p. v). That was in 1844; in later years Marsh continued to augment his Scandinavian collection.

18. Francis A. March, *A Comparative Grammar of the Anglo-Saxon Language* (New York, 1870), p. iv. For another acknowledgment of Medlicott's help see n. 30 below.

19. See J. R. Hall, "William G. Medlicott (1816–1883): An American Book Collector and His Collection," *Harvard Library Bulletin*, NS 1 (1990), 13–46; on the Anglo-Saxon collection see pp. 27, 38–44. I would like to take the opportunity to correct a major editorial error in the essay: the leaf from Medlicott's catalogue reproduced on p. 37 should be captioned "A Medlicott family copy, p. 27, with annotations in the hands of family members" (not "A Harvard copy, p. 27, with annotations recording some books purchased in 1894"). A photograph of the Medlicott Company's mill and another of one of its stock houses can be found in a pamphlet, "The Canal of the Connecticut River Company, and the Industries on its banks in Windsor Locks, Connecticut" (1909), available in the Hagley Library, Imprints Department, Wilmington, DE. I am grateful to my sister, Barbara D. Hall, of the Hagley, for bringing the photographs to my attention.

20. On Louis F. Klipstein see Henneman, "Two Pioneers," pp. xlvii–xlix; Callaway, pp. 10–12; the DAB, vol. 5, pp. 446–47; and, for consideration of his historical or cultural doctrines, Frantzen, pp. 207–08.

21. In "Some Turning Points in the History of Teaching Old English in America," OEN, 13.2 (1980), 9, Robert F. Yeager observes, "Anglo-Saxon did not, in fact, become standard fare at the University of Virginia, or anywhere, until the middle of the [19th] century. As the turning point, we may cite 1848, when Louis F. Klipstein issued his *Grammar of the Anglo-Saxon Language*. . . ." Klipstein's grammar seems rather early to designate as "the" turning point. A decade after the grammar was published only four colleges—the Univ. of Virginia, Harvard, Lafayette, and the Univ. of Mississippi—offered Anglo-Saxon (Hall, "William G. Medlicott," p. 41); in the late 1860's Anglo-Saxon was available at only half a dozen schools (n. 29 below); by 1875, however, it was taught at about two dozen schools (March, "The Study," p. 479; idem, "Recollections," p. xx). Klipstein's grammar had little to do with the sudden growth of Anglo-Saxon as an academic discipline in the 1870's.

22. In "*Exodus* 488b, *helpendra pað*," *ANQ*, NS 5 (1992), 5, I adopt a suggestion of Klipstein's that *he* in line 489b has as its antecedent *merestreames* in line 489a, a reading proposed otherwise only (and almost 75 years later) by W. J. Sedgefield, *An Anglo-Saxon Verse-Book* (Manchester, 1922), p. 182.

23. So Henneman, "Two Pioneers," p. xlviii; Henneman, "English Studies in the South," *The South in the Building of the Nation*, 7 (Richmond, 1909), p. 120; and Callaway, p. 10.

24. Walther Fischer, "Aus der Frühzeit der amerikanischen Anglistik: Louis F. Klipstein (1813–79)," *Englische Studien*, 62 (1927), 250–64.

25. On Henry David Thoreau see Bernbrock, pp. 79–81. Another Transcendentalist who studied Anglo-Saxon was Theodore Parker; see Horsman, p. 178.

26. See Bernbrock, esp. pp. 1–31, 109–57.

27. On John S. Hart see the DAB, vol. 4, pt. 2, pp. 359–60; and my essay, "Mid-Nineteenth-Century American Anglo-Saxonism: The Question of Language," in *Anglo-Saxonism and the Construction of Social Identity*, ed. Allen J. Frantzen and John D. Niles (Gainesville, FL, 1997), pp. 133–56. Hart's "On the Study of the Anglo-Saxon Language; or, the Relations of the English Language to the Teutonic and Classic Branches of the Indo-European Family of Languages," *American Journal of Education*, 1 (1856), 33–60, shows him widely learned in philology. The "Discussion upon Prof. Hart's Lecture," pp. 60–66, contains a lively exchange of views. Details on Hart's life and his administration of Central High School are given by Franklin Spencer Edmonds, *History of the Central High School of Philadelphia* (Philadelphia, 1902), pp. 98–157, 328. On the teaching of Anglo-Saxon, see pp. 131–33 and Appendix G (after p. 386). On the dropping of Anglo-Saxon from the curriculum, Edmonds says, p. 132: "The period of Know-Nothing agitation was not an auspicious time for the advocacy of the study of foreign languages." The number of students who took Anglo-Saxon each year is placed at 250 by March, "The Study," p. 478.

28. William D. Moore was born in Harper's Ferry, VA, and attended Western Univ. of Pennsylvania (now the Univ. of Pittsburgh) and Western Theological Seminary (Allegheny, PA). After ordination in 1845 he served as pastor in Pennsylvania churches until he assumed teaching duties at Oakland College (near Rodney, MS), 1855, and then the Univ. of Mississippi, 1858–61, where he was the first to hold the Chair of English Literature (one of the first such chairs in the South). He did not return to the university after the Civil War—he supported the North—but practiced law in western Pennsylvania. See S. W. Geiser, "William D. Moore (1824–96): Amateur Geologist of Mississippi," *Field and Laboratory*, 17.3 (1949), 116–20. For finding the article, calling it to my attention, and sending me a copy I am grateful to Peter S. Baker. On the teaching of Anglo-Saxon at the Univ. of Mississippi, see my Medlicott essay (n. 19 above), p. 41, n. 87.

29. On Samuel M. Shute see Callaway, p. 20; and ACAB, vol. 5, p. 520. Shute's *A Manual of Anglo-Saxon for Beginners; Comprising a Grammar, Reader, and Glossary, with Explanatory Notes* (New York, 1867) is reasonably well informed; there was nothing quite like it in America at the time. Shute declares at the outset, "The study of the Anglo-Saxon language in this country, is limited to a very small number of students. Instruction in it is given, probably, in six or eight of our colleges, and but little time is allotted to it" (p. iii). There is support for Shute's lower estimate. I know of but five colleges—in addition to Shute's own Columbian College—that taught Anglo-Saxon in 1867: the Univ. of Virginia (Maximilian Schele De Vere), Harvard College (F. J. Child), Lafayette College (Francis A. March), the Univ. of Mississippi (S. G. Burney), and Haverford College (Thomas Chase). The subject may also have been taught, as part of "historical English," at Washington and Lee by Edward S. Joynes (as at n. 66 below). A decade later the number of schools offering Anglo-Saxon had grown to about two dozen (n. 21 above).

30. On Hiram Corson see Callaway, pp. 20–21; and the DAB, vol. 2, pp. 453–54. Corson's *Hand-Book of Anglo-Saxon and Early English* (New York, 1871) is an intelligently conceived anthology of literature to the end of the 14th century. On p. x Corson thanks Medlicott for lending him books from his "extensive Anglo-Saxon and early English library." Corson's own Anglo-Saxon collection, bequeathed to Cornell, was not meager. In one of the volumes, entitled on the spine "Tracts ¦ Anglo-Saxon" and containing a table of contents in what I take to be Corson's own lucid (and childlike) hand, are bound five Anglo-Saxon scholarly works (plus two other works seemingly out of place here), including N. F. S. Grundtvig's very rare *Bibliotheca Anglo-Saxonica* (London, 1830). Like another Anglo-Saxonist, England's great Henry Sweet, Corson was fascinated by spiritualism. As befits the subject, Corson's book *Spirit Messages, with an Introductory Essay on Spiritual Vitality* (Rochester, NY, 1911) was published posthumously; the messages in it were delivered through the mediumship of one Mrs. Minnie Meserve Soule. Among the spirits Corson records contacting are the Brownings, Tennyson, Whitman, Longfellow, and Hawthorne. (He was friends with the Brownings and Whitman when they were "in the body.") The poets from whom Corson received messages communicate, alas, in prose, nor is their prose especially spirited.

31. On Thomas R. Lounsbury see Callaway, pp. 22–26, and the DAB, vol. 7, pp. 429–31. Lounsbury, a great Chaucerian, seems to have published nothing exclusively on Anglo-Saxon. He deals with the subject at length, however, in his *History of the English Language* (New York, 1879, 1894, 1907).

32. On Stephen H. Carpenter see Callaway, pp. 21–23, and the DAB, vol. 2, pp. 513–14. Carpenter's *An Introduction to the Study of the Anglo-Saxon Language*

(Boston, 1878) was, according to the DAB, a widely used textbook. On Carpenter's *Introduction* see also n. 84 below.

33. On Morgan Callaway see the *Dictionary of Georgia Biography*, ed. Kenneth Coleman and Charles Stephen Gurr, vol. 1 (Athens, GA, 1983), pp. 153–54; and Callaway, p. 17. For information on the elder Callaway I am grateful to Kathy Shoemaker, Department of Special Collections, Emory University. Morgan Callaway, Jr., says his father was asked "to relinquish his chair of Latin in Emory College, Georgia, in order to inaugurate a chair of English Language and Literature in the same institution; and, though in his 40's, he buckled down to learning at first-hand and then to teaching Old English and Middle English in addition to Rhetoric and Modern English Literature." The entry on Morgan Callaway, Jr., in the DAB Supplement, vol. 2, pp. 88–89, gives a few details on the elder Callaway. It is no surprise that at Emory the holder of the Latin chair should be assigned Anglo-Saxon; many Anglo-Saxon teachers in 19th-century America were also classics scholars, the closest one could come to being a linguist. March, "The Study," p. 478, says the "professorship of the English language and comparative philology" created at Lafayette College in 1858—and held by March himself—"was supposed to be the first authoritative recognition of the English and Anglo-Saxon as a separate department of philological study coördinate with Greek and Latin, and the central object of comparative study." March himself taught the classics. See also n. 48 below.

34. On Georg Blaettermann see the *Cyclopædia of American Literature*, ed. Evert A. Duyckinck and George L. Duyckinck (New York, 1866), vol. 2, p. 730; Philip Alexander Bruce, *History of the University of Virginia, 1819–1919*, 5 vols. (New York, 1920–22), vol. 1, pp. 341, 359–60, 366, and vol. 2, pp. 3–4, 8–9, 34, 90–92, 157–60, 293, 296, 323; Callaway, pp. 7–8; O. W. Long, *Thomas Jefferson and George Ticknor: A Chapter in American Scholarship* (Williamstown, MA, 1933), pp. 26–27, 35, 37; Thompson, pp. 246–47; Virginius Dabney, *Mr. Jefferson's University: A History* (Charlottesville, 1981), pp. 14–15 ("Prussian personality"); and Hauer, p. 891. Frantzen, p. 207, asserts that Blaettermann (along with Schele, see n. 36) "published significant scholarship" but cites none, nor do I know of any. I am now editing a letter in French, dated 26 June 1824, which Blaettermann wrote to Jefferson accepting the professorship in modern languages. Blaettermann refers to preparing himself to teach Anglo-Saxon. Although he held a doctorate from Leipzig, the university did not then teach the language, and Blaettermann had to learn it on his own.

35. On Charles Kraitsir see ACAB, vol. 3, p. 574; Bruce, vol. 2, pp. 160–62; and Callaway, p. 8.

36. On Maximilian Schele De Vere see Bruce, vol. 3, pp. 81–84; Callaway, pp. 8–9; the DAB, vol. 8, pp. 423–24; and Dabney, pp. 15–16.

37. On the number of students Schele taught see March, "The Study," p. 478.

38. Neither the brief obituary on John Petheram published by the (London) *Bookseller*, 14 (24 Feb. 1859), 727–28, nor the brief entry on him in the DNB, vol. 15, p. 967, discusses his devotion to Anglo-Saxon. But see the valuable account by T. A. Birrell, "The Society of Antiquaries and the Taste for Old English 1705–1840," *Neophilologus*, 50 (1966), 114–15. Birrell also brings to light a diary Petheram kept while he was a young man, preserved as Oxford Bodleian Lyell Empt 38–39. As Birrell does not describe the diary, a few remarks may be in order. The first volume is a small booklet with a marbled blue and brown cardboard cover, containing 44 leaves, paginated on the recto in pencil. The first entry is for "Sept 5 [1831]"; the last, "Saturday April 14 [1832]." The second volume has hard covers covered in white calf and contains 174 leaves (including the inside back cover). The first entry is for "May 11 Sn 1834"; the last formal entry is dated "131 Vanck St New York. Augt 17. 1835. Finis" (fol. 172), but there are book titles listed on fol. 172v, and fol. 173 contains a note. In his entry for 6 July 1834 (fol. 12) Petheram says he started out for America a few days earlier, and in his entry for 15 August (fol. 16) he notes he first set foot in the country on 11 August. After his initial excitement Petheram grew disenchanted with the new land, declaring in his entry for 17 May 1835 (fol. 130) a strong desire to return to England—"I never saw an elegant American man or woman. . . ." The Bodleian catalogue entry is not certain whether the J. Petheram of the diary is to be identified with John Petheram the author and publisher. The hand of the diary, however, is the same as that of the annotations in Petheram's *Historical Sketch* (see below).

39. The copy of Petheram's *Historical Sketch* owned by Emory Univ. contains the autograph "Richard Paul Wülcker. 1881." Karen Thomson, an antiquarian bookseller in Edinburgh, owns a copy of still greater interest—one annotated by Petheram. I am grateful to her for supplying copies of the annotations and for permission to quote one appearing on p. 180. After saying that Bosworth plans a duodecimo version of his Anglo-Saxon dictionary, Petheram continues, "our friends on the other side of the Atlantic would take one half of the impression! It would appear from the Doctors account that his Dictionary sells much better there than at home, & the subject of Anglo-Saxon has been taken up very warmly by some of the Professors." The annotation, which must be dated no earlier than 1840 (when *Historical Sketch* was published) and probably no later than 1848 (the year Bosworth published his abridgment, *A Compendious Anglo-Saxon and*

English Dictionary), attests the increasing interest in Anglo-Saxon in America near the middle of the 19th century, perhaps not long after 1840.

40. In any case there are various links or parallels between the two men. Medlicott and Petheram were from the same part of England, Petheram's Oldmixon, near Weston-super-Mare, being only about fifteen miles from Bristol, where Medlicott was born. Petheram came to America in 1834, Medlicott in 1835. Neither could afford a university education; each established his own business; both became non-professional scholars devoted to Anglo-Saxon. Medlicott owned a copy of Petheram's *Historical Sketch* (Medlicott catalogue no. 399), which may have helped guide him in forming his collection of Anglo-Saxonica.

41. To date I know of only two German-born philologists in 19th-century America who promoted Anglo-Saxon, Flügel and Klaeber. There were certainly other German-born philologists in America at the time, e.g., Hans Carl Günther von Jagemann (who taught at Earlham College, Indiana Univ., and Harvard); I have found no evidence that these others promoted the language.

42. On Ewald Flügel see the DAB, vol. 3, pt. 2, pp. 484–85; and two items in the *Flügel Memorial Volume* (Stanford, 1916), "Outline of Ewald Flügel's Life," p. [7], and William Dinsmore Briggs, "Dr. Flügel as a Scholar," pp. 36–48.

43. See *The Leland Stanford Junior University First Annual Register 1891–92* (Palo Alto, 1892), p. 48; and *The Leland Stanford Junior University Second Annual Register 1892–93* (Palo Alto, 1893), p. 54. I am grateful to David Sullivan, Dept. of Special Collections, Stanford Univ. Libraries, for copies of pages of the catalogues and for copies of three other documents: M[elville] B[est] A[nderson], "Words Spoken at the Obsequies of Dr. Ewald Flügel, 17 November, 1914" (3 pp.) ("Hardly can there be in this part of the world a more sacred temple than was his library,—a temple wherein to labor was to pray"); "Bericht über die erste Sitzung der 'Vereinigung Alter Deutscher Studenten in Amerika, Zweigverein San Francisco' am 20. Nov., 1914" (5 pp.); and "Professor Ewald Flügel: A Tribute by Karl G. Rendtorff at the Memorial Exercises held in the Unitarian Church of Palo Alto, Nov. 29, 1914" (8 pp., rpt. from "The Pacific Unitarian"). Anderson was not only the first to teach Anglo-Saxon at Stanford; he also introduced the subject to Knox College a decade earlier. See Harold S. Wilson, *'McClure's Magazine' and the Muckrakers* (Princeton, 1970), p. 7. For the reference I am grateful to my wife, Joan Wylie Hall.

44. Ewald Flügel, "The History of English Philology" (delivered in 1902 as a presidential address to the Pacific Coast Branch of the American Philological Association), *Flügel Memorial Volume*, pp. 8–35. In *An Annotated Bibliography of North American Doctoral Dissertations on Old English Language and Literature* (East Lansing and Woodbridge, 1988), Phillip Pulsiano cites a dissertation accepted by Stanford in 1896, "The Ethics of Beowulf," by Kathryne Janette Wilson (no. 441). According to Pulsiano, Stanford reports no reference to the dissertation in its catalogues. If the dissertation was in fact accepted by Stanford in 1896, it seems likely that the director was Flügel.

45. See Malone and Ruud, eds., *Studies in English Philology* (n. 1 above), p. vii. For a brief *vita* of Frederick Klaeber see p. 486.

46. According to Callaway, p. 38, Klaeber spent twenty years on his first edition of *Beowulf* (1922). In "Diminished by Kindness: Frederick Klaeber's Rewriting of Wealhtheow," *Journal of English and Germanic Philology*, 93 (1994), 183–203, Josephine Bloomfield cogently argues that Klaeber's Prussian heritage influenced his treatment of Wealhtheow as strongly maternal. On Klaeber's personal life see Helen Damico, "Klaeber's Last Years: Letters from Bad Koesen," OEN, 22.2 (1989), 41–54, and her essay in the present volume.

47. The first Anglo-Saxon dissertation Klaeber directed appears to be C. Abbetmeyer's (presumably begun in 1899 or earlier): *Old English Poetical Motives Derived from the Doctrine of Sin, A Dissertation Presented to the Faculty of the University of Minnesota for the Degree of Doctor of Philosophy, 1900* (New York, 1903). Abbetmeyer thanks Klaeber both for advice and for "placing at my disposal from his own library books otherwise inaccessible" (p. [2]); Abbetmeyer dedicates the study, however, to Prof. Theodore Buenger, Director of Concordia College, St. Paul, MN.

48. In discussing Americans abroad my chief focus is on their study of Anglo-Saxon or Germanic philology. It should be noted, however, that most of them studied a range of subjects and that for many the study of the classics was paramount, Germanic philology claiming secondary interest (if any). (See n. 33 above.) Even so, the number of Americans who went to Germany to study Germanic philology or the classics was evidently but a fraction of the overall American influx. According to Lawrence McNamee, *Ninety-Nine Years of English Dissertations* (Commerce, TX, 1969), p. 5, "there were over 10,000 Americans who matriculated in Germany during the nineteenth century." It should be noted that there was a strong German presence in America. By the 1880's two million native-born Germans were living in the country: W. T. Hewett, "The Aims and Methods

of Collegiate Instruction in Modern Languages," *Transactions of the Modern Language Association of America 1884–5* [later *PMLA*], 1 (1886), 28. Two million would be about four percent of the population at the time.

49. On Edward D. Sims see the NCAB, vol. 7, p. 131; A. A. Kern, "A Pioneer in Anglo-Saxon," *Sewanee Review*, 11 (1903), 337–44; and Callaway, pp. 12–13.

50. As Callaway points out (p. 13, n. 10), sources differ on when Sims resumed teaching at Randolph-Macon, one giving 1838, another, 1839. The latter seems correct: Sims studied at Halle 1836–38, spent a year in European travel, then returned to his college. Kern, p. 339, mentions only Prof. Tholuck as a teacher under whom Sims studied, but Heinrich Leo, a notable early Anglo-Saxonist, was then at Halle, and it seems reasonable to suppose Sims attended Leo's lectures as well. Leo's *Altsächsische und Angelsächsische Sprachproben* (Halle) was published in 1838. On Leo see Müller (n. 9 above), pp. 255–57.

51. Presumably the law had been changed by 21 March 1860, when the Univ. of Virginia's Prof. Schele married a sister of his deceased wife (DAB, vol. 8, p. 424).

52. On the notebooks see Kern, pp. 340–44, who does his best to show that Sims' grammar-in-progress was not as primitive as it seems.

53. On Francis James Child see Callaway, pp. 31–36; and the DAB, vol. 2, pp. 66–67.

54. On the teaching of Anglo-Saxon at Harvard (of which a detailed study is a desideratum), see Edmonds (n. 27 above), p. 132; March, "The Study," p. 478; March, "Recollections," pp. xx–xxi; and Thompson, p. 250.

55. On Thomas Chase see the DAB, vol. 2, pt. 2, p. 37.

56. See Callaway, p. 22, n. 14.

57. On Theodore W. Hunt see the DAB, vol. 5, p. 393; and Thompson, pp. 252–53.

58. See Hall, "William G. Medlicott" (n. 19 above), p. 27.

59. Hunt's *Cædmon's Exodus and Daniel* is vol. 2 of Harrison's Library of Anglo-Saxon Poetry, for which see Henneman, "English Studies," p. 131. Harrison is discussed below.

60. On Albert S. Cook see the DAB, vol. 2, pp. 370–71; and Thompson, p. 252.

61. Cook's presence at Berkeley in 1883 gives the lie to my statement in "William G. Medlicott," p. 40, n. 83, that Berkeley did not then teach Anglo-Saxon. Contrary to my discussion in the same note, it now seems possible that as early as 1883 Berkeley acquired its copy of Franciscus Junius, ed., *Cædmonis Monachi Paraphrasis Poetica Geneseos ac Præcipuarum Sacræ Paginæ Historiarum* (Amsterdam, 1655); the Berkeley copy of another rare volume, Grim. Johnson Thorkelin, ed., *De Danorum Rebus Gestis Secul. III & IV* (Copenhagen, 1815)—the first edition of *Beowulf*—bears on its bookplate (inside the front cover) "Received August 1883."

62. Fred C. Robinson, "Medieval English Studies at Yale University," in *Medieval English Studies Past and Present*, ed. Akio Oizumi and Toshiyuki Takamiya (Tokyo, 1990), p. 166.

63. Many of the foregoing details come from the entry on Francis A. Blackburn in the Univ. of Chicago's *Annual Register Covering the Academic Year Ending June 30, 1914, with Announcements for the Year 1914–1915* (Chicago, 1914), pp. 39–40. For finding and supplying the information, I am grateful to Richard L. Popp, Dept. of Special Collections, Univ. of Chicago Library. The Univ. of Michigan did not teach Anglo-Saxon when Blackburn attended. In answer to a survey sent out in 1875 on the teaching of the language, an official at the Univ. of Michigan remarked, "Sorry to say that the study is not pursued at all" (March, "The Study," p. 479). Although I have been unable to find any reference to Blackburn's dissertation in Richard Mummendey, *Language and Literature of the Anglo-Saxon Nations as Presented in German Doctoral Dissertations 1885–1950: A Bibliography / Die Sprache und Literatur der Angelsachsen im Spiegel der deutschen Universitätsschriften 1885–1950: Eine Bibliographie* (Charlottesville, VA, and Bonn, 1954), Blackburn's dissertation was in fact published: *The English Future; Its Origin and Development* (Leipzig, 1892).

64. Kenneth Sisam, "The Authority of Old English Poetical Manuscripts," *Studies in the History of Old English Literature* (Oxford, 1953), p. 30, n. 1.

65. J. R. Hulbert, "On the Text of the Junius Manuscript," *Journal of English and Germanic Philology*, 37 (1938), 533. Blackburn's editorial conservatism—in which possible emendations are relegated to the notes and not introduced into the text—is best seen in his edition, *Exodus and Daniel* (Boston, 1907), another early, great American edition of Anglo-Saxon verse.

66. A possible addition to the list is Edward S. Joynes (1834–1917), who graduated from the Univ. of Virginia, studied at the Univ. of Berlin (1856–58), and taught courses in French and German and "historical" English at several southern schools, most notably at South Carolina College (later the Univ. of South Carolina) in 1882–1908. It is unclear how much (if any) Anglo-Saxon Joynes taught in his historical English course. On Joynes see the DAB, vol. 5, pp. 226–27; Henneman, "English Studies," p. 124; and "A Tribute to Dr. Edward Southey Joynes on His Eightieth Birthday, March 2, 1914," *Bulletin of the University of South Carolina*, 37.2 (Apr. 1914).

67. On Thomas R. Price see the DAB, vol. 8, pp. 219–20; Charles Sears Baldwin, "Thomas Randolph Price," *Journal of English and Germanic Philology*, 5 (1903–05), 239–52; and Callaway, pp. 14–16. Price was not the first to teach Anglo-Saxon at Columbia. Marsh's aforementioned *Lectures on the English Language*, which includes a fine discussion of Anglo-Saxon, is based on lectures delivered at Columbia in 1858–59. Anglo-Saxon was first regularly taught there, 1879–84, by Charles P. G. Scott (1853–1936), trained by March at Lafayette College (A.B. 1879, Ph.D. 1881) and known to his students at Columbia as "Great Scott." See Callaway, p. 22, n. 14; and William R. Parker, "The MLA, 1883–1953," *PMLA*, 68.4.2 (1953), 9. For Scott's doctoral dissertation see the Appendix above.

68. On the special connection between Randolph-Macon and Leipzig and between Wofford and Vanderbilt, see Henneman, "English Studies," pp. 126–30. For furnishing the date of Robert Sharp's death, I am grateful to Roy Liuzza, who kindly consulted the archives at Tulane. While he was at Vanderbilt, William M. Baskervill published an edition of *Andreas* (Boston, 1885), dedicated "to My Teachers in English, Thomas R. Price and Richard P. Wülker." Baskervill's text is based upon Wülker's examination of the manuscript in 1884 at Vercelli. The edition is vol. 3 in Harrison's Library of Anglo-Saxon Poetry: Henneman, "English Studies," p. 131. On Baskervill see the sketch by Randall G. Patterson in *Southern Writers: A Biographical Dictionary*, ed. Robert Bain, Joseph M. Flora, and Louis D. Rubin, Jr. (Baton Rouge, 1979), pp. 16–17. I am grateful to my wife, Joan Wylie Hall, for the reference.

69. On James H. Kirkland see the DAB, vol. 11, pt. 2, pp. 360–62. Kirkland received a Ph.D. from Leipzig in 1885 (his studies expressly including Anglo-Saxon), after which he studied for a term in Berlin. In 1893, at age 34, he assumed the presidency of Vanderbilt, a post he held for 44 years. On C. C. Ferrell see the *vita* at the end of his Leipzig dissertation (written under the guidance of Wülker and Sievers), *Teutonic Antiquities in the Anglosaxon* [*sic*] *Genesis* (Halle, 1893).

70. On James M. Garnett see the DAB, vol. 4, pp. 157–58. That Garnett taught Anglo-Saxon at St. John's is stated by March, "The Study," p. 478.

71. On James A. Harrison see the DAB, vol. 4, pp. 343–44; and ACAB, vol. 3, p. 100.

72. Earlier Harrison published *Beowulf, I. Text: Edited from M. Heyne* (Boston, 1882), without a glossary. The 1883 edition added a glossary, Sharp sharing the labor.

73. On Charles W. Kent see the NCAB, vol. 18, p. 143.

74. On J. Douglas Bruce see the NCAB, vol. 21, pp. 115–16. Bruce enrolled at Johns Hopkins in 1889; a decade earlier no one had written an Anglo-Saxon dissertation at an American institution. Things soon changed. During the 1880's nine doctorates in Anglo-Saxon were awarded by American schools; see the Appendix above. It is nonetheless notable that Kent preferred to pursue a doctorate in America despite his study in Germany.

75. Bruce or his heirs must have donated at least part of his personal Anglo-Saxon collection to the Univ. of Tennessee. The university's copy of Rudolf Imelmann's *Forschungen zur altenglischen Poesie* (Berlin, 1920) bears Bruce's signature at the top of the title page.

76. On James M. Hart see the DAB, vol. 4, pt. 2, pp. 357–58. Presumably Hart graduated from Central High School about 1856; as the school ceased teaching Anglo-Saxon in 1854, he would have had at least a year of Anglo-Saxon. In any case it is easy to believe that his father, who held knowledge of the language in high esteem, would have acquainted him with Anglo-Saxon. For the younger Hart's basic ideas on teaching Anglo-Saxon (including a recommendation that "if any one of the longer Anglo-Saxon poems is to be read" *Elene* be taken rather than *Beowulf*), see his "The College Course in English Literature, how it may be Improved," *Transactions of the Modern Language Association of America 1884–5*, 1 (1886), 84–95. The essay is briefly discussed by Frantzen, pp. 75–76.

77. Unfortunately for the present purpose, Hart's narrative centers on his earlier stay in Germany, when he studied law, rather than on his later stay, when he pursued philology. There is but a single direct reference to his work under C. W. M. Grein (p. 93). An unlooked-for bonus, however, is Hart's giving the abstract of a dissertation on the

Gospel of Nicodemus "defended by an acquaintance of mine at Marburg, in 1872" (p. 280), who can be none other than Richard P. Wülker. Another fascinating source on the experiences of an American studying in Germany is Joynes' "Old Letters of a Student in Germany"; first published in various issues of a Richmond weekly, *Magnolia*, in 1863–64, the letters were integrated and reprinted in *Bulletin of the University of South Carolina*, 45 (1916). On Joynes see n. 66 above.

78. On Francis B. Gummere see the DAB, vol. 4, pp. 48–49; and the *vita* printed at the end of *The Anglo-Saxon Metaphor* (Halle, 1881).

79. On James W. Bright see the DAB, vol. 2, p. 45. For Bright's dissertation see Pulsiano (n. 44 above), no. 787. The dissertation is reported as "not owned by university."

80. So the DAB. Further, as the Appendix above shows, eighteen of the 39 Anglo-Saxon dissertations completed in America before 1900 were done at Johns Hopkins, most or all, I suppose, directed by Bright; Bright's own Johns Hopkins dissertation would make nineteen.

81. One of the first great American Anglo-Saxon editions appeared in the series, George Philip Krapp, ed., *Andreas and the Fates of the Apostles: Two Anglo-Saxon Narrative Poems* (Boston, 1906). Krapp dedicated the book to "James Wilson Bright | Scholar and Guide of Scholars."

82. See the Appendix for a list of the 39 authors, dates, and schools. In *Ninety-Nine Years of English Dissertations* (n. 48 above), p. 24, McNamee gives figures showing that 128 doctoral dissertations on Anglo-Saxon had been written worldwide from 1871 through 1899; if this is accurate, America's 39 would represent about 30 percent of the total. (In "William G. Medlicott," p. 42, n. 89, I misinterpreted McNamee's statistics; I should have said only eleven Anglo-Saxon doctoral dissertations were written in the world—not in America—from 1871 through 1883, the year of Medlicott's death. In America during this period only three had been written, making Medlicott's Anglo-Saxon collection, begun in 1845, all the more farsighted.) As noted, more than a quarter of the American doctorates in Anglo-Saxon went to women. March, "The Study," p. 478, quotes Corson of Cornell in 1875 as saying of his Anglo-Saxon classes, "The lady students do the best."

83. On Francis Andrew March see the DAB, vol. 6, pp. 268–70 (sketch by Kemp Malone); Bright, "An Address" (n. 7 above), pp. cxvii–cxxxvii; and, on March's cultural or pedagogic doctrines, Frantzen, pp. 208–13.

84. March's *Reader* is the first American book I know to use a space to divide long verse lines into half-lines, a technique apparently borrowed from Moritz Heyne, ed., *Beovulf, mit ausführlichem Glossar* (Paderborn, 1863; 2nd ed. 1868). Carpenter also uses caesural space in his *Introduction*, 1878 (n. 32 above).

85. Bright, "An Address," pp. cxxviii–cxxix. My own experience on first looking into March's grammar accords with Bright's. When, more than a decade ago, I came upon it, I returned to the book repeatedly over the course of two months, each time with renewed admiration.

86. The MLA, for example, was founded largely by philologists (for which, I suppose, they will have to be forgiven, as they could not have foreseen "the one-winged, sinister-listing beast a century later"): Parker (n. 67 above), pp. 3–32. Many Anglo-Saxonists mentioned in the present article were MLA officers at one time or other, including Garnett, Harrison, Kent, James M. Hart, March, Bright, Gummere, Cook, Price, and Bruce (the last seven of them serving as president). Other members of the MLA among those mentioned are Baskervill, Klaeber, Schele, Scott, and Sharp. Lounsbury attended the first meeting but never joined. On other early societies or philological journals see Callaway, pp. 18–19; and Parker, pp. 8, 10, 25, 27, 30–32.

"My Professor of Anglo-Saxon Was Frederick Klaeber": Minnesota and Beyond

Helen Damico

In 1893, after having received his Ph.D. at the University of Berlin the year before with a thesis on Chaucer under Julius Zupitza, Frederick Klaeber took up teaching duties at the University of Minnesota, where he spent his entire formal academic career. From his entry status of Instructor he rose progressively to the rank of Assistant Professor of English Philology in 1896; Professor of English and Comparative Philology in 1898 (a department which he founded); and Professor Emeritus on his retirement in 1931.[1] Klaeber had a particular fondness for Minnesota (he declined numerous offers from other universities, especially after the publication of the first edition of *Beowulf* in 1922), but his affection for Berlin and for Germany was equally strong. This double attachment caused him political difficulties—first during World War I, at which time he was charged with disloyalty, a charge he successfully refuted and for which he received an apology; and, second, during World War II, when he found himself in dire difficulties with both governments.[2]

After his tenure at Minnesota, Klaeber returned to Germany, where he lived in active retirement as Adjunct Professor of Anglo-Saxon at the University of Berlin. For a time he had the best of both worlds: he ran an advanced seminar on *Beowulf*, lectured extracurricularly, published voluminously, and was the unofficial faculty in residence for the University of Minnesota in Berlin.[3] The Hitler years, especially those between 1936 and 1940, and World War II cut short that blissful existence, so that towards the end of his life Klaeber experienced much suffering before his death on 4 October 1954, almost 91 years to the day after his birth (1 October 1863).[4]

At the time of his emigration Klaeber knew little about the university system in America and still less about Minnesota, never even having heard the name Minneapolis, the city which was to be his home for 38 years. Shortly after his retirement, in a lecture to students at Schulpförta, Klaeber's gymnasium from 1876 to 1881 (fig. 1), Klaeber characterized the call to Minnesota as something that happened "by chance" but added philosophically, "if there is such a thing as chance."[5] The appointment had been arranged by Zupitza, and it was a call by which the young Klaeber was tempted and which he could not refuse. In the early 1890's the University of Minnesota was, as Klaeber described it, a "young institution" with "childhood sicknesses." In the succeeding period of some 40 short years it became an institution of some standing. To have participated in the development of such an important research and teaching center had been, for Klaeber, "a glorious task," and he had been caught by the "magic power of the strongly . . . optimistic life."[6]

In time Klaeber came to know the shortcomings of the American educational system. Not all those institutions that were called "universities" were bona fide research centers in the German sense of the word. Nor were the students committed to serious study. Klaeber found the quality of the curriculum—again by German standards—acceptable only at the advanced degree levels. Preparatory studies leading to the baccalaureate degree were quite inferior. For Klaeber, the essential flaw in the American educational system was that it lacked the German gymnasium. In Klaeber's estimation, it was the exemplary training he had received at Pförta that had enabled him to achieve the "personal excellence" which he felt had been required of him as an expatriate professor in an American university and which he attempted to instill in his students at Minnesota.[7]

One of Klaeber's contributions to the University of Minnesota was his attempt to transpose the European tradition of comparative philology into the curriculum. Klaeber had been trained by Julius Zupitza and

Figure 1. Schulpförta. Klaeber's gymnasium. Photo: Helen Damico.

Adolf Tobler.[8] His thought had been shaped by such men as Wilhelm Dilthey and Johann Gustav Droysen. Before Berlin he had followed studies at the universities of Halle, Leipzig, and Kiel. And he was a product of Pförta, the school of Friedrich Nietzsche, Gotthold Lessing, and Leopold von Ranke. To attempt to transpose the intellectual sophistication of Germany to an amorphous midwestern institution was no small task—and in the end he had to learn to be less demanding of both his students and his administration. Klaeber's responsibilities upon taking the post had been to teach Germanic philology, principally Old English and *Beowulf*, but also Middle English, History of the English Language, and Gothic. During Klaeber's tenure all doctoral candidates in English were required to take the Old English-*Beowulf* sequence. The late John Clark, who himself came to hold the position of Professor of Old English at the University of Minnesota, was fond of relating an anecdote (told to him by Martin B. Ruud) which suggests that Gothic, if not strictly a requirement, had been a desideratum. It seems that Klaeber, who was always on the examining committee for the Ph.D. oral preliminaries, invariably would open the examination proceedings by glancing up at the candidate with his piercing eyes and requesting, "Will the candidate now pray in Gothic?"[9] To midwestern American students interested in James Fenimore Cooper the request must have seemed somewhat bizarre. Nonetheless, Klaeber's standing was such that the opening proceedings became a tradition: all doctoral candidates in English recited the Lord's Prayer in Gothic. Professor Clark, who remembered Klaeber from over a 50-year distance at the time I interviewed him, described him as "a product of the German university right through his life"—in his preoccupation with scholarship, in his disregard for grades, in his primary concern for graduate students, and in behavioral patterns that were thought idiosyncratic by young midwesterners. They were at a loss to understand, for example, why he persisted in entering the classroom fifteen minutes after the appointed class time, and he did not explain to them or to anyone else that this late entry was a tradition in German universities.

As would be expected, the course of study Klaeber had established slowly began to erode after his retirement. Martin B. Ruud, who had taken over Klaeber's courses, attempted to continue the program as long as he was able, but by the end of the 1930's only Old English and *Beowulf* remained as requirements. Doctoral candidates in English no longer had to pray in Gothic, and it was only due to the efforts of Clark and Ruud that Old English continued as a requirement for the Ph.D. By the end of the 1970's, however, both Old English and *Beowulf* had become electives.

Unfortunately, I have not been able to find sets of classroom lectures or lengthy written reminiscences of Klaeber in the classroom. Three sources give a general picture of Klaeber conducting his class: the first is a brief recollection by Mary Ellen Chase, from which part of the title of this paper was taken; the second is a notebook that belonged to Cleora Clark Wheeler, who had taken Klaeber's Old English course during her freshman year in 1900; and the third is the interview reminiscence by Professor Clark.[10] A fourth source is a poetic spoof entitled "Klaeber" that appeared in the University of Minnesota *Gopher Yearbook* of 1909, accompanied by a cartoon sketch of Klaeber.[11]

Mrs. Chase describes her professor of Anglo-Saxon as a "marvelous teacher," whose engagement with his subject was passionate. What to other teachers might have been dull, to Klaeber was "full of color and light." Once when Mrs. Chase had protested a letter grade Klaeber had given her, he "looked at [her] vaguely with his small blue eyes and said, 'Why do you mind? Those letters, they are nothing'" (*A Goodly Fellowship*, p. 208). Klaeber had wit, and he was humorous in action and appearance. The tailed coat (which became his trademark), Mrs. Chase remembers, "reached below his knees and was always getting in the way" (ibid.).

Cleora Clark Wheeler's *Notebook* contains her lecture notes taken during Klaeber's Introductory Old English course given between January and June in 1900. The text used was Klaeber's own *Old English Historical Prose Texts*, an anthology compiled and published in 1896. From Mrs. Wheeler's notes it is possible to see Klaeber's interest in historical linguistics, for the bulk of the notes deal with Old English in the context of other Indo-European languages, along with traditional lectures on the characteristics of the Germanic languages, Grimm's and Verner's laws, the Great Vowel Shift, foreign influences on Old English, morphology, and a brief section on Old English dialects. The notes are especially full and complete on the consonantal shifts, with complete diagrams of the laws. Only occasionally is literature mentioned. In the context of what must have been a lecture on the Old English alliterative line, *Cædmon's Hymn* is referred to as possibly being stanzaic. As would be expected, there is a section on Bede, and what appears to have been a full lecture on Alfred and his work. Mrs. Wheeler's notebook reveals that Klaeber spent time preparing students for his examinations, for he apparently drew up a list of some 21 items for their study, which included the representative topics mentioned above and a separate category for the Norse element in Old English.

By the late 1920's when John Clark was an undergraduate, Klaeber's *Beowulf* course numbered some twenty to 25 students, graduate and undergraduate combined. Professor Clark, who described himself as a not-yet serious student of Old English, sat in the back row and participated along with the other students in "translating or attempting to translate the text." Clark remembered few details—Klaeber's customary entrance into the classroom fifteen minutes after the hour, his piercing eyes, his crisp closure at the hour's end, and his speech. Klaeber spoke English flawlessly, except for a very heavy German accent. Clark suspected that he retained the accent consciously, for although Klaeber "was very heavily Germanic in his ordinary speech," he could "at will produce every conceivable sound."[12] Clark felt that this was part of his "Germanness," of Klaeber's never having fully assimilated himself into American culture.[13]

Klaeber's strong German accent was the source of the comic bit of verse in the *Gopher Yearbook* of 1909 (p. 154):

Klaeber

There was a man in our U,
And he was wondrous wise;
But he had trouble to pronounce
His "e's" and "o's" and "y's."

"But as for modern English
I do not give a dern,
I know Old English forms," he said,
"In every crook and turn."

"So I'll say 'poihaps,' and 'voib' and scorn
All criticism rude;
For it's by my Early English
That I earn my daily food."

Figure 2. Cartoon of Klaeber. *Gopher Yearbook* (1909). Courtesy of the University of Minnesota Archives.

One wishes the verse were somewhat cleverer, but it and the accompanying cartoon (fig. 2) do indicate what an aura of strangeness Klaeber must have held for his midwestern students.

Klaeber's History of the English Language course had less of an enrollment, about seven or eight students, with the syllabus of readings consisting of articles from periodicals. There was no textbook: the approach was empirical and the method Socratic. It was unsettling to the undergraduate Clark, who found the class

> extremely unsystematic—random discussions, random referenda, random subjects. And he did not restrict himself to English, come to think of it. . . . One day I remember, we must have been discussing the vagaries of English spelling somehow, and I remember him turning to me and saying, "Mr.

> Clark, how do you spell 'weird'?" And I misspelled it. And he was most gratified. And he then proceeded to explain why I had misspelled it and so on, and so on, and I've never misspelled it since.

In Clark's recollection, Klaeber was more stimulated by scholarship than by his teaching, a situation caused by non-serious students.[14] He felt it unfortunate that Klaeber had had to learn to be undemanding in the American university system, and perhaps, in Clark's words, he had "overlearned" it.

Being an undergraduate, Clark had little social contact with Klaeber, visiting neither his home on 616 Ninth Avenue South (figs. 3 and 4) nor his office at 216 Folwell Hall. He was present, however, at a banquet that may have been Klaeber's farewell dinner. This was the only time Clark had occasion to see Charlotte Klaeber, whom he described as a short woman (as Klaeber himself was short) and a "confirmed hausfrau," or so it seemed to him (fig. 5):

> I remember them in 1931, when he was on the point of leaving to go to Germany. . . . There was an Honor Society here [at the University of Minnesota] of students of languages, and they had an annual initiation banquet, and of course the faculty who owned a dinner jacket wore them . . . and Klaeber showed up in a costume nobody there had ever seen before—it wasn't a tailcoat—it was a frock coat literally—not cutaways either—a black broadcloth, double-breasted frock coat, and, I suppose, that was the common continental evening costume in the Germany of the 1890s.

Klaeber's trademarks—the tailed coat he wore in the classroom and the frock coat on formal occasions—were a sign of Klaeber's difference, his "Germanness" among the university community.

In Clark's estimation, Klaeber's sense of "Germanness" caused him to be socially retiring, having "virtually no social life with his colleagues in the Department of English, and certainly none with students, and certainly not with undergraduates." Not that he was cold or forbidding. This was not even a consideration in describing his character. Nonetheless, from Klaeber's correspondence we know that the Klaebers had friends from the educated German community and colleagues from the

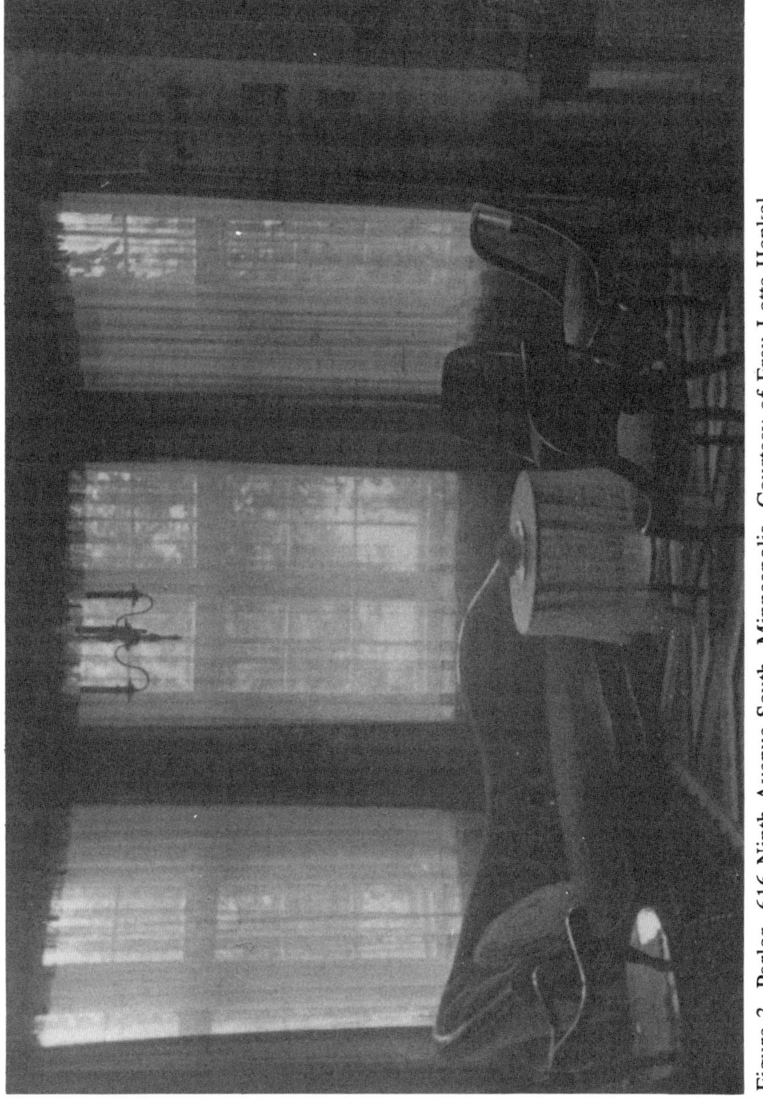

Figure 3. Parlor. 616 Ninth Avenue South, Minneapolis. Courtesy of Frau Lotte Henkel.

Department of German.[15] Klaeber's letters reveal a warm, collegial relationship with several of his colleagues in English, Joseph W. Beach and Kemp Malone, for instance. To be sure, the Beach-Malone letters are from the last years, after his retirement to Germany, but

Figure 4. The Klaebers in their sitting room at 616 Ninth Avenue South, Minneapolis. Courtesy of Frau Lotte Henkel.

Figure 5. Charlotte Klaeber. Courtesy of Frau Lotte Henkel.

nonetheless those documents and the Malone-Ruud Miscellany point to strong professional ties in the early years as well.[16]

Klaeber's contribution to the life of the German-American community in the Twin Cities was considerable. He was one of the directors of the Germanistische Gesellschaft of St. Paul-Minneapolis, for whom he published *Deutsche Worte* in 1917, an anthology of prose excerpts from renowned German writers, and *Deutsche Kriegsgedichte* in 1915, a year after the beginning of World War I, an anthology of war poems by German poets, which in his words "successfully captured with deep understanding and inner sympathy the terrible fateful struggle of Germany, and one senses in the poems the spirit that fills the fighting brothers."[17]

In a 1916 article discussing German war poetry published since the outbreak of the war in 1914, Klaeber sees the ten thousand printed poems—in a variety of German dialects—as the combined voice of the German people, responding to the treachery and violence of those first days of August. Obviously moved by the poetry while recognizing that a large portion of these works lack merit, Klaeber nonetheless sees the circumstances of the war as having sparked a literary renaissance whereby "we feel the true pulse of the people like it hasn't been felt in a long time."[18] He calls the war "the holy war of the people"; the "true hero" is the German people; and the "true content" is "the unfolding of the soul of the people."[19] It was perhaps the publication of the two anthologies, his approval and praise of German poetic production in print, his open affection for his native land, his active participation in the Germanistische Gesellschaft, and his close associations with members of both the German community and the Department of German that led to the disloyalty charges brought against him in 1917.

It was an unfortunate time. A Minnesota Commission of Public Safety had been formed in the capital, St. Paul, and what amounted to sanctioned witch hunts began to take place. Charges of disloyalty were brought against administration and faculty alike, especially the high-ranking professorial segment in the Department of German, although the Departments of Biology and Chemistry were also singled out.[20] On 17 September 1917 a letter from T. G. Winter, reporting charges of disloyalty against select members of the Department of German and against Klaeber, was sent to the Honorable Fred B. Snyder, President of the Board of Regents, who in turn informed Marion L. Burton, President of the University: "Professor Klaeber is as radical as ever Shafer [another accused individual] was and certainly should not be allowed to remain in the University; he has done and is doing everything he can to further the German cause."[21] The accuser, who (in Winter's words) was "absolutely reliable," remained anonymous, but all who were named in the letter were asked to await the pleasure of the Regents. Marion L. Burton responded to what must have been a volatile situation with temperance and sensitivity. He asked Klaeber to refute the charges in writing, while he himself would present the case to the Regents. I quote a portion from Klaeber's refutation of the charge of disloyalty:[22]

> I have given the best years of my life to the service of this university and country, I have helped to educate a generation of American (not German) men and women, I have proved my loyalty every day during the past twenty-four years. To be told, in the twenty-fifth year of my service, that I am regarded as a disloyal citizen, is a blow, in fact an outrage which I shall not easily forget.

Klaeber was vindicated, as were his colleagues. Nonetheless, it was for him a sad and painful time.

Yet in point of fact Klaeber felt himself to be German. In a note to his niece Lotte Henkel, he wrote: "May my thought, action and yearning be German, German my love, German my song, and German my death bell toll."[23] But he was not fully of Germany. He identified himself most closely with those German-American intellectuals who offered much to American culture in the late nineteenth and early twentieth centuries. Despite his American citizenship and loyalty to the government, Klaeber was sensitive to and proud of his expatriate status. What pleased him most about receiving an honorary doctorate from the University of Wisconsin was that in the introductory remarks he was praised not only for having promoted knowledge in America but also for having done so in the orderly, German scholarly tradition.

Klaeber assessed the contribution made to the rise of the American university system and culture by German researchers and German-American educators as "extraordinary."[24] As a branch of study in the American educational system of the first third of the twentieth century, German had what Klaeber called a "decisive advantage" over other foreign languages because of the high standard of language proficiency of teachers who had been trained in German church and private schools and who spoke German in the home. The development of Germanic Philology in the American universities—which came more vigorously and earlier than in England—was a direct result of Americans "flocking" to study at German universities and of the creative activity of German-American scholars, such as Hermann Collitz, the linguist and founder of *Hesperia*; Gustaf Karsten, the founder of *The Journal of Germanic Philology* in 1897; Edward Prokosch; and the literary historian Kuno Francke, disseminator of German culture and founder of the German Museum at Harvard University.[25]

On 13 February 1940, at a meeting of The Berlin Society of the Study of Modern Languages, Klaeber defended these German-Americans.[26] In the course of a lecture on the topic of what he called American German (a type of language mingling that springs up in immigrant cultures), Klaeber discoursed on the characteristics of being an immigrant in America, in a non-particularized way to be sure, but nonetheless in a manner that betrayed a sensitivity to the duality of the immigrant's position. He felt that the most profound contribution to both German and American culture was that which had been contributed by German-American writers composing in German, especially on the theme of expatriation. He quotes from Konrad Krez's *An Das Vaterland* (1869), which expresses the writer's enduring attachment to Germany, and from a poem by Kuno Francke, which articulates the pull the poet feels for his native land: "Oh, Germany, none of all your children loves you more than we do, the estranged, the Germans across the sea. You are more than a mother to us, you are our life's peace."[27] Klaeber's comments on these poems reflect the complexity of his own emotional attachment to both Germany and America. Characteristically, he concludes his remarks first by citing a homespun maxim that the "loyalty to the chosen wife does not exclude attachment to the mother," then by reaffirming the Germanic spirit in which "there is an inherent unique life power."[28] To be loyal to the new land while entertaining the reality of one's own German spirit is at the center of the dilemma that informs the character of the immigrant, caught between two loves and two loyalties, a psychic condition with which Klaeber lived to the end of his days.

By far, Klaeber's main contribution, which brought international recognition to the University of Minnesota as an institution, rested on his publication of the 1922 edition of *Beowulf*, wherein he "settles" (his words) the three main issues of Beowulfian scholarship: single over multiple authorship, Christian over pagan authorship, and the author's familiarity with the *Aeneid*.[29] To American students and scholars he came to be, and (I would venture to say) he remains, the authority on *Beowulf*. His Minnesota colleagues looked upon him as a German expatriate who contributed the best years of his life to the enhancement of Anglo-Saxon Studies in the American university curriculum. Ironically, Klaeber carried this expatriate status when he returned to his native land. Martin Lehnert remembered that between 1936 and 1940 Klaeber was looked upon as "an American" by the students and younger faculty at the Englisches Seminar in Berlin.[30] Those students who had even heard of him saw him as a "marginal figure" with little if any standing in the educational fervor that characterized the University of Berlin in the late 1930's. The introductory courses in Old English and *Beowulf* were then taught not by Klaeber but by the charismatic young Lehnert, then assistant to Wilhelm Horn, the Professor of Anglo-Saxon. Lehnert had just published his *Altenglisches Elementarbuch*, which quickly came to be known as *Der kleine Lehnert* and for which he received praise from Klaeber,[31] and a year later his *Beowulf: Eine Auswahl mit Einführung* was published, again with praise from Klaeber.[32] Lehnert was a young man rising to fame, and his appeal was to the young. The lecture halls filled to capacity. In contrast, Klaeber's advanced seminar on *Beowulf*, which dealt with the poem's etymology and its linguistic and stylistic beauty rather than with ideology, drew in three or four students at a time.

This indifference from the student body seemed not to touch Klaeber. Professor Lehnert remembered some dozen times he had been present at interviews between Klaeber and Wilhelm Horn in the latter's office. There was detachment in Klaeber's composure, with a formality that was warm and cordial but removed. The discussions between the two in Lehnert's presence had to do with scheduling the *Beowulf* seminar, which, although poorly enrolled, was nevertheless continuously offered, and with other departmental matters that touched upon Klaeber's position as an adjunct professor. Klaeber and Horn had been friends as well as colleagues. It was Horn who wrote the congratulatory 80th-birthday tribute to Klaeber in the *Archiv für das Studium der neueren Sprachen* in 1943 (fig. 6),[33] and it may have been Horn's presence at the University of Berlin that had prompted Klaeber upon his retirement to Germany in 1931 to choose that institution as his home base rather than the universities at Halle and Leipzig, which had also been possibilities and which were closer to his beloved Schulpförta and to his wife's family at Bad Kösen.[34] Klaeber proved to be a good friend to Horn. Sensitive to Horn's need for solitude to complete his *Laut und Leben—Englische Lautgeschichte der neueren Zeit*, Klaeber gave his colleague the use of his home in Bad Kösen during the violent air raids over Berlin.[35]

What is somewhat disconcerting in assessing Klaeber as a teacher is that we cannot point to a line of individual and identifiable students on whom he had an influential and lasting effect. His situation is like that of Beowulf, who had no son to whom he could leave his country. In Minnesota, Klaeber was an expatriate scholar holding fast to a culture that was foreign to the majority of his colleagues and students. In Germany, at the University of Berlin of the 1930's, Klaeber was thought of as marginal, not fully German, not fully American. As

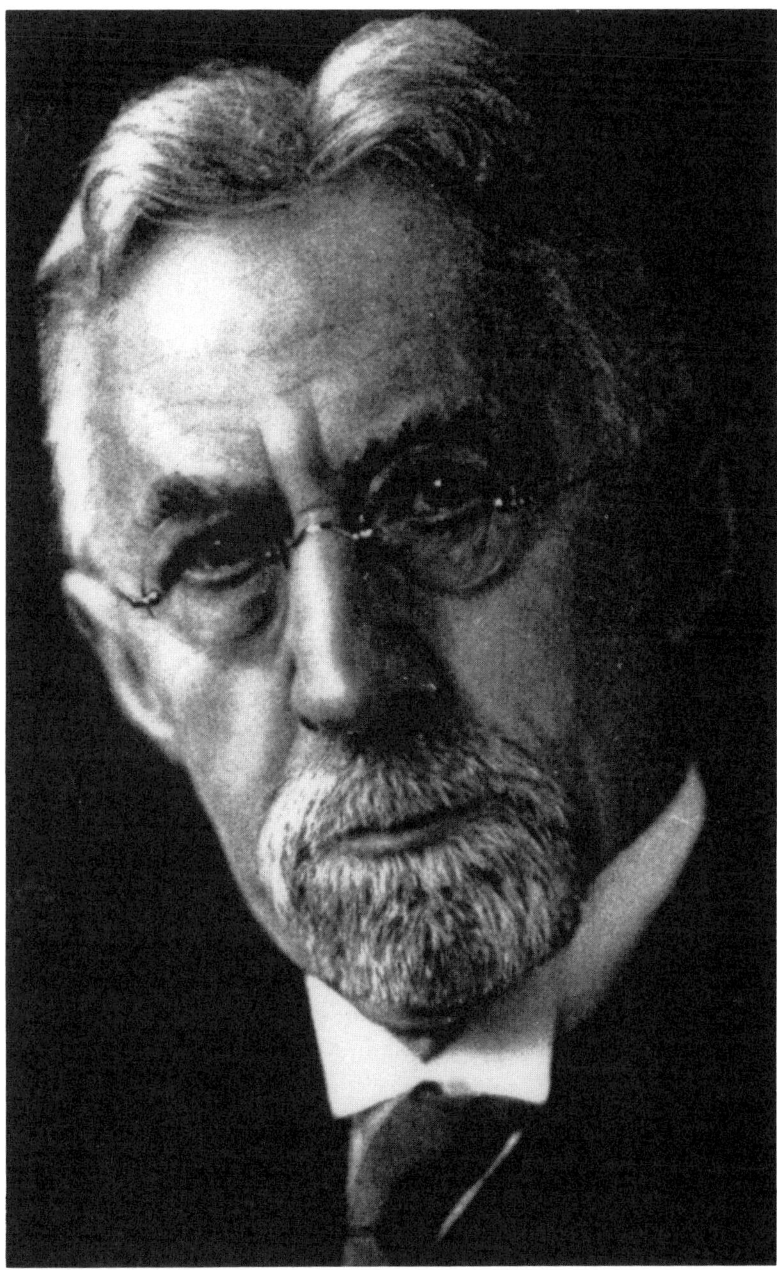

Figure 6. Klaeber at 80. Courtesy of Professor Dr. Martin Lehnert.

Lehnert candidly pointed out, Klaeber could do nothing to advance the careers of the young German scholars in the Germany of the 1930's. Humane, gracious, and gentle, he continued to offer his advanced seminar on *Beowulf* as long as he could to the one or two students who might be interested in the first English epic.

When his home in Berlin-Zehlendorf West (and, apparently, only his on the street [fig. 7]) was bombed by an American plane in 1944,[36] he removed himself to Bad Kösen, where he remained until the end of his days. These later days were harsh, filled with sickness and poverty. Yet he continued an active professional life as best he could until the end: the last item in the Lehnert bibliography lists an entry for 1953, and Klaeber was obviously a part of the professional circle in post-war Germany. In one of his letters to Kemp Malone he notes the scholarly activities of mutual colleagues, Max Förster, Ferdinand Holthausen, Schirmer, Wilhelm Horn;[37] in another he reports the death of Johannes Hoops in April 1949; and in the same letter he praises Malone for his scrutiny of the Thorkelin manuscripts, which examination gave Klaeber new readings on *unsnyttrum* and *ge(l)denne* in *Beowulf*.[38] His attitude toward his work is best described by his own words in a letter to Lehnert (9 October 1953), thanking him for his article in the *Berliner Zeitung* honoring him on his 90th birthday:

> To reach one's ninetieth year is no achievement, at most it could be considered an "act of grace." The only thing I can rightfully claim is that, during these long years, I took great care over my research, but the accomplishment lags far behind all good intentions. My "superbiblical" age reminds me of the familiar proverb, which, with a syntactical alteration from Luther's version, might go like this: If life has been full of trouble and work, it has been glorious.[39]

In Bad Kösen, Klaeber continued his customary work schedule, working from late evening to sunrise, until the morning they found him collapsed in his home, having slipped and broken his hip. For ten years, following his move to Bad Kösen, the study on the second floor of Berbigstrasse 3 (fig. 8) was the scene of unceasing intellectual

Figure 7. The Klaeber house at 15 Niklasstrasse, Berlin-Zehlendorf West. Courtesy of Frau Lotte Henkel.

Figure 8. Klaeber's second-floor study. 3 Berbigstrasse, Bad Kösen. Photo: Helen Damico.

activity, despite the harassments from the Russian police, despite the hunger and the loneliness and the cold. It was there that he completed in scholarly solitude the supplement to the third and final edition of *Beowulf*, which (as he noted in a letter to Beach) he hoped would "perhaps outlive" him.[40] It is that edition—finished as he lay partially paralyzed in his bed those last years—that is his legacy, and it is in the context of that work that all Anglo-Saxonists who follow him emerge as students of Klaeber.

UNIVERSITY OF NEW MEXICO

NOTES

This paper is dedicated with gratitude to the late John Clark, Prof. Emeritus of the Univ. of Minnesota, the late Martin Lehnert, Prof. Dr. Emeritus of Humboldt University, and Frau Lotte Henkel, Frederick Klaeber's niece. It was their generosity in sharing their reminiscences of Klaeber with me that made this piece possible. The materials cited in the present essay were made available to me by Frau Henkel and Profs. Clark and Lehnert; Klaeber's remaining letters are found at the Univ. of Minnesota Archives. The correspondence between Kemp Malone and Klaeber cited herein is housed at The Robert W. Woodruff Library at Emory Univ. My thanks to Prof. Dr. Klaus Ostheeren of the Univ. of Münster, who facilitated my meeting with Prof. Lehnert, and I owe a special debt to Dr. Helga Spevack-Husmann of the Univ. of Münster, whose help was indispensable in the interviews with Frau Henkel.

1. "Frederick Klaeber 1863–1954." Obituary written by Prof. John Clark, Chairman of the Dept. of English, and presented to the University Senate of the Univ. of Minnesota at its meeting on 10 Nov. 1955.

2. Klaeber's trials with the U.S. Government are discussed in my article "Klaeber's Last Years: Letters from Bad Koesen," OEN, 22.2 (Spring 1989), 41–54.

3. Letter to Lotus D. Coffman, President of the Univ. of Minnesota, 25 February 1935; Univ. of Minnesota Archives.

4. Klaeber (born in Beetzendorf, Prussia) is buried at the cemetery in Bad Kösen a short distance from his house on Berbigstrasse 3, next to Charlotte Klaeber. He died alone at 7 A.M. in a private clinic in Naumburg to which he had been taken some two weeks before (interview with Frau Lotte Henkel). He was buried at 1:30 P.M. on 8 October 1954.

5. Fr. Klaeber, "Aus den Erfahrungen eines Alten Pförtners in Amerika," pp. 11–12, on p. 11 ("Es geht oft merkwürdig zu im Leben. Durch Zufall—wenn es einen Zufall gibt—wurde ich vor nahezu vierzig Jahren nach Minneapolis gerufen . . ."). Only these two pages are found in a notebook of Klaeber's with a cover sheet in his handwriting, in Frau Henkel's possession. I have not been able to locate the journal. Schulpförta is located outside of Bad Kösen, on the road to Naumburg.

6. Klaeber, "Aus den Erfahrungen," p. 12 (". . . zu Anfang der 90er Jahre des vorigen Jahrhunderts war es eine junge, ganz und gar unfertige Anstalt, die noch manche Kinderkrankheit zu überwinden hatte. . . . Und zu diesem Aufbau einer wichtigen Lehr- und Forschungsstätte mitbestimmend beizutragen war eine herrliche Aufgabe, die unser einen mit hoher Genugtuung erfüllen musste. Wer hätte sich dem Zauberbann des mächtig flutenden, zukunftsfrohen Lebens entziehen können?").

7. Ibid.: (". . . denn auf den Beweis persönlicher Tüchtigkeit kommt es drüben ganz besonders an"). Klaeber was a true Pförtner. In his later years, his niece would wheel him from his home to the school on pleasant afternoons. He had much affection for it, and he requested that the young students from Pförta sing the traditional Latin hymn at his funeral, which they did at the cemetery service.

8. In Klaeber's Latin *vita* appended to his dissertation, *Das Bild bei Chaucer*, Teil I, Abschnitt 1: *Sammlung der Bilder aus der Tierwelt* (Berlin, 1892), and in the Klaeber *Festschrift*, *Studies in English Philology, A Miscellany in Honor of Frederick Klaeber*, ed. Kemp Malone and Martin B. Ruud (Minneapolis, 1929), p. 486.

9. I interviewed the late Prof. John Clark on 4 August 1982 at his home in Minneapolis, a meeting that he graciously allowed me to tape.

10. Mary Ellen Chase, *A Goodly Fellowship* (New York, 1939), pp. 207–08; Cleora Clark Wheeler's *Notebook* is found at the Univ. of Minnesota Archives. Pages 32–84 inclusive of the *Notebook* are given over to Klaeber's class, concluding with a closing citation, "(Work under Dr. Frederick Klaeber ends here)."

11. The Univ. of Minnesota Archives, the *Gopher Yearbook* files.

12. This was undoubtedly a result of his early training in pronunciation of Latin and English at Schulpförta under the tutelage of Theodor Plüss, who was a strict taskmaster to the young Klaeber. Klaeber relates an anecdote of his standing in a corner in the Plüss study and being taught the "then unknown art of pronouncing correctly, clearly, intelligibly and of reciting adequately" ("Kaum hatte ich drei Worte gesprochen: Hoc die solemni, so rief der Plüss: 'Halt, ich habe das **h** nicht gehört. Und nun unterwies er mich in der unbekannten Kunst, richtig, deutlich, verständlich auszusprechen und angemessen vorzutragen" ["Aus den Erfahrungen," p. 12]). The young Klaeber was subsequently criticized for pronouncing Latin too correctly.

13. For a discussion of the influence of Klaeber's "Germanness" on the *Beowulf* edition see Josephine Helm Bloomfield's dissertation, "The Canonization of Editorial Sensibility in *Beowulf*: A Philological and Historical Reassessment of the Klaeber Edition," Diss. Univ. of California-Davis 1991.

14. Clark was primarily referring to himself in this instance and was, after many years of teaching Old English, sympathetic to the wearing effect non-responsive students might have on a teacher.

15. Letters in the archives at the Univ. of Minnesota Archives indicate that the Klaebers had a large circle of friends from the university community.

16. Perhaps the most poignant are those Klaeber sent to Beach in which he describes the hardships of his later years and, in particular, the death of Mrs. Klaeber. (See Damico, "Klaeber's Last Years.") Klaeber was a devoted correspondent, responding to every letter that was sent to him. His niece recalls his sitting at his chair or in his bed, answering his mail, even on those days when he was not feeling well.

17. *Deutsche Kriegsgedichte*, ed. Fr. Klaeber (Minneapolis-St. Paul, 1915); *Deutsche Worte*, ed. Fr. Klaeber, Germanistische Gesellschaft von Minnesota, Nos. 4, 5 (Minneapolis-St. Paul, 1917). The quotation is from a review article by Klaeber of German war poetry written from the beginning of World War I: "Ein neues Blatt deutscher Dichtung," *Monatshefte für deutsche Sprache und Pädagogik*, 16.10 (Milwaukee, 1916), 1–4 ("Mit tiefem Verständnis und innigem Mitgefühl für das furchtbare Schicksalsringen Deutschlands ist die Auswahl getroffen, und man spürt in den Dichtungen den Geist, der die kämpfenden Brüder beseelt" [n. 1]).

18. "Hier fühlen wir den wahren Pulsschlag des Volkes, wie man ihn seit langem nicht gefühlt hat"; "Ein neues Blatt," p. 4.

19. "Wie dieser Krieg ein allgemeiner, heiliger Volkskrieg ist, so ist der wahre Held dieser Dichtung das deutsche Volk, die Gesamtheit der Kämpfenden, Arbeitenden, Leidenden. Und den wahren Inhalt bildet die Entfaltung der Volksseele" ("Ein neues Blatt," p. 3).

20. The letters pertaining to the charges of disloyalty and the Minnesota Commission of Public Safety are found in the files of the Board of Regents in the Office of the President at the Univ. of Minnesota.

21. Letter of T. G. Winter to Fred B. Snyder; Files of the Board of Regents, Office of the President, Univ. of Minnesota.

22. Klaeber's letter to the Board of Regents, 15 October 1917; Files of the Board of Regents, Office of the President, Univ. of Minnesota.

23. The original is in the possession of Frau Lotte Henkel (n.d.): "Deutsch sei mein Denken / Tun u. Streben / Deutsch meine Liebe/ deutsch mein Sang/ und deutsch mein Sterbeglockenklang." Quoted with the permission of Frau Henkel.

24. Fr. Klaeber, "Die deutsche Sprache in den Vereinigten Staaten von Amerika," *Neuphilologische Monatsschrift*, 11.6 (1940), 121–34, esp. pp. 126–29, 133–34.

25. "Wenn wir Zeit hätten, würde ich gern über Deutsch als Lehrfach sprechen. Hier nur zwei Sätze. 1. Der Deutschunterricht an Mittel- und höheren Schulen [high schools, colleges] hat insofern einen entschiedenen Vorsprung vor dem Unterricht in anderen Fremdsprachen, als ihm noch viele Lehrer zur Verfügung stehen, denen Deutsch als Sprache des Elternhauses hinreichend vertraut ist. (Es ist kein Zufall, dass sich darunter eine grosse Zahl von Pastorensöhnen befindet.) 2. Wenn die germanische Philologie an den amerikanischen Universitäten sich viel früher und kräftiger entwickelt hat als in England, so rührt dies von dem starken deutschen Einfluss her, sowohl dem Einfluss, der direkt von den deutschen Universitäten ausging, vielfach durch Vermittlung lernbegieriger Amerikaner, die scharenweise nach Deutschland geströmt waren, als auch von der zielbewussten, schaffensfrohen Tätigkeit deutschamerikanischer Forscher im Lande" (Klaeber, "Die deutsche Sprache," p. 133).

26. The address was later published in *Neuphilologische Monatsschrift* (see n. 24 above).

27. "O Deutschland, von all deinen Kindern liebt keines dich so sehr / Wie wir, die fremdgewordnen, die Deutschen überm Meer. / Du bist uns mehr als Mutter, du bist unsers Leben Ruh'. . ."; quoted in "Die deutsche Sprache," p. 134, from Kuno Francke, "Deutsche Arbeit in Amerika" (Leipzig, 1930).

28. "Wie ist eine Synthese möglich? Gewöhnlich beruhigt man sich bei dem Satze, dass die Treue gegen das erwählte Weib die Anhänglichkeit an die Mutter nicht ausschliesst. . . . Es muss doch der Germania eine einzigartige Lebenskraft innewohnen" ("Die deutsche Sprache," p. 134).

29. Interview in the *Minneapolis Daily*, 29 April 1926.

30. My interview with the late Prof. Dr. Martin Lehnert took place on 2 July 1988, at his home in Berlin-Köpenick, at which time he spoke openly about Klaeber and the years between 1936 and 1939 at the Univ. of Berlin.

31. Klaeber's letter to Lehnert, 28 December 1938; courtesy of Prof. Dr. Lehnert.

32. Klaeber's letter to Lehnert, 14 November 1939; courtesy of Prof. Dr. Lehnert.

33. Wilhelm Horn, "Friedrich Klaeber, zum achtzigsten Geburtstag am 1. Oktober 1943," *Archiv für das Studium der neueren Sprachen*, 184.1–2 (1943), 1.

34. Interview with Frau Lotte Henkel. Frau Henkel described the 1929 sabbatical visit by the Klaebers to Germany during which time Klaeber moved back and forth from Berlin to Halle and Leipzig, before he decided to go to Berlin with Horn.

35. Lehnert interview; also in Lehnert's 90th-birthday tribute to Klaeber, "Friedrich Klaeber zum 90. Geburtstag am 1. Oktober 1953," *Zeitschrift für Anglistik und Amerikanistik*, 2 (1953), 122–28. At the end of this tribute Lehnert offers a continuation of the Klaeber bibliography that appeared in *Studies in English Philology* (see n. 8 above) covering the years 1929–53. See also Lehnert's tribute in *Berliner Zeitung* (1 Oct. 1953). Klaeber's obituary written by Lehnert appeared in *Zeitschrift für Anglistik und Amerikanistik*, 4 (1954), 455–56. *Laut und Leben* was published in 1954 after Horn had died, with Lehnert as editor: *Laut und Leben: Englische Lautgeschichte der neueren Zeit (1400–1500)*, 2 vols. (Berlin, 1954).

36. The address of the Klaebers' house in Berlin changed street names between 1934 and 1936 (Letters to Malone, 5 July 1934; 1 May 1936), from Niklasstrasse 15 to Chamberlainstrasse 15. Today the street has its former name. There is some discrepancy as to the date of the bombing. With his characteristic reserve, Klaeber noted the particularly painful loss of his comprehensive and priceless library in a footnote: "It may be added, by the way, that after the completion of this paper (June 1943), my library was wiped out by an American bomb"; in "Some Further Additions to Beowulf Bibliography and Notes," *Beiblatt zur Anglia*, 54/55 (1944), 274–80, quotation from p. 274. In a letter to Kemp Malone (6 April 1946), Klaeber states that the bombing took place "two years ago," and in another letter to Malone (18 January 1950) he states that all his books "(and all other worldly possessions)" were burned "five years ago." The photograph of the Klaeber residence in Berlin carries a caption on the reverse side in Klaeber's handwriting: "Our house in Berlin-Zehlendorf—29.4.1944." Perhaps the June 1943 date refers only to Klaeber's completion of his paper and not to the bombing, which must have occurred sometime after April 1944 and before January 1945.

37. Klaeber letter to Kemp Malone, 8 June 1946, at The Robert W. Woodruff Library, Emory Univ.

38. Klaeber letter to Kemp Malone, 30 May 1950, at The Robert W. Woodruff Library, Emory Univ.

39. "Neunzig Jahre alt zu werden ist kein Verdienst, könnte höchstens eine Gnade sein. Nur das dürfte ich in Anspruch nehmen, dass ich in langen Jahren mich ernstlich um Forschung bemüht habe, aber die Leistung ist weit hinter dem guten Willen zurückgeblieben. Das 'überbiblische' Alter lässt mich an den bekannten Spruch denken, in dem man, in syntaktischer Umwendung von Luthers Version, sagen könnte: Wenn das Leben Mühe und Arbeit gewesen ist, so ist es köstlich gewesen."

40. In his 90th-birthday tribute to Klaeber, Lehnert calls the edition the "*Beowulf* Bible of international studies" ("ist nach wie vor die *Beowulf*-Bibel in der internationalen Wissenschaft" [p. 124]).

"Writ in Ancient Character and of No Further Use": Anglo-Saxon Manuscripts in American Collections[1]

William P. Stoneman

Prior to the Cortlandt Field Bishop sale, *The New York Times Book Review* of 27 March 1938 reported that the manuscript of the Blickling Homilies "is the only Anglo-Saxon [vernacular] manuscript in private hands and the first to be offered for sale in America. There is not a single leaf of Anglo-Saxon in any American institution today."[2] Eight days later, on 5 April 1938, at the American Art Association–Anderson Galleries, New York, lot no. 285, the manuscript of the Blickling Homilies was purchased by A. S. W. Rosenbach for John H. Scheide of Titusville, Pennsylvania. The manuscript had formerly belonged to the city council of Lincoln and on 24 March 1724 was given by the city council as "writ in ancient character and of no further use" to William Pownall, who later sold it to Richard Ellys, and thence it came by descent to the Marquess of Lothian.[3] Scheide had been the underbidder when six years earlier the manuscript was up at auction in New York and went to the bookseller Barnet J. Beyer (as lot no. 2 in the Marquess of Lothian sale, 27 January 1932). Beyer had purchased the manuscript with funds supplied by the owner of the auction galleries, Cortlandt Field Bishop. The two men quarreled when Beyer was unable to sell the manuscript and the manuscript was put up at auction again.[4] Now six years later Scheide paid substantially less than Beyer had paid for the manuscript.

Philip Brooks of *The Times* was very much interested in the fate of the manuscript and commented that "the beauty of the language is comparable to that of the King James Version of the Bible. Its basic significance in the development of English prose has been recognized in histories of English literature."[5] Rowland Collins has written that "Scheide was particularly pleased to have this book which he saw as a vital vernacular link between his great collection of Bibles and his extraordinary collections of Americana. It was a unique part of the linguistic and religious heritage of American civilization."[6] William H. Scheide, son of John H. Scheide, has written,

> I am convinced that the impulse to acquire this book came from my father's interest in Americana. Here was a unique milestone in Anglo-American culture. Here was an outstanding specimen of proto-English, giving opportunity to penetrate farther into the ancestry of our language than could be done anywhere else in the western hemisphere. My father had a typically modest but very real pride in this fact, quite justifiable in my opinion. He bought an Anglo-Saxon grammar and was settling down to a long-term attack on the manuscript when death intervened.[7]

The Blickling Homilies (now Princeton, Scheide Library 71; Gneuss 905) (see References, below) may have been the first vernacular manuscript from Anglo-Saxon England to come to America, but the Chronology appended to this paper makes clear that other manuscript artifacts of this Anglo-American culture had preceded it. In 1907, Pierpont Morgan had purchased a now imperfect copy of the gospels written under Anglo-Saxon influence on the Continent (now New York, Pierpont Morgan Library 333; Temple 30 [xiii]). In 1912, Coella Lindsay Ricketts purchased from the London bookseller Tregaskis a bound volume of early manuscript fragments. The fragments had previously been in the collection of Sir Thomas Phillipps (1792–1872), a self-described "vello-maniac" and indefatigable collector; his is a name that will be repeated frequently in this paper. Included in the volume were "Anglo-Saxon MSS Fragments of two ninth-century MSS on vellum, one being a portion of a constitutional treatise, apparently on the kingdom of the Franks, the other a portion of the life of a saint. . . ." These two manuscript fragments, then, were the first Anglo-Saxon manuscripts to reach America.

In 1976, Rowland Collins described these fragments as "not to be found,"[8] but in an uncharacteristic momentary lapse he was searching for an Anglo-Saxon *vernacular* manuscript. In 1961 the Lilly Library of Indiana University in Bloomington, Indiana, acquired the bulk of the Coella Lindsay Ricketts collection. Included in the collection is a leaf of Bede's *Historia Ecclesiastica*, V.13 (s. ix^{in}). The Bede fragment (now Lilly Library Ricketts 177; Gneuss 797) was part of the collection purchased by Ricketts from Tregaskis, and the nature of the text of the fragment (an unnamed man near death is shown a book by devils, a book in which his sins are recorded), suggests that the "lost" life of a saint and the Bede fragment are, in fact, the same fragment. Additional evidence confirms this identification.

In 1988 the bound volume of Ricketts fragments was given to the Newberry Library in Chicago, the gift of Alma Schmidt Petersen. The volume apparently had been given or traded to Mrs. Petersen's father, Dr. Otto L. Schmidt, by Ricketts. The eighth fragment in the volume is a fragment of *Epistula Hieronimi de Gradus Romanorum* (now Newberry Library 1.5, Fragm. 8); this is certainly the "lost" constitutional treatise.

In 1914, John Frederick Lewis of Philadelphia purchased a leaf of Aldhelm's prose *De Laude Virginitatis* (s. ix^{in}) with seven glosses in Old English (s. x^{2}); at his death in 1932 his widow presented his collection of manuscripts to the Free Library of Philadelphia; it is now Lewis ET 121 (Gneuss 857). It is from a group of *membra disiecta* now in Philadelphia, New Haven, Oslo/London, Cambridge, Oxford, and London.

Ricketts and Lewis, however, were really only minor, albeit early, players in the acquisition of Anglo-Saxon manuscripts by Americans at this time. The period is dominated by Pierpont Morgan and Henry Huntington and their librarians and agents buying on a vast scale. In 1924, Huntington through A. S. W. Rosenbach purchased the Gundulf Bible (now San Marino, Henry E. Huntington Library HM 62; Gneuss 934), then the property of the heirs of Sir Thomas Phillipps. The two-volume Latin Bible (Rochester, s. xi^{ex}) has a thirteenth-century inscription attributing ownership to Gundulf, Bishop of Rochester (1077–1108). In 1926 the Pierpont Morgan Library acquired four illuminated manuscripts from Holkham Hall, one of the seats of the earls of Leicester. We are interested in two, Holkham Hall 15 and 16, gospel books associated with Judith, Countess of Flanders. These are now Pierpont Morgan Library 708 and 709 (Gneuss 860 and 861). In 1932 the Pierpont Morgan Library acquired the Blickling Psalter at the New York sale of the library of the Marquess of Lothian (now Pierpont Morgan Library 776; Gneuss 862). In 1948 the Pierpont Morgan Library acquired a leaf of Bede's *Historia Ecclesiastica*, formerly in the collection of Sir Thomas Phillipps (now Pierpont Morgan Library 826; Gneuss 863), and in 1954 a manuscript of the gospels written and decorated at Christ Church, Canterbury (s. x^{ex}) from the dukes of Arenberg (now Pierpont Morgan Library 869; Gneuss 864).

William S. Glazier of New York formed another important private collection of manuscript fragments. His first purchase of Anglo-Saxon material was of fragments of two folios of Gregory's *Moralia in Job* in November 1954 (now Pierpont Morgan Library Glazier 30); his second in 1961, four leaves of *Exodus* in Old English from H. P. Kraus (now Pierpont Morgan Library Glazier 63; Gneuss 866). Glazier died in 1962, and his collection was deposited at the Morgan Library and is now part of its holdings.

In 1954 the Kenneth Spencer Research Library at the University of Kansas purchased a leaf (now Lawrence, Spencer Library Pryce P2A.1). This acquisition was the first by an American university research library, and such purchasers gradually replaced private collectors as acquirers of Anglo-Saxon manuscripts in America. This leaf purchased by the University of Kansas and another in the Bodleian Library (Lat. Misc. a. 3, fol. 49) were once part of the British Library's Harley glossary (Harley 3376; Ker 240; Gneuss 436). In 1957 the Spencer Library purchased an STC book in the binding of which they afterwards found two fragments of Old English homilies, one (Pryce C2.1) related to CCCC 557, the other (Pryce C2.2) related to Bodleian Library Hatton 115.[9]

In 1958 a bifolium of Aldhelm, *De Laude Virginitatis*, passed through H. P. Kraus to Germany, but will appear again at the Getty Museum in Malibu, California. This transaction is also important because it marks the rise of H. P. Kraus to replace A. S. W. Rosenbach (d. 1952) as the great supplier of manuscripts and fragments to American collectors and institutions.

Also in 1958 the Lilly Library at Indiana University entered upon the scene for a brief but significant period. In 1958 it acquired the George A. Poole, Jr., collection of manuscript fragments, including two fragments (now Poole 40; Gneuss 146) of Ælfric's *Lives of Saints* (s. xi^{med}). Acquired by Poole from Robinson Brothers, London, in 1947 (formerly Sir Thomas Phillipps 22229; Phillipps purchased them at the sale of the notorious book thief Guglielmo Libri, Sotheby's, London, 28 March 1859, lot no. 1111). The fragments are from the same manuscript as fragments now in New Haven, Oxford, and Cambridge.

Included in the same collection is a leaf (Poole 41; not in Gneuss) from a Latin missal (s. x^{ex}), in the same lot in the Libri sale and therefore presumably by the same route to Poole. The leaf includes prayers for Good Friday, which correspond exactly with *The Leofric Missal*, and it also includes instructions and prayers for the ceremony for the Veneration of the Cross and preparations for the Mass of the Presanctified on that day. Also in the same collection are a leaf (Poole 47; not in Gneuss) of Bede's *Historia Ecclesiastica* III.19 (s. x/xi) and a leaf (Poole 43; not in Gneuss) from the anonymous *Life of St. Ermin* (BHL 2614; s. xi). This is a saint's life that previously had not been known to have been known in Anglo-Saxon England.

In 1960 the Lilly Library acquired a fragment of Ælfric's *Grammar* (s. xi^{1}) from Herbert Reichner of Stockbridge, Massachusetts; it is now Additional 1000 (Gneuss 441). Earlier the fragment had been in the Fürstlich Hohenzollern'sche Bibliothek, Sigmaringen. This fragment is from the same group of manuscripts as another bifolium, London, BL Harley 5915, fols. 8–9 (Ker 242); this London Harley manuscript, like the Missouri *Fragmenta Manuscripta*, is a collection put together by John Bagford. Finally, in 1961 the Lilly Library purchased the bulk of the Ricketts collection and that leaf (now Ricketts 177) of Bede's *Historia Ecclesiastica* (s. ix^{in}) discussed earlier in this paper, which was the first Anglo-Saxon manuscript to come to America.

In 1963 the Beinecke Rare Book and Manuscript Library was officially opened at Yale University. The year 1964 marks the entry into our list of Edwin Beinecke and other members of the Beinecke family. In 1964 Beinecke purchased a leaf of Bede's commentary on the Gospel of Luke, a leaf which may be from Anglo-Saxon England or from an Anglo-Saxon center on the Continent (New Haven, Beinecke Library 441; not in Gneuss). In 1965 he purchased a leaf of a pontifical (Beinecke Library 320) with a provenance similar to that of the Scheide will of Æthelgifu (see below). The leaf is probably from the same manuscript as flyleaves in a Cambridge, Trinity College manuscript (Gneuss 157). In 1969, 28 leaves of the Aldhelm *De Laude Virginitatis* came up for auction at Sotheby's in London. It was purchased by Kraus, and in 1970 he sold it to Beinecke for the Yale Library; they are now Beinecke Library 401 and 401A (Gneuss 857). Other leaves are now in Cambridge, Oxford, London, Philadelphia, and Oslo/London. In 1972 the Beinecke Library purchased a fragment of Gregory's *Moralia in Job* (Beinecke Library 516; Gneuss 858) and in 1975 the West Saxon translation of the gospels of Mark and Matthew (Beinecke Library 578; Gneuss 859). In 1984, Barbara Shailor reported that in the period 1963–84 Yale had purchased 350 medieval and Renaissance manuscripts and that "no fewer than 115 items were selected by Edwin J. Beinecke personally or were purchased with the gifts and endowment funds contributed by members of the family."[10]

In December 1968 the University of Missouri purchased a bound collection of *Fragmenta Manuscripta*, mostly derived from John Bagford (1650–1716), a man who for a long time had a reputation as a mutilator of manuscripts and printed books to make these kinds of collections. Milton McC. Gatch has demonstrated that Bagford has been unnecessarily maligned and that he used imperfect copies and binding fragments to make up his volumes. The Missouri Bagford collection was once Sir Thomas Phillipps MS 15758 and was also once in the collection of Sir Sidney Cockerell, and was lot no. 2 at his sale at Sotheby's, London, 3 April 1957. It sold again at Sotheby's, London, on 12 December 1967, and then passed through a number of rare book dealers before being acquired by the University of Missouri Library, Columbia, from William Salloch of Ossining, New York.[11] Fragmenta Manuscripta 1 is a leaf from an Anglo-Saxon Latin liturgical manuscript, perhaps, as Linda Voigts has suggested, from a reading book (Glastonbury[?], s. x^{med}). The leaf contains part of Lamentations; after the last verse, a note places the reading of passages from Lamentations as part of the night offices during the last three days of Holy Week.[12] Fragmenta Manuscripta 3 (Gneuss 810) is a leaf from an Anglo-Saxon sacramentary (s. x/xi). Strictly speaking, a sacramentary contains only prayers that are to be said by the celebrant of the Mass, namely the Collect, the Secret, the Preface, and the Post-communion. This fragment includes these prayers for the fourth, fifth, sixth, and seventh Sundays after Pentecost (here described as [third], fourth, fifth, and sixth Sundays after the Octave of Pentecost). The texts are the same as *The Leofric Missal*.[13] Fragmenta Manuscripta 4 (Gneuss 811) is a leaf from a manuscript of the Bible, or of the Old Testament or of the Minor Prophets (s. x^2). Because of cropping the fragment includes parts of Micah, Nahum, and Habakkuk.

On 10 December 1969 at Sotheby's, London, lot no. 29, the will of Æthelgifu (s. x^{ex}) (now Scheide Library 140) was purchased by H. P. Kraus for William H. Scheide. The will was probably from the collections of John Selden (1584–1654) and Sir Matthew Hale (1609–76); it was purchased in 1939 by James Fairhurst from a descendant of Hale. Manuscripts from the Fairhurst collection were sold at Sotheby's, London, on 10 June 1963 as the property of Messrs. Morgan Grenfell; the will was held back by Lord Rennell, a partner in Morgan Grenfell, to study and publish as his contribution to the Roxburghe Club.

Up to the mid-1980's the British Library and the Bodleian Library were acquiring Anglo-Saxon manuscripts and fragments with some regularity. In 1971 the British Library acquired the manuscript of a Latin pontifical with some Old English glosses from Christ Church, Canterbury (now BL Additional 57337; Gneuss 302); in 1979, a sheet of Ely Abbey farm accounts sold by Queens' College, Cambridge (Additional 61735); in 1981, a fragment of an Exeter missal with neumes (now Additional 62104); in 1984, a leaf from a gospel book (now Additional 63143); and as late as 1985, a leaf containing prayers in Latin (now Additional 63651). In 1967 the Bodleian Library was able to acquire a leaf from Ælfric's *Catholic Homilies I* (Bodleian Library Eng. th. c. 74; Gneuss 146), from the same manuscript as fragments now in Bloomington, New Haven, and Cambridge.

The Beinecke Library at Yale University from 1964 to 1975 and earlier from 1958 to 1961, and to a lesser extent the Lilly Library at Indiana University, were making themselves a presence in the market. But after the mid-1980's the buyers were private individuals again. In 1988 the Philadelphia Free Library (although not, I suspect, very seriously, as it is a publicly funded civic institution) and particularly Yale were after the Aldhelm leaf sold by the Getty Museum. In 1989 the Kent County Record Office and the British Library were after the Anglo-Saxon charter. But they simply are unable to compete with private collectors in the current market. Toshiyuki Takamiya of Tokyo and particularly Martin Schøyen of Oslo (note the last five items in the Chronology are now his) are determined private collectors and competitors with large financial resources at their command—remember Huntington, Morgan, Beinecke. The situation has not changed so very much, only the location of the players in the world market who have the money, and although they are generous in granting scholars access to their manuscripts, they have not yet created institutions to house them.

What has changed is that the manuscript material still in England requires an export license if it is to leave the country. For example, the sheet of farm accounts from Ely Abbey sold by Queens' College,

Cambridge, in 1979 is now in the British Library as BL Additional 61735 because Professor Takamiya, to whom the manuscript was knocked down at auction, was denied an export license. Mr. Schøyen was denied an export license for the eleventh-century Kentish charter he purchased in 1989 (Oslo/London, Schøyen Collection 600) and so now he simply keeps it in England. I think there is no doubt that a good number of the manuscripts and fragments now in the United States would not be permitted to leave England if they were to come up for sale there now.

Another curious, but related, observation about the source of this Anglo-Saxon manuscript material: Two of the sellers on the recent market are American institutions which might have been thought to be permanent homes (St. John's Seminary in Camarillo, California, and the Getty Museum, also in California). The buyers in these two cases, Takamiya and Schøyen, recognized the limited opportunity to acquire English material outside of England, which is effectively sealed up by its export legislation. This institutional selling, a pattern in Anglo-Saxon material started in 1979 by Queens' College, Cambridge, is, in my opinion, likely to continue. In June of 1991 Manhattan College in New York sold a small collection of manuscripts and about 80 incunables. The costs of maintaining manuscript collections, that is, in appropriate climatic conditions with adequate insurance coverage and qualified staff to enable public access, are very great indeed. Add to these costs the infrequent use of this material by faculty and students, particularly at theological seminaries and undergraduate colleges, and it is possible to see why budget-conscious administrators are eyeing these assets. A lot of salaries can be paid and a lot of buildings built by using funds derived from deaccessioning this material. I do not mean to suggest that this is done lightly or quickly and without a real evaluation of the goals of the institution, or without opposition. A comparable situation was the controversy at the Barnes Foundation in Philadelphia, which contemplated selling paintings to pay the bills; this is only one of a number of examples I could name. And administrators are not the only ones who have seen the money to be made here. The recent sale of a copy of the first printing of the American Declaration of Independence to a group calling itself Visual Equities Limited is extremely alarming. These are businessmen buying material for eventual resale, having realized the capital gains that could be made in a few years' time. This is a trend established by the British Rail Pension Fund. The Fund did make a tidy profit in less than ten years. I find this situation alarming because the traditional pattern of private collectors eventually finding or creating institutional homes for their collections may be disrupted by economic factors. The thought of manuscripts as commodities too valuable to take out of an increasingly limited market is not pleasant.

Another observation about the nature of this material: Notice how much of it is composed of fragmentary or single-sheet documents. This kind of material exists in some quantity and is still essentially unnoticed and unexplored in American institutions.[14] We in America owe a lot to Sir Thomas Phillipps and John Bagford. Look at the results from the University of Missouri *Fragmenta Manuscripta* (perhaps evidence for a type of manuscript otherwise not known to have survived)[15] and at the Lilly Library (evidence of a saint's life otherwise not known to have survived). Phillipps and Bagford, however, are not the last to have made up large collections of fragments to illustrate the history of handwriting. A number of institutions have such collections, and they remain largely unexplored. For example, in 1966, H. P. Kraus, an important source for a number of the manuscripts discussed in this paper, gave to the Beinecke Library two collections of manuscript fragments (MSS 481 and 482). These have not yet been published in Barbara Shailor's *Catalogue* of the Yale manuscripts, but Robert Babcock has provided a brilliant demonstration of how they can be used in research.[16]

I want to conclude by suggesting another type of Anglo-Saxon manuscript material that deserves more study than it has received in the past, and that is the remains of the work of Anglo-Saxonists, men and women, who worked with materials which may no longer be extant. Columbia University MS (X837.95.M319) is an undated 44-

page manuscript with rules of Gothic grammar and a collection of prayers in an imitation Anglo-Saxon hand. Phillip Pulsiano showed in an *Old English Newsletter* that the prayers are copied from BL Cotton Tiberius A.iii from transcripts by William L'Isle and Francis Junius in Bodleian Library Laud Misc. 201 and Junius 63.[17] They could equally well have been from manuscripts that no longer survive, as could the sources of annotations in a copy of Lambarde's *Archaionomia* (London, 1568) offered for sale in 1991 by the bookseller Karen Thomson of London.[18] This copy of a printed book has numerous manuscript notes by William Lambarde himself and by John Joscelyn, the Latin secretary of Matthew Parker, and John Parker, the son of Matthew. There is clear evidence that the book has been collated with a manuscript of the laws, now BL Cotton Nero A.i. What other treasures it holds remain to be seen.

This report on Anglo-Saxon manuscripts in American collections is only a beginning and is bound to be incomplete. I would be grateful for any additions or corrections to it. I hope that this introduction has provided some insight into one aspect of the preservation and transmission of Anglo-Saxon culture in America.

THE SCHEIDE LIBRARY, PRINCETON UNIVERSITY LIBRARY

CHRONOLOGY[19]

(See References below.)

1907

Pierpont Morgan acquired this now imperfect copy of the gospels (s. xi^{in}) from the collection of the comte de Troussures, near Beauvais. Formerly in the collection of Beauvais Cathedral. The text is now Matthew 8:36–John 10:16. Written and illuminated in the monastery of Saint-Bertin at Saint-Omer under Abbot Odbert.

Now New York, **Pierpont Morgan Library 333.**

de Ricci, p. 1428; de Ricci, *Supplement*, p. 342; Temple 30 (xiii) (plate); Ohlgren, *Iconographic Catalogue* 130.

F. Wormald, "The Survival of Anglo-Saxon Illumination after the Norman Conquest," *Proceedings of the British Academy*, 30 (1944), 127–45, at p. 133; rpt. *Francis Wormald Collected Writings*, vol. 1, *Studies in Medieval Art from the Sixth to the Twelfth Centuries*, ed. J. J. G. Alexander, T. J. Brown, and Joan Gibbs (London, 1984), pp. 153–68, at 158.

1912

Coella Lindsay Ricketts of Chicago purchased from Tregaskis, *Catalogue* 720 (London, 1912), no. 36, a bound collection of early fragments; the same collection had been Tregaskis, *Catalogue* 706 (London, 1911), no. 17. The fragments were previously in the collection of Sir Thomas Phillipps (his MS 22254). Included in the collection were "Anglo-Saxon MSS Fragments of two ninth-century MSS on vellum, one being a portion of a constitutional treatise, apparently on the kingdom of the Franks, the other a portion of the life of a saint. . . ." Collins (pp. 66–67) describes the fragments as "not to be found." The bound volume of fragments was given in **1988** by Alma Schmidt Petersen to the Newberry Library, Chicago.[20] The volume was apparently given or traded to Mrs. Petersen's father, Dr. Otto L. Schmidt, by Ricketts. Fragment VIII in the volume is labelled "Historica-theologica" and is a fragment of *Epistula Hieronimi de Gradus Romanorum* (s. ix^{in}). The text of this fragment was first published by Spangenberg, but the fragment could not be traced until now. Thus, the first of the two missing fragments "not to be found" by Collins has been located.

Now Chicago, **Newberry Library 1.5, Fragm. 8.**

D. A. Rath Spangenberg, *Göttingische gelehrte Anzeigen*, 3 (1832), 1661–63.
P. S. Barnwell, " 'Epistula Hieronimi de Gradus Romanorum': An English School Text," *Historical Research*, 64 (1991), 77–86.

A second fragment in the same bound volume also has Anglo-Saxon connections. A damaged leaf containing excerpts of Isidore, *Etymologiae*, Books I–III (s. viii–ix).

Now Chicago, **Newberry Library 1.5, Fragm. 26.**

"Addenda *CLA* II" 1869, p. 290; de Ricci, p. 660.

Bischoff, Brown, and John ("Addenda *CLA* II") suggest that the fragment was "written probably in an Anglo-Saxon centre in Germany."

Fragment XXIV in the volume, labelled "E legenda Sanctorum," is now missing. In pencil is the note "Removed by C. L. R. 5/14/12." In **1961** the Lilly Library acquired the bulk of the Ricketts collection. Included in the collection was a leaf of Bede's *Historia Ecclesiastica* V.13 (s. ix^{in}); de Ricci (p. 644) records that the Bede fragment was purchased by Ricketts from Tregaskis, *Catalogue* 720 (London, 1912), part of no. 36; additional evidence, including the nature of the text of the fragment, confirms that the portion of the life of a saint "not to be found" by Collins and the Bede fragment are the same fragment.

Now Bloomington, Indiana, **Lilly Library Ricketts 177.**

Gneuss 797; de Ricci, p. 660.

The text is Bertram Colgrave and R. A. B. Mynors, eds., *Bede's Ecclesiastical History of the English People* (Oxford, 1969), p. 498, line 32, to p. 502, line 12.

Related to Düsseldorf, Universitätsbibliothek K 1: B 216, and described as "eighth-century insular" by R. A. B. Mynors in Colgrave and Mynors, p. xliv, n. 5, but omitted by Bischoff and Brown as "saec. IX in." in "Addenda *CLA*," p. 317.

1914

John Frederick Lewis purchased a leaf of Aldhelm's prose *De Laude Virginitatis* (s. ix^{in}) with glosses in Old English (s. x^2); at his death in **1932** his widow presented his collection of manuscripts to the Free Library of Philadelphia.

Now Philadelphia, **Free Library Lewis ET 121.**

Ker 12; Collins 1b (plate); Gneuss 857; de Ricci, *Supplement*, p. 545 (no. XXIV:1). Jennifer Morrish, "Dated and Datable Manuscripts Copied in England During the Ninth Century: A Preliminary List," *Mediaeval Studies*, 50 (1988), 527.

From a group of *membra disiecta* now in Philadelphia, New Haven, Oslo/London, Cambridge, Oxford, and London.

May 1924

Phillipps 3504, a two-volume Latin Bible (Rochester, s. xi^{ex}) with a thirteenth-century inscription attributing ownership to Gundulf, Bishop of Rochester (1077–1108). Subsequently the Bible was in the library of John, Lord Lumley (1534?–1609). The manuscript was acquired by private treaty from the heirs of Sir Thomas Phillipps by A. S. W. Rosenbach, who sold it to Henry E. Huntington; Huntington died in **1927**.

Now San Marino, **Henry E. Huntington Library HM 62.**

Gneuss 934; de Ricci, p. 48.
Consuelo W. Dutschke, *Guide to Medieval and Renaissance Manuscripts in the Huntington Library* (San Marino, 1988), vol. 1, pp. 124–30.
Leslie A. Morris, *Rosenbach Abroad: In Pursuit of Books in Private Collections* (Philadelphia, 1988), p. 41 (Medieval Manuscripts no. 1).

The most recent and extensive discussion of the manuscript is Mary P. Richards, "The Medieval Vulgate Tradition at Rochester," in *Texts and Their Traditions in the Medieval Library of Rochester Cathedral Priory*, Transactions of the American Philosphical Society, 78.3 (1988), 61–84.

1926

The Pierpont Morgan Library acquired four illuminated manuscripts from Holkham Hall, one of the seats of the earls of Leicester. Among the manuscripts are two gospel books, Holkham Hall 15 (s. xi^{med}) and 16 (s. xi^{med}), associated with Judith, Countess of Flanders (1032–94).

Now New York, **Pierpont Morgan Library 708 and 709.**

Gneuss 860; de Ricci, p. 1485; de Ricci, *Supplement*, p. 354; Temple 94 (plate); Ohlgren, *Iconographic Catalogue* 199; Ohlgren, *Textual Illustration* 12 (plates); Voelkle 9 (plate).
Gneuss 861; de Ricci, pp. 1485–86; de Ricci, *Supplement*, pp. 354–55; Temple 93 (plates); Ohlgren, *Iconographic Catalogue* 198; Ohlgren, *Textual Illustration* 11 (plates); Voelkle 8 (plate).

Meta Harrsen, "The Countess Judith of Flanders and the Library of Weingarten Abbey," *Papers of the Bibliographical Society of America*, 24 (1930), 1–13.
Mary P. Richards, *Texts and Their Traditions in the Medieval Library of Rochester Cathedral Priory*, Transactions of the American Philosphical Society, 78.3 (1988), 66.
T. A. M. Bishop, *English Caroline Minuscule* (Oxford, 1971), pp. xvi–xvii.

1927

Two separate folios survive from a manuscript (s. viii–ix) of Isidore's *Synonyma* (I.36–41 and 65–68), probably once forming the outer bifolium of a quire (of which the Morgan leaf is the first and the Plimpton leaf the last). Written in an Anglo-Saxon center in Germany. The leaves were acquired from Giuseppe Martini in Paris. The Columbia leaf was bequeathed by George Plimpton to Columbia University in **1936**.

Now New York, **Columbia University Library Plimpton 129** and New York, **Pierpont Morgan Library 559.**

de Ricci, pp. 1471 (Morgan) and 1775 (Plimpton); *CLA* 1655.
E. A. Lowe, "Membra Disiecta," *Revue Bénédictine*, 39 (1927), 193–94.
Bernhard Bischoff, "Panorama der Handschriftenüberlieferung aus der Zeit Karls des Grossen," *Karl der Grosse*, II, Lebenswerk, pp. 233–54, at 251n.

27 January 1932

American Art Association–Anderson Galleries, New York, the property of the Marquess of Lothian, lot no. 1, the Blickling Psalter (s. viii^{med}) with Old English glosses (s. ix–x^{2}), was purchased by A. S. W. Rosenbach and later sold to the Pierpont Morgan Library.

Now New York, **Pierpont Morgan Library 776.**

Ker 287; Collins 10 (plate); Gneuss 862; de Ricci, pp. 1502 and 2320; *CLA* 1661; Alexander 31; Ohlgren, *Iconographic Catalogue* 31; Voelkle 1 (plate).

This manuscript, and the Blickling Homilies (see the next entry) belonged to the city council of Lincoln and were given by the council to William Pownall (**24 March 1724**), who later sold them to Richard Ellys, and so by descent to the Marquess of Lothian. Pownall also tried to sell the manuscripts to Humfrey Wanley, librarian to Edward Harley, second Earl of Oxford on **14 April 1725**. Harley apparently agreed to buy the manuscripts, but Pownall failed to close the deal, probably having sold the manuscripts in the meantime to Ellys.

C. E. Wright and Ruth C. Wright, eds., *The Diary of Humfrey Wanley, 1715–1726*, 2 vols. (London, 1966), vol. 2, p. 352 (14 April 1725), 353 (20 and 21 April 1725) and 399 (16 December 1725).

5 April 1938

American Art Association–Anderson Galleries, New York, the property of Cortlandt Field Bishop, lot no. 285, the Blickling Homilies in Old English (s. x/xi), was purchased by A. S. W. Rosenbach for John Hinsdale Scheide of Titusville, Pennsylvania.

Now Princeton, **Scheide Library 71.**

Ker 382; Collins 8 (plate); Gneuss 905; de Ricci, p. 2323 (no. 55); de Ricci, *Supplement*, p. 314 (no. 66).

The Blickling Homilies, ed. Rudolph Willard, EEMF 10 (1960).

The Blickling Homilies of the Tenth Century, ed. Richard Morris, EETS OS 58, 63, 73 (1874–80; rpt. with corrections as one vol. 1967). John Scheide had been the underbidder when the manuscript (as lot no. 2 in the Marquess of Lothian sale, **27 January 1932**) was previously up at auction (with the Blickling Psalter, see the previous entry) and went to the bookseller Barnet J. Beyer. Beyer had purchased the manuscript with funds supplied by the owner of the auction galleries, Cortlandt Field Bishop. The two men quarreled when Beyer was unable to sell the manuscript, and the manuscript was put up at auction again. Six years later Scheide paid substantially less than Beyer had paid.

Wesley Towner, *The Elegant Auctioneers* (New York, 1970), pp. 468, 472, 480–85, 529.

1948

The Pierpont Morgan Library purchased from H. P. Kraus this leaf from a manuscript of Bede, *Historia Ecclesiastica* (s. viii^{ex}), formerly in the collection of Sir Thomas Phillipps (his MS 36275) and Sir A. Chester Beatty.

Now New York, **Pierpont Morgan Library 826.**

Gneuss 863; de Ricci, *Supplement*, pp. 361–62; *CLA* 1662.

E. A. Lowe, "A New Manuscript Fragment of Bede's *Ecclesiastical History*," *English Historical Review*, 41 (1926), 244–46.

Item no. 22 in the list of books donated by Sæwold, sometime abbot of Bath, to the church of Saint-Vaast in Arras (**c. 1070**).

Philip Grierson, "Les Livres de l'Abbé Seiwold de Bath," *Revue Bénédictine*, 52 (1940), 96–116.

Michael Lapidge, "Surviving Booklists from Anglo-Saxon England," in *Learning and Literature in Anglo-Saxon England: Studies Presented to Peter Clemoes*, ed. Michael Lapidge and Helmut Gneuss (Cambridge, 1985), list VIII, no. 22.

1948

Also purchased by the Morgan Library from H. P. Kraus in the same year were the Anhalt–Morgan Gospels (s. x). Written in continental caroline minuscule in Arras, perhaps at Saint-Vaast, or at Corbie. Anglo-Saxon additions could have been made in either place, or at Saint-Bertin, where the artist is known to have worked. It was in the collection of the dukes of Anhalt-Dessau from the sixteenth century. Sold at Sotheby's, London, **31 May 1927**, thence to Gabriel Wells.

Now New York, **Pierpont Morgan Library 827.**

de Ricci, *Supplement*, p. 362; Temple 45 (plate); Ohlgren, *Iconographic Catalogue* 150; Voelkle 7 (plate).

Hans Swarzenski, "The Anhalt Morgan Gospels," *Art Bulletin*, 31 (1949), 77–83 (plates).

1954

The Kenneth Spencer Research Library, University of Kansas, Lawrence, Kansas, acquired a leaf from Frank Glenn of Kansas City, who had acquired it earlier that year from Robinson Brothers, London (formerly Phillipps 1118). This leaf and another leaf (now Oxford, Bodleian Library Lat. misc. a. 3, fol. 49; also formerly Phillipps 1118) were once part of London, BL Harley 3376 (s. x/xi), an alphabetical glossary in Latin with Old English glosses.

Now Lawrence, Kansas, University of Kansas, **Spencer Library Pryce P2A.1.**

Ker 240; Collins 5 (plate); Gneuss 436.

1954

The Pierpont Morgan Library purchased from the library of the dukes of Arenberg a manuscript of the gospels written and decorated at Christ Church, Canterbury (s. x^{ex}).

Now New York, **Pierpont Morgan Library 869.**

Gneuss 864; de Ricci, *Supplement*, p. 366; Temple 56 (plates); Ohlgren, *Iconographic Catalogue* 161; Ohlgren, *Textual Illustration* 6 (plates); Voelkle 6 (plate).
The Golden Age of Anglo-Saxon Art 966–1066, ed. Janet Backhouse, D. H. Turner, and Leslie Webster (London, 1984), no. 47.

November 1954
William S. Glazier of New York purchased fragments of two folios of Gregory, *Moralia in Job* (s. vii^{ex}), from Arthur Rau in Paris. At his death in **1962** his manuscript collection was deposited at the Pierpont Morgan Library, New York, and given to the library in **1984**.
Now New York, **Pierpont Morgan Library Glazier 30.**

de Ricci, *Supplement*, p. 396; *CLA* 1664.
Bernhard Bischoff, *Mittelalterliche Studien: Ausgewählte Aufsätze zur Schriftkunde und Literaturgeschichte*, vol. 2 (Stuttgart, 1967), p. 339.
John Plummer, *The Glazier Collection of Illuminated Manuscripts* (New York, 1968), no. 4.
Wolfgang Milde, "Paläographische Bemerkungen zu den Breslauer Unzialfragmenten der Dialoge Gregors des Grossen," *Wolfenbütteler Forschungen*, 30 (1986), 149, no. 1.
Gregory T. Clark, "Medieval and Renaissance Manuscripts," *Twenty-First Report to the Fellows of the Pierpont Morgan Library, 1984–1986*, ed. Charles Ryskamp (New York, 1989), p. 69.

Purchased at the same time from the same dealer was a single leaf of the gospel of Luke (s. viii–ix). The text is Luke 23:29–24:8. Probably written in an Anglo-Saxon center in Germany, probably in the Main region. Related to fragments now in Stuttgart, Munich, Vienna, and Würzburg.
Now New York, **Pierpont Morgan Library Glazier 26.**

de Ricci, *Supplement*, p. 396; *CLA* 1339; *Supplement CLA*, p. 20.
William S. Glazier, "Contemporary Collectors XV: A Collection of Illuminated MSS," *The Book Collector*, 6.4 (1957), 361–68, at p. 363.
John Plummer, *Manuscripts from the William S. Glazier Collection* (New York, 1959), no. 2.
John Plummer, *The Glazier Collection of Illuminated Manuscripts* (New York, 1968), no. 5.

Gregory T. Clark, "Medieval and Renaissance Manuscripts," *Twenty-First Report to the Fellows of the Pierpont Morgan Library, 1984–1986*, ed. Charles Ryskamp (New York, 1989), p. 68.

1957 (1961)

The Kenneth Spencer Research Library, University of Kansas, Lawrence, Kansas, acquired a copy of *Barclay his Argenis*, tr. Kingsmill Long, 2nd ed., London, 1636 (STC 1392.5) from Pearson's Book Rooms, Cambridge, in **1957**; in **1961** in the binding were discovered fragments of *The Legend of the Cross* (Worcester, s. xi^{med}) and Ælfric's *De Uno Confessore* (Worcester, s. xi^{2}).

Now Lawrence, Kansas, University of Kansas, **Spencer Library Pryce C2.1 and C2.2.**

Ker 73; Collins 6 (plate); Gneuss 117 and Ker 332; Collins 7 (plate); Gneuss 639.

Pryce C2.1 is related to CCCC 557, and Pryce C2.2 to Oxford, Bodleian Library Hatton 115.

Described by Bertram Colgrave and Ann Hyde, "Two Recently Discovered Leaves from Old English Manuscripts," *Speculum*, 37 (1962), 60–78.

On CCCC 557 see R. I. Page, Mildred Budny, and Nicholas Hadgraft, "Two Fragments of an Old English Manuscript in the Library of Corpus Christi College, Cambridge," *Speculum*, 70 (1995), 502–29.

1958

In H. P. Kraus *Catalogue* 88 (New York, 1958), no. 4, is a fragment of a sylloge of Latin inscriptions (s. x^{med}).

Now Urbana, **University of Illinois at Urbana MS 128.**

Gneuss 938.

Luitpold Wallach, "The Urbana Anglo-Saxon Sylloge of Latin Inscriptions," in *Poetry and Poetics from Ancient Greece to the Renaissance: Studies in Honor of James Hutton*, ed. G. M. Kirkwood (Ithaca, NY, 1975), pp. 134–51.

Michael Lapidge, "Some Remnants of Bede's Lost *Liber Epigrammatum*," *English Historical Review*, 90 (1975), 798–820.

Daniel J. Sheerin, "John Leland and Milred of Worcester," *Manuscripta*, 21 (1977), 172–80.

Dieter Schaller, "Bemerkungen zur Inschriften-Sylloge von Urbana," *Mittellateinisches Jahrbuch*, 12 (1977), 9–21.

In the same H. P. Kraus *Catalogue* 88 (New York, 1958), no. 5, and again in H. P. Kraus *Catalogue* 95 (New York, **1961**), no. 3, is a bifolium of Aldhelm, *De Laude Virginitatis* (s. ix^{in}).
Gneuss 857; Ker 12 (as Wilfred Merton 41; acquired from Merton's estate by Martin Breslauer and appeared in their *Catalogue* 90 [London, **1958**], no. 3, and passed through an English dealer to Kraus and sold by him to Dr. and Mrs. Peter Ludwig, Aachen, Germany; subsequently sold with the rest of the Ludwig collection in **1983** to the J. Paul Getty Museum, Malibu, California, and subsequently sold by them, see **6 December 1988**).
Hans P. Kraus, *A Rare Book Saga: The Autobiography of H. P. Kraus* (New York, 1978), pp. 209–10.

For the same H. P. Kraus *Catalogue* 88 (New York, 1958), no. 3, see **1964**.

1958
The Lilly Library, Indiana University, Bloomington, Indiana, acquired the George A. Poole, Jr., collection, including two fragments of Ælfric's *Lives of Saints* (s. xi^{med}). Acquired by Poole from Robinson Brothers, London, in **1947** (formerly Sir Thomas Phillipps 22229, purchased at the sale of the notorious book thief Guglielmo Libri, Sotheby's, London, **28 March 1859**, lot no. 1111).
Now Bloomington, Indiana, **Lilly Library Poole 40.**

Ker 81; Gneuss 146; Collins 3b (plate); de Ricci, *Supplement*, p. 181.
From the same manuscript as fragments now in New Haven, Oxford, and Cambridge.
Described by Rowland L. Collins and Peter Clemoes, "The Common Origin of Ælfric Fragments at New Haven, Oxford, Cambridge, and Bloomington," in *Old English Studies in Honour of John C. Pope*, ed. Robert B. Burlin and Edward B. Irving, Jr. (Toronto, 1974), pp. 285–326.

Included in the same collection is a leaf from a Latin missal (s. x^{ex}), in the same lot in the Libri sale and therefore presumably by the same route to Poole. It was Poole's MS 98:6.
Now Bloomington, Indiana, **Lilly Library Poole 41.**

de Ricci, *Supplement*, p. 181.
The fragment includes prayers for Good Friday (*The Leofric Missal*, ed. F. E. Warren (Oxford, 1883), pp. 95–96; *The Sarum Missal*, ed. J. Wickham Legg [Oxford,

1916], p. 112); it also includes instructions and prayers for the ceremony of the Veneration of the Cross and preparations for the Mass of the Presanctified on that day (*Sarum Missal*, pp. 112–14).

In the same collection is a leaf (s. xi) from the anonymous *Life of St. Ermin* (BHL 2614). It was Poole's MS 98:11 and purchased with other Phillipps manuscripts from the Robinson Brothers in **1947**.

Now Bloomington, Indiana, **Lilly Library Poole 43.**

de Ricci, *Supplement*, p. 181.

The text is *Passiones Vitaeque Sanctorum Aevi Merovingici*, ed. B. Krusch and W. Levison, MGH, Scriptorum Rerum Merovingicarum 6 (Hanover, 1913), p. 462, line 2, to p. 468, line 8.

Also in the same collection is a leaf of Bede, *Historia Ecclesiastica* III.19 (s. x/xi). It was Poole's MS 98:7, purchased from the Robinsons, and is the end leaf from Sir Thomas Phillipps MS 13153.

Now Bloomington, Indiana, **Lilly Library Poole 47.**

de Ricci, *Supplement*, p. 181.

The text is Bertram Colgrave and R. A. B. Mynors, eds., *Bede's Ecclesiastical History of the English People* (Oxford, 1969), p. 270, line 30, to p. 272, line 30.

1960

The Lilly Library acquired a fragment of Ælfric's *Grammar* (s. xi[1]) from Herbert Reichner of Stockbridge, Massachusetts; earlier the fragment had been in the Fürstlich Hohenzollern'sche Bibliothek, Sigmaringen.

Now Bloomington, Indiana, **Lilly Library Additional 1000.**

Ker 384; Collins 4 (plate); Gneuss 441; de Ricci, *Supplement*, p. 186 (no. 132).
Described by Rowland Collins, "Two Fragments of Ælfric's Grammar: The Kinship of Ker 384 and Ker 242," *Annuale Mediaevale*, 5 (1964), 5–12.

From the same group of manuscripts as another bifolium, London, BL Harley 5915, fols. 8–9 (Ker 242); this London manuscript, like the Missouri *Fragmenta Manuscripta*, is a Bagford collection.
See Milton McC. Gatch, "John Bagford as a Collector and Disseminator of Manuscript Fragments," *The Library*, 7 (1985), 95–114, esp. p. 109.

1961

H. P. Kraus *Catalogue* 95 (New York, 1961), no. 4, four leaves of Exodus in Old English (s. xi^2), were purchased by William S. Glazier. His manuscript collection was deposited upon his death in **1962** at the Pierpont Morgan Library and given to the library in **1984**. Kraus acquired the leaves from Quaritch, who found them in an eighteenth-century atlas of Irish provenance. They were originally flyleaves in a sixteenth-century dictionary now in the Cashel Diocesan Library.

Now New York, **Pierpont Morgan Library Glazier 63.**

Ker 418; Collins 11 (plate); Gneuss 866.
John Plummer, *The Glazier Collection of Illuminated Manuscripts* (New York, 1968), no. 11.

10 June 1963

Sold at Sotheby's, London, lot no. 155, see **1965**.
Sold at Sotheby's, London, lot no. 156, see **25 April 1983**.

1964

A leaf of Bede, *Expositio in Lucae Evangelium* (England or an Anglo-Saxon center in Germany, s. viii/ix), was acquired from Goldschmidt by Edwin J. Beinecke for the Beinecke Library. It had been in the collection of Wilfred Merton (1889–1957) and was his MS 42; it then appeared in Martin Breslauer *Catalogue* 90 (London, **1958**), no. 2, and H. P. Kraus *Catalogue* 88 (New York, **1958**), no. 3. The manuscript was purchased in **1959** by Mark Lansburgh (*An Illustrated Checklist of Manuscript Leaves in the Collection of Mark Lansburgh* [Santa Barbara, 1962], no. 2).

Now New Haven, Yale University, **Beinecke Library 441.**

de Ricci, *Supplement*, p. 24 (no. 2, Mark Lansburgh); *CLA* 220; *Supplement CLA*, pp. 10 and 47; "Addenda *CLA*," p. 363.
Barbara A. Shailor, *Catalogue of Medieval and Renaissance Manuscripts in the Beinecke Rare Book and Manuscript Library, Yale University*, vol. 2, *MSS 251–500* (Binghamton, 1987), p. 380.
M. L. W. Laistner and H. H. King, *A Handlist of Bede Manuscripts* (Ithaca, NY, 1943), p. 46.

Two other leaves from the same manuscript are Hannover, Kestner Museum CUL.I. 71/72 (393/394).

1965

A leaf of a pontifical (s. x^{med}) was acquired by Edwin J. Beinecke for the Beinecke Library. Actually two fragments of a single leaf patched together, they were in H. P. Kraus *Catalogue* 107 (New York, 1965), no. 2, and were bought by Kraus at Sotheby's, London, on **10 June 1963**, lot no. 155. The leaf was the property of Messrs. Morgan Grenfell and previously belonged to James Fairhurst of Oxford, and it once formed part of the collection of John Selden (1584–1654) and later his friend and one of his executors, Sir Matthew Hale (1609–76). Hale gave the majority of Selden's books to the Bodleian Library at Oxford.

Now New Haven, Yale University, **Beinecke Library 320.**

Barbara A. Shailor, *Catalogue of Medieval and Renaissance Manuscripts in the Beinecke Rare Book and Manuscript Library, Yale University*, vol. 2, *MSS 251–500* (Binghamton, 1987), pp. 126–28.

David N. Dumville, "On the Dating of Some Late Anglo-Saxon Liturgical Manuscripts," *Transactions of the Cambridge Bibliographical Society*, 10.1 (1991), 40–57, at pp. 42–43.

Probably from the same manuscript as Cambridge, Trinity College B. 1. 30A (Gneuss 157).

Simon Keynes, *Anglo-Saxon Manuscripts and Other Items of Related Interest in the Library of Trinity College, Cambridge*, OEN, Subsidia 18 (Binghamton, 1992), no. 3.

Helmut Gneuss, "Liturgical Books in Anglo-Saxon England and Their Old English Terminology," in *Learning and Literature in Anglo-Saxon England: Studies Presented to Peter Clemoes*, ed. Michael Lapidge and Helmut Gneuss (Cambridge, 1985), pp. 91–141, at 132.

1965

The Pierpont Morgan Library acquired a manuscript of 77 leaves containing *Lives of Saints* and *Hymns* (St. Albans, s. xi/xii) previously in the collection of the Library Company of Philadelphia, bequeathed to the Library Company in **1803** by the Rev. Samuel Preston of Chevening, Kent.

Now New York, **Pierpont Morgan Library 926.**

Gneuss 865; de Ricci, *Supplement*, pp. 468–69 (no. 13, Library Company of Philadelphia).

K. D. Hartzell, "A St. Albans Miscellany in New York," *Mittellateinisches Jahrbuch*, 10 (1975), 20–61.

Rodney M. Thomson, *Manuscripts from St. Albans Abbey, 1066–1235*, rev. ed. (Woodbridge, 1985), no. 64.

29 July 1965

At Sotheby's, London, lot no. 576, two strips from a binding fragment of Ælfric, *Catholic Homilies I*, Homily for Palm Sunday (s. x^{in}).

Now New Haven, Yale University, **Beinecke Library Osborn Collection.**

Ker 81; Collins 3a (plate); Gneuss 146.

From the same manuscript as fragments now in Bloomington, Oxford, and Cambridge.

Described by Rowland L. Collins and Peter Clemoes, "The Common Origin of Ælfric Fragments at New Haven, Oxford, Cambridge, and Bloomington," in *Old English Studies in Honour of John C. Pope*, ed. Robert B. Burlin and Edward B. Irving, Jr. (Toronto, 1974), pp. 285–326.

20 January 1967

At Hodgson's, London, lot no. 630, a leaf containing Ælfric, *Catholic Homilies I*, the end of the homily for the second Sunday after Easter and the beginning of the homily for Wednesday in Rogationtide (s. x^{in}).

Now Oxford, **Bodleian Library Eng th. c. 74.**

Ker 81; Gneuss 146.

From the same manuscript as fragments now in Bloomington, New Haven, and Cambridge.

Described by Rowland L. Collins and Peter Clemoes, "The Common Origin of Ælfric Fragments at New Haven, Oxford, Cambridge, and Bloomington," in *Old English Studies in Honour of John C. Pope*, ed. Robert B. Burlin and Edward B. Irving, Jr. (Toronto, 1974), pp. 285–326.

December 1968

The University of Missouri purchased a bound collection of manuscript fragments, mostly derived from John Bagford, from William Salloch; it was item 2 in his *Catalogue 258: Manuscripts* (Ossining, NY [1968]). The collection was once Phillipps 15758, and at the Phillipps sale (Sotheby's, London, **19 May 1913**, lot no. 742) it was bought by Sir Sidney Cockerell and was lot no. 2 at his sale at Sotheby's, London, **3 April 1957**. Bought by Edwards, it sold again at the

H. C. Drayton sale (Sotheby's, London, **12 December 1967**, lot no. 51) and passed through a number of book dealers before being acquired by Salloch and then the University of Missouri.

The collection (Rare-L PA 3381/.A1/.F7) included an Anglo-Saxon Latin liturgical leaf, perhaps from a reading book (Glastonbury[?], s. x^{med}).

Now Columbia, Missouri, **University of Missouri Library Fragmenta Manuscripta 1.**

Described by Linda Ehrsam Voigts, "A Fragment of an Anglo-Saxon Liturgical Manuscript at the University of Missouri," ASE, 17 (1988), 83–92.

Rejected by David N. Dumville, "On the Dating of Some Late Anglo-Saxon Liturgical Manuscripts," *Transactions of the Cambridge Bibliographical Society*, 10.1 (1991), 40–57, at pp. 43–44.

Christopher de Hamel, "Medieval and Renaissance Manuscripts from the Library of Sir Sydney Cockerell (1867–1962)," *British Library Journal*, 13.2 (1987), 187–210, at p. 203 (no. 69).

Because of cropping the leaf now contains the following texts: recto: Lamentations 2:22–3:14 and 3:19–35 and recto: Lamentations 3:40–56 and 3:60–66. After the last verse a note places the reading of passages from Lamentations as part of the night offices during the last three days of Holy Week.

On the collection see Milton McC. Gatch, "*Fragmenta Manuscripta* and *Varia* at Missouri and Cambridge," *Transactions of the Cambridge Bibliographical Society*, 9.5 (1990), 434–75.

Included in the same collection is a leaf from an Anglo-Saxon sacramentary (s. x/xi).

Now Columbia, Missouri, **University of Missouri Library Fragmenta Manuscripta 3.**

Gneuss 810.

Included are prayers for the fourth, fifth, sixth, and seventh Sundays after Pentecost (here described as [third], fourth, fifth, and sixth Sundays after the Octave of Pentecost). The texts are the same as *The Leofric Missal*, ed. F. E. Warren (Oxford, 1883), pp. 116–17.

Included in the same collection is a leaf of Old Testament Minor Prophets (s. x^2).

Now Columbia, Missouri, **University of Missouri Library Fragmenta Manuscripta 4.**

Gneuss 811.

The texts included are: recto: Micah 7:15–20 and Nahum 1:1–6 and verso: Habakkuk 2:5–17.

Included in the same collection is a leaf of Gregory's *Moralia in Iob* (s. viii–ix).

Now Columbia, Missouri, **University of Missouri Library Fragmenta Manuscripta 8.**

"Addenda *CLA*," p. 350.

Related to fragments at Durham, Kassel, and Hersfeld.

25 November 1969

At Sotheby's, London, lot no. 442, 26 leaves and another bifolium of Aldhelm's prose *De Laude Virginitatis* (s. ix^{in}) with Old English glosses (s. x^{2}). Formerly Phillipps 8071 and 20688; purchased by H. P. Kraus and in **1970** acquired by Yale University as the gift of Edwin J. Beinecke.

Now New Haven, Yale University, **Beinecke Library 401 and 401A.**

Ker 12; Collins 1a (plate); Gneuss 857.

Barbara A. Shailor, *Catalogue of Medieval and Renaissance Manuscripts in the Beinecke Rare Book and Manuscript Library, Yale University*, vol. 2, *MSS 251–500* (Binghamton, 1987), pp. 280–84.

Jennifer Morrish, "Dated and Datable Manuscripts Copied in England during the Ninth Century: A Preliminary List," *Mediaeval Studies*, 50 (1988), 527.

From a group of *membra disiecta* now in Philadelphia, New Haven, Oslo/London, Cambridge, Oxford, and London.

10 December 1969

At Sotheby's, London, lot no. 29, the will of Æthelgifu (s. x^{ex}). The will was purchased by H. P. Kraus for William H. Scheide. Originally in the archives of St. Albans Abbey and thence probably to the collections of John Selden (1584–1654) and Sir Matthew Hale (1609–76); purchased in **1939** by James Fairhurst from a descendant of Hale. Hale was one of Selden's executors and gave the majority of his books to the Bodleian Library at Oxford. Manuscripts from the Fairhurst collection were sold at Sotheby's, London, **10 June 1963**, as the property of Messrs. Morgan Grenfell; the will was held back by Lord Rennell, a partner in Morgan Grenfell, to study and publish as his contribution to the Roxburghe Club.

Now Princeton, **Scheide Library 140.**

Collins 9 (plate); Sawyer 1497.
The Will of Æthelgifu: A Tenth Century Anglo-Saxon Manuscript, ed. Dorothy Whitelock, Neil Ker, Lord Rennell (Oxford [for the Roxburghe Club], 1968).
Simon Keynes, "A Lost Cartulary of St. Albans Abbey," ASE, 22 (1993), 253–79, at pp. 260–61 and 268.
Margaret Gelling, *The Early Charters of the Thames Valley*, Studies in Early English History 7 (Leicester, 1979), no. 171.
Facsimiles of Anglo-Saxon Charters, ed. Simon Keynes (Oxford, 1991), no. 15.

12 July 1971
At Sotheby's, London, lot no. 35, a Latin pontifical of 144 leaves (Christ Church, Canterbury, s. x) with some Old English glosses (s. xi), found in the stables at Brodie Castle, Forres, Elginshire, in **June 1970**.

Now London, **BL Additional 57337 (the Anderson Pontifical).**

Ker 416; Gneuss 302.

before 1972
Two leaves containing portions of three letters of Alcuin (second quarter of s. x). There are no records to show when and where the fragment was acquired. Masi noted the existence of the fragment but was unable to identify the texts in 1972.

Now Chicago, **Newberry Library, Fragm. 15 (olim A–2).**

Michael Masi, "Newberry MSS Fragments, S. VII–S. XV," *Mediaeval Studies*, 34 (1972), 99–112, at p. 103.
David Ganz, "An Anglo-Saxon Fragment of Alcuin's Letters in the Newberry Library, Chicago," ASE, 22 (1993), 167–77.[21]

The text is from *Ep.* 149, 155, and 136, but are consecutive in the extant manuscripts. *Epistolae Karolini Aevi* II, ed. Ernst Dümmler, MGH, Epistolae 4 (Berlin, 1895), pp. 242–43, 205, and 253.

1972
A fragment of Gregory, *Moralia in Job* (s. viii[1]).

Now New Haven, Yale University, **Beinecke Library 516.**

Gneuss 858; "Addenda *CLA*" 1849, pp. 340–41.
Cora E. Lutz, "A Manuscript Fragment from Bede's Monastery," *Yale University Library Gazette*, 48 (1973), 135–38.

21 November 1972
Three leaves from a benedictional (s. x^1) were sold at Sotheby's, London, lot 532, and have subsequently been separated.
One leaf appeared as Maggs *Catalogue* 973 (London, **1976**), no. 150.
Now Cambridge, Massachussetts, **Houghton Library Typ 612.**

Catalogue of Manuscripts in the Houghton Library, Harvard University (Alexandria, VA, 1986–87), vol. 2, p. 115.

The leaf contains the conclusion of the benediction for the beginning of Lent and the beginning of the benediction for the first Sunday in Lent. *The Benedictional of Saint Æthelwold, Bishop of Winchester, 963–984*, ed. George Frederic Warner and Henry Austin Wilson (Oxford, 1910), pp. 14–15.
For no. 151 in the same Maggs catalogue see June 1976.

The second leaf appeared as Maggs *Catalogue* 982 (London, **1977**), no. 23. It was purchased by B. S. Cron and sold again in **1986** by Bernard Quaritch.
Now Tokyo, **Takamiya Collection.**

The leaf contains the benediction for the Saturday before Easter and two benedictions for Easter Day. *The Benedictional of Saint Æthelwold, Bishop of Winchester, 963–984*, ed. George Frederic Warner and Henry Austin Wilson (Oxford, 1910), pp. 19–20.

The third leaf appeared as Maggs *Catalogue* 1002 (London, **1980**), no. 6.
Now London, **Collection of S. J. Keynes, Esq.**

The leaf contains the conclusion of the benediction for Easter, benedictions for Monday and Tuesday, and the beginning of the benediction for Wednesday after Easter. *The Benedictional of Saint Æthelwold, Bishop of Winchester, 963–984*, ed. George Frederic Warner and Henry Austin Wilson (Oxford, 1910), pp. 20–21.

25 March 1975
At Sotheby's, London, the property of Major J. R. Abbey (his 3243), lot no. 2955, an endleaf and two binding strips of the West Saxon translation of Mark

and Matthew (s. xi) in a Latin psalter (s. xiv), bought by H. P. Kraus. The manuscript was formerly in the collections of Sir Sidncy Cockerell, who acquired it in or before **1924** and gave it to C. H. St. John Hornby (his MS 70). It was bought from his executors by Abbey on **15 September 1946**.

Now New Haven, Yale University, **Beinecke Library 578.**

Ker 1; Collins 2 (plate); Gneuss 859.

Roy Michael Liuzza, ed., *The Old English Version of the Gospels*, EETS OS 304 (1994), pp. xli–xlii.

Walter Cahn and James Marrow, "Medieval and Renaissance Manuscripts at Yale: A Selection," *Yale University Library Gazette*, 52 (1978), 182.

Christopher de Hamel, "Medieval and Renaissance Manuscripts from the Library of Sir Sydney Cockerell (1867–1962), *British Library Journal*, 13.2 (1987), 186–210, at pp. 205–206 (no. 93).

Described by Roy Michael Liuzza, "The Yale Fragments of the West-Saxon Gospels," ASE, 17 (1988), 67–82.

June 1976

A fragment of Prudentius, *Contra Symmachum* (Christ Church, Canterbury, s. x/xi). Purchased from Maggs *Catalogue* 973 (London, 1976), no. 151.

Now Christchurch, New Zealand, **private collection.**

Margaret M. Manion, Vera F. Vines, and Christopher de Hamel, *Medieval and Renaissance Manuscripts in New Zealand Collections* (Melbourne, 1989), no. 165.

T. A. M. Bishop has identified this as the work of his scribe (xv), the scribe of four other Anglo-Saxon manuscripts. They are: (1) Oxford, Bodleian Library Auct. F.1.15 (gloss to pt. 1); (2) London, BL Royal 6.A.VI; (3) Cambridge, Trinity College B.14.3 (289); and (4) Taunton, County Record Office, Marquess of Ailesbury deposit, a charter of Æthelred II for Muchelney, Somerset, dated 995 (E. H. Bates [Harbin], *Two Cartularies of the Benedictine Abbeys of Muchelney and Athelney in the County of Somerset*, Somerset Record Society 14 [1899], frontispiece). See T. A. M. Bishop, "Notes on Cambridge Manuscripts," *Transactions of the Cambridge Bibliographical Society*, 3 (1959–63), 412–23, at p. 422, and his *English Caroline Minuscule* (Oxford, 1971), no. 9.

1977

Two leaves from a Latin Bible, containing Deuteronomy 30:9–32:6 and 32:12–34:12 (Mercian [?], s. viii/ix). Purchased from Quaritch *Catalogue* 969

(London, 1977), no. 8. Formerly Phillipps 36183, they were acquired by Quaritch from H. P. Kraus in **1976**; acquired by Kraus from Dr. Martin Bodmer of Geneva in **1971**.

Now Tokyo, **Takamiya Collection 21.**

CLA II.259; N. R. Ker, *Medieval Libraries of Great Britain: A List of Surviving Books* (London, 1964), p. 175, n. 3.

Teresa Webber, *Scribes and Scholars at Salisbury Cathedral, c. 1075–c. 1125* (Oxford, 1992), pp. 77 and 79.

The leaves were once used as flyleaves in Salisbury manuscripts and are related to the flyleaves in Salisbury Cathedral MS 117 and to the flyleaf in Oxford, Bodleian Library Bodley 516, now kept separately as Lat. bib. c. 8 (P).

11 December 1979

At Sotheby's, London, the property of Queens' College, Cambridge, lot no. 25, a sheet of farm accounts of Ely Abbey (s. xi^{in}–xi^{1}) now in three strips, two recovered from the binding of a sixteenth-century printed book in the college library and the third strip from the collection of a Lincolnshire antiquary, for some time on deposit at the college, acquired outright by the college the year before the sale. It was advertised as "probably the largest piece of Anglo-Saxon writing ever likely to come on the market."

Now London, **BL Additional 61735.**

Ker 80.

The Golden Age of Anglo-Saxon Art, 966–1066, ed. Janet Backhouse, D. H. Turner, and Leslie Webster (London, 1984), no. 150.

December 1981

A fragment of a leaf from a manuscript of Gregory of Tours, *Miraculorum Libri Octo* (s. xi^{1}). The fragment is of the account of the miracles of St. Martin. Formerly in the collections of Philip Bliss, Sir Thomas Phillipps, E. H. Dring, E. M. Dring. For other fragments of similar provenance see Bernard Quaritch, *Bookhands of the Middle Ages*, pts. I and II (London, 1984 and 1985).

Now London, **Richard A. Linenthal Collection.**

8 December 1981

At Sotheby's, London, lot no. 8, a fragment of a missal in Latin with neumes (Exeter, s. xi^{med}).

Now London, **BL Additional 62104.**

Illustrated in Christopher de Hamel, *A History of Illuminated Manuscripts* (Boston, 1986), pl. 210. Related to other fragments enumerated in N. R. Ker, *Fragments of Medieval Manuscripts Used as Pastedowns in Oxford Bindings* (Oxford, 1954), 285a.

25 April 1983

At Sotheby's, London, lot 5 (plate), a fragment of a sacramentary leaf (s. xi). With part of the vigil for Ascension Day and a lection from Mark 11:23–26. From the leaf collection of the late Esther Rosenbaum. Sold at Sotheby's, London, **10 June 1963**, lot 156, and afterwards A. G. Thomas *Catalogue* 17 (London, **1966**), no. 22. From the materials found in **1939** at Alderley, Gloucestershire, by James Fairhurst, which probably belonged to John Selden (1584–1654) and later his friend and executor, Sir Matthew Hale (1609–76). This is the same provenance as the Scheide Library will of Æthegifu. Hale gave the majority of Selden's books to the Bodleian Library at Oxford.

Now London, **Collection of S. J. Keynes, Esq.**

1984

Bernard Quaritch, *Bookhands of the Middle Ages*, pt. I, Catalogue 1036 (London, 1984), no. 56, is a leaf from a gospel book (s. x/xi).

Now London, **BL Additional 63143.**

The fragments in this catalogue were from the collection of the Oxford antiquary Philip Bliss (1787–1857) and were sold at the Bliss sale on **21 August 1858**, lot nos. 100 and 119, and became, in part, Sir Thomas Phillipps 18133, which was lot no. 390 in the Phillipps sale of **24 April 1911**. They were acquired by E. H. Dring, thence to E. M. Dring, through whom to Quaritch.

Included in the same catalogue, no. 124, is a flyleaf from a manuscript containing a collection of Latin verse texts (s. x/xi), including verse riddles with answers in cipher, verses on the seven days of creation with responses in cipher, and questions and answers on the tribes and languages of the world.

Now USA, **private collection.**

13 December 1984

At Christie's, London, lot no. 123, two leaves from a gospel book or lectionary (Canterbury?; s. xi^{in}), formerly Musée van Maerlant, Damme, Belgium. The leaves were acquired in **1952** from the De Tracy collection, Ghent. Two badly mutilated leaves with three full-page miniatures and lections from Matthew 8:23–27 and 8:28.

Now Malibu, **J. Paul Getty Museum 9.**

Gneuss 817; Temple 53 (plate); Ohlgren, *Iconographic Catalogue* 158.
"Acquisitions: Manuscripts," *J. Paul Getty Museum Journal*, 14 (1986), no. 98.
A Thousand Years of the Bible: An Exhibition of Manuscripts from the J. Paul Getty Museum, Malibu, and Printed Books from the Department of Special Collections, University Research Library, UCLA (Malibu, 1991), no. 13 (plate).
André Boutemy, "Les feuillets de Damme," *Scriptorium*, 20 (1966), 60–65 (plates).
J. J. G. Alexander and C. M. Kauffmann, *English Illuminated Manuscripts 700–1500* (Brussels, 1973), no. 7.
J. J. G. Alexander, "Some Aesthetic Principles in the Use of Colour in Anglo-Saxon Art," ASE, 4 (1975), 145–54, at pp. 150–53 (color plates).

before 1985

Two leaves of Isidore, *In Libros Veteris ac Novi Testamenti Prooemia* (s. viii[2]) preserved as a front pastedown and flyleaf in Robert Holcot, *Super Sapientiam Salomonis*, Cologne, Conrad Winters de Homborch, c. 1479 (Goff H-288), which formerly belonged to the Benedictine abbey of Werden. The leaves are cleaned, scraped, and much faded. From the same manuscript as Düsseldorf Universitätsbibliothek K.1: B. 210 (*CLA* 1184).

Now San Marino, **Henry E. Huntington Library RB 99513 (PR 1188).**

"Addenda *CLA*," p. 358.

Given the provenance, the same as that of a leaf from a Bible sold on **2 December 1987**, perhaps the manuscript is more likely the product of an Anglo-Saxon center in Germany.

1985

Bernard Quaritch, *Bookhands of the Middle Ages*, pt. II, Catalogue 1056 (London, 1985), no. 46, is a leaf containing prayers in Latin (s. x/xi).

Now London, **BL Additional 63651.**

25 June 1985

At Sotheby's, London, the property of the Folger Shakespeare Library, Washington, DC, lot no. 50, the major part of a bifolium of Rufinus' Latin translation of Eusebius, *Historia Ecclesiastica* (s. vii[1], Northumberland or Ireland). Originally the vellum wrapper of two sixteenth-century medical texts, *An Hospital for the Diseased*, London, 1578 (STC 4303.5) and *Orders . . . in such Townes . . . infected with the Plague*, London, c. 1578 (STC 9187.10), bought by the Folger Library in **1935** from E. M. Lawson, Sutton Coldfield, nr. Birmingham (*Catalogue* 110, no. 500). Purchased by the British Rail Pension Fund; sold again privately in **1988**.

Now London, **J. Paul Getty, Jr., Collection.**

"Addenda *CLA*" 1864, pp. 348–49.
Folger Library Newsletter, 16.3 (February 1985), 1 (plate).
Bischoff and Brown ("Addenda *CLA*") suggest that the manuscripts were "written presumably in Ireland."

2 December 1987

At Christie's, London, the Estelle Doheny Collection, the property of St. John's Seminary, Camarillo, California, lot no. 137, a single leaf from a Latin Bible containing Judges 10:8–11:26 (s. ix[1]). Originally from a collection of manuscript leaves belonging to Professor E. A. Lowe through H. P. Kraus (*Catalogue 60: Fifty Select Books, Manuscripts and Autographs* [New York, 1953], no. 7) to Doheny, presumably in **1953**. Lowe appears to have acquired the leaf from the library of Schloss Arenfels, Bad Hönningen.

Now Tokyo, **Takamiya Collection.**

de Ricci, *Supplement*, p. 14 (no. 59 [6558]); *Supplement CLA*, no. 1685.
Described by Michelle P. Brown, "A New Fragment of a Ninth-Century English Bible," ASE, 18 (1989), 33–43.
Related to 32 further leaves preserved in Düsseldorf, Heinrich-Heine-Universitätsbibliothek A.19. The leaves may be the remains of an Octateuch and are convincingly attributed to Werden by B[ruce] C. Barker-Benfield, "The Werden 'Heptateuch,' " ASE, 20 (1991), 43–64. Werden is also the provenance of two leaves of Isidore, see **before 1985.**
Sigrid Krämer, *Handschriftenerbe des deutschen Mittelalters*, Mittelalterliche Bibliothekskataloge Deutschlands und der Schweiz Ergängzungsband 1 (Munich, 1989–1990), vol. 2, p. 827.
G. Karpp in G. Gattermann, ed., *Kostbarkeiten aus der Universitätsbibliothek Düsseldorf: Mittelalterliche Handschriften und Alte Drucke*, Schriften der Universitätsbibliothek Düsseldorf 5 (Wiesbaden, 1989), no. 2.

1988
In a copy of Thomas Elyot's *The Castle of Helthe* [London, 1557] (STC 7649) was discovered a fragment of a manuscript in Old English. Unfortunately the fragment is too narrow to allow the text to be identified.
Now Washington, DC, **Folger Shakespeare Library.**

Richard W. Clement, "An Anglo-Saxon Fragment at the Folger Shakespeare Library," OEN, 22.2 (1989), 56–57.

6 December 1988
Sotheby's, London, the property of J. Paul Getty Museum, Malibu, California, lot no. 33, a bifolium of Aldhelm, *De Laude Virginitatis*, in Latin prose (s. ix^{in}) with Old English glosses (s. x^{2}). Once in the collection of Dr. and Mrs. Peter Ludwig, Aachen; it was their MS XI 5. The collection was bought en bloc by the Getty in **1983**.
Now Oslo/London, **Schøyen Collection 197.**

Ker 12; Gneuss 857.
Anton von Euw and Joachim M. Plotzek, *Die Handschriften der Sammlung Ludwig* (Cologne, 1982), vol. 3, pp. 66–69.
Jennifer Morrish, "Dated and Datable Manuscripts Copied in England during the Ninth Century: A Preliminary List," *Mediaeval Studies*, 50 (1988), 527.
"Objects Removed from the Collection since 1983," *J. Paul Getty Museum Journal*, 19 (1991), 145.
From a group of *membra disiecta* now in Philadelphia, New Haven, Oslo/London, Cambridge, Oxford, and London.

20 June 1989
At Sotheby's, London, lot no. 27, a charter of Godwine granting Leofwine the Red the swine pasture of Swiþrædingdænne (Christ Church, Canterbury, 1013–20). Bought by Quaritch and in **December 1989** purchased by Martin Schøyen. Originally from the archives of Christ Church, Canterbury, thence to the antiquary Sir Edward Dering (1598–1644), who believed it referred to his family estate at Surrenden Dering, but more likely it refers to land in Southerden, also in Kent. At auction, Puttick & Simpson, London, **7 February 1863**, lot no. 1155, but seems to have remained in the Dering family.
Now Oslo/London, **Schøyen Collection 600.**

Sawyer 1220; Robertson 75; Kemble 1315.

Facsimiles of Anglo-Saxon Charters, ed. Simon Keynes (Oxford, 1991), no. 19.

C. E. Wright, "Sir Edward Dering: A Seventeenth-Century Antiquary and His 'Saxon' Charters," in *The Early Cultures of North-West Europe (H. M. Chadwick Memorial Studies)*, ed. Cyril Fox and Bruce Dickins (Cambridge, 1950), pp. 369–93, at 378, n. 3, and 379 and 380.

L[ambert] B. L[arking]. "On the Surrenden Charters," *Archaeologia Cantiana*, 1 (1858), 50–65, at pp. 62–64 (plate).

"John Bruce [Vice President of the Society] by permission of the Rev. Lambert Larking, exhibited a Saxon Charter, belonging to Sir Edward Dering, . . . of which the following is a copy," *Proceedings of the Society of Antiquaries*, 4 (1856–59), 76.

J. K. Wallenberg. *Kentish Place-Names: A Topographical and Etymological Study of the Place-Name Material in Kentish Charters Dated Before the Conquest*, Uppsala Universitets Årsskrift, Filosofi, Språkvetenskap och Historiska Vetenskaper 2 (Uppsala, 1931), pp. 331–32.

19 June 1990

At Sotheby's, London, lot no. 10, a fragment of an office book with the lection from John 6:54–65 used at Corpus Christi (s. xi^{med}).

Now Oslo/London, **Schøyen Collection 674.**

1991

Inspeximus of King Henry III of the grant to the abbey of Wherwell made by King Ethelred in 1002 with the addition of 1008, dated 26 October 1259. The original charter is now lost, and this charter preserves a line of Old English text. Purchased 1991 from Quaritch.

Now Oslo/London, **Schøyen Collection 1354.**

Sawyer 904; Harmer, p. 551; Kemble 707.

H. P. R. Finberg, *The Early Charters of Wessex* (Leicester, 1964), no. 149.

17 December 1991

At Sotheby's, London, lot no. 4, a fragment of a missal (s. xi^{med}) for 17–18 February. From the collection of George Salt; a gift to him from Peter Croft (1929–84).

Now Oslo/London, **Schøyen Collection 1542.**

REFERENCES

Alexander

J. J. G. Alexander, *Insular Manuscripts, 6th to the 9th Century*, A Survey of Manuscripts Illuminated in the British Isles, ed. Alexander, vol. 1 (London, 1978).

Collins

Rowland Collins, *Anglo-Saxon Vernacular Manuscripts in America* (New York, 1976).

CLA

E. A. Lowe, *Codices Latini Antiquiores*, 11 vols. (Oxford, 1934–72).

Supplement CLA

E. A. Lowe, *Codices Latini Antiquiores: Supplement* (Oxford, 1971).

"Addenda *CLA*"

Bernhard Bischoff and Virginia Brown, "Addenda to *Codices Latini Antiquiores*," *Mediaeval Studies*, 47 (1985), 317–66.

"Addenda *CLA* II"

Bernhard Bischoff, Virginia Brown, and James J. John, "Addenda to *Codices Latini Antiquiores* (II)," *Mediaeval Studies*, 54 (1992), 286–307.

de Ricci

Seymour de Ricci, with the assistance of W. J. Wilson, *Census of Medieval and Renaissance Manuscripts in the United States and Canada* (New York, 1935–40).

de Ricci, *Supplement*

C. U. Faye and W. H. Bond, *Supplement to the Census of Medieval and Renaissance Manuscripts in the United States and Canada* (New York, 1962).

Goff

Frederick R. Goff, *Incunabula in American Libraries: A Third Census of Fifteenth-Century Printed Books in North American Collections*, rev. ed. (Millwood, NY, 1973) and *Supplement* (New York, 1972).

Gneuss

Helmut Gneuss, "A Preliminary List of Manuscripts Written or Owned in England up to 1100," ASE, 9 (1981), 1–60.

Harmer

F. E. Harmer, *Anglo-Saxon Writs* (Manchester, 1952).

Kemble

J. M. Kemble, *Codex Diplomaticus Aevi Saxonici*, 6 vols. (London, 1839–48).

Ker

N. R. Ker, "A Supplement to *Catalogue of Manuscripts Containing Anglo-Saxon*," ASE, 5 (1976), 121–31.

Mary Blockley, "Addenda and Corrigenda to N. R. Ker's 'A Supplement to *Catalogue of Manuscripts Containing Anglo-Saxon*,'" *Notes and Queries*, NS 29 (1982), 1–3.

Ohlgren, *Iconographic Catalogue*

Thomas H. Ohlgren, *Insular and Anglo-Saxon Illuminated Manuscripts: An Iconographic Catalogue, c. A.D. 625 to 1100* (New York, 1986).

Ohlgren, *Textual Illustration*

Thomas H. Ohlgren, *Anglo-Saxon Textual Illustration: Photographs of Sixteen Manuscripts with Descriptions and Index* (Kalamazoo, 1992).

Robertson

A. J. Robertson, *Anglo-Saxon Charters*, 2nd ed. (Cambridge, 1956).

Sawyer

P. H. Sawyer, *Anglo-Saxon Charters: An Annotated List and Bibliography* (London, 1968).

Temple

Elżbieta Temple, *Anglo-Saxon Manuscripts, 900–1066*, A Survey of Manuscripts Illuminated in the British Isles, ed. J. J. G. Alexander, vol. 2 (London, 1976).

Voelkle

William Voelkle, *Mediaeval and Renaissance Manuscripts: Major Acquisitions of The Pierpont Morgan Library, 1924–1974* (New York, 1974).

NOTES

1. Initial research for this paper was begun in 1986 with the assistance of a Bibliographical Society of America Fellowship for which I am most grateful. The paper, in its original form, was meant to accompany a one-day exhibition of manuscripts which was mounted in the Burke Library of Union Theological Seminary in New York City. My thanks go to Margaret Howell, Special Collections Librarian at the Univ. of Missouri, Columbia, MO, and Saundra Taylor, Curator of Manuscripts at the Lilly Library, Indiana Univ., Bloomington, IN, for their courtesy and trust in permitting the manuscript fragments in their care to be exhibited. Thanks also to Richard Spoor, Librarian Emeritus, and Milton McC. Gatch, Librarian, of the Burke Library, to Paul Szarmach, naturally, and to colleagues in the Department of Rare Books and Special Collections at Princeton and to William H. Scheide, for assistance, advice, and encouragement. In my research I have relied heavily on the work of Neil Ker, Rowland Collins, and Helmut Gneuss, among others. Corrigenda and addenda to their work are offered with the deepest respect and are possible only because their work was there to begin with.

2. Philip Brooks, *The New York Times Book Review*, 27 March 1938, p. 25.

3. On the provenance of the manuscript see Rudolph Willard, "Modern Ownership," in his *The Blickling Homilies*, EEMF 10 (1960), pp. 15–17.

4. The long and complicated story of the relationship of Beyer and Bishop is related in Wesley Towner's *The Elegant Auctioneers* (New York, 1970), pp. 468, 472, 480–85, 529. See also Douglas Gordon, "Cortlandt Field Bishop and the Death Struggles of the American-Anderson Galleries," *The Book Collector*, 34.4 (1985), 452–60.

5. Brooks, p. 25.

6. Rowland Collins, *Anglo-Saxon Vernacular Manuscripts in America* (New York, 1976), pp. 15–16.

7. William H. Scheide, "Love for the Printed Word as Expressed in the Scheide Library," *Papers of the Bibliographical Society of America*, 51 (1957), 221–22.

8. Collins, pp. 66–67.

9. Bertram Colgrave and Ann Hyde, "Two Recently Discovered Leaves from Old English Manuscripts," *Speculum*, 37 (1962), 60–78.

10. Barbara A. Shailor, *Catalogue of Medieval and Renaissance Manuscripts in the Beinecke Rare Book and Manuscript Library, Yale University*, vol. 1 (Binghamton, 1984), p. xvii.

11. On Bagford see Milton McC. Gatch, "John Bagford as a Collector and Disseminator of Manuscript Fragments," *The Library*, 6th series, 7 (1985), 95–114, and "John Bagford, Bookseller and Antiquary," *British Library Journal*, 12 (1986), 150–71. On the collection see Milton McC. Gatch, "*Fragmenta Manuscripta* and *Varia* at Missouri and Cambridge," *Transactions of the Cambridge Bibliographical Society*, 9.5 (1990), 434–75.

12. Described by Linda Ehrsam Voigts, "A Fragment of an Anglo-Saxon Liturgical Manuscript at the University of Missouri," ASE, 17 (1988), 83–92. On reading books see Helmut Gneuss, "Liturgical Books in Anglo-Saxon England and Their Old English Terminology," in *Learning and Literature in Anglo-Saxon England*, ed. Michael Lapidge and Helmut Gneuss (Cambridge, 1985), pp. 120–21.

13. *The Leofric Missal*, ed. F. E. Warren (Oxford, 1883), pp. 116–17.

14. On medieval manuscript fragments see Rowan Watson, "Medieval Manuscript Fragments," *Archives*, 13 (1977), 61–73; Elisabeth Pellegrin, "Fragments et Membra Disiecta," in *Codicologica 3: Essais Typologiques*, ed. A. Gruys and J. P. Gumbert, Litterae Textuales (Leiden, 1980), pp. 70–95; Bernard M. Rosenthal, "Latin Scripts before 1600," *The Professional Rare Bookseller*, 7 (1984), 3–7; William P. Stoneman, "Medieval Manuscript Fragments at Princeton," *Princeton University Library Chronicle*, 51 (1989), 91–101.

15. Voigts, article as above, but see David N. Dumville, "On the Dating of Some Late Anglo-Saxon Liturgical Manuscripts," *Transactions of the Cambridge Bibliographical Society*, 10.1 (1991), 40–57 at pp. 43–44.

16. Robert Babcock, *Reconstructing a Medieval Library: Fragments from Lambach* (New Haven, 1993).

17. Phillip Pulsiano, "A *Gothic Grammar* with a Transcript of Anglo-Saxon Prayers," OEN, 23.1(1989), 40–41.

18. Karen Thompson, *Catalogue* (London, 1991), no. 68; now in a private collection in Tokyo.

19. This chronology includes Latin and vernacular manuscripts written in Anglo-Saxon England or on the Continent under Anglo-Saxon influence. It also includes some manuscripts purchased by individuals and institutions outside the United States in order to provide a more accurate picture of market conditions operating upon all these buyers.

20. I am grateful to Paul Saenger, Curator of Manuscripts at the Newberry Library, for his assistance with these fragments, and especially to Milton McC. Gatch, who examined the Newberry Library fragments on my behalf.

21. I am grateful to David Ganz for allowing me to read his article while it was still in page proof.

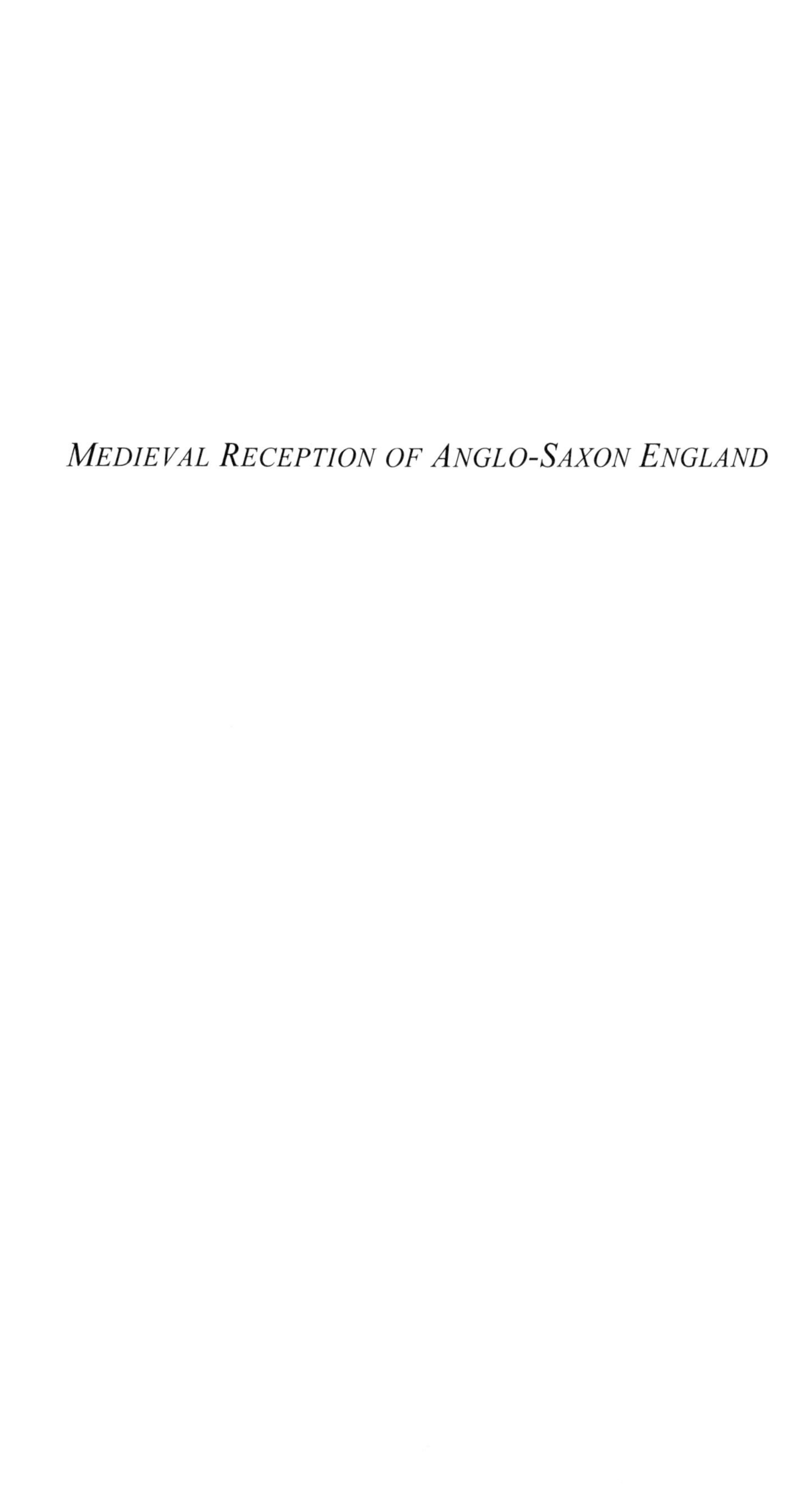

Medieval Reception of Anglo-Saxon England

THE FRANKS AND THE ENGLISH IN THE NINTH CENTURY RECONSIDERED

JANET L. NELSON

Before the Roman came to Rye or out to Severn strode
The rolling English drunkard made the rolling English road. . . .
A merry, a mazy road, and such as we did tread
The night we went to Birmingham by way of Beachy Head.[1]

I have taken my cue from Chesterton, not because I intend to talk about Anglo-Saxon trackways, or drinking habits, but to signal this paper's point of departure: that direct routes are not always the ones people take, nor are direct links therefore the only ones upon which historians ought to focus. Time-travelers to the ninth century need a map covering more than the English Channel. For ninth-century contacts between the Franks and the English often went a long way round: not rolling drunkenly, I hasten to add, but *carefully choosing* a route via Rome. Rome's unique combination of imperial and apostolic traditions was reinforced in the ninth century by the new historical reality of a western empire and by the papacy's newly asserted claims to jurisdictional authority. Anglo-Frankish contacts were pulled into a transalpine ellipse—and they can scarcely be understood unless we too feel the pull of Rome.

Over 40 years ago Michael Wallace-Hadrill argued that it was "Danish pressure" that "drew the English and the Franks—or at any rate their rulers—closer together than they had ever been before." It was in these "years of crisis" that "the full force of Frankish example hit England"—and Wallace-Hadrill saw the evidence in the historical writing of Alfred's reign—the Anglo-Saxon Chronicle and Asser's *Life*.[2] Twenty years later, Wallace-Hadrill developed these insights in the latter part of *Early Germanic Kingship in England and on the Continent*.[3]

Ninth-century historical writing supplies evidence for political strategies in which a motive and motor, even more powerful than common concern with external defense, was competition. Wallace-Hadrill rightly diagnosed dynastic insecurity as a major problem for all ninth-century rulers; but his account of ninth-century remedies underestimated one that I see as of fundamental importance: the renewal of empire. This necessarily embroiled Franks and Anglo-Saxons in rivalry rather than in mutual support. Which brings me back to my starting point. The rulers and leaders of both Franks and English aspired—precisely because of their insecurity—to extend and defend their power by attaching it to imperial or papal authority. Ideologically speaking, and very often literally as well, all roads led to Rome. What follows is an investigation of three cases in point. They may seem only obliquely relevant to the continental reception of Anglo-Saxon culture. In fact, they should be read as evidence of the profound impact of that culture on the Franks. For it was not only Anglo-Saxon texts[4] but also Anglo-Saxon regimes that, through a variety of personal and institutional contacts, helped to re-focus the Franks' attention on Rome in the mid- and later-ninth century. Of course, that orientation was already congenial: short of legitimacy, Pippin, the first Carolingian king, had looked to papal authority, while his successors Charlemagne and Louis the Pious had drawn heavily on sanctity imported from Rome.[5] All that is well known. Later in the ninth century, however, established receptivity stimulated further kinds of reception of Roman models and Roman inspiration. Here too—and this is less well known—Anglo-Saxon culture continued to play an essential role. The very indirectness of the evidence is testimony to contacts so pervasive, influences so thoroughly absorbed, that they had become part of the air breathed in the Frankish world.

I. Imperial Strategies and Roman Legitimacy: Æthelwulf King of Wessex and Charles the Bald of West Francia

In recent years there have been two interesting accounts of the marriage of Æthelwulf with Charles the Bald's daughter Judith and its political context, both concentrating primarily on West Saxon interests.[6] If the focus is shifted to West Francia, the scene is dominated by Charles the Bald, restless, ambitious, inventive. He suffered the first major defeat of his career in August 851 at the hands of the Bretons; Charles salvaged his pride (at least) and put relations with the Breton leader Erispoë on a new footing: Erispoë "gave Charles his hands," and Charles granted him "royal vestments" but withheld a royal title. Charles himself thus implicitly assumed a superior "imperial" position.[7] In 855 he set up his second son as sub-king in Aquitaine; and in February 856 he set up his eldest son as sub-king in Neustria (the region between the Seine and the Loire), at the same time arranging the boy's betrothal to Erispoë's daughter.[8] These relationships, reinforced by public rituals, created a family of kings and princely allies, reminiscent of the Byzantine model. Charles was no emperor yet—but he had aspirations to imitate his grandfather Charlemagne.[9] The death of Charles' eldest brother, the emperor Lothar, in 855 had been followed by a parceling out of Lothar's realm among his three sons: the eldest of them ruled, as the West Frankish annalist put it, as "so-called emperor of Italy."[10] After 855, Carolingian political relationships altered fundamentally, and north of the Alps new prospects of empire-building opened up. Charles the Bald's initiatives in later 855 and early 856 must be seen in the light of a response to the new conditions. So too must the marriage of Charles' daughter to Æthelwulf: it brought the West Saxon king into Charles' "family of kings," succeeding where Charlemagne had in a sense failed with Offa. But Charlemagne was certainly his grandson's model for (at this stage) a *Romfrei* imperial ideal.[11]

In 849–50 when the Breton chief Nominoë deposed "his" five bishops, defying their Frankish metropolitan, the Archbishop of Tours,

King Charles had, it seems, sent a trusted agent, Lupus of Ferrières, to Rome to mobilize the authority of Pope Leo IV (847–55), and it was Lupus who could then draw on papal letters in composing the conciliar admonition sent to Nominoë by the assembled West Frankish bishops.[12] Æthelwulf of Wessex took a similar tack: in 853 (or end of 852?) he "sent his son Alfred to Rome. The Lord Leo was then pope in Rome, and he consecrated him king and stood sponsor to him at confirmation."[13]

Æthelwulf's decision can be seen in part as a defensive one: contacts with Charles' kingdom had been exceptionally close during the early 850's,[14] and Æthelwulf probably knew enough of Charles' imperial vision to wish to forestall any extension of it across the Channel. But Æthelwulf's frame of mind in 853 was less likely to have been defensive than quite positively assertive: in 850, at Sandwich in Kent, his son Athelstan had "slain a great army," while the following year Æthelwulf and his son Æthelbald "inflicted the greatest slaughter on a heathen army that we have ever heard tell of" at Aclea in Surrey.[15] In 853 the Anglo-Saxon Chronicle records—immediately before the sending of Alfred to Rome—a West Saxon campaign across Mercia (at the Mercians' request) against the Welsh, and the Welsh "submission";[16] and the same annal ends with the marriage on Æthelwulf's territory[17] of Æthelwulf's daughter Æthelswith to the Mercian king. She may well have been crowned queen on this same occasion, following a Mercian precedent.[18]

There were new possibilities here. Could Æthelwulf set up his own family of kings? There is no evidence that in 853 or later he had set his face against a division of his realm: Asser c. 16 shows him dividing it in 856/58.[19] Given high mortality (Æthelwulf's eldest son, Athelstan, may have died in or soon after 851[20]) and the availability of potential sub-kingdoms, even a fourth son might hope for a realm. Contemporary arrangements were much more flexible than is often realized. Carolingian rulers who were Æthelwulf's contemporaries made and unmade succession arrangements to suit their own desires, and they created *regna* that modern historians call sub-kingdoms, without, apparently, staging formal king-makings for the recipients or conferring royal titles on them. Thus Charlemagne's eldest son and namesake got a *regnum* in 790 but was crowned king by the pope only in 800, and apparently he did not have the title *rex* before that.[21] Louis the Pious' youngest son, Charles (the Bald), got a series of *regna* in the 830's and in 838 even received a crown without actually being consecrated king, or using the title *rex* before his father's death in 840.[22] It was not clear that Lothar's son Louis would rule in Italy rather than (as Lothar himself had finally succeeded in doing) in Francia. Only on his deathbed did Lothar make his final dispositions, and (evidently to some observers' surprise) carved out a *regnum* for his youngest son.[23] Æthelwulf in 853, I suggest, invoked papal authority to legitimize a similar possibility. Like Louis the Pious, like Lothar, Æthelwulf wanted his youngest son to succeed to a share in his composite realm, and in 853 he seemed in position to secure that. While Leo did not (strictly speaking) make Alfred a king, he set the seal of throne-worthiness on him: Alfred was now a prospective, a potential heir. The claim that Alfred was "consecrated king" in 853 simply drew out the implication of papally invented rituals that were probably intended anyway to be ambiguous.[24] Whoever, c. 890, entered this statement in the Anglo-Saxon Chronicle had no intention of being controversial. The question of Alfred's truthfulness or otherwise seems to me a red herring.[25]

For two things seem certain. First, in sending Alfred to Rome, Æthelwulf was imitating Carolingian examples of the designation of kings' sons as potential heirs.[26] Charlemagne in 781 had taken (rather than sent) his third and fourth sons (aged four and three) to Rome, to be confirmed and consecrated kings by the pope,[27] and in 800 he had done the same with his son Charles the Younger.[28] Lothar I in 844 had sent his eldest son (aged eighteen) to Rome, where the pope (Sergius II) "anointed him king and invested him with a swordbelt"; and in 850, Lothar sent the same son again to Rome, where Pope Leo IV consecrated him emperor.[29] Second, Alfred was being kept in the running by being marked out for secular life; this is clear from Leo IV's own account of his reception of Alfred: as well as confirming him, he conferred the title of consul and invested him with a sword and belt.[30] In sending Alfred to Rome in 853, Æthelwulf was forging his own direct link with Leo IV and also registering his own *imitatio imperii*: just as Lothar had had his son girded with a sword by the pope, so too would the king of a West Saxon kingdom recently extended to include Kent, and Devon, and Cornwall, and already with sights set northwards to Mercia and Wales.[31] There is a striking contrast, though, with what Charles the Bald did the very next year in the case of his own four-year-old son, Carloman, the third of three sons borne by Charles' wife between 846 and 849: "Charles had [Carloman] tonsured and dedicated him to the church"—that is, he meant to exclude him from the succession.[32] Charles' plans envisaged a limitation of partibility from early on—just the opposite of Æthelwulf's. As if to underline the significance of *his* strategy, Æthelwulf himself visited Rome in 855–56, bearing gifts that rivaled those of Carolingian benefactors (a golden crown weighing five pounds, golden armrings and a gold-decorated sword, two golden statues, four silver-gilt Saxon platters, and some embroidered vestments)[33] and taking Alfred with him "for a second journey on the same route, because he loved him more than his brothers."[34]

But ninth-century royal family planning was a hit-and-miss affair; and even today strange things can happen at home when rulers take trips abroad. The involvement of Æthelwulf's eldest surviving son in a major revolt during his absence meant that Æthelwulf dropped his own quasi-imperial pretensions and instead attached himself to Charles the Bald's; that was surely what it meant to become Charles' son-in-law (though the bride's consecration, and coronation, as queen may have owed something to Æthelswith's example).[35] In 856 Æthelwulf was no longer in any position to maintain Alfred's claims to a *regnum* in the face of his elder sons' hostility: by the terms of the will drawn up during the last two years of Æthelwulf's life, his youngest son had to be content with a share of his father's personal property, and some money.[36]

II. Military Service, Frankish, Anglo-Saxon, and Roman

In the Edict of Pîtres (June 864), Charles the Bald enacted that "those who cannot perform military service in the army must, according to the custom of antiquity and of other peoples (*aliae gentes*), work at building new *civitates* and bridges and ways across marshes, and perform watch-duty in the *civitas* and on the march."[37] Despite the formulation, Charles was not referring here to *a single custom* that was both antique and practiced by contemporary foreign peoples. He was making a distinction: he recognized that while Christian Roman emperors required work on the construction of "public and sacred buildings," roads and bridges, and on the repair of walls, there was in fact no Late Antique precedent for demanding work on the building of *civitates,* that is, of walls around them; nor was there a precedent in earlier Carolingian legislation.[38] Hence Charles had to appeal, uniquely in his extensive capitularies, to an alternative model, acknowledging that in this respect the West Saxons had extended the scope of the state's demands further than the Franks themselves—and further than the Christian Roman emperors who elsewhere in the Edict of Pîtres were Charles' role models.

The earliest West Saxon charter references to the reservation of the royal right to demand fortification work—*arcis* (or *arcium*) *munitio*—belong, as Nicholas Brooks pointed out, to the reign of Æthelbald. The first appearance is in a grant of 858 to Winchester.[39] That Charles knew about a recent extension of West Saxon royal claims is entirely plausible: contacts between the two kingdoms and courts had surely been closer than ever from 856 to 860, when Charles' daughter was married to Æthelwulf, then, on his death in 858, to his son Æthelbald;[40] and in 860 a group of Danes who had crossed the Channel from West Francia (where Charles was attempting to recruit them into his service) were repulsed from Winchester—an event recorded by the Annals of Saint-Bertin as well as the Anglo-Saxon Chronicle—perhaps because *munitio arcis* had successfully been required by the West Saxon king and was already paying dividends.[41] If Æthelbald and his successor had been implementing a burghal program during those years, Charles would have heard about it—and it may well have inspired his own program in 864, implemented in the later 860's.[42]

What inspired the West Saxons? Mercian and Kentish example, no doubt. But those had been available before, yet not followed. Again the route to the answer leads via Rome. When Alfred and his large entourage[43] reached Rome in 853, Pope Leo had just the year before completed the fortifications linking St. Peter's with the city of Rome itself on the other side of the Tiber. Leo's biographer says that work teams were required from all the estates and towns in the duchy of Rome. Surviving inscriptions make it clear that each team, called a *militia*, was responsible for a stretch of wall.[44] Forty feet high with 44 towers and stretching for something over two thousand meters, the new walls protected, as well as St. Peter's, the *schola Saxonum*,[45] where Alfred surely stayed during his two visits. In the OE version of Augustine's *Soliloquies*, Alfred says there is a difference between seeing a thing and being told about it: "me þincð nu þæt ic wite hwa *R*omeburh timbrode, and æac feala oðra þincga þe ær urum dagum geweordon wæs, þa ic ne mæg æalla ariman. nat ic no ði hwa (Rome)burh timbrede þe ic self hyt gesawe."[46] He is referring to the ancient city—*ær urum dagum*; but the point perhaps had extra piquancy because everyone knew that Alfred had only *just* missed seeing a modern timbering of Rome.

III. Fulk of Rheims, Alfred, and the Roman Model of Mission

Archbishop Fulk of Rheims was a key participant in the last phase of Frankish contacts with the English in the ninth century. It was Fulk to whom Alfred applied for a scholar who would help restore the learning and morale of the church in his kingdom.[47] Grimbald's arrival in 886 may not have been the necessary stimulus to the Anglo-Saxon Chronicle's production, but it seems to have contributed, sufficiently, to the annals' content. On events in 885, continental information reached Wessex from East as well as West Francia: like the East Frankish Annals of Fulda, the Anglo-Saxon Chronicle called Charles the Bald's grandson "Carl" instead of "Carloman";[48] and Asser knew that Charles the Fat had been king of the Alamans (not, *pace* Whitelock, "Germans").[49] The account of events s.a. 887 has not so much a West Frankish as a Fulk-ish slant—or to be more accurate, reflects Fulk's views on Carolingian legitimacy in 888 (but not before) and Fulk's persisting interest in Guy of Spoleto. Fulk had supported Guy for the

West Frankish throne in 887, despite Guy's lack of Carolingian blood in male or female line. Only once it became clear that Guy's bid would fail did Fulk switch his support to Odo, yet he remained keen to give the impression that Odo had become king only with Arnulf's permission: the *Annals of St-Vaast* reflect this in the story about Arnulf's sending a crown with which Odo was crowned on 13 November at Rheims— presumably by Fulk—and acclaimed by *omnis populus*, those who had previously opposed Odo now being received into "fellowship" (*societas*). Fulk had in fact pushed Guy's candidature because the two men were close kinsmen,[50] but he could offer the justification that Guy had been picked by the pope as an adoptive son.[51] Like Æthelwulf, and like the emperor Lothar, Fulk was playing the card of papal authority to legitimize a succession strategy.

The same authority underpinned Fulk's dealings with the English, as is directly evidenced in his letter to Alfred. Dorothy Whitelock resented that letter's "patronizing tone."[52] But patronage—*patrocinium*—in heaven as well as on earth was exactly the name of Fulk's game. Reading the letter to Alfred in the light of the quite substantial dossier on Fulk's career and political contacts before 886, one becomes aware of the Roman dimension to Fulk's conception of his own primatial position at Rheims. Fulk himself had been to Rome[53] (he continued to hope for a return visit that never materialized); and his first act on becoming Archbishop of Rheims early in 883 was to write to Pope Marinus, whom he already knew personally. In 884 he was writing to Hadrian III, and in 886 to Stephen V.[54] His repeated invocations of papal authority, and assertions of Rheims' primatial status, were two sides of a coin. Rheims was a Petrine foundation: its first bishop had been endowed with the primacy of Gaul by Peter himself. Peter's successors had held the see of Rheims in special honor. And the purpose and substance of this claim, in Fulk's mind, was quite literally its apostolic role. *Quamdiu apostolus sum gentium, ministerium meum honorificabo*: Fulk could quote St. Paul (Romans 11:13) with a real sense of historic unity between past and present in Rheims' specific task of mission.[55] Of Fulk's ninth-century predecessors, Ebbo had evangelized the Danes in the 820's, and Hincmar had identified St. Remi as the apostle of the Franks, inventing the tradition of Remi's baptism of Clovis that was also a royal anointing, with oil sent from heaven.[56] Fulk fused these two themes—patronage and mission—in his letter to Alfred. Of course the English had already been evangelized; they already had their apostle, Gregory (in Fulk's eyes, and he had history on his side, the *apostolus Anglorum—apostolus vester*—was modeled on the *apostolus Francorum* rather than vice versa[57]): but the English, unlike the Franks, urgently needed a second dose of mission. Alfred had knocked on the right door—"quia una est catholica et apostolica ecclesia, sive Romana sive transmarina."[58] Fulk did not quite claim jurisdiction over the church of the English, though he came close in suggesting that church councils had assembled "non solum ex vicinis civitatibus vel provinciis, sed etiam ex transmarinis regionibus." (Was Fulk thinking of the Council of Frankfurt in 794?[59]) But what he did have to offer was *patrocinium*: and Grimbald too, endowed with Remi's authority, would extend his *patrocinium* over those who received him in England—descendants of the *gens rudis et barbara* to whom Gregory's decrees had been sent. Remi's successor did not have to pose as the middleman between the English and Rome: he actually functioned as such, writing to the pope after 886 *pro quorundam susceptione Anglorum*.[60] Like Charles the Bald with Æthelwulf, Fulk with Alfred exploited his strategic location on the route to Rome. At the outset of his pontificate, with *timor hostilis* real and immediate at Rheims, Fulk could understand all too well Alfred's anxieties about the irruption of pagans: Rheims' safety was credited to St. Remi's protection—but Fulk then rebuilt the city walls. His successor, Harvey, was to take the lead in converting Viking settlers in Normandy.[61] Mission and defense were necessary responses at Canterbury or Winchester as well as at Rheims. Fulk, and Alfred, had their sights set on a more distant destination even than Rome, but *patrocinium* with all it entailed of responsibility as well as power imposed a busy agenda meanwhile—one which both Fulk and Alfred (like Chesterton[62]) contemplated with zest and ultimately with optimism.

KING'S COLLEGE, UNIVERSITY OF LONDON

NOTES

1. "The Rolling English Road," G. K. Chesterton, *Collected Poems*, 10th ed. (London, 1943), p. 203. I should like to thank Joel Rosenthal and Paul Szarmach for scholarly inspiration over the years, and, in reference to the present paper, for their moral support and editorial patience.

2. J. M. Wallace-Hadrill, "The Franks and the English in the Ninth Century: Some Common Historical Interests," *History*, 35 (1950), 202–18, rpt. in his collected essays, *Early Medieval History* (London, 1975), pp. 201–16, at p. 209. The title of the present paper is intended to suggest a coda to Wallace-Hadrill's work.

3. J. M. Wallace-Hadrill, *Early Germanic Kingship in England and on the Continent* (Oxford, 1969), chs. 5 and 6.

4. For that type of Anglo-Saxon cultural influence see the masterly paper by George H. Brown in the present volume.

5. P. Riché, "Les Carolingiens en quête de sainteté," in *Les fonctions des saints dans le monde occidental (IIIe–XIIIe siècles)* (Rome, 1991), pp. 217–24.

6. M. J. Enright, "Charles the Bald and Æthelwulf of Wessex: The Alliance of 856 and Strategies of Royal Succession," *Journal of Medieval History*, 5 (1979), 291–302; P. Stafford, "Charles the Bald, Judith and England," in M. T. Gibson and J. L. Nelson, eds., *Charles the Bald: Court and Kingdom*, 2nd ed. (London, 1990), pp. 139–53, stresses Æthelwulf's wish to concert a common defense policy with Charles, against Enright's view of the marriage as Æthelwulf's response to the rebellion of his son. Stafford thinks the marriage provoked the son's revolt. See below, p. 144.

7. *Annales de Saint-Bertin* 851, ed. F. Grat, J. Vielliard, and S. Clémencet (Paris, 1964) (hereafter AB), pp. 63–64, tr. J. L. Nelson, *The Annals of St-Bertin* (Manchester, 1991), p. 73. For the significance of Charles' dealings with Erispoë see now J. M. H. Smith, *Province and Empire: Brittany and the Carolingians* (Cambridge, 1992), pp. 108–15.

8. AB 855, 856, pp. 70, 856, tr. Nelson, pp. 80–82; and cf. on the latter episode the supporting evidence of charters: G. Tessier, *Receuil des Chartes de Charles II le Chauve*, 3 vols. (Paris, 1943–55), vol. 1, nos. 113, 114.

9. See Nelson, "Translating Images of Authority: The Christian Roman Emperors in the Carolingian World," in M. M. Mackenzie and C. Roueché, eds., *Images of Authority: Essays in Honour of Joyce Reynolds* (Cambridge, 1989), pp. 196–205. For the broader context see A. Angenendt, *Kaiserherrschaft und Königstaufe* (Berlin, 1984).

10. AB 863, 864, pp. 96, 105, tr., pp. 104, 112. Cf. AB 858, 859, pp. 78, 82, tr., pp. 87, 91, where Louis is called "king."

11. "Rome-free" empire was the phrase coined by C. Erdmann, *Forschungen zur politischen Ideenwelt des Frühmittelalters* (Berlin, 1951). See further Nelson, "Kingship and Empire," in J. H. Burns, ed., *The Cambridge History of Medieval Political Thought* (Cambridge, 1988), pp. 230–34.

12. Lupus of Ferrières, *Correspondance*, ed. L. Levillain, 2 vols. (Paris, 1935), vol. 2, Epp. 75–77, 81, pp. 16–23, 56–65. See also W. Hartmann, ed., *Die Konzilien der karolingische Teilreiches 843–859* (Hanover, 1984), MGH *Concilia* 3, pp. 185–93; and Smith, pp. 154–55. Lupus' mission may well have had several other objectives: see E. Lockwood, "Lupus of Ferrières," Ph.D. thesis Univ. of London 1992, ch. 9.

13. *The Anglo-Saxon Chronicle: A Collaborative Edition*, general eds. D. Dumville and S. Keynes, vol. 3, *MS A*, ed. J. M. Bately (Woodbridge, 1986) (hereafter ASC), s.a. 853, p. 45, tr. G. N. Garmonsway (London, 1953), p. 64. Asser, *Life of King Alfred*, c. 8, ed. W. Stevenson (Oxford, 1904), p. 7, tr. S. Keynes and M. Lapidge, *Alfred the Great* (Harmondsworth, 1981), p. 69, translates this into Latin, with additions: see below, p. 143.

14. The victory at Sandwich (ASC 851, p. 44, tr., p. 64) was recorded in northern Francia within months if not weeks of the event (AB 850, pp. 59–60, tr., p. 69); and Lupus of Ferrières wrote to congratulate Æthelwulf on his victory at Aclea (*Correspondance*, vol. 2, Ep. 84, p. 70). Further, at Æthelwulf's court, acting not just as a scribe but (if we take Lupus literally) head of the royal chancery (*Correspondance*, vol. 2, Ep. 84, p. 70, "epistolarum vestrarum officio fungebatur"; cf. vol. 1, Ep. 17, p. 98, on Charles' chancellor Louis, "epistolare in palatio gerens officium"), was a Frank called Felix, an old acquaintance of Lupus and also the recipient of a letter from him (Ep. 85) in 851. Lupus had just recovered control of Ferrières' dependent church of Saint-Josse near Quentovic, hence on the obvious route for English travelers to the Continent: see Stafford, pp. 140–41; and S. Lebecq, "La Neustrie et la mer," in H. Atsma, ed., *La Neustrie*, Beihefte der *Francia*, 2 vols. (Sigmaringen, 1989), vol. 1, pp. 405–40,

esp. 427–28. West Saxons were certainly interested in Breton affairs a generation later: ASC 885, 890; and Æthelwulf had very probably learned about dealings between Franks and Bretons very soon after the event.

15. See preceding note. Note Æthelwulf's contact right at the beginning of his reign with Louis the Pious, AB 839, pp. 28–30, tr., pp. 42–43. Could this be linked with the journey of Archbishop Wigmund of York (to whom Lupus also wrote c. 851) to Rome to collect his pallium, c. 839?

16. ASC, pp. 44–45; tr. Garmonsway, pp. 64–66.

17. Asser, *Life of King Alfred*, c. 8, ed. Stevenson, p. 8, tr. Keynes and Lapidge, p. 69: "at the royal estate called Chippenham."

18. See Stafford, p. 149 and n. 65.

19. Asser, *Life of Alfred*, ed. Stevenson, pp. 14–15: "regni inter filios suos, duos scilicet seniores, . . . divisionem ordinabiliter literis mandari procuravit." Cf. tr. Keynes and Lapidge, p. 72. On Æthelwulf's intentions see D. P. Kirby, *The Earliest English Kings* (London, 1991), pp. 198–204. I read Kirby's book only after delivering this paper; though my conclusions differ somewhat from his, I have found his discussion characteristically thought-provoking.

20. Cf. Keynes and Lapidge, pp. 231–32: "[Æthelstan] is not heard of again after 851."

21. See P. Classen, "Karl der Grosse und der Thronfolge im Frankenreich," in *Festschrift für H. Heimpel*, vol. 3 (Göttingen, 1972), pp. 109–34.

22. See Janet L. Nelson, *Charles the Bald* (London, 1992), pp. 92–97.

23. AB 855, p. 71; cf. 856, p. 73, tr., pp. 81, 83.

24. Cf. AB 869, p. 155, tr., p. 156, for symbolic papal gifts to Lothar II, and their interpretation. There is of course no question of confusing distinct liturgical rites in 853: the ambiguity centers on the status of *regna* and *reges* in kingdoms that were family firms.

25. I took a rather different view in "The Problem of King Alfred's Royal Anointing," *Journal of Ecclesiastical History*, 18 (1967), 145–63, rpt. in my essays, *Politics and*

Ritual in Early Medieval Europe (London, 1986), pp. 309–27 (cited hereafter from the reprint).

26. He may also have been mindful of the Mercian precedent of Offa, whose son Ecgfrith had perhaps been consecrated by papal legates in England; see Wallace-Hadrill, *Early Germanic Kingship*, p. 114. If so, Æthelwulf meant to go one better.

27. *Annales Regni Francorum*, ed. F. Kurze, MGH *Scriptores Rerum Germanicarum in Usum Scholarum* (Hanover, 1895), pp. 56–57.

28. Unmentioned in the *Annales Regni Francorum*, but clearly stated in *Vita Leonis III*, c. 24, *Liber Pontificalis*, ed. L. Duchesne, rev. C. Vogel, 3 vols. (Paris, 1955–57), vol. 3, p. 8; tr. R. Davis, *The Lives of the Eighth-Century Popes (Liber Pontificalis)* (Liverpool, 1992), p. 191.

29. AB 844, pp. 45–46: ". . . Hlodouuicum pontifex Romanus unctione in regem consecratum cingulo decoravit," tr., p. 57 (taking *cingulum* to imply 'sword'), and AB 850, p. 59, tr., p. 69.

30. ". . . consulatus cingulo honore vestimentisque ut mos est Romanis consulibus decoravimus," ed. A. de Hirsch-Gereuth, MGH *Epistolae* 5 (Berlin, 1899), p. 602. I argued 25 years ago that the consulship and investiture with sword were anachronisms branding the letter fragment of Leo IV an 11th-century forgery. I am now fairly sure that I was wrong: the so-called *Tract on Offices*, convincingly argued by P. S. Barnwell, "*Epistula Hieronimi de Gradus Romanorum*: An English School Book," *Historical Research*, 64 (1991), 77–86, to be an Anglo-Saxon schoolbook diffused on the Continent in the 9th century, shows *consul* a familiar term for viceroy; and for instances of papal *imitatio imperii* in the Donation of Constantine (where c. 15 specificies the papal right to appoint consuls) and elsewhere, see my "Problem of King Alfred's Royal Anointing," pp. 312–13. The appointment of Alfred as consul does fit within this context.

31. The significance of Æthelwulf's reign is underlined by P. Wormald, "The Ninth Century," in J. Campbell, ed., *The Anglo-Saxons* (Oxford, 1982), pp. 140–42, and also by Kirby, p. 195.

32. AB p. 70, tr., p. 79. See Nelson, "A Tale of Two Princes: Politics, Text and Ideology in a Carolingian Annal," *Studies in Medieval and Renaissance History*, 10 (1988), 105–41, at p. 109.

33. *Vita Benedicti III*, *Liber Pontificalis*, vol. 2, p. 148: "gabatae saxiscae de argento exaurato IIII, saraca de olovero cum chrisoclavo I, camisa alba sigillata olosyrica cum chrisoclavo I, vela maiora de fundato II."

34. Asser, *Life of Alfred*, c. 11, ed. Stevenson, p. 9: "iterum in eandem viam secum ducens. . . ." In my 1967 article, pp. 325–26, I mistakenly rejected Asser's unequivocal statement about Alfred's second journey. For suggestive observations on important, and hitherto neglected, evidence see S. Keynes, "Anglo-Saxon Entries in the 'Liber Vitae' of Brescia," in J. Roberts and J. L. Nelson, eds., *Alfred the Wise. Studies in Honour of Janet Bately* (Woodbridge, 1997), pp. 99–119.

35. See above, p. 142; for Æthelwulf's intentions cf. Enright, "Charles the Bald and Æthelwulf of Wessex."

36. Asser, *Life of Alfred*, c. 16, ed. Stevenson, pp. 14–15, tr., p. 72.

37. MGH *Capitularia Regum Francorum*, ed. A. Boretius and V. Krause (Hanover, 1897), vol. 2, no. 273, c. 27.

38. See N. Brooks, "The Development of Military Obligations in Eighth- and Ninth-Century England," in P. Clemoes and K. Hughes, eds., *England before the Conquest: Studies Presented to Dorothy Whitelock* (Cambridge, 1971), pp. 69–84.

39. B 495/S 1274. In this and following references to Anglo-Saxon charters, B signifies the number in W. de G. Birch, *Cartularium Saxonicum*, 4 vols. (London, 1885–99), and S, the number in P. Sawyer, *Anglo-Saxon Charters: An Annotated List and Bibliography* (London, 1968). B 451/S 298 shows Æthelwulf already reserving host- and bridge-service in 847. See Brooks, p. 81, for further references to reservation of *arcis* [*arcium*] *munitio* in B 500/S 326 (860); B 504–5/S 335 (862); and B 508/S 336 (863—for 868). To these may be added B 520/S 340 (868) and B 886/S 341 (869), both with a possibly authentic base.

40. Judith's marriage to her stepson evoked "magna infamia," according to Asser, *Life of Alfred*, c. 17, ed. Stevenson, p. 16, tr. Keynes and Lapidge, p. 73, but it is recorded without comment in AB 858, p. 76, tr., p. 86.

41. AB 860, p. 83, tr., p. 92, records the Anglo-Saxons' repulse of Danes from the Somme; ASC 860, p. 46, tr., p. 68, says they had attacked Winchester, and Asser, *Life*

of Alfred, c. 18, ed. Stevenson, p. 18, tr. Keynes and Lapidge, p. 74, adds that they fled "like women." AB 861, p. 85, tr. p. 95, records the return of this group (now naming their commander as Weland) from England. Charles seems to have employed a Dane named Ansleic as cross-Channel negotiator with these Danes while they were in England: *Miracula Sancti Richarii*, *Acta Sanctorum Aprilis III*, p. 456. See F. Lot, "La Grande Invasion normande de 856–862," *Bibliothèque de l'École des Chartes*, 69 (1908), 5–62, rpt. in Lot, *Receuil des travaux historiques*, 3 vols. (Geneva, 1968–73), vol. 2, p. 756, n. 1.

42. At Angoulême, *Annales Engolismenses* 868, ed. O. Holder-Egger, MGH *Scriptores* 16 (Hanover, 1859), p. 486; and at Pîtres, Le Mans, and Tours, AB 868, 869, pp. 150, 166, tr., pp. 151, 163–64. For later-9th-century royal demands for "maintenance and defence" of fortifications in Wessex see the Burghal Hidage, tr. Keynes and Lapidge in *Alfred the Great*, pp. 193–94.

43. Asser, *Life of Alfred*, c. 8, ed. Stevenson, p. 7: "magno nobilium et etiam ignobilium numero constipatus."

44. On 27 August 846 the basilica of St. Peter had been sacked by Saracens and St. Peter's tomb desecrated. Though his biographer says the pope acted on Lothar's orders, Leo himself organized the building project, celebrated its successful completion, and reaped the propaganda harvest; Frankish annalists credit the work to Leo and say nothing about the emperor. For this and Leo's other projects, including frescoes and mosaics, see *Vita Leonis IV*, *Liber Pontificalis*, vol. 2, pp. 123–24 and nn. at pp. 137–38.

45. On this hostel for Anglo-Saxon pilgrims and visitors see P. Llewellyn, *Rome in the Dark Ages* (London, 1972), pp. 178–79, and map at pp. 16–17.

46. *King Alfred's Version of St Augustine's Soliloquies*, ed. T. Carnicelli (Cambridge, MA, 1969), p. 97. 'Now it comes into my mind that I know who built Rome, and also many other things that happened before our days, so many that I can't list them all. It's not because I saw it myself that I know who built Rome.' Cf. the text of Augustine that Alfred is following here, quoted by Carnicelli, p. 107: ". . . unde sciremus civitates ubi numquam fuimus; vel a Romulo conditam Romam. . . ?" Augustine's point was that knowledge comes from sources other than direct experience; Alfred takes this on board but adds an allusion to his own visit to Rome.

47. Alfred's request is described in Fulk's reply: D. Whitelock, M. Brett, and C. N. L. Brooke, eds., *Councils and Synods with Other Documents Relating to the English Church*,

I (Oxford, 1981), vol. 1, pp. 6–12, tr. Keynes and Lapidge, *Alfred the Great*, "Fulk's Letter to Alfred," pp. 182–86. Despite the doubts I expressed in "'A King across the Sea': Alfred in Continental Perspective," *Transactions of the Royal Historical Society*, 36 (1986), 45–68, at pp. 48–49, about the authenticity of this letter as it stands, I have been persuaded that its substance is genuine. See below and also my "'. . . *sicut olim gens Francorum . . . nunc gens Anglorum*': Fulk's letter to Alfred Revisited," in Roberts and Nelson, eds., *Alfred the Wise*, pp. 135–44.

48. ASC 885, p. 52, tr. p. 79; cf. the Mainz Continuator of the *Annales Fuldenses* 884, ed. F. Kurze, MGH *Scriptores Rerum Germanicarum in Usum Scholarum* (Hanover, 1891), p. 101 (though not the Regensburg Continuator, 885, p. 113); see now the translation by T. Reuter, *The Annals of Fulda* (Manchester, 1992), p. 96, with comment on the divergent continuations at pp. 5–9.

49. Asser, *Life of Alfred*, c. 70, ed. Stevenson, p. 52, tr. Keynes and Lapidge, p. 87; cf. D. Whitelock, ed., *English Historical Documents*, vol. 1, 2nd ed. (London, 1979), p. 198, n. 12.

50. Flodoard, *Historia Remensis Ecclesiae IV*, c. 1, pp. 555–56, says Guy was Fulk's *affinis*; at c. 3, p. 565, his *propinquus*.

51. For Guy's adoption by Pope Stephen V see G. Schneider, *Erzbischof Fulco von Reims (883–900) und das Frankenreich* (Munich, 1975), pp. 44–45. Curiously enough, Schneider has nothing to say about Alfred.

52. *English Historical Documents*, ed. Whitelock, vol. 1, p. 883.

53. Flodoard, *Historia* IV, c. 1, p. 555—with Charles the Bald in 875–76.

54. See Schneider, pp. 30–38.

55. Flodoard, *Historia* III, c. 5, p. 566 (addressing the dowager empress Richildis). P. Depreux, *Étude sur la devotion à Saint Remi de Reims*, unpub. Mémoire de Maitrise, Paris, 1989, has invaluable comments on the 9th-century association of Rheims with mission. I am very grateful to Philippe Depreux for sharing his insights with me. He does not deal with Fulk's letter to Alfred, however.

56. AB 869, pp. 162–63, tr., p. 161. The author of the AB at this point was Hincmar himself. For Hincmar's sense of Rheims' history see Wallace-Hadrill, "History in the

Mind of Archbishop Hincmar," in R. H. C. Davis and J. M. Wallace-Hadrill, eds., *The Writing of History in the Middle Ages: Essays Presented to R. W. Southern* (Oxford, 1981), pp. 43–70, esp. 48, 54–55.

57. ". . . sicut olim gens Francorum . . . nunc gens Anglorum. . . .": letter to Alfred, ed. Whitelock, Brett, and Brooke, p. 7, tr. Keynes and Lapidge, p. 183.

58. Ibid., p. 11: ". . . for the Catholic and Apostolic Church is one, whether Roman or across the sea."

59. To this council Alcuin brought back from Britannia a formal letter to add to the synodical letters of other *gentes*: *Annales Nordhumbrani*, MGH *Scriptores* 13, ed. J. Heller and G. Waitz (Hanover, 1881), p. 155; MGH *Concilia* 2, ed. A. Werminghoff (Hanover, 1908), i, no. 19, pp. 120–21. Cf. *Libri Carolini* IV, 28, MGH *Concilia* 2, Supplement, ed. H. Bastgen (Hanover, 1924), p. 227, on the participation at councils of "praesules duarum vel trium provinciarum—et fortasse dici potest universale, quoniam, quamvis non sit ab omnibus orbis praesulibus actum, tamen ab universorum fide et traditione non discrepat."

60. Flodoard, *Historia* IV, c. 1, p. 556.

61. D. Bates, *Normandy before 1066* (London, 1982), pp. 11–12.

62. "For there is good news yet to hear and fine things to be seen / Before we go to Paradise by way of Kensal Green" (Chesterton, "The Rolling English Road").

The Preservation and Transmission of Northumbrian Culture on the Continent: Alcuin's Debt to Bede

George H. Brown

> Die führende Gestalt freilich unter den Schriftstellern und Gelerhten am fränkischen Hof [Karls des Grossen] ist der Angelsachse Alkuin gewesen. Er war überhaupt die bedeutendste Persönlichkeit in der Geschichte des geistigen Lebens seit Beda, dessen Tradition er fortgesezt und weiter ausgebaut hat.
>
> —Franz Brunhölzl[1]

Like all great leaders, Charlemagne had vision and a goal. Like all great administrators, he knew how to attract, select, hold, and release his staff. By the time he encountered Alcuin in March of 781 at Parma, he was well aware that Anglo-Saxon clerics were a rich resource for the programmatic establishment of religion, education, and culture in his broad realm.[2] Even while serious problems festered in the political and religious life of Anglo-Saxon England, the Anglo-Saxon missionaries had been working persistently and ultimately successfully on the Continent among the Franks and Frisians. Although the two Anglo-Saxon Hewalds had been martyred for their missionary efforts, Willibrord (658–739), founding abbot of Echternach (whose *vita* Alcuin was to rewrite), and his twelve companions energetically proselytized the pagan Frisians. Duke Pippin II (of Heristal), Charlemagne's great-grandfather, had supported these Anglo-Saxons with his might and sent Willibrord, as Bede says, "with the favorable consent of all," to the pope to be made archbishop of the Frisians, establishing his see at Utrecht (695).[3] Later, Boniface

(c. 675–754) came to assist Willibrord. Likewise working closely with the pope, Boniface proved to be an even more powerful missionary. Establishing the bishoprics of Freising, Regensburg, and Salzburg and the abbey of Fulda in addition to his missionary work among the pagans, Boniface set out to reform the entire Frankish church, organizing a series of regional councils in an attempt to impose discipline on both clergy and laity.[4] The Anglo-Saxons also proved to be politically useful. Deposing the last of the Merovingians, Childeric III, Pippin III sent Burchard, the Anglo-Saxon bishop of Würzburg, with Fulrad, the abbot of Saint Denis and head of the clergy in Pippin's *curia*, to Rome in 750 to request Pope Zacharias' support for Pippin's becoming king.[5]

Later, Anglo-Saxon clergy living in Charlemagne's lands were actively supportive during Charlemagne's campaigns and consolidation of the realm. Although Lull, Boniface's successor at Mainz, in 775 registered some concern about Charlemagne's high-handed ways, Cathwulf wrote to the monarch, congratulating him on his triumphs, pleasing to God and men. There is the case of Alubert, pupil of Egbert and Ælberht at York, who went to the Continent as a missionary and returned to York to be consecrated by Archbishop Ælberht as Bishop of Utrecht. Anglo-Saxons continued to prove ardent missionaries. In the 780's the Northumbrian Willehad, who had come to missionize the Frisians where Boniface had been killed, was asked by Charles to extend his mission further east.[6]

So when Alcuin joined Charles in 782, the king already had a great deal of positive proof of Anglo-Saxon and especially Northumbrian zeal and learning benefiting his realm. Moreover, Charles recognized in this schoolmaster a person who could help him develop educational, cultural, and religious programs in his court and in his empire. Charles had decided to expand his *curia* by systematically acquiring learned men as educators and advisors.[7] Alcuin was brought not as a substitute for Angilram of Metz, who had taken on the position of head chaplain when Fulrad left the court (about four years before he died), but as an addition to the *palatini.* Alcuin joined an already prestigious group of scholars—Peter of Pisa, Paulinus of Aquileia, and others—who had come eagerly at Charles' behest. Later they were joined by the Italian scholar Paul the Deacon and the especially talented Spanish Goth Theodulf, in addition to a number of less well-known Anglo-Saxons and Irishmen. What attracted all these great men? Donald Bullough furnishes a convincing answer:

> Even in the largest and most prosperous religious community books were still few and contact with other scholars was at best intermittent: hence the unique attraction of a court where both these needs were generously met. In the 780s a combination of this magnetic pull and the initiative of the king in summoning educated men to his court brought together scholars from many parts of Europe. Incomparably the most important among them was the Northumbrian Alcuin.[8]

Alcuin soon became director of the educational *renovatio*. Charles was remarkably canny in choosing Alcuin for that major role. Although *magister* of the School of York and already 50 years old, Alcuin had not yet published much—three poems, as far as we know. Alcuin's years of incredible productivity were still ahead. As he undertook the great task of establishing the educational system of Charlemagne's realm, he naturally used the resources he himself had drawn from his Northumbrian education. The greatest resource was Bede.

Alcuin, like Bede, was conscious of his Englishness, of his being a member of the *gens Anglorum*. In the famous letter Alcuin wrote in 793 to Æthelred, King of Northumbria, about the sack of Lindisfarne, he said, "By a double bond of kinship we are fellow citizens of one city in Christ: that is, as sons of Mother Church and as natives of one fatherland (*unius patriae indigene*)."[9] Kept from returning to his *patria*, Alcuin even in his last days as abbot of Saint-Martin in Tours still looked upon himself as an expatriate from Britain. He wrote poignantly to his brethren at York:

> Keep me in mind, dearest of fathers and brothers, for I shall be yours, in death as in life. And it may be that God in his compassion will grant that

> you, who nurtured my childhood, will also bury my old age. But if another grave be assigned to my body, yet I think that God will listen to the prayers of men like you and give me somewhere some haven of peace for my soul. For—as our young Seneca declares he saw—we believe that the souls of our brotherhood must be gathered together in one and the same place and joy.[10]

Some of Alcuin's Frankish monks resented his nationalism. The *vita* relates the story of how the Anglo-Saxon priest Aigulf came to visit Alcuin in his last days at Saint-Martin: one of four of the local monks, thinking he would not be understood, remarked that "That Brit [*iste Britto*] has come to visit the other Brit lying inside. O God, free this monastery of these Brits; for just as bees return to their mother, they all swarm to him."[11] Wallace-Hadrill makes the point that in the opinion of Alcuin's contemporaries, there existed an English *patria*: "It distinguished all Englishmen from the Celtic and continental peoples, though not from the Old Saxons. . . . Beyond this, however, we must recognize in Alcuin a narrower patriotism. He was a Northumbrian."[12] Peter Godman, commenting on Alcuin's great poem, *The Bishops, Kings, and Saints of York*, adds:

> Patriotism, centred on York and Northumbria, is a major theme of Alcuin's work. It shaped his sense of relevance. . . . In this regional emphasis, stated at the beginning and sustained in the course of the poem, Alcuin differs from Bede, who sees Northumbria, his native land, partly in the perspective of Canterbury. . . . Alcuin's view is strictly Northumbrian and Romanist.[13]

It is ironic that Bede, who never traveled more than 50 miles (that is, to York) from his Northumbrian place of birth, located on the very land of the monastery in which he spent his life, possessed a trans-regional vision, whereas Alcuin, who traveled widely, was familiar with international society, and established an imperial school system on the Continent, remained loyally local.

Alcuin's school of York was most closely tied, if perhaps not literally filiated to, Bede's school of Wearmouth-Jarrow. There is a congruity in the historical origins of Wearmouth-Jarrow and of York.

Just as the founders of Wearmouth-Jarrow were the nobles Benedict Biscop and Ceolfrith, and their finest scholar, Bede, was among the first generation of students there, so at York the founders were the noble Egbert and Ælberht, and Alcuin had been instructed by both.[14] In the first case, Benedict Biscop established the monastery with furniture and books but was frequently engaged in affairs outside the monastery; Ceolfrith was active as abbot and teacher and doubled the size of the library. In the second case, Egbert was cousin to King Ceolwulf, to whom Bede dedicated his *Historia Ecclesiastica Gentis Anglorum,* and brother of the king, Eadbert, who succeeded Ceolwulf (737); Egbert, first archbishop of York, established the school and was honored by Alcuin as "ecclesiae rector clarissimus atque egregius doctor," ['most illustrious ruler of the Church and renowned teacher'] but as Bishop and then first Archbishop of York he was taken up with duties outside the school.[15] Egbert, as the *Vita Alcuini* states, had been Bede's student; Bede's candid and powerful letter to him (734) about the need to reform the Northumbrian church demonstrates the strength of the student-pupil relationship. Otherwise, such a candid criticism by a simple monk (famed for his discretion) to a great prelate would constitute *lèse majesté.* Ælberht, who served under Egbert as master in the school, was, like Ceolfrith, a venerated teacher and an effective administrator who greatly enhanced the library holdings.[16] Ælberht apparently received his education at York under Egbert.[17] Alcuin worked closely under him, succeeding him as master of the school when Ælberht became Archbishop. Manifestly, the links between the northern schools of Wearmouth-Jarrow and York were direct and strong. Alcuin's own testimony and his own educational ideals and practice make that clear.

Other data complete the Jarrow-York-Continent connection. The history of manuscript transmission and Alcuin's letters indicate that the library at York served as a clearinghouse for Northumbrian texts, particularly Bede.[18] When Anglo-Saxon missionaries on the Continent wanted copies of the works of Bede, they sent their requests to Egbert and Ælberht at York.[19] Godman attempts to make a case for Alcuin's using the Insular M-type of Bede's *Historia Ecclesiastica* in composing the York poem.[20] The evidence that Alcuin used the chapter (IV.14) in the M-type, not found in the other main class of *Historia* manuscripts, for some details in lines 1600ff. of his York poem is slight and questionable. Still, since the source of the M-type is the Moore Bede (CUL Kk. 5. 16), written in Northumbria in 737 during Alcuin's youth and deposited in Charlemagne's palace library, as Bischoff asserts, it is altogether possible that Alcuin himself brought it there. It then served as the exemplar for many continental copies of the *Historia*.[21] Most of Bede's writings, except for his historical and homiletic works, survived the tumultuous ninth century only in continental manuscripts and had to be re-imported into England in calmer times.

In any case, Bede's works had become the staple of continental education, and Alcuin was in large measure responsible for it. Charlemagne's General Admonition on Education (789), composed by Alcuin, stipulates: "Let schools be created in every monastery and episcopal see for boys to study *psalmos* [psalms], *notas* [notation], *cantus* [chants], *compotum* [computus], *grammaticam* [grammar], and *libros catholicos* [catholic literature] properly edited."[22] This curriculum derives from that of Theodore and Hadrian at Canterbury by way of Bede's Wearmouth-Jarrow, through York to Francia. We find the very form and contents of this program, as Charles Jones has shown, in Bede's educational works.[23] Alcuin was the primary transmitter of that program and, indeed, as we know from his letters, of his works.[24] No Anglo-Saxon writer, not even King Alfred or Ælfric, uses Bede's ideas and Bede's texts as often and as extensively as does Alcuin.[25] To students, Alcuin held up Bede as the best guide and shining example.[26]

It is important, however, to register the point that the Jarrow curriculum was not taken over without modification at York and then at Charlemagne's palace school. Such simple imitation was not the mode in the Middle Ages. Each *magister*, weighing the conflicting principles of Late Antique and Early Medieval educational programs and dealing with his own particular school needs, added and expanded or abolished and diminished parts of the inherited systems. Alcuin's curriculum gave greater scope to the liberal arts than Bede's monastic program did. Alcuin's *The Bishops, Kings, and Saints of York* lists a number of texts in dialectic and rhetoric. Some parts of these two subjects had been absorbed into the larger compass of grammar in the Late Antique schools. Since in the earlier monastic tradition (excluding Cassiodorus) these disciplines were considered downright dangerous, because they taught students how to persuade regardless of truth, Bede's school excluded them as subjects in the curriculum.[27] However, inspired by the *Consolatio Philosophiae* of Boethius (which Bede seems not even to have known),[28] Alcuin acknowledges in his little educational pamphlet, *Disputatio de Vera Philosophia*, the full worth of secular learning and depicts the seven liberal arts as seven steps, *gradus*, leading to wisdom.[29] The two subjects rhetoric and dialectic Alcuin fully reinstates as part of the trivium. He composes his own texts for the school and court, mostly by lifting from other sources. Over 90 percent of the *Rhetoric* is borrowed material, most of it from Cicero's *De Inventione* interlarded with passages from Julius Victor.[30] As for dialectic, "He was responsible," as John Marenbon has pointed out, "for putting the *Categoriae Decem* into general circulation, and in his *De Dialectica* he provided a useful, though entirely derivative, compendium of logical doctrine."[31]

In composing these educational texts that Bede would not provide Alcuin was nonetheless following the example of Bede, who, wherever he perceived a need, tailored a text for his pupils. Bede wrote textbooks that took into account both the monastic program he directed at Wearmouth-Jarrow and the capacities of the students he taught.[32] Although Bede was more learned and original in certain fields, particularly science and history, and Alcuin ventured into philosophy and dogmatic theology, both Bede and Alcuin as schoolmasters with curricular pressures engaged in excerpting and editing earlier texts; they plundered the available sources. If a suitable text existed, then it was put into service. Manuscript history and remarks made in letters indicate that Alcuin made available Bede's educational works, such as the *De Metris* and the *De Schematibus et*

Figuris.[33] But here too there are differences between Bede and Alcuin. While Bede often gives credit to a source by some form of citation, Alcuin generally does not. Alcuin lifts large amounts of matter and even whole texts, edited but without acknowledgment. In his *De Orthographia*, for instance, Alcuin incorporates (in the thirteen pages of the modern critical edition) two hundred entries, many slightly abridged, from Bede's *De Orthographia* and supplies most of the rest from Cassiodorus; though he cites Priscian thrice in the work, he does not once mention Bede or Cassiodorus.[34]

Fortunately for Alcuin, Bede's two books on computus, the *De Temporibus* and *De Temporum Ratione*, were the best available sources for the classroom and for the occasions when Alcuin needed scientific information to answer Charlemagne's eager astronomical and calendrical questions. In his letters and works Alcuin frequently alludes to these treatises.[35] Thus, in Letter 155, written in 798, he parries Charlemagne's queries about planetary orbits with "What can be said more clearly on the agreement of the paths of the sun and moon through the signs of the zodiac than what such an investigator as Master Bede has left us in his writings?"[36] Alcuin uses explanations and sections directly taken from Bede's computistical works, of which there was a "swift multiplication of manuscripts during Alcuin's domination of the schools of France and for years thereafter."[37] Alcuin's disciples even composed didactic poems, *Rhythmi Computistici,* based on Bede's manual, such as "Anni Domini Notantur" (71 stanzas), "De Ratione Temporum" (45 couplets), and "Ex Novenis atque Denis" (52 stanzas).[38]

In some fields, which Bede had not entered, Alcuin draws heavily upon earlier writers. For instance, for his moral philosophical treatise, *De Animae Ratione,* Alcuin turned to Augustine, Jerome, Cassian, Lactantius, and Isidore. It is noteworthy, as Malcolm Godden has pointed out, that Alcuin modifies the views of his authorities and develops his own distinctive position, namely, that the soul and the mind are identical. With this work the "the psychological literature of the Christian Middle Ages is said to begin."[39]

In exegesis Alcuin's debt to Bede is heavy; he borrows extensively from Bede's commentaries and sermons, usually lifting whole sections verbatim.[40] A good example of Alcuin's dependence on Bedan hermeneutics is his late work (801) *Commentary on St. John's Gospel*. Alcuin obviously knew Augustine's *Tractatus in Iohannem*, for he names it as his paramount authority and frequently refers to it elsewhere. In writing his commentary for the royal nuns of Chelles, Gisla and Rotruda (respectively daughter and sister of Charlemagne), however, Alcuin uses Bede almost exclusively for the first one-and-one-half books (and also thereafter). According to Donald Bullough, Alcuin uses Bede and not Augustine for his exposition of these chapters because Augustine answered none of the questions foremost in the eighth-century religious mind: "Bede's Homilies on the other hand were, like Alcuin's interests and sympathies, Christ-centered—His co-eternity with the Father, His Incarnation, His coming to save fallen man, the calling of the first Apostles."[41] To Bullough's theological reason I would add that the text indicates that Alcuin exploited Bede's homilies on John's gospel first; he drew upon fully nineteen of Bede's 21 Johannine homilies.[42] When Alcuin needed more to complete the text, he *then* turned to Augustine.

Bede had not engaged in apologetic or dogmatic theology, so for usable texts in those disciplines in which he was involved in later life Alcuin resorted to patristic and synodal sources. However, Bede's profound abhorrence of heresies, and especially Christological heresies, is reflected in Alcuin's polemics against Adoptionism. That Alcuin personally possessed a good theological mind not totally derivative is proved by the quality of his late piece *De Fide Sanctae Trinitatis et de Incarnatione Christi*, in which he transcends his sources; but here too, like Bede, to a great extent he is a transmitter of earlier thought.[43] In this he is again the best representative of Northumbrian and Carolingian culture. John Contreni has perceptively written,

> What strikes me as typical of intellectual life from about 750 to 900 is its programmatic and very self-conscious nature. The Carolingian dynasts and their clerical advisers were not intellectual innovators. They certainly would

> disown any such label. The significance of Carolingian efforts lay in another direction. Carolingian leaders promoted and Carolingian scholars executed the organization and dissemination of what had, by their time, become an accepted body of knowledge and attitude toward learning.[44]

Alcuin's production of biblical commentaries and texts and his work on liturgical reform correspond to Bede's own love of the Bible, reflected in his numerous biblical commentaries, and his devotion to the liturgy, represented by his hymns and prayers.

Alcuin's poems, composed at York and on the Continent, owe much to the Bedan tradition of *De Arte Metrica*, which served generations of Carolingians as a poetic handbook.[45] It is clear that Alcuin owed his early poetic training to Bede. Most of the metrics and the forms employed by Alcuin in his 320 extant poems are represented and demonstrated in Bede's handbook and exemplified in a wide range of Bede's own writings. Among the various types of poems that Alcuin knew from Bede and then himself wrote are metrical letter conclusions, dedicatory verses, epigrams, epitaphs, and *tituli*, panegyrics, elegies, hymns, historical narratives, and poetic saints' lives. I should not claim that Alcuin was totally dependent on Aldhelm and Bede for all his verse training, since Alcuin demonstrably learned much from pagan and Christian poets of Antiquity as well from the poems of Carolingian court writers such as Paul, Paulinus, Angilbert, and Theodulf. However, the poetic influence of both Aldhelm and Bede is amply evident in the Anglo-Latin elements, themes, and frequent phrasal borrowings from their verse.[46] Two-thirds of Alcuin's great poem on York is a poetic rendition of Bede's *Historia*, with some borrowing from Bede's metrical Life of Cuthbert. The last third, however, is all from Alcuin and contains precious information about the school and library of York found nowhere else.

In the genre of hagiography, Alcuin composed lives in prose and verse of his relative, Willibrord, at the behest of his Anglo-Saxon friend, Archbishop Beornrad of Sens. In these works Alcuin followed the tradition of the *opus geminatum* made famous by Aldhelm and by Bede, in which an author writes first a narrative in prose, then in poetry.[47] Just as Bede wrote a simple prose version of Cuthbert's life for public reading to the community and a more elaborate, artful poetic version for private reading, so Alcuin wrote the prose version for paraliturgical use and the poetic version for the private reflection, a *libellus* "qui in secreto cubili inter scholasticos tuos tantummodo ruminari debuisset" ['which ought to be ruminated upon by students only in their private room'].[48]

Alcuin's admired correspondence is more prolific and wide-ranging than Bede's, from whom only a few formal letters survive. However, Alcuin's epistolary prose style emulates Bede's clear, unpretentious Latin, which is free from the Late Antique mannerism fostered by Aldhelm and the Irish schools. Moreover, Alcuin's correspondence with royalty and prelates bespeaks not only his own noble background but also the religious and political ideology modeled in Bede's *Historia*—for instance, the positive relations between Augustine and Ethelbert, Paulinus and Edwin, Aidan and Oswald, and the negative example of Wilfrid and Ecfrid.

The filial relationship of Alcuin to Bede and the continuation of religious and ideological Northumbrian tradition in Francia is well exemplified by the shared principles enunciated in Bede's and Alcuin's formal letters—to take but one major example, their mutual condemnation of ecclesiastical extortion in the form of tithes. In Bede's famous letter to Egbert, bishop and later Archbishop of York, Bede warns Egbert repeatedly "not to presume to demand and receive temporal advantages," especially from those who have not benefited from his service; he cites Matthew 10:8–9, "Freely have you received; freely give." After a number of denunciations of clerical greed, Bede concludes this powerful letter with the statement that he intentionally has concentrated not on "drunkenness, feasting, loose living, and other pollutions of this kind" but on "the venom of avarice."[49] It is against the same kind of "tributis antistiti reddendis" ['levies that must be rendered to the bishop'] that Alcuin writes his urgent appeals in letters to Carolingian bishops and Charlemagne himself, especially in his pleas to go more easily on the newly subjugated Saxons. He repeatedly warns that in his clerics the emperor "tantos non habet iustitiae adiutores, quantos etiam subversores, nec tantos praedicatores, quantos praedatores" ['does not have so much helpers as subverters of justice, nor so much preachers as predators'].[50] Even though Alcuin's lifestyle was far more courtly and gregarious than Bede's, he nonetheless shared many of the same attitudes and concerns of the Northumbrian monk in his dealings with the church and the crown.

I hope that even in the brief span of this paper it is clear why Alcuin thought of Bede as his own "praeclarus magister," and how his own life and career at York and on the Continent were modeled on Bede's. I suppose there is a consensus that of the two, Bede had the better mind, was the better scholar and writer; but without Alcuin, Bede's writings would never have had the central position they held in the Carolingian *renovatio,* for which the master Bede and the Northumbrian school system formed the heart. The other Northumbrians in the Carolingian realm and Alcuin's own disciples, such as Einhard and Hrabanus Maurus, continued the reverent tradition, so much so that in 836 the Council of Aachen decreed that Bede had the same kind of authority as the earlier Fathers of the Church. By drawing upon Bede's religious, historical, and political ideas, texts, and educational program, the Carolingian renaissance furthered by Alcuin had its source in the Northumbrian renaissance.

STANFORD UNIVERSITY

NOTES

1. Franz Brunhölzl, *Geschichte der lateinischen Literatur des Mittelalters*, vol. 1 (Munich, 1975), p. 268. ['The guiding figure among the writers and scholars at the Frankish court of Charlemagne was surely the Anglo-Saxon Alcuin. He was altogether the most important personality in the history of the intellectual life after Bede, whose tradition he continued and further extended.']

2. The publication a century ago in the MGH of the correspondence of Boniface, Lull, and Alcuin, of various Lives of Anglo-Saxon missionaries on the Continent, and the

famous lectures by the MGH editor Wilhelm Levison, *England and the Continent in the Eighth Century* (Oxford, 1946), made Anglo-Saxonists aware of the impact of Anglo-Saxons on continental culture. Charles W. Jones, J. M. Wallace-Hadrill, Pierre Riché, and, most recently, Donald Bullough, John Contreni, Peter Godman, and Michael Lapidge have added important information, details, and corrections to that topic. What this paper contributes to the discussion is a specific awareness of the particular contributions of the Northumbrian culture to the Carolingian court through Alcuin, especially through the textual and programmatic links between Bede and Alcuin.

3. Bede, *Historia Ecclesiastica*, ed. Bertram Colgrave and R. A. B. Mynors (Oxford, 1969), V.10–11; *Venerabilis Baedae Opera Historica*, ed. Charles Plummer, 2 vols. (Oxford, 1896–97), II.287–88, 538; Wilhelm Levison, "St. Willibrord and His Place in History," in *Aus rheinischer und fränkischer Frühzeit* (Düsseldorf, 1948), pp. 314f., and *England and the Continent*, pp. 53–69; Donald Bullough, *The Age of Charlemagne* (New York, 1966), pp. 29–30.

4. Levison, *England and the Continent*, pp. 70–93; *Dictionary of the Middle Ages*, vol. 1 (New York, 1982), p. 441.

5. Bullough, *Age of Charlemagne*, pp. 30–31; Rosamond McKitterick, "England and the Continent," in *The New Cambridge Medieval History*, vol. 2, *c. 700–c. 900*, ed. Rosamond McKitterick (Cambridge, 1995), pp. 64–84.

6. Bullough, *Age of Charlemagne*, pp. 51–52, 57.

7. Josef Fleckenstein, "Karl der Grosse und sein Hof," in *Karl der Grosse*, ed. Wolfgang Braunfels, 5 vols. (Düsseldorf, 1965–68), vol. 1, pp. 5–39.

8. Bullough, *Age of Charlemagne*, p. 101.

9. *Alcuini Epistolae*, Ep. 16 in MGH, *Epistolae* 4, ed. E. Dümmler (Hannover, 1895), p. 42, cited and tr. by Peter Godman, ed., "Alcuin," in *The Bishops, Kings, and Saints of York* (Oxford, 1982), p. xlvii.

10. Alcuin, Ep. 42 in MGH, *Epistolae* 4, p. 86.

11. *Vita Alcuini*, c. 18, in MGH, *Scriptores* 15.1 (Hannover, 1887), p. 193.

12. J. M. Wallace-Hadrill, "Charlemagne and England," in *Karl der Grosse*, ed. Braunfels, vol. 1, p. 684. He quotes Ep. 17 in MGH, *Epistolae* 4, pp. 47f.: "fiat haec patria ab illo nobis nostrisque nepotibus conservata in benedictione sempiterna" ['May this fatherland be preserved by him for us and our offspring in perpetual blessing'].

13. Godman, "Alcuin," pp. xlviii, xlix.

14. "Traditions of learning and education are commonly supposed to have existed at York under the predecessors of Archbishop Egbert, but the evidence for them is slight. . . . Not until the reigns of the archbishops of Alcuin's own lifetime, Egbert and Ælberht, is there firm evidence for a school of York," Godman, "Alcuin," p. lxi. For more on the school of York see Michael Lapidge, "Aediluulf and the School of York," in *Lateinische Kultur im VIII. Jahrhundert*, ed. Albert Lehner and Walter Berschin (St. Ottilien, 1989), pp. 161–78, esp. 163–67.

15. Alcuin, *Bishops, Kings, Saints of York*, ed. Godman, lines 1259–60.

16. See Peter Hunter Blair, "From Bede to Alcuin," in *Famulus Christi*, ed. Gerald Bonner (London, 1976), pp. 254–55. Godman, "Alcuin," p. lxii, seconding Hunter Blair, claims that Alcuin "hardly describes Egbert as a teacher. . . . The man who made the school of York what it represented to Alcuin was not Egbert, but his successor Ælberht." But Alcuin does describe Egbert as a teacher, line 1260. Alcuin in his extended period as student at York, and then as master when Ælberht succeeded Egbert as archbishop, no doubt was more familiar with Ælberht, whose qualities he rightly admired; but this should not detract from Egbert's role as founder of the school any more than Bede's extensive details about Ceolfrith in *Historia Abbatum* should be interpreted as a slighting of Benedict Biscop.

17. Alcuin, *Bishops, Kings, Saints of York*, ed. Godman, lines 1415–26.

18. See, e.g., MGH, *Epistolae* 4, Ep. 121, pp. 175–78.

19. MGH, *Epistolae Selectae* 1 (*S. Bonifatii et Lulli Epistolae*), ed. Michael Tangl (Munich, 1916), Epp. 75, 91, 125, 126.

20. See Godman's note to lines 1600ff. of *Bishops, Kings, Saints of York*, pp. 130–31.

21. Bernhard Bischoff, "Die Hofbibliothek Karls der Grossen," in *Karl der Grosse*, ed. Braunfels, vol. 2, p. 56.

22. *Admonitio Generalis Karoli Magni, Anno 789*, in MGH, *Legum Sectio II, Capitularia Regum Francorum*, vol. 1, ed. Alfred Boretius (Hanover, 1883), 1:60, cited by Charles W. Jones, "Bede's Place in Medieval Schools," in *Famulus Christi*, ed. Bonner, p. 263.

23. Jones, "Bede's Place," pp. 265–67.

24. See MGH, *Epistolae* 4, Epp. 88, 101, 216; Stephen Allott, *Alcuin of York—His Life and Letters* (York, 1974), nos. 90, 130, 146.

25. For the evidence of the extent of Alcuin's use of Bede, see my entry on Bede the Venerable in *Sources of Anglo-Saxon Literary Culture* [SASLC], ed. Frederick M. Biggs, Thomas D. Hill, Paul E. Szarmach, forthcoming.

26. See Alcuin's Letter to the monks at Wearmouth-Jarrow, MGH, *Epistolae* 4, Ep. 29, p. 55, lines 23–26; also Wolfgang Edelstein, *Eruditio und Sapientia: Weltbild und Erziehung in der Karolingerzeit* (Freiburg, 1967), p. 80.

27. See my *Bede the Venerable* (Boston, 1987), pp. 29–31; Pierre Riché, *Écoles et enseignement dans le Haut Moyen Âge*, 2nd ed. (Paris, 1989), p. 59. Riché, however, oversimplifies the position of the Fathers on the matter of the worth of the liberal arts; they were ambivalent about them, as their contradictory statements show.

28. Hunter Blair, pp. 243, 253.

29. The little piece is printed as the first part of *Grammatica* in PL 101, 850–54; its title, *Disputatio de Vera Philosophia*, is found in Munich Clm 6404, fol. 1v, the oldest witness (c. 800). See Brunhölzl, pp. 270, 547.

30. Luitpold Wallach, *Alcuin and Charlemagne* (Ithaca, NY, 1959), p. 36; Wilbur Samuel Howell, *The Rhetoric of Alcuin and Charlemagne* (Princeton, 1941), pp. 22–33.

31. John Marenbon, *From the Circle of Alcuin to the School of Auxerre* (Cambridge, 1981), p. 31. As Brunhölzl notes in *Geschichte*, p. 273, "Was den Inhalt angeht, hat der Verfasser nahezu alles wörtlich übernommen: aus den pseudo-augustinischen Kategorien, aus Boethius de topicis differentiis und aus Eytmologien Isidors" ['As to content, the author has taken over nearly everything word for word, from the pseudo-Augustinian *Categories*, from Boethius' *De Topicis Differentiis*, and from Isidore's *Etymologies*'].

32. See Bede's *Historia Ecclesiastica*, V.24, pp. 566–69; Brown, *Bede the Venerable*, pp. 19, 41.

33. On "The Bedan Tradition and Carolingian Education" see C. W. Jones' preface to *Bedae Opera Didascalia*, CCSL 123A (Turnhout, 1969), p. xv; Brown, *Bede the Venerable*, p. 98.

34. See *Orthographia Alcuini*, ed. Aldo Marsili (Pisa, 1952), pp. 14, 83.

35. See my SASLC Bedan sources list under *Opera Didascalia*; cf. Dieter Schaller, "Alkuin," in *Die deutschen Literatur des Mittelalters: Verfasserlexicon*, ed. Wolfgang Stammler, Karl Langosch, and Kurt Ruh, vol. 1 (Berlin, 1978), p. 252: "wichtigste Autorität ist Beda" ['the most important authority is Bede'].

36. Allott, tr., no. 76; MGH, *Epistolae* 4, Ep. 155, p. 250.

37. *Bedae Opera de Temporibus*, ed. Charles W. Jones (Cambridge, MA, 1943), p. 142.

38. MGH, *Poetae Latini Aevi Carolini* 4.2, ed. Karl Strecker (Berlin, 1914), pp. 674–97. These *Rhythmi Computistici* sometimes accompanied as appendices Bede's *De Temporibus* and *De Temporum Ratione*; see pp. 667–69, 698–701.

39. M. R. Godden, "Anglo-Saxons on the Mind," in *Learning and Literature in Anglo-Saxon England*, ed. Michael Lapidge and Helmut Gneuss (Cambridge, 1985), pp. 271–72.

40. Schaller, p. 248: In biblical theology, Alcuin "schloss sich eng an seine Quellen an: Hieronymus, Augustinus, Beda, Chrysostomus (lat.), Ambrosius Autpertus" ['closely copied his sources: Jerome, Augustine, Bede, (Latin) Chrysostom, Ambrosius Autpertus'].

41. Bullough, "Alcuin and the Kingdom of Heaven: Liturgy, Theology, and the Carolingian Age, " in *Carolingian Essays*, ed. Uta-Renate Blumenthal (Washington, DC, 1983), p. 62; see also pp. 60–61; rpt. in Bullough, *Carolingian Renewal* (Manchester, 1991), pp. 201–03.

42. I list Alcuin's excerpts and borrowings from Bede's *Homeliarum Evangelii Libri II* in my SASLC entry on Bede the Venerable.

43. Bullough, "Alcuin and the Kingdom," p. 63; *Carolingian Renewal*, p. 202.

44. John J. Contreni, "Carolingian Biblical Studies," in *Carolingian Essays*, ed. Blumenthal, pp. 71–72.

45. Charles Jones, CCSL 123A, p. x, remarks about Bede's *De Arte Metrica*, "This useful tract became indispensable in the age of Charlemagne because it was directly vocational." See also C. D. Kendall's remarks on p. 74 of this edition.

46. See my SASLC list of Bedan sources, under *Opera Poetica, Hagiographica, et Historica;* and Godman, "Alcuin," in *Bishops, Kings, Saints of York*, Index of Quotations and Allusions, pp. 143–47.

47. See Peter Godman, "The Anglo-Saxon Opus Geminatum: From Aldhelm to Alcuin," *Medium Ævum*, 50 (1981), 215–29, who claims in "The Rise of the Opus Geminatum and the Form of Alcuin's Poem on York," part of his introduction to "Alcuin" in *Bishops, Kings, and Saints*, pp. lxxviii–lxxxviii, that in creating the poem Alcuin's use of Bede's *Historia Ecclesiastica* was influenced by the *opus geminatum* format; see also Gernot Wieland, "Geminus Stilus: Studies in Anglo-Latin Hagiography," in *Insular Latin Studies*, ed. Michael W. Herren (Toronto, 1981), pp. 113–33; Michael Lapidge, "Bede's Metrical *Vita S. Cuthberti*," in *St. Cuthbert, His Cult and His Community,* ed. Gerald Bonner, David Rollason, and Clare Stancliffe (Woodbridge, 1989), pp. 86–90; Levison, "St. Willibrord," p. 311.

48. *Biblioteca Rerum Germanicarum*, vol. 6: *Monumenta Alcuiniana*, ed. Philippe Jaffé (Berlin, 1873), p. 39; quoted in Lapidge, "Bede's Metrical *Vita S. Cuthberti*," p. 93.

49. Letter of Bede to Egbert, Archbishop of York (5 November 734), no. 170 in *English Historical Documents*, vol. 1, *c.500–1042*, 2nd ed., ed. and tr. Dorothy Whitelock (London, 1979), pp. 799–810. The original Latin document is printed in *Venerabilis Baedae Opera Historica,* ed. Plummer, vol. 1, pp. 405–23. In his commentary in vol. 2, pp. xxxv and 381–82, Plummer calls attention to other places in Bede's works where he inveighs against episcopal extortion.

50. *Alcuini Epistolae* in MGH, *Epistolae* 4, Ep. 254, p. 411, lines 24–25; see the same phrasing in Ep. 111, p. 1621, lines 9–10. Other admonitory letters against such unjust tithing are Epp. 107, 110, 174.

THE PRESERVATION OF ANGLO-SAXON CULTURE AFTER 1066: GLASTONBURY, WALES, AND THE NORMANS

DAVID A. E. PELTERET

Hastings was not a profitable battle for the monks of Glastonbury, whose abbey had been the wealthiest in Anglo-Saxon England. Their abbot, Æthelnoth, was kept under William the Conqueror's control until he was finally deposed by Lanfranc's Council of London in late 1077 or 1078. Though Domesday Book shows that theirs was still the richest abbey in the country in 1086, the monks were deprived of a great deal of property by the Conqueror and his followers. Worse, however, was to follow. Thurstan, a Norman monk from Caen, replaced the ousted Æthelnoth. His relationship with the monks was an unhappy one. He attempted to change their old way of chanting and, when the monks proved recalcitrant, employed a technique much beloved of political dictators, though unusual in the case of abbatial ones: he called in the troops. Taking full advantage of the architecture of the abbey, from the triforium the archers skewered the terrified monks, who had fled to the high altar for sanctuary. Three monks died and another eighteen were wounded. This was bit excessive, even by the standards of the time. Thurstan was sent back to Caen, though it is reported that he regained his monastery from William Rufus with the help of five hundred pounds of silver donated by his relatives and evidently returned "before meeting a miserable end (far from there, as was appropriate)."[1]

The monks must have heard the name of his successor with the same horror that bibulous dons might feel on learning of the election of a new master dedicated to the selling of their college's wine cellar. Not only did Herluin also come from Caen—but he was reputed to be an ascetic! Fortunately for the monks, like many men unused to the exercise of power but eager to be thought well of, Herluin went to the other extreme. He rebuilt the church at Glastonbury and energetically sought to redeem properties seized by various Normans. In consequence, he was held in good repute by the abbey's historians, such as William of Malmesbury.[2]

Herluin's desire to aggrandize his new monastic house helps provide an explanation for the existence of the document that I shall now examine. The text in question records that a Norman, Robert de la Haye, made over to Glastonbury, with the approval of Robert fitz Hamo, the church of Bassaleg near Newport in Monmouthshire (now called Gwent), together with some attached churches and other appurtenances.[3] The charter, whose authenticity there is no reason to doubt, should interest Anglo-Saxonists for several reasons. Here is a document in which a Norman gives to an English monastery ecclesiastical property in Wales. The document preserves the Anglo-Saxon diplomatic tradition of employing Old English in the boundary clause nearly 40 years *after* the Conquest of England—and, what is more, this clause has the clear intention of precluding arguments amongst *English*-speaking locals.

This paper will restrict itself to the examination of only three matters arising out of the document. First, I shall focus on the text and its context. What does it say? What precisely was being presented? Why was it given to Glastonbury and what made it attractive for the monastery to accept the gift? Turning from the text, I then shall succumb to the temptation of speculating on the possible implications of the evidence for the later literary and cultural history of England. Finally, in the manner of a good homily, I shall point out some precepts for Anglo-Saxonists to bear in mind when examining material in the future.

First let us examine what the text itself says. This is by no means straightforward. Our main textual guide is a fourteenth-century transcript in a Glastonbury volume containing copies of numerous charters as well as Adam of Damerham's *History of Glastonbury*. The gaps in the text show that the Glastonbury copyist's original was not in good condition: some words were either lost or illegible. Fortunately, there is a second text that forms part of a confirmation of 10 April 1330 recorded in a patent roll of 4 Edward III. Though this version lacks the vernacular boundary clause and the witness list, it at least enables one to make some reasonable conjectures as to the words missing from the Glastonbury text.[4] The textual critic is presented, however, with yet further challenges. The Glastonbury copyist seems not to have given his full mind to what the text was saying. His version tells us that the vernacular boundary clause is appended so that it will be more intelligibly understood "by the unworthy." This is nonsensical, and Hearne pointed out the obvious emendation in his edition of 1727: the conversion of *indignis* to *indigenis* makes perfect sense.[5] In other words, English is being used to define the boundaries so that the *natives* will not get into arguments about the limits of the parish.

When the copyist came to words in Welsh and Old English he was even more at sea. For instance, mention of the chapel of *Coit-carneu* (present-day Coedkernew) threw him into confusion. The *c* in *carneu* he read as a *t* and the final *u* he read as an *n*, turning it into *Coittarnen*. Then, apparently not recognizing *inne*, a late Old-English form of *innan*, he consistently divided it into two words, *in ne*, thereby rendering his text unintelligible. He created a ghost word, *ahas*, which at first sight seems incomprehensible. When one recalls, however, that the alder is a tree typical of a marshy locality, it becomes clear that the original document must have read *alras*.[6] In one case we must allow for the possibility that the scribe did what every textual critic fears: he used his intelligence. At one point he makes reference to *montaynes* in the north of the parish. The word first appears in English at the beginning of the thirteenth century. In 1100 we might expect to find the Old English *muntas* rather than the Old French *montaigne*. Perhaps the word was borrowed from French earlier than we might have expected, but I would urge caution upon lexicographers.[7]

An emended text (with some puzzles still remaining) and a translation are provided in the Appendix below. Landscape geographers and those doughty few who spend their weekends doggedly tramping round in an attempt to identify English charter bounds will be disappointed that a detailed map of the charter boundaries has not been provided. It must be said in exculpation that in this part of Wales circumstances are somewhat different from the rolling downs of the South or West Midlands of England.

In the east of the parish we have the River Ebbw (or Ebboth as it was evidently called in 1100).[8] Several major floods occurred near its mouth and along the Wentlooge Level between 1100 and 1800—indeed, the church of Peterstone Wentlooge still bears a plaque recording the flood level attained in the year 1606–07.[9] Giraldus Cambrensis records a ford over a stream called Pencarn—but the stream seems now to have disappeared and the name has been transferred to some nearby farms.[10]

The Wentlooge Level is to be found to the south of the parish. This low-lying area of salty marsh bordering the Mouth of the Severn seems first to have been reclaimed in Roman times.[11] Further accretions of soil, now evident as low cliffs to the east of Cardiff, occurred in the thirteenth century and after.[12] Precision as to the southern boundary is thus in all probability unattainable, even with the assistance of a geologist. When we move north up the Rhymney River we reach *Henbon*. If this is interpreted as a reference to an old bridge, there is little chance of locating it. And if the name, in fact, is Welsh for an 'old stump', we have even less chance of identifying it. While the salt and silt of the Wentlooge Level have preserved timbers from the sixteenth century A.D.,[13] a nine-hundred-year-old stump is unlikely to have survived in a freshwater context. But at least we can be fairly confident about identifying the "brode stone" that is mentioned. This is in all likelihood the "Standing Stone" in the grounds of Druidstone House shown in the current 1:50 000 Ordnance Survey map[14] (though local lore holds that if a cock crows at a midnight hour, the stone uproots itself and goes down to the Rhymney for a bathe!).[15]

It is more profitable to try to locate the chapels and churches that were attached to Bassaleg. These reveal an interesting distribution. They are all to be found within the area between the rivers Rhymney and Usk, the old territory of Gwynllŵg.[16] I have not been able to locate the chapel of *Pulcrud*, but the small settlement of Coedkernew survives. It even has a chapel, though this is a nineteenth-century rebuilding of an older church.[17] Bedwas still possesses its church, as does Lower Machen. Manmoil has sunk in ecclesiastical status: a village set in a slight declivity up in the hills some twelve miles from Bassaleg as the crow flies, it now possesses only a minute evangelical meeting house. Mynyddislwyn perhaps most readily enables you to move back over nine centuries. You ascend a narrow winding hedge-rowed lane, moving steadily further away from the former mining settlements that crowd the valley down below. Your destination provides food for mind, soul, and body. As you crest the hill, there is the graveyard, with a curious mound beyond it, a strong incentive to contemplation. Nearer at hand is the church, dedicated in the name of St. Tewdwr ap Hywel and declaring the site to be of sixth-century origin. But the Devil is even nearer . . . the first building you meet after your thirst-inducing ascent is an isolated pub. We may conclude that what was being presented to Glastonbury was an old *clas* church (the leading ecclesiastical community in a district, led by an abbot and staffed by a group of secular canons).[18] Its antiquity is suggested by its name, Bassaleg. This appears to be derived from *basilica*, a word that was used by Gildas in the sixth century.[19] Bassaleg may thus be seen as the equivalent of the mother-churches found in early Anglo-Saxon England.[20]

Gwynllŵg itself was one of the three regions into which the old kingdom of Glywysing was divided. The origin of the name of this kingdom is uncertain; allegedly it was named after one Glywys, whom the genealogies appear to place in the early sixth century.[21] Gwynllŵg is supposed to have been named after Gwynllyw, one of the three sons of Glywys.[22] It is clear, not merely from de la Haye's charter but also from other sources such as the *Life of Saint Cadog*, the *Life of Saint*

Gwynnlyw, the *Brut y Tywysogyon*, and chronicle material in the *Book of Llandaff*, that Gwynllŵg was still considered a distinct region into the twelfth century, even though it had long been incorporated into larger (and frequently shifting) kingdoms.[23] Its bounds were evidently still remembered and can be reconstructed, rather like the territory of the Hwicce, who had been absorbed quite early into the kingdom of Mercia.[24] By the end of the eleventh century only the mountainous northern part of Gwynllŵg retained any kind of separate existence, being controlled by the shadowy Owain Wan, son of King Caradog, who had ruled over Glamorgan and parts of Gwent before his death in battle in 1081.[25]

The ecclesiastical *territorium* of Bassaleg was a well-balanced economic unit within Gwynllŵg. The church itself is located on a narrow upland shelf containing good arable land. The marshy ground in the south would have provided fowl and rich pasture for horses and cattle. The Ebbw offered excellent prospects for fishing. We know that in the early fourteenth century the tidal Usk was providing salmon in abundance, as well as trout, eels, and lampreys;[26] the Ebbw, flowing into the Usk, is likely to have been no less abundant in the twelfth century. The Welsh, who were a people of the hillsides, would also have exploited the pastoral possibilities of the lands round the upland churches and the wildlife of the abundant woodland in the area.[27]

David Crouch has suggested that Bassaleg had a secular counterpart in Lower Machen, which was the seat of the Caerleon dynasty in the twelfth century: it still bears evidence of an earth and timber castle there.[28] This is strikingly like Anglo-Saxon mother-churches, which frequently were associated with, but separately located from, a *villa regalis*.[29]

It is interesting that the bounds of Bassaleg do not seem to have incorporated the whole of the Wentlooge Level; excluded, for instance, are the present parishes of St. Brides Wentlooge, Peterstone Wentlooge, Marshfield, St. Mellons, and Rumney. If other ecclesiastical *capita* in Gwynllŵg were to have a balanced mix of land within their *parochia*, then obviously this should include a portion of the rich Wentlooge

Level. I would suggest that indeed the remainder of Wentlooge was originally under the ecclesiastical control of other *clas* churches. These might have included St. Gwynnlyw in Newport, an obvious *clas* church, and St. John Baptist at Rumney, which is called a *monasterium* in a Bristol Abbey charter and thus probably at some time held a similar status.[30] Much more work will have to be done on the published and unpublished documents of this region,[31] the place-names they contain,[32] and the topographical and archaeological features of the region[33] before we can be confident about the political and ecclesiastical lineaments of Gwynllŵg. What might be observed here are the similarities to the early Anglo-Saxon kingdoms presented by this evidence.

By the time of the Norman conquest of this area, Bassaleg had ceased to be important as an ecclesiastical center.[34] Perhaps for that reason its bounds had to be well defined in this charter. Just over half a mile to the west of the River Rhymney flows the Taff, which was the eastern ecclesiastical boundary of Llandaff. Llandaff's claims to metropolitan status and to ecclesiastical prerogatives in the region were shortly to be assiduously argued by the ambitious prelate Urban, once he became bishop in 1107.[35] To the east was Newport, a Norman stronghold.[36] Definition of Bassaleg's territory was simple prudence.[37]

Why should Robert de la Haye have offered this property to Glastonbury? Here a brief sketch of the political background in the late eleventh century is useful. One of William Rufus' most loyal supporters was Robert fitz Hamo, whom he rewarded with many of the lands that the late Queen Matilda had possessed, *inter alia*, in nearby Gloucestershire.[38] These Gloucestershire estates provided fitz Hamo with a base from which to exercise control over much of the area known as Morgannwg (roughly Glamorganshire and much of Monmouthshire).[39] After Rufus' death, fitz Hamo transferred his allegiance to Henry, and it was when he was fighting in the latter's cause at the Battle of Falaise in 1105 that he received a lance-wound that rendered him *non compos mentis*—thus inadvertently enabling us to date our document to before 1104, when fitz Hamo last left England, but after 1100, when Herluin became Abbot of Glastonbury.[40]

A sixteenth-century legend recounts that fitz Hamo conquered Morgannwg with the help of twelve companions.[41] The precise details of this account are a historiographical minefield which I had best leave to Welsh historians to enter.[42] All I will observe is that the surnames of two of these companions were Le Sor and St. Quintin, names that appear in this witness list and in an unpublished charter donating property in Newport to Montacute Priory.[43] Since de la Haye is not included among the twelve companions, however, the legend is obviously inaccurate.

When precisely fitz Hamo conquered Morgannwg is uncertain. He probably undertook the invasion in 1093. There is evidence of a Welsh uprising in 1096, so possibly territory had to be recaptured in the last few years of the century. A parceling out by fitz Hamo of lands to his supporters would mark the successful conclusion of such a campaign.[44]

Fitz Hamo himself, like William the Conqueror, took out insurance against the spiritual consequences of his martial endeavors by generously endowing ecclesiastical foundations, notably Tewkesbury, where he is buried, and Gloucester. What was more natural than that de la Haye should follow his example? Since he could hardly rival his overlord in the esteem of the monks of Gloucester and Tewkesbury, it made eminent sense instead to contribute towards another English monastery near the lands that were the source of his lord's power.[45] Thus Glastonbury benefited.

What marked the Normans' conquest of southern Wales was their willingness to employ English colonists to subdue the area, especially the lowland coastal region.[46] Robert de la Haye's charter with its vernacular bounds was there to assist these settlers in knowing their rights.

The subduing of the Welsh who inhabited the hills was more problematic for the Normans.[47] To grant property and rights to Glastonbury can be seen as something of a masterstroke, different in practice but similar in consequence to the advance of the missionaries into the hinterland of Africa. Wales, unlike Anglo-Saxon England, seems to have had a continuous tradition of Christianity from the

Roman period.[48] Opposition to a Christian community such as Glastonbury was thus likely to be muted, especially if Bassaleg no longer had a strong community of canons. But even if it was ecclesiastically weak, Bassaleg may still have preserved its economic rights in outlying areas such as Manmoil and Machen: tithes, alms, burial dues, rights of pannage, all probably stayed in place. Skillful handling by English ecclesiastics might keep the turbulent but Christian Welsh pacific while reaping rich economic profits.

Glastonbury had every incentive to accept de la Haye's offer. We have already seen that Abbot Herluin was eager to ingratiate himself with his new house—and what better way to do that than by adding to its property? Glastonbury was sure to have among its members those like Chaucer's monk who chafed at the discipline of the mother house and might welcome the independence that a distant priory offered.

The simple facts of geography, furthermore, are likely to have made this area attractive to Glastonbury. The monastic house had long had associations with the Celts in general and Wales in particular. St. Gildas was buried at Glastonbury, and the monastery claimed also to possess the bones of St. David.[49] We might suspect that Glastonbury had ties with Gwynllŵg going back over several centuries. The River Brue leading northwest to the coast was navigable as far as Glastonbury,[50] affording ready access to the Mouth of the Severn; from there the estuaries of the Ebbw and Usk were within easy sailing distance.[51]

And Gwynllŵg itself must have seemed physically a home-from-home for the Glastonbury monks. Here were the same combination of marshes and precipitous hillsides that would have reminded them of the Somerset levels and the neighboring Quantocks and Mendips. This was topography which they knew how to exploit, even if recent research suggests that they did not always utilize their lands in the Somerset to the full.[52]

So much, then, for the document itself and its direct implications. We have seen that it provides material for political, economic, and ecclesiastical historians, for geographers, place-name experts, students of charters, textual critics, and philologists. But it also has interesting implications for literary historians.

Glastonbury showed a considerable interest in the twelfth century in things Welsh. For instance, it employed a Welshman, Caradoc of Llancarfan, to write a biography of St. Gildas in which Guinevere and Arthur were brought into association with Glastonbury, although not in the most favorable of ways.[53] Caradoc was a contemporary of that marvellous storyteller (or mendacious historian, depending on your intellectual disposition), Geoffrey of Monmouth.[54] Geoffrey created—or recreated—the figure of Arthur, whose exploits had an immediate appeal to his contemporaries. But an innovative and imaginative creation is of no value in itself, as any businessman will tell you: to be successful, it must be marketed. And it was Glastonbury that did the marketing, in part through that entertaining scribbler Gerald of Wales.[55] In 1184 the abbey suffered a severe blow: its church burned down. Money was needed to rebuild. Just seven years later, in 1191, a remarkable discovery was made at the abbey—nothing less than the bones of King Arthur and his wife, Guinevere. This is not the place to retell the story.[56] What is more interesting is why Glastonbury was receptive to the exploitation of the Arthur fantasy. It may be suggested—and it can be no more than a suggestion—that the intimate contact with Wales afforded the monks through their property in Bassaleg gave them continuous access to the world of early British myth and legend.[57] We might note that when the abbey received some further property at Bassaleg in the early twelfth century, one of the chaplains who witnessed the gift had the good Norman name of Ralph—but another possessed a Welsh name, Wurgan. The discovery of the remains of "Arthur" 90 years after Glastonbury received Bassaleg is not such a long time when you realize that the monks, whose cultural origins must have remained largely Anglo-Saxon and Norman, had to make the world of Celtic story their own to such a degree that they could with confidence accept as genuine the discovery that was so materially to benefit their house. If this suggestion has merit, the obscure benefaction recorded in this document has a part in the development of the Arthurian legend, one of the most productive story cycles ever created.[58]

Our discussion has drifted insensibly forward in time. We shall conclude by moving into the present day and away from the document towards Anglo-Saxon Studies, which is the focus of this volume. The Bassaleg charter has lain buried in the Cambridge, Trinity College library for some centuries. Hearne brought it to light in 1727; G. T. Clark resurrected it again late in the nineteenth century.[59] Until now, however, it has received no extended analysis. There are several reasons for this. First of all, we tend to keep within the boundaries that must necessarily be drawn in order to impose intellectual order and discipline on a subject. Anglo-Saxonists have a natural tendency to use the political boundary of 1066 as an all-encompassing one for the subject. Yes, we all know that the Peterborough Chronicle was continued in English until 1154.[60] Yes, we know that perfectly competent copies of Ælfrician manuscripts were made well into the twelfth century.[61] But we only "know" this with part of our minds; in practice, we assume that the literary culture died in 1066.

Then, we also employ the boundaries imposed by our intellectual disciplines. The English philological tradition of the past century has sanctioned the study of exquisite literary texts such as *The Dream of the Rood* and linguistically interesting glosses such as those found in the Vespasian Psalter. Charters (with a handful of exceptions) have not been deemed suitable material for students of English language and literature —they are the province of historians and Latinists.

Finally, there has been since the origin of our subject in the sixteenth century a certain nationalistic tinge: students have tended either to be "little" Anglo-Saxonists or "little" Normanists. What they have had in common is a focus on England. England has had a Place-Name Society since the early 1920's, which has published some 60 volumes to date. Wales has produced only a few monographs on Welsh place-names that meet modern onomastic standards[62] and a handful of specialists who are interested in utilizing the 250,000 place-name records amassed by the late Melville Richards. Current events reveal the folly of fostering nationalism, and this paper has no such intention in mind. But the failure of most Anglo-Saxonists to recognize the constant interaction between England and Wales has diminished the recognition of the importance for English cultural life—for both good and ill—of the stubborn survival of the Western British Celts.

It says much for the openness of our subject, however, that this paper was accepted for delivery before an audience of Anglo-Saxonists rather than specialists in Welsh or Anglo-Norman Studies. This acceptance says much for the vitality of Anglo-Saxon Studies when one reflects on the fact that the lecture, which discussed a Norman document concerning Wales, was originally given in New York State—itself a former Dutch and English colony obtained by dubious means from its indigenous inhabitants.

UNIVERSITY OF TORONTO

APPENDIX

Sources: A = Cambridge, Trinity College R.5.33, fol. 106v. B = London, PRO, Patent Rolls, 4 Ed. III, Part 1, m. 32, no. 1 (C.66/173).

The A text is one of a number of fourteenth-century transcripts of documents relating to Bassaleg inserted in the Trinity College manuscript of the *Historia de Rebus Glastoniensibus* by Adam of Damerham (c. 1252–92). The original text was apparently illegible in places, as gaps were left in the manuscript, which Hearne has faithfully reproduced on pp. 604–07 of his two-volume edition of the *Historia*, published in Oxford in 1727. B was written in 1330; the text contains some variant spellings and, more significantly, some passages that appear to represent the words missing from A.

It is likely that at about the time when the original transaction took place, several copies were made of the charter recording this legal act. Glastonbury, as the beneficiary, obviously would have kept in its archives a written record in the form of a single-leaf charter, and it is this document (or a copy of it) that was transcribed, evidently after it had suffered some damage. Single-leaf charters were frequently folded, and so wear could easily have occurred along the line of the folds.

It would also have been prudent to keep a copy of some of the charters relating to Bassaleg at the priory itself and especially this text, as it established Glastonbury's right to the property. Charters originally kept at Bassaleg may have been the ultimate source of the version of the two Bassaleg records transcribed in the confirmation in mortmain granted on 10 April 1330 to John de Eclescliff (Eaglescliffe), Bishop of Llandaff (translated from Connor on 20 June 1323; d. 2 January 1347), and his chapter. Since, as we shall see, these two charters are abbreviated in B, one must assume that what the Chancery scribe saw was a composite document or documents compiled by the see of Llandaff in order to record for posterity the transfer of Bassaleg and its appurtenant churches and property from Glastonbury to Llandaff. The Chancery confirmation consists of the following elements:

1. The text of the grant of Bassaleg and associated churches made by Robert de la Haye to Glastonbury. Omitted in B are the vernacular bounds and the witness list of the A text. B is presumably a transcript

of a copy made at Llandaff of the putative Bassaleg text of the charter. When the copy was made, the bounds were most likely unintelligible to the clerks at Llandaff, and it probably seemed unimportant to preserve the names of the original witnesses to the transaction, so both elements were omitted.

2. A grant in frank almoin of these same churches by Gilbert de Clare, Earl of Gloucester and Hereford (1180–25 October 1230).
3. The text of a charter of William de Bercherolles assigning further property to Bassaleg. This same charter immediately follows Robert de la Haye's charter in the Trinity College manuscript but, as in the case of the latter document, we can assume that Glastonbury's copy was damaged because of two gaps left in the Trinity transcript. The B text (presumably also a transcript of a Llandaff copy of a Bassaleg document) enables one to conjecture that the first gap may have contained the words *in perpetuam elemosinam* and that the word following the first gap should read "quae" instead of "qui" in order to agree with the phrase "omnem terram," which appears three lines before. The phrase in B that equates to the second gap in the A text is "in ebbodh cu*m* o*mn*ib*us* alnetis." B has "Deny" for A's "Dens" and "Blainfrot" for A's "Blainfort." As with the B text of the first Bassaleg charter, the names of the witnesses are not recorded in B; they are in the A text.
4. A record of the grant of Bassaleg and associated chapels made by Michael, Abbot of Glastonbury (1235–52), to Elias de Radnor, Bishop of Llandaff (consecrated 1 December 1230; d. 13 May 1240), in return for a perpetual farm of 35 marks.
5. A confirmation of the latter grant made, according to the Chancery text, by the "aforesaid" ("p*re*fatus") Gilbert de Clare "p*er* l*itt*eras suas patentes" to the aforesaid ("p*re*fatis") abbot and convent, approving and ratifying the grant made by the abbot to the bishop and his successors.
6. Release granted by "Mareduch de K*er*lionn" (i.e., Maredudd of Caerleon) "per scrip<tum> suu*m*" to William, sometime ("dudu*m*") Bishop of Llandaff and his successors, wherein he waives any right and claim to the advowson of the churches ("ecclesiarum") of Machen ("Macheyn"), Bedwas ("Bedewas"), and Mynyddislwyn ("Menydhestelon"). This obviously must post-date the transfer of Bassaleg to Llandaff. There were no fewer than four Williams who were elected as bishops

of Llandaff between 1240 and 1266; the last of them, William de Breuse, died in office on 19 March 1287. On the basis of the present evidence it does not seem possible to decide which of the four bishops is referred to in this release.

This B text exists because John de Eclescliff evidently decided to protect his episcopal claims to Bassaleg and associated churches in Monmouthshire by securing this royal confirmation from Edward III. Following the tradition of tampering with Llandaff's documents in the interests of advancing the cause of the see that Bishop Urban had initiated in the twelfth century, John, or perhaps his predecessor at the time of Maredudd's grant of advowson, apparently decided to fortify Llandaff's claims by having Glastonbury's transfer of the property (which took place c. 1237) ostensibly confirmed in writing by the person who was thought to be the local overlord at that time, viz., Gilbert de Clare. Unfortunately, as alert readers will already have noticed, Gilbert died over a month before Elias was consecrated Bishop of Llandaff and five years before Michael became Abbot of Glastonbury.

Luckily for us, the Chancery scribe's source preserved in some sections better texts of Robert de la Haye's and John of Bercherolles' charters than did the texts that had been kept at Glastonbury—possibly, as I have suggested, because the scribe's source was derived from older copies that had been kept in better condition at Bassaleg. We can thus reconstruct with tolerable certainty the missing words in A's Latin text of Robert's charter, just as we have done in the case of John of Bercherolles' charter. In the edition of Robert's charter below such reconstructions are enclosed within square brackets. The capitalization and punctuation follow modern practice. Expansions are italicized; forms whose expansions may be questioned are recorded in the notes.

The Chancery scribe records the document in the third person, at times summarizing the original, and so his text cannot verify the A text in all details. It does, however, preserve some variant spellings of place-names, which are noted in the edition below. As has been mentioned, the vernacular bounds are not recorded in B, which is most frustrating. Kitson and Roberts have suggested to me some emendations and translations of the bounds and place-names that are found in the A text.

The text of A is reprinted by the kind permission of the Master and Fellows of Trinity College, Cambridge, and that of B, which is Crown copyright, by permission of the Controller of Her Majesty's Stationery Office.

TEXT

Ego Rob*er*tus de Haia *et* sponsa mea Gundred*a* concessu[a] d*omi*ni mei Rob*er*ti filii Hamonis *et* sponse sue Sibilie[b] p*ro* salute a*nimaru*m n*ostraru*m *et* antecessor*um* n*ostr*or*um* *et* successor*um* damus Deo *et* S*anct*e Marie ecc*les*ie Glaston[*iensis et* monachis ibide*m*][c] ecc*les*iam de Basselec in elemosinam in p*er*petuu*m* possidenda*m*, lib*er*am *et* quietam ab o*mn*ib*us* geldis donis auxiliis [op*er*ib*us et* ab o*mn*ib*us* consuetudinib*us*][d] in bosco in plano in aquis *et* in o*mn*ib*us* o*mn*in*o* locis, *et* h*oc* p*ro* beneficiis tantu*m et* or*aci*onib*us* co*ngr*egacio*n*is facim*us*. Concedimus *eciam* ecc*les*ie Glaston*iensi* ecclesias [pertinentes ad ecclesiam][e] de Basselech cu*m* dec*im*is *et* elemosinis om*n*ib*us* *et* defunctor*um* corp*or*ib*us* que ad parrochiam de Basselech p*er*tinent, scilic*et* ecc*les*iam de Mahhayn[f] *et* ecc*les*iam de Bedewas *et* eccl*es*iam de Menedwiscleluyn[g] *et* eccl*es*iam de Mapmoil *et* capellam de Coitcarneu *et* capellam de Pulcrud.[h] Et ne dissensio u*e*l scandalu*m*, quod absit, int*er* parrochiam de Basselech *et* alias parrochias sibi p*r*oximas oriat*ur*, t*er*minos parrochie de Basselech in cartula ista Anglice notari uolum*us*, ut ab indigenis[i] intelligat*ur* clari*us*. Parrochia de Basselech incipit a fonte Cadoci dunwardes þurh þa alras[j] inne[k] þene mor, an esthalf[l] Pencarn, 7 swa inne[k] þene pul[m] þe sceadeð[n] inne Ebboth.[o] Of Eboth ut inne[k] þa se 7 endelanges[p] thare sa to Tenbrith.[q] 7 swa upricht[r] þurch thane mor inne[k] Dufeles, 7 swa to þe brode stone 7 swa into[s] Remni 7 swa to Henbon 7 swa to Inweri 7 swa to Kemelin[t] allang the[u] montaynes ofdun linch[v] to Rid Cambren.[w] 7 swa to miðe[x] Kemeli and[y] swa dunewardes to Kadokes pulle. Dedim*us eciam* eis una*m* p*ar*tem de terra n*ost*ra in marisco, cui*us* hii su*n*t t*er*mini. De uado Merepul usq*ue* Kemelin,[z] *et* s*ic* p*ro*tendit*ur* usq*ue* in Ebboth.[aa] Ip*s*a u*er*o cingit IIIIor hammas t*er*re *et* t*er*ra ista extendit*ur* in altu*m*, usq*ue* in pullam q*ue* uocat*ur* Kenerad. De pulla Kenerad ducit*ur* usq*ue* ad quendam quaceolu*m* spinis consitum. De isto u*er*o reducit*ur* ad alt*eru*m minore*m* et dehinc reu*er*tit*ur* in Merepul. Concedim*us* itaq*ue* monachis Glasto*nie*, ut accipiant in bosco n*ost*ro qua*n*tu*m*cu*n*q*ue* eis expedierit ad op*us* ecc*les*ie Glaston*iensis* et Basselech[bb] *et* ad op*us* officinar*um* suar*um* lib*er*e *et* quiete[cc] absq*ue* om*n*i calumpnia *et* s*er*uic*i*o[dd] *et* co*n*suetudine om*n*iq*ue* querela. Porcor*um* suor*um* pastio*n*em in bosco n*ost*ro sine pasnagio[ee] liberam h*ab*eant. Portu*m eciam et* piscinas suas *et* licencia*m* piscandi libere *et* absolute h*ab*eant, scil*ic*et qua*n*tu*m* flume*n* de Ebboth[ff] ex una p*ar*te illa*m* t*er*ram influit. Curiam uero suam[gg] plene lib*er*e *et* quiete in om*n*i negoc*i*o *et* consuetudi*n*e h*ab*eant, sic*ut et* nos [curiam habemus. Concedimus] eciam[hh] eis licenciam essartandi[ii] boscum circa locum qui dicitur As dormanz usque fontem qui dicitur contra Werthin.[jj] Inde usque stan hus.[kk] Inde per iungeta *et* [guaceolos usq*ue* Glissyn].[ll] Inde usq*ue* Penbur. Inde in Ebboth.[mm] Concedim*us* q*uoque* monachis S*anct*e Marie Glaston*iensis* ecc*les*ie[nn] q*ui* h*ab*itant apud Basselech[oo] ad supplementu*m* sui uestit*us* singulis annis XX sol*idos* de n*ost*ra elemosina, scil*ice*t de dec*im*is de Gunleonc.[pp] Dedim*us* aut*em* eis que*n*dam ho*min*em n*ost*rum no*min*e Wrghi[qq] filiu*m* Wrgan cu*m* te*r*ra sua[rr] lib*er*um ad s*er*uiciu*m* illor*um*. *Et* si q*ui*s hom*inum* n*ost*ror*um* tam Francor*um* q*ua*m Anglor*um* u*e*l Gualensiu*m* ecc*les*ie de Basselech donac*ion*em u*e*l uendic*ion*em de te*r*ra sua fec*er*it u*e*l ibi cu*m* te*r*ra sua ad monachatu*m* acced*er*e uoluerit, a D*eo* *et* nob*is* lib*er*am h*ab*eat licencia*m*. Hiis testib*us*: Will*elmo* uiceco*mite* Kard*iff*; Rob*erto* le Sor; Rog*ero* de Sumeri; Rog*ero* fil*io* Joze; Hereb*erto* de S*anc*to Q*u*intino; Laudomaro Aze. Et ex p*ar*te Herlewini abbatis: Widone monacho;[ss] Samuele m*onach*o;[tt] Moyse m*onach*o;[tt] Aluredo de Nichol*as*[uu] *et* filio suo, Rob*er*to; Osm*u*ndo G*ra*netario; Walt*er*o le Chamb*erlain*; Aluredo pinc*erna* abb*a*tis; *et* multis aliis.

TEXTUAL VARIANTS

[a] Gundreda ux*or* ei*us* . . . concensu B
[b] sibille ux*or*is ei*us* B
[c] B; A *omits the suspension and et* monachis ibide*m*
[d] donis *et* auxiliis *followed by a space* A; ab o*mn*ib*us* geldis donis auxiliis op*er*ib*us* *et* ab o*mn*ib*us* consuetudinib*us* B; *cf.* monachis Glastoniae *below and Adami de Domerham Historia, ed. Hearne, p. 608*
[e] *Reconstructed from B*: de eccl*es*iis . . . ad d*ic*tam eccl*es*iam de Basselec p*er*tinentib*us*; *space in* A
[f] mahhain B
[g] menedyistelinn B
[h] *et* capellam de Coittarnen *et* capellam de Pulcrud A; de capellis de coitcarnen *et* pulcrud B; B *om.* Et ne dissensio . . . to Kadokes pulle
[i] indignis A
[j] ahas A
[k] in ne A
[l] esthalf *Kitson*; es half A
[m] þeneful A

n sceadeð *Kitson*; þe sað A

o in Newboth A

p endelanges *Kitson*; eadela ses A

q to me Tenbrith A; melenbrith *Kitson*

r upricht *Kitson*; up rich A

s in to A

t Namelin A

u allang the *Kitson*; allathe A

v ofdun linch *Kitson*; of Sunlinch A

w Cambrem A

x miþe *Kitson*; mire A

y an A

z kemelyn B

aa s*ic* p*ro*tendit*ur* usq*ue* in Elboth A (*on the form* Ebboth, *see n. 8 below*); *om*. B

bb Bassclcc B

cc lib*er*e quiete *et* B

dd s*er*uicis B

ee de porcis suis pascond*is* in eod*em* bosco sine pannagio B

ff Elboth A; Ebboth*o* B

gg necno*n* curiam suam B

hh curiam suam h*ab*erunt. Concessione*m* insup*er* . . . fecer*un*t B

ii essarttandi A; de essartand*o* B

jj weichin B

kk Stanhus A; stanhus B

ll guaceolos vsq*ue* Glissyn B; *space in* A

mm Elboth A; Ebboth*um* B

nn B *om*. ecclesie

oo Basselegh*um* B

pp de viginti solid*is* p*er*cipiend*is* sing*u*lis annis de decimis de Gunleonc B

qq Worchi B

rr B *omits the remainder of the text*

ss modo A (*see n. 5 below*)

tt m̊ A (*see n. 5 below*)

uu Nichol A

TRANSLATION OF THE BOUNDS

The parish of Bassaleg begins from *Cadoc's well* downwards through the alders into the marshy land on the east side of [the stream called] Pencarn and so into the pool which flows into the Ebbw. From the Ebbw out into the sea and along the sea to *Tenbrith.*[63] And so up directly through the marshy land within [the manor of] Diflais[64] and so to the broad stone and so to the Rhymney [River]. And so to the old bridge[65] and so to *Inweri* and so to *Kemelin.*[66] All the mountains down the linch to *Rhyd Cambren,*[67] and so to the lake *Kemelin*, and so downwards to *Cadoc's pool.* We have also given to them a part of our land in the marsh, of which these are the boundaries. From the ford *Merepul*[68] up to *Kemelin* and so it extends to the Ebbw. The [river] encloses four water meadows and that land extends into the upland to the pool that is called *Kenerad.* From the pool *Kenerad* it leads to a certain little wash[69] surrounded by thorn trees. From there it leads back to another smaller one and from there it turns back into the *Merepul.*

[There is] also [granted] to them the right of assarting the woodland round the place which is called *As dormanz* up to the spring which is called *contra Werthin.* From there to a stone house.[70] From there through the reedbeds and little washes to *Glissyn.* From there to *Penbur.* From there into the Ebbw.

NOTES

I wish to thank Frederick Case, Principal of New College, Univ. of Toronto, for the financial assistance that enabled me to present the original version of this paper at the 1991 ISAS conference at Stony Brook; I also gratefully acknowledge the grant awarded by the Humanities and Social Sciences Committee of the Univ. of Toronto that permitted me to undertake further research in England and Wales during December 1991. Ms. Helen Rowett generously lent me her car at an early stage in my researches, which enabled me to explore the region round Bassaleg. The late Cecily Clark, to whom I owe many debts that I am sad to say now cannot be repaid, initiated a chain of academic contacts which was of significant help to me. Gwynedd Pierce, Madeleine Gray, David Crouch, and Peter Kitson all freely offered information and helpful criticism for which I am deeply grateful. G. Aled Williams put me in touch with Tomos Roberts, who consulted Melville Richards' archive of Welsh place-name records at the Univ. College of North Wales in Bangor and provided me with invaluable assistance. Richard Sharpe spared my committing a number of blunders to print and alerted me to several recent publications. Naturally, they do not necessarily subscribe to the views expressed in this paper and I alone remain responsible for all errors of commission and omission.

1. For a history of the abbey see James P. Carley, *Glastonbury Abbey: The Holy House at the Head of the Moors Adventurous* (Woodbridge, 1988), and Thomas Scott Holmes, "The Abbey of Glastonbury," in *The Victoria History of Somerset*, vol. 2, ed. William Page (London, 1911), pp. 82–99. My account of Thurstan is taken from *The Early History of Glastonbury: An Edition, Translation and Study of William of Malmesbury's De Antiquitate Glastonie Ecclesie*, ed. John Scott (Woodbridge, 1981), ch. 78, pp. 156–59; his end, "(longe ab ipso, ut dignus erat,) misere uitam finiuit," is mentioned on p. 158. Herluin is discussed in ch. 79, pp. 158–61. Details about Thurstan's relationship with Glastonbury and the attack in the abbey church inevitably vary somewhat from source to source: see esp. also *The Peterborough Chronicle 1070–1154*, ed. Cecily Clark, 2nd ed. (Oxford, 1970), p. 7, s.a. 1083, tr. in *The Anglo-Saxon Chronicle: A Revised Translation*, ed. and tr. Dorothy Whitelock with David C. Douglas and Susie I. Tucker (London, 1961), p. 160, and, for further references, see *The Early History of Glastonbury*, ed. Scott, p. 173, n. 14. The numbers of the dead and wounded are taken from the *Chronicle* account; William of Malmesbury mentions two dead and fourteen injured. I have interpreted the *uppflor* of the *Chronicle* account to be the triforium, as William evidently did, since he mentions "solaria inter columpnas erecta," but possibly a gallery at the back of the church is being referred to instead. Harold M. and Joan Taylor simply refer to it as "a gallery" in *Anglo-Saxon Architecture*, vol. 1 (Cambridge, 1965),

p. 252. On the music of Glastonbury see David Hiley, "Thurstan of Caen and Plainchant at Glastonbury: Musicological Reflections on the Norman Conquest," *Proceedings of the British Academy*, 72 (1986), 57–90 and pls. III–V.

2. See William of Malmesbury's discussion of Herluin cited in the previous note.

3. On Robert de la Haye (La Haye-du-Puits, Manche), see John Le Patourel, *Normandy and England 1066–1144* (Reading, 1971), pp. 34–35, and Judith A. Green, *The Government of England under Henry I* (Cambridge, 1986), p. 258. On Robert fitz Hamo see T. F. T[out], "Fitzhamon, Robert," in DNB, vol. 7, pp. 159–62, and Ralph A. Griffiths, "The Norman Conquest and the Twelve Knights of Glamorgan," *Glamorgan Historian*, 3 (1966), 153–69, pp. 157–61.

4. The description of the Glastonbury manuscript (Cambridge, Trinity College R.5.33) by Montague Rhodes James in *The Western Manuscripts in the Library of Trinity College, Cambridge: A Descriptive Catalogue*, vol. 2 (Cambridge, 1901), pp. 198–202 (the charter in question is no. 724.16 on p. 201), has been superseded by Julia Crick's detailed analysis of the manuscript and its contents: "The Marshalling of Antiquity: Glastonbury's Historical Dossier," in *The Archaeology and History of Glastonbury Abbey*, ed. Lesley Abrams and James P. Carley (Woodbridge, 1991), pp. 217–43, as Richard Sharpe has pointed out to me. Tomos Roberts in a letter of 28 June 1991 drew my attention to the existence of the Public Record Office (PRO) copy (Patent Roll, 4 Ed. III, Part 1, m. 32, no. 1), which is calendared in *Calendar of the Patent Rolls Preserved in the Public Record Office. Edward III. A.D. 1327–1330* (London, 1891), p. 507.

5. *Adami de Domerham Historia de Rebus Gestis Glastoniensibus*, ed. Thomas Hearne, vol. 2 (Oxford, 1727), pp. 604–07. A similar inattention to the text explains the curious title of *modo* borne by one of the witnesses. Seeing an *o* above an *m*, the copyist automatically transcribed this as "modo"; with the other two names he retained the abbreviation, not recognizing it as representing m*onach*o. For another example of a confused spelling see n. 8 below.

6. *An Anglo-Saxon Dictionary: Based on the Manuscript Collections of the Late Joseph Bosworth*, ed. T. Northcote Toller (Oxford, 1898), s.v. *alor*.

7. See *The Oxford English Dictionary*, 2nd ed., ed. John A. Simpson and Edmund S. C. Weiner (Oxford, 1989), s.v. *mountain* I.1.a; *Middle English Dictionary*, ed. Sherman M. Kuhn, s.v. *mountain* (a). It should be noted that Peter Kitson has pointed out

to me that *muntas* never appears in charter boundaries. Observing that topographical words often appear earlier in charter boundaries than elsewhere, he rejects my suggestion that it is a scribal substitution and believes that *montaynes* is a genuine reflection of the mixed language of southeast Wales of this period.

8. The name of the River Ebbw is completely mangled on one occasion in A; three times it appears in that manuscript as "Elboth," and once as "Eboth." In B it appears as "Ebboth," and in a 13th-century document it is spelled "Eboth." See *Llandaff Episcopal Acta 1140–1287*, ed. David Crouch, South Wales Record Society 5 (Cardiff, 1988), p. 2, no. 2. The scribe of A or his source has evidently mistaken an open *b* for an *l*.

9. G. C. Boon, "Caerleon and the Gwent Levels in Early Historic Times," in *Archaeology and Coastal Change*, ed. F. H. Thompson, Society of Antiquaries of London, Occasional Papers, NS 1 (London, 1980), pp. 24–36, p. 30. The 1606–07 flood was very extensive: for a reproduction of the plaque commemorating it in the church at Goldcliff, east of the Usk, see *Archaeology and Coastal Change*, p. 31, fig. 16.

10. Giraldus de Barri (i.e., Giraldus Cambrensis), *The Itinerary of Archbishop Baldwin through Wales A.D. MCLXXXVIII*, tr. Richard Colt Hoare (London, 1806), pp. 120–31. Hoare, p. 130, equates Pencarn with the Ebbw, but this is clearly wrong. For an edition of the original text see *Itinerarium Kambriae* I.6 in *Giraldi Cambrensis Opera*, ed. James F. Dimock, Rolls Series, 21.6 (London, 1868), pp. 61–62.

11. J. R. L. Allen and M. G. Fulford, "The Wentlooge Level: A Romano-British Saltmarsh Reclamation in Southeast Wales," *Britannia*, 17 (1986), 91–117. For more recent evidence see J. R. L. Allen, "Reclamation and Sea Defence in Rumney Parish (Monmouthshire)," *Archaeologia Cambrensis*, 137 (1988), 135–40 and pl. XXVI, and M. G. Fulford, J. R. L. Allen, and S. G. Rippon, "The Settlement and Drainage of the Wentlooge Level, Gwent: Excavation and Survey at Rumney Great Wharf 1992," *Britannia*, 25 (1994), 175–211.

12. For an illustration of the cliffs known as Rumney Great Warth see Boon, p. 27, fig. 12.

13. Allen and Fulford, p. 108, mention an L-shaped double row of oak stakes with a composite radiocarbon age of 410±40 bp. One must allow (as the two authors do) that these may be a much more recent revetment using old timbers.

14. Ordnance Survey, "Cardiff and Newport," Sheet 171, 1:50 000 Landranger Series, 1986 ed. (British National Grid reference ST 235836).

15. Chris Barber and John G. Williams, *The Ancient Stones of Wales* (Abergavenny, 1989), p. 134, no. 169, and cf. pp. 67–68, with illustrations on pp. 67 and 135.

16. For the territory of Gwynllŵg see Melville Richards, *Welsh Administrative and Territorial Units: Medieval and Modern* (Cardiff, 1969), p. 281, Map 61. For a physical description of the region see the chapter on Monmouthshire in Dorothy Sylvester, *The Rural Landscape of the Welsh Borderland: A Study in Historical Geography* (London, 1969), pp. 377–410.

17. I owe this information to David Crouch, who notes that it has an old churchyard, which he believes is next to a manorial site.

18. On the *clas* church see R. R. Davies, *Conquest, Coexistence, and Change: Wales 1063–1415* (Oxford, 1987), pp. 174–79. For a physical description of Llandaff, a typical *clas* church in the 11th century, see David Crouch, "Urban: First Bishop of Llandaff, 1107–34," *Journal of Welsh Ecclesiastical History*, 6 (1989), 1–15, pp. 4–5.

19. Tomos Roberts, "Welsh Ecclesiastical Place-Names and Archaeology," in *The Early Church in Wales and the West: Recent Work in Early Christian Archaeology, History and Place-Names*, ed. Nancy Edwards and Alan Lane (Oxford, 1992), pp. 41–42, and Melville Richards, "Ecclesiastical and Secular in Medieval Welsh Settlement," *Studia Celtica*, 3 (1968), 9–18, p. 12, both support this identification, originally made by Hugh Williams, ed., in *Gildas*, vol. 1 (London, 1899), pp. 28–29. As Roberts points out in "Welsh Ecclesiastical Place-Names" (p. 41), *basilica* has been identified by Charles Doherty in "The Basilica in Early Ireland," *Peritia*, 3 (1984), 303–15, p. 308, as the origin of *Baislec* in Ireland (*Annals of Ulster*, s.a. 734) and by Margaret Gelling, W. F. H. Nicolaisen, and M. Richards, *The Names of Towns and Cities in Britain* (London, 1970), p. 149, as the source of Paisley in Scotland (through Irish *baslec* 'church'). For the use of *basilica* by Gildas see *The Ruin of Britain and Other Works*, ed. and tr. Michael Winterbottom (London, 1978), ch. 12.2, p. 20 (tr.) and p. 93 (text). The derivation of Bassaleg from *Maes-aleg* 'the field of Aleg' ("a name commemorative of a battle") made in Thomas Nicholas, *Annals and Antiquities of the Counties and County Families of Wales*, vol. 2 (London, 1872), pp. 722 and 786, may be regarded as fanciful; it is rebutted by Ifor Williams, "Maesaleg, Basaleg," *Bulletin of the Board of Celtic Studies*, 7 (1933–35), 277.

20. Some scholars have used the word *minster* to denote these churches, but it is apparent that the Old English *minster* and its Latin cognate *monasterium* were not used with such precision in the Anglo-Saxon period. "Mother church" is employed by P. H. Hase in his paper "The Mother Churches of Hampshire," in *Minsters and Parish Churches: The Local Church in Transition 950–1200*, ed. John Blair (Oxford, 1988), pp. 45–66. Sarah Foot recommends in her paper "Anglo-Saxon Minsters: A Review of Terminology," in *Pastoral Care before the Parish*, ed. John Blair and Richard Sharpe (Leicester, 1992), pp. 212–25, p. 225, that the (hyphenated) form "mother-church" be employed to describe "those institutions which maintained communities of clergy assuming pastoral responsibility for their neighbours. . . ." I have followed her advice.

21. On the origin of the name Glywysing see Wendy Davies, *An Early Welsh Microcosm: Studies in the Llandaff Charters* (London, 1978), p. 99, n. 1, and references there cited.

22. *The Text of the Book of Llan Dâv: Reproduced from the Gwysaney Manuscript*, ed. J. Gwenoguryn Evans (Oxford, 1893), pp. 278–79; David Crouch, "The Slow Death of Kingship in Glamorgan, 1067–1158," *Morgannwg*, 29 (1985), 20–41, p. 23.

23. Lifris, *Vita Sancti Cadoci, Prefatio*, in *Vitae Sanctorum Britanniae et Genealogiae*, ed. Arthur W. Wade-Evans, Board of Celtic Studies, Univ. of Wales, History and Law Series 9 (Cardiff, 1944), p. 24 (text) and p. 25 (tr.); *Vita Sancti Gundleii* (Gwynnllyw) 1, in *Vitae Sanctorum Britanniae et Genealogiae*, p. 172 (text) and p. 173 (tr.); *Brut y Tywysogyon: Or The Chronicle of the Princes; Red Book of Hergest Version*, ed. and tr. Thomas Jones, Board of Celtic Studies, Univ. of Wales, History and Law Series 16 (Cardiff, 1955), p. 34 (text) and p. 35 (tr.); *Book of Llandaff* as cited in n. 22 above. On the history of the region see Wendy Davies, *Wales in the Early Middle Ages* (Leicester, 1982), pp. 102–04, and Crouch, as cited in n. 22 above.

24. On the Hwicce see A. H. Smith, "The *Hwicce*," in *Medieval and Linguistic Studies*, ed. Jess B. Bessinger, Jr., and Robert P. Creed (London, 1965), pp. 56–65; Della Hooke, *The Anglo-Saxon Landscape: The Kingdom of the Hwicce* (Manchester, 1985); and Patrick Sims-Williams, *Religion and Literature in Western England 600–800* (Cambridge, 1990), pp. 29–39. One should note, however, that the analogy is not complete. Most early Anglo-Saxon kingdoms seem to have had a tribal basis; Wendy Davies insists that the early divisions of Wales had a *political* rather than a tribal basis. In other words, they were associated with a specific territory and with particular dynasties rather than with tribes or ethnic groups: see W. Davies, *Patterns of Power in Early Wales* (Oxford, 1990), esp. pp. 37–38.

25. Crouch, "The Slow Death of Kingship," pp. 23–24, 27, and 30. For the genealogical relationships of Owain and Caradog see K. L. Maund, *Ireland, Wales, and England in the Eleventh Century* (Woodbridge, 1991), p. 32, fig. 14, p. 73, fig. 39, and p. 75, fig. 41.

26. William Rees, *South Wales and the March 1284–1415: A Social and Agrarian Study* (Oxford, 1924), p. 198.

27. The frequent appearance in place-names of the Welsh word *coed* 'wood' is evidence in support of this statement.

28. I owe this suggestion to Crouch, who points to Llandeilo-Dynevor and Aberffro-Llangadwaladr as other examples. On the Caerleon dynasty and Machen see R. R. Davies, pp. 274–75, 282, and 291.

29. In "Minster Churches in the Landscape" John Blair observes that in Anglo-Saxon England "early minsters usually lay at some distance from their counterpart royal *villae* . . ." (*Anglo-Saxon Settlements*, ed. Della Hooke [Oxford, 1988], pp. 35–58, at 35).

30. Crouch drew my attention to the existence of the Bristol Abbey charter: presumably it is to be found in the Bristol Abbey cartulary in the Berkeley Castle Muniments (microfilm in Bodleian Library, MS film dep. 912), which I have not seen. It should be noted that Risca, Henllys, Betws, and Malpas in the uplands and the whole northern part of Gwynllŵg including Bedwellty are also excluded from de la Haye's charter. (St. Brides Wentlooge, Risca, and Henllys had come under Bassaleg's control, however, by the time it was handed over to Llandaff in 1235x1240 as the fourth document recorded in the confirmation of A.D. 1330, discussed in the Appendix above, makes clear.) Madeleine Gray has pointed out to me that documents in the Glamorgan Record Office (CL/Deeds II/Mon. 11 December 1585 and 13 July 1594) show that the later parish of St. Woolos (derived from St. Gwynllyw) included lands in Christchurch, Peterstone Wentlooge, Marshfield, and Betws, which probably reflect the earlier *territorium* of the *clas*. I wonder whether some of the eastern and northern portions of Gwynllŵg originally might also have been included in the former *parochia*, though the possible existence of yet another *clas* church whose *parochia* embraced these parts of Gwynllŵg, including the far north of the territory, should also be explored. Malpas is a potential candidate: founded by Winibald of Caerleon before 1122, it was a daughter house of the Cluniac monastery of Montacute. As with Bassaleg, there may, however, have been an antecedent foundation; *clas* churches could have a lasting impact on a region

after their institutional form had disappeared, as J. Wyn Evans shows in "The Survival of the *Clas* as an Institution in Medieval Wales: Some Observations on Llanbadarn Fawr," in *The Early Church in Wales and the West*, ed. Edwards and Lane, pp. 33–40.

31. Many parts of England and Wales have been well served by county historians, who have recorded information based on oral, written, and archaeological sources that have since been lost. Gwynllŵg has been most unfortunate in this regard. William Coxe's tour through Monmouthshire provided a useful record, but he never wrote up his notes from a subsequent visit. W. Haines in his "Memoir of the Author," published in the 2nd edition of Coxe's *A Historical Tour Through Monmouthshire*, ed. Edwin Davies (Brecon, 1904), states (p. xxviii): "Of his Tour through Monmouthshire, he evidently contemplated a second edition, as I have a large quantity of his notes—in MS.—taken on a subsequent tour through the county, many years afterwards." It is to be hoped that someone will trace these notes. Joseph Bradney's multi-volume *History of Monmouthshire* did not include Newport and Wentlooge. Madeleine Gray discovered among other notes and transcripts in the Bradney papers in the National Library of Wales at Aberystwyth "final drafts of chapters on most of the parishes in the Hundred of Newport, virtually ready to be printed" (Gray, "Bradney and the Hundred of Newport," *Gwent Local History*, 62 [Spring 1987], 17–18). Unfortunately, her edition for the South Wales Record Society appeared too late to be used in this paper: Sir Joseph Alfred Bradney, *A History of Monmouthshire from the Coming of the Normans down to the Present Time*, vol. 5, *The Hundred of Newport* (Cardiff, 1993). Included in Bradney's notes are early-17th-century surveys of the manors of Machen and Mynyddislwyn. Charles A. H. Green's useful *Notes on Churches in the Diocese of Llandaff*, 3 pts. (Aberdare, 1906–07), unfortunately does not add much of value on the churches contained in de la Haye's charter. Primary sources that need to be examined include the Bassaleg charters printed in Hearne's *Adami de Domerham* (n. 5 above), vol. 2, pp. 607–12, as well as other charters for Goldcliffe and Malpas Priories, surveys of the various manors in the district such as those for Wentlooge and Bassaleg in the Newport Central Library, and other records that will assist in determining parish boundaries such as the Kemeys Tynte Estate Plans (D/O KT E/1), fols. 20 and 39 in the Glamorgan Record Office, Cardiff, and stray literary references to Bassaleg such as *Vita Sancti Cadoci* 59, in *Vitae Sanctorum Britanniae et Genealogiae*, ed. and tr. Wade-Evans, p. 128 (text) and p. 129 (tr.).

32. The Bassaleg charters in Hearne (*Adami de Domerham*, vol. 2, pp. 607–12) mention a number of place-names not found in de la Haye's charter. The tithe maps for the area in the Gwent County Record Office in Cwmbran are less helpful than I had hoped, but some of the field names may provide insights. (Unfortunately, some of these maps

seem to have gone astray: I could trace them neither in Cwmbran nor in the Newport Central Library.) I doubt whether the work submitted by "Shon" to the National Eisteddfod of Wales held in Pontypool in 1924 entitled "Place Names of Monmouthshire" (the original is in the National Library of Wales with a copy in the Gwent County Record Office) will prove to be very useful, which is regrettable, as it is obviously a labor of love.

33. The area is ideal for a multidisciplinary landscape history project. Bassaleg church itself is a 19th-century building, but an examination of its environs might be revealing. Coxe reports in his *Historical Tour*, "A small gothic edifice, now a school-room, stands a few paces from the south side of the church, and was probably an ancient chapel" (p. 74). Roberts rightly urges that this should be investigated ("Welsh Ecclesiastical Place-Names," p. 42). I am reminded of the small Anglo-Saxon chapel separated only by a narrow road from the parish church in Bradford-on-Avon, Wilts. Multiple churches are a common feature of important ecclesiastical centers; it would be intriguing to know whether this "small gothic edifice" might originally have been a baptistery. Equally intriguing is Coxe's reference on p. 74 to "a ruined building at the distance of about a mile, in the midst of a deep sequestered forest, not far from the Rumney, on the confines of the Machen parish, which is by some supposed to be part of the original cell."

34. An 11th-century source reports it as represented only by a *presbyter*: W. Davies, *Early Welsh Microcosm*, pp. 125 and 137. She discusses the meaning of the word *presbyter* on pp. 126–27.

35. On Urban, see Crouch, "Urban: First Bishop of Llandaff," and R. R. Davies, pp. 179–80 and 182–83.

36. See Albert C. Reeves, "Newport," in *Boroughs of Mediaeval Wales*, ed. Ralph A. Griffiths (Cardiff, 1978), pp. 188–217.

37. In fact, in due course Bassaleg succumbed to Newport and Newport to Llandaff, so that eventually Bassaleg was to be found in the archdeaconry of Newport in the see of Llandaff: see *Taxatio Ecclesiastica Angliae et Walliae Auctoritate P. Nicholai IV. Circa A.D. 1291*, ed. Thomas Astle, Samuel Ayscough and John Caley, Record Commission (London, 1802), p. 278, and Arthur W. Wade-Evans, "Parochiale Wallicanum," *Y Cymmrodor*, 22 (1910), 22–124, p. 74.

38. Fitz Hamo was regularly in the company of Rufus, as numerous charters attest, and he was present on the fateful afternoon when Rufus was mortally wounded by an

arrow shot by a hunting companion. On Rufus see Frank Barlow, *William Rufus* (Berkeley, 1983).

39. Lynn H. Nelson discusses this event in *The Normans in South Wales, 1070–1171* (Austin, 1966), pp. 94–111. The "conquest of Glamorgan" has been rather overblown, as Crouch shows in "The Slow Death of Kingship," pp. 29–30. For Norman relationships with the area in the preceding reign of William the Conqueror, see A. G. Williams, "Norman Lordship in South-East Wales during the Reign of William I," *Welsh History Review*, 16 (1993), 445–66.

40. For the chronology of Herluin's abbacy see *The Heads of Religious Houses: England and Wales 940–1216*, ed. David Knowles, Christopher N. L. Brooke, and Vera C. M. London (Cambridge, 1972), p. 51.

41. The list appears in Sir Edward Stradling's "Winning of the Lordship of Glamorgan," written between 1561 and 1566, and in Rice Merrick's *Morganiae Archaiographia*, probably composed between 1578 and 1584. For an edition of the two works see Rice Merrick, *Morganiae Archaiographia: A Book of the Antiquities of Glamorganshire*, ed. Brian L. James, South Wales Record Society 1 (Barry Island, 1983). The date of composition of Merrick's book is given on p. xvi, that of Stradling's work on p. 147. The latter is edited on pp. 150ff.

42. Griffiths, "The Norman Conquest and the Twelve Knights of Glamorgan," provides strong evidence that the story of the twelve knights is a fiction. See also James' well-considered comments on the bardic origin of the story in *Morganiae Archaiographia*, pp. 147–49. Cennydd G. Traherne, "Presidential Address: The Conquest of Glamorgan," *Archaeologia Cambrensis*, 133 (1984), 1–7 and pls. I–IV, obviously would like to believe the story, though he cautiously suggests on p. 7 that it was formulated in the reign of Edward I as a result of the *Quo Warranto* inquests that followed the promulgation of the Statute of Gloucester in 1278.

43. The witness list reads (expansions italicized; modern punctuation): "His testib*us*: d*omi*no meo H. regis; d*omi*no Rob*er*to de Haia; Rannulfo d*omi*ni regis cancellario; Winebaldo de Balu*n*; Will*elm*o tunc vice*comi*te de Kaerd*iff*; Rob*er*to Sor; Rog*er*o de Sum*eri*; Rob*er*to fil*io* Joce; Herb*er*to de Sancto Q*ui*ntino; Laudomaro Ace; Aluredo de Nichol*as* 7 Rob*er*to fil*io* suo; & multis aliis." See Oxford, Trinity College 85 (Montacute Cartulary), fol. 86v (deposited in the Bodleian Library), calendared in *Two Cartularies of the Augustinian Priory of Bruton and the Cluniac Priory of Montacute in the County*

of Somerset, ed. Members of the Council (including H. C. Maxwell-Lyte and Thomas Scott Holmes), Somerset Record Society, 8 (London, 1894), pp. 182–83, no. 164, and *Regesta Regum Anglo-Normannorum, 1066–1154*, vol. 2, ed. Charles Johnson and Henry A. Cronne (Oxford, 1956), p. 168, no. 1307.

44. For further discussion of Rufus and Wales see Edward A. Freeman, *The Reign of William Rufus and the Accession of Henry the First*, 2 vols. (Oxford, 1882). On the feudal ties among fitz Hamo, de la Haye, and others see Charlotte A. Newman, *The Anglo-Norman Nobility in the Reign of Henry I: The Second Generation* (Philadelphia, 1988), p. 150, and for fitz Hamo's noble standing by A.D. 1100, p. 95.

45. Robert de la Haye also endowed Boxgrove Priory on his honor of Halnaker in Sussex: see *Chartulary of Boxgrove Priory*, ed. and tr. Lindsay Fleming (Lewes, 1960), pp. 16–17, and Newman, p. 76.

46. On the Norman colonization of Wales see R. R. Davies, pp. 97–100, esp. 99.

47. Later in the 12th century the Welsh were to provide the fastnesses for a temporarily successful assault on the Norman lands: see John E. Lloyd, *A History of Wales: From the Earliest Times to the Edwardian Conquest*, 3rd ed., 2 vols. (London, 1939), and R. R. Davies, pp. 274–75.

48. W. Davies, *Wales in the Early Middle Ages*, pp. 169–71.

49. The bones of David were allegedly deposited there, according to John of Glastonbury, by a "nobilis matrona, nomine Elswitha" in 962: *The Chronicle of Glastonbury Abbey: An Edition, Translation and Study of John of Glastonbury's Cronica sive Antiquitates Glastoniensis Ecclesie*, ed. James P. Carley, tr. David Townsend, rev. and enlarged ed. (Woodbridge, 1985), ch. 69, p. 130 (text) and p. 131 (tr.). Both saints were commemorated at Glastonbury, Gildas on 29 January and David on 1 March: see Francis Wormald, "The Liturgical Calendar of Glastonbury Abbey," in *Festschrift Bernhard Bischoff zu seinem 65. Geburtstag*, ed. Johanne Autenrieth and Franz Brunhölzl (Stuttgart, 1971), pp. 325–45, esp. 340–41.

50. James F. Edwards and Brian P. Hindle, "The Transportation System of Medieval England and Wales," *Journal of Historical Geography*, 17 (1991), 123–34, p. 131, Table 1, no. 52.

51. The sea route would have led up the coast past Weston-super-Mare and then north across the Mouth of the Severn to the estuary of the Usk, into which the Ebbw flowed.

52. M. D. Costen, "Dunstan, Glastonbury and the Economy of Somerset in the Tenth Century," in *St Dunstan: His Life, Times and Cult*, ed. Nigel Ramsay, Margaret Sparks, and Tim Tatton-Brown (Woodbridge, 1992), pp. 25–44, esp. 31–32 on the exploitation of the Somerset marshes and pp. 35–36 on the poor economic management of Glastonbury's large Somerset estates at the end of the Anglo-Saxon period. I owe this reference to R. Sharpe.

53. J. S. P. Tatlock, "Caradoc of Llancarfan," *Speculum*, 13 (1938), 139–52. On Arthur, Guinevere, and Glastonbury see "Vita Gildae," in *Chronica Minora Saec. IV. V. VI. VII*, vol. 3, ed. Theodor Mommsen, MGH, *Auctores Antiquissimi* 13 (Berlin, 1898), pp. 109–10.

54. Publications on Geoffrey are legion. A new series of editions of his *Historia* is now in progress: see *The Historia Regum Britannie of Geoffrey of Monmouth*. Vol. 1. *Bern, Burgerbibliothek, MS. 568*, ed. Neil Wright (Cambridge, 1985), which provides a helpful introductory bibliography. For a translation of his *Historia*, which was probably completed by 1138, see *The History of the Kings of Britain*, tr. Lewis Thorpe (Harmondsworth, 1966). Antonia Gransden provides an excellent critical introduction to the Glastonbury writings in "The Growth of the Glastonbury Traditions and Legends in the Twelfth Century," *Journal of Ecclesiastical History*, 27 (1976), 337–58, rpt. in her *Legends, Traditions and History in Medieval England* (London, 1992), pp. 153–74.

55. *De Principis Instructione Liber* I.20, in *Giraldi Cambrensis Opera*, ed. George F. Warner (London, 1891), pp. 3–329, pp. 126–29. For a translation see *The Autobiography of Giraldus Cambrensis*, ed. and tr. Harold E. Butler (London, 1937), pp. 119–21. Gerald has further comments in his *Speculum Ecclesiae* I.9, in *Giraldi Cambrensis Opera*, ed. John S. Brewer (London, 1873), pp. 48–50.

56. A convenient introduction is provided by Reginald F. Treharne, *The Glastonbury Legends: Joseph of Arimathea, The Holy Grail and King Arthur* (London, 1967), pp. 93–97. Gransden examines the story more critically in "The Growth," pp. 350–58.

57. Some of these arguments are presented by Clark H. Slover in "Glastonbury Abbey and the Fusing of English Literary Culture," *Speculum*, 10 (1935), 147–60; Bassaleg is

mentioned on p. 156. Certainly Arthur was later well-known in the region round Bassaleg. William Coxe noted at the beginning of the 19th century that there was a meadow about a mile from Bassaleg called Maes Arthur or 'field of Arthur' and that the Roman amphitheater was called by the locals "Arthur's Round Table": see *Historical Tour*, ed. Edwin Davies, pp. 74–75 and 94. Regrettably, it would obviously be improper to argue this as presumptive evidence of a knowledge of Arthur in the area in the early 12th century before Geoffrey of Monmouth wrote, more especially in the light of Gerald of Wales' charming story told in the *Itinerarium Kambriae* I.5 of the Welshman called Meilyr, who lived in the vicinity of Caerleon: when evil spirits oppressed him, they could be banished by the placing of St. John's Gospel on his breast, but they would return and linger for a greater length of time when Geoffrey of Monmouth's *Historia Regum Brittanie* was put there! See Giraldus Cambrensis, *Itinerarium Kambriae* I.5, in *Opera*, pp. 57–58. Apart from this nice insight into Gerald's view of Geoffrey's veracity, this does at least suggest that the literary portrayal of Arthur's exploits was already known in southeast Wales before the end of the 12th century.

58. For an introduction to the Arthurian cycle see *Arthurian Literature in the Middle Ages: A Collaborative History*, ed. Roger S. Loomis (Oxford, 1959). Unfortunately, there is no evidence that there were any reciprocal benefits for Bassaleg or for south Wales. Once Arthur's remains had been discovered, Glastonbury had more than enough pilgrims and local property for its monks to be fully engaged in the West Country. At some point between 1235 and early 1240, Bassaleg was farmed out to Llandaff in return for an annual payment; on the date, see the Appendix. It continued to be profitable for Glastonbury: the great *Valor Ecclesiasticus* undertaken on behalf of Henry VIII in 1535, just four years before the doughty last abbot of Glastonbury was hanged on the Tor, reveals that it was still providing an annual return in rent of £23 6s.8d.: *Valor Ecclesiasticus temp. Henr. VIII: Auctoritate Regia Institutus*, ed. John Caley, vol. 2 (London, 1802), p. 364.

59. Hearne, ed., *Adami de Domerham*, vol. 2, pp. 604–07; *Cartae et Alia Munimenta quae ad Dominium de Glamorgancia Pertinent*, ed. George T. Clark, 4 vols. (Cardiff, 1885–93). I have used the 2nd edition in six vols., ed. Godfrey L. Clark (Cardiff, 1910), 1.38, no. 35. The text was also inaccurately printed (*ex* Hearne) in William Dugdale, *Monasticon Anglicanum*, ed. John Caley, Henry Ellis, and Bulkeley Bandinel, 6 vols. in 8 (London, 1817–30, rpt. 1846), vol. 4, pp. 633–34. The document is no. 58 in my *Catalogue of English Post-Conquest Vernacular Documents* (Woodbridge, 1990), p. 84.

60. *The Peterborough Chronicle*, ed. Clark.

61. For example, CUL Ii.1.33 (s. xii[2]) and CCCC 303 (s. xii[1]). The two manuscripts are listed by Ker, *Catalogue*, pp. 23–27 and 99–105 (nos. 18 and 57, respectively). For other 12th-century manuscripts containing English see ibid., pp. xviii–xix.

62. For instance, Gwynedd O. Pierce, *The Place-Names of Dinas Powys Hundred* (Cardiff, 1968). Some place-name material is to be found in T. J. Morgan and Prys Morgan, *Welsh Surnames* (Cardiff, 1985).

63. Rather hesitantly I have retained the reading of A, with the sense 'the dappled fort', interpreting the first element as a variant of Welsh *din* 'a fort', which can be seen in the place-name Tenby (Pembrokeshire). There are, admittedly, problems with this reading: the provection of *d* to *t*, though not uncommon in English representations of Welsh, is unattested in this place-name element before 1230 (see M. Richards, "Some Welsh Place-Names Containing Elements Which Are Found in Continental Celtic," *Études Celtiques,* 13 [1972–73], p. 368, s.v. *DINBYCH*). The representation of *e* for *i* first appears (without provection) in this element only in 1294 (see Richards, p. 379, s.v. *DINAN*). Kitson has suggested the reading *melenbrith* 'speckled mill', though he notes it is an "odd name." Oliver J. Padel discusses the second element of the name in his *Cornish Place-Name Elements* (Nottingham, 1985), p. 32, s.v. **bryth*, where he notes the Old Welsh *i main brith* 'the speckled stone' and *lapis in i guoun breith* 'a stone in the mottled marsh'.

64. Kitson believes that this must refer to a river-name since he believes *inne* could not be used to signify attachment to a manor. The extent of the manor of "Dyueleis" is given in an Inquisition Post Mortem of 31 September 8 Ed. III (PRO, C.134/43), calendared in *Calendar of Inquisitions Post Mortem and Other Analogous Documents Preserved in the Public Record Office*, vol. 5, *Edward II* (London, 1908), p. 335. I owe this reference to Roberts.

65. *Henbon* could mean 'old stump', but Kitson has pointed out to me that the final *t* in Welsh *bont* 'bridge' is often lost. *Henbon* for *Henbont* thus seems more plausible.

66. The closeness of *Namelin* to *Kemelin* seems more than coincidental. Roberts notes that *Kemelin* represents Welsh *Cemlyn* 'curved lake'.

67. Roberts suggests that this represents **Rhyd y Cambren* 'ford of the bent tree'. Kitson argues that it instead should be interpreted (without *y*) as 'gambrel or swingle-tree ford'.

68. Roberts notes the Welsh *merbwll* 'stagnant pool', but I prefer to follow Kitson in interpreting this as Old English 'boundary creek'.

69. Kitson points out that this must be a small submersible place rather than a little inlet. One might suggest that it is the equivalent of the apparently Welsh word **pil* or **pyl* seen in such place-names as Pill, Milford Haven. See further Padel, pp. 185–86, s.v. **pyll*.

70. Alternatively, this may be interpreted as a place-name, 'to Stonehouse'.

The Influence of Anglo-Saxon Genesis Iconography on Later English Medieval Manuscript Art

Herbert R. Broderick

In his landmark article of 1944, "The Survival of Anglo-Saxon Illumination after the Norman Conquest,"[1] the late Francis Wormald presented a number of examples of the stylistic continuity between post-Conquest English manuscript art and its Anglo-Saxon antecedents, taking his examples as far forward in time as the early fourteenth-century Holkham Bible Picture Book (London, BL Add. 47682). That this continuity is also iconographic has been demonstrated most recently by K. E. Haney in her 1986 study of the twelfth-century Winchester Psalter (BL Cotton Nero C.iv).[2] I propose to show that this stylistic and iconographic continuity, especially in later English Genesis imagery, includes broader modes of pictorial organization as well as framing systems.[3]

For example, on fol. 5v (fig. 1) of the early thirteenth-century Bible of Robert de Bello (BL Burney 3),[4] the events of the six days of creation plus the seventh day of rest are presented within a series of overlapping discs that fill the confines of a great initial *I* at the beginning of the text of Genesis, followed by six additional roundels at the bottom of the folio that take the Genesis narrative up to the Sacrifice of Isaac at the bottom right. Although it is generally agreed that the earliest extant historiated Genesis *I* initial with scenes of the Creation in discs is to be found on fol. 6r of the late eleventh-century Goderannus Bible from Lobbes (Tournai, Bibl. du Seminaire 1),[5] it should be noted that the earlier Creation images on pages 6 (fig. 2) and 7 (fig. 3) of the so-called "Cædmon" manuscript at Oxford

(Bodleian Library Junius 11)[6] of c. 1000 are the first extant images to our knowledge that present the familiar cosmic discs essentially as frames, overlapping each other on a vertical axis as they do in the later de Bello Bible image. While not associated in the Anglo-Saxon Junius manuscript with the letter *I* of a Latin Vulgate text, and by no means an initial, the striking format of the Junius images may well have been dictated, as I have demonstrated in detail elsewhere, by the often ill-suited and irregular blank spaces left to the illustrator either by the scribe or by the "designer" of the manuscript's illustrative program.[7] The artist of the Junius manuscript was most likely working from a model more on the order of what one sees in the Cotton Genesis—inspired imagery of the thirteenth-century San Marco mosaics, where the Creator stands at the left of the cosmic circle to the right.[8] In choosing to stack as well as overlap his cosmic circles like so many poker chips, the Junius artist incorporated his Creator-figures within their circumference, in all three instances located centrally on axis, unlike the de Bello artist who retains his Creator figures at the left.

Unfortunately, it is not known where the de Bello Bible was created,[9] but the traditional hypothesis of a Canterbury provenance might be strengthened by virtue of the association of the Genesis initial's composition with the format of the Anglo-Saxon Junius illustration, a manuscript, however, whose own Canterbury provenance is also by no means certain.[10]

One further detail serves to link the de Bello initial with Anglo-Saxon tradition, and that is the representation of the Creation of Light and the Separation of Light from Darkness by the Fall of the Rebel Angels into the upturned jaws of Hell at the far right of the first disc at the top of the initial. On fol. 2r of the so-called Hexateuch of Ælfric (fig. 4) (BL Cotton Claudius B.iv), as pointed out already by C. R. Dodwell, we have possibly the earliest extant example in medieval art of the Creation of Light as the Creation of the Angels, which is in conformity with an exegetical tradition subscribed to by Augustine, among others, as well as the earliest surviving illustrated example of the Separation of Light from Darkness as the Fall of Lucifer and the Rebel Angels,[11] although the actual Fall is illustrated even earlier (c. 1000) on page 3 (fig. 5) of the Junius manuscript where the motif of the upturned jaws of Hell is quite prominent and the depiction of Lucifer/Satan as a demonic, animalized creature is to be seen.[12]

Looking forward to the fourteenth century, it is possible to see the continued influence of many of the Anglo-Saxon pictorial devices discussed above. On fol. 1v of the early fourteenth-century Queen Mary Psalter (BL Royal 2 B.vii),[13] for example, the Creation of the World (fig. 6) is directly associated with the Fall of Lucifer and the Rebel Angels in a spare and elegant schematic illustration. In fact, almost all the individual elements of this composite image are anticipated in Anglo-Saxon manuscript art of the late tenth and early eleventh centuries. The distinctive "diagrammatic" mode of representing the Creation in the Queen Mary image as a series of interlinked circles, for instance, as well as the large compass held by the Creator in his right hand, recall the specifically Anglo-Saxon creation "diagram" to be found on fol. 7v (fig. 7) of the mid-eleventh-century Tiberius Psalter (BL Cotton Tiberius C.vi) as explicated by Adelheid Heimann.[14] Yet the particular symmetrical presentation in the Queen Mary Psalter image of the upturned jaws of Hell with the Creator seated frontally on axis above may owe much to the Fall of Lucifer scene, on the first of the Fitzwilliam Museum leaves (fig. 8) illuminated by William de Brailes in the second quarter of the thirteenth century (Cambridge, Fitzwilliam Museum 330, leaf 1).[15]

In major, as well as minor, ways the continuity of Anglo-Saxon iconographic innovation as well as the transmission of much older pictorial iconography is evident in post-Anglo-Saxon manuscript illustration. A seemingly minor detail, again also from the Queen Mary Psalter, further enhances this assessment. In an article entitled "History, Typology and Homily: The Joseph Cycle in the Queen Mary Psalter,"[16] the author, Kathryn A. Smith, makes a number of interesting suggestions with reference to establishing more clearly the *Sitz im Leben* of the manuscript and its imagery. In the author's own words,

> The starting point for this study is the discovery of a representation of the dove-topped *virga*—an element of the royal regalia depicted in several works associated with Plantagenet patronage—in the Joseph narrative in the Old Testament cycle at the beginning of the manuscript.[17]

In the lower of the two illustrations on fol. 15v of the manuscript (fig. 9), Joseph is shown being presented to Pharaoh seated at the right holding in his hand the distinctive bird-topped scepter.[18] While noting that this distinctive dove-topped "rod of virtue and equity" appears on the seals of most of the English kings, starting with Edward the Confessor (1042–66),[19] the author does not mention that Pharaoh is shown prominently enthroned and bearing a bird-topped scepter on fol. 68v of the Anglo-Saxon illustrated Hexateuch of Ælfric of c. 1050 (fig. 10).[20] Such a bird-topped staff is an attribute of Roman gods and emperors,[21] but it may well be a contemporary royal reference in the Hexateuch as well. The presence of this seemingly minor motif in the Hexateuch in no way diminishes Smith's interpretation of Plantagenet program in the later Queen Mary Psalter, but it does indeed demonstrate the important role that Anglo-Saxon manuscript art sometimes plays in the transmission of iconographic motifs often quite far forward in time.

On fol. 4v of New York, Pierpont Morgan Library 791 (fig. 11), the Frontispiece to the so-called "Lothian Bible," an English work of c. 1220,[22] we find a significant number of individual iconographic details as well as aspects of format and framing that point directly toward Anglo-Saxon sources. In 1967 George Henderson indicated this. He suggested a possible connection to Anglo-Saxon manuscript art in the depiction in the first roundel at the bottom left of the page (fig. 12) of the Creation of Light represented by two angels holding bowls of "flaming" light similar to those unusual symbols of light carried upside down by angels on pages 6 (fig. 2) and 7 (fig. 3) of the Junius 11 manuscript.[23] While it is unusual, this motif of bowls of light is not unique, as it was also found on fol. 8v of the now destroyed twelfth-century *Hortus Deliciarum* manuscript, as John Plummer pointed out in his 1953 study of the Lothian Bible.[24] What is unusual about the Junius 11 image is the action of the angels on pages 6 and 7 pouring light out of an overturned vessel.[25] This mode of representing Day or Light as angels with bowls of light is distinctly different from the iconographic traditions of both the Cotton Genesis and the Byzantine Octateuchs, where, for example, in Vatican Library, Codex graecus 747 Day or Light is represented on fol. 15r as a torch-bearing figure.[26] What we may have in the motif of angels with bowls of light is a distinctly Latin, Western, and perhaps specifically Anglo-Saxon mode of representing this phenomenon.[27] That this motif was more widely available in Anglo-Saxon England is attested to, as Barbara Raw has pointed out, by its presence on fol. 81v of Oxford, St. John's College 28, as well as a related image on fol. 81r of the Anglo-Saxon Psalter from Bury St. Edmunds (Vatican, Reg. lat. 12).[28]

Further evidence of Anglo-Saxon influence on the Lothian composition is provided by a closer look at fol. 2v (fig. 13) of BL Cotton Galba A.xviii, one of two pictorial additions of the tenth century thought to have been added at Winchester to the ninth-century Athelstan Psalter,[29] where, at the upper left of a composition organized into horizontal registers showing Christ at the center with choirs of saints and angels at left and right, one can see an angel to the left of Christ who appears to hold a flaming vase of light.[30] Whether this "light-bearing" angel is meant to be Lucifer before his fall is not clear, but the fact that light is presented in this form is indeed significant, as are other aspects of this image. Of special note are the four ferocious lion-like beasts who both grasp and bite the frame at its four corners. This nice bit of Anglo-Saxon brutishness[31] is echoed in the Lothian image by the two tiny beast heads at the lower left of the composition, the finale, if you will, of a complex framing system consisting of these beasts' elaborately intertwined bodies (fig. 11).

The seated Trinity at the top center of the Lothian folio gives evidence as well of additional Anglo-Saxon influence, as God the Father is shown grasping the frame at left and right from within its confines. The manner is reminiscent of such powerful and expressive images as that of Satan at the lower left of the Frontispiece to the

Hexateuch of Ælfric (fol. 2r), who grasps his once bright frame of light with his own hands from within the frame itself (fig. 4), or perhaps in an even more compelling image, of the frightful *Blemmya* represented on fol. 82r (fig. 14) of the eleventh-century illustrated *Marvels of the East* (BL Cotton Tiberius B.v). This peculiarly Anglo-Saxon penchant for representing figures in the field grasping from within its confines the frame that surrounds them, thus rendering the frame a tactile and reified object,[32] can be observed in the context of an English twelfth-century representation of the Trinity on fol. 6r of Cambridge, Pembroke College 120, an illustrated gospels possibly from Bury St. Edmunds.[33] The probable relationship of both the Pembroke Trinity and the Lothian image to the extraordinary Anglo-Saxon Trinity on fol. 1r of BL Harley 603 is worth reiterating at this point.[34]

Further and even more curious details of the Lothian image may find their explanation in Anglo-Saxon iconography. In his study of the Lothian manuscript John Plummer noted that some of the angels on fol. 4v of that manuscript are shown, oddly enough, as tonsured figures,[35] to be seen at the left and right of the seated Trinity in the second register up from the bottom (figs. 11 and 12). Although one might seriously question whether these figures are really meant to be angels at all, they nevertheless might be seen as resembling very closely the tonsured members of the chorus of Martyrs and Confessors to be seen on fol. 21r (fig. 15) of the Athelstan Psalter (BL Cotton Galba A.xviii). Finally, might not the four "enigmatic" heads observed by Plummer at the four corners of the frame of the Lothian image[36] (fig. 11) be seen as the four winds, such as they are depicted at the top left and right of fol. 21r of the Athelstan image?

In terms of several specific iconographic details, then, as well as broader modes of pictorial organization and framing, the thirteenth-century Lothian Bible Frontispiece would indeed seem to owe much to Anglo-Saxon precedent, especially the several motifs that we were able to indicate on fols. 2v and 21r of the Athelstan Psalter. Konrad Hoffmann, in the 1970 catalogue to *The Year 1200* exhibition at the Metropolitan Museum of Art in New York, attempted to cast serious doubt on Henderson's 1967 suggestion of a link to earlier Anglo-Saxon manuscript art in this important masterpiece of thirteenth-century English illumination.[37] We have been able to bring forward here even more compelling evidence of the preservation of earlier Anglo-Saxon iconography and compositional predilections by linking the de Bello Bible initial, the Lothian Frontispiece, and the Creation diagram of the Queen Mary Psalter to specific Anglo-Saxon works of the tenth and eleventh centuries.

A final word about the transmission of iconographic motifs as well as their preservation reminds us to recall that, as Robert Deshman has indicated, Cain and Abel appear at either side of Christ on fol. 2v (fig. 13) of the Athelstan Psalter with their respective offerings in their hands. Deshman convincingly demonstrated the important connection of Cain and Abel to Last Judgment iconography.[38] It is worth noting at this point that the image of God as Christ seated *between* Cain and Abel is an important Early Christian iconography,[39] a motif, interestingly enough, extremely rare in later medieval art but to be seen quite clearly and prominently on fol. 8v (fig. 16) of the eleventh-century Hexateuch of Ælfric. We find a later, and much altered, version of this unusual image on fol. 5r (fig. 17) of the fourteenth-century Holkham Bible Picture Book (BL Add. 47682), where the seated Creator has been replaced by a fleece-clad Adam, shown between his sons Cain and Abel.[40]

Anglo-Saxon manuscript art, then, plays an important role in preserving and transmitting multiple iconographic motifs, often greatly transformed, from the art of Early Christian Rome to the High Middle Ages in England as well as on the Continent.

LEHMAN COLLEGE, CUNY

Figure 1. London, BL Burney 3, fol. 5v. By permission of the British Library.

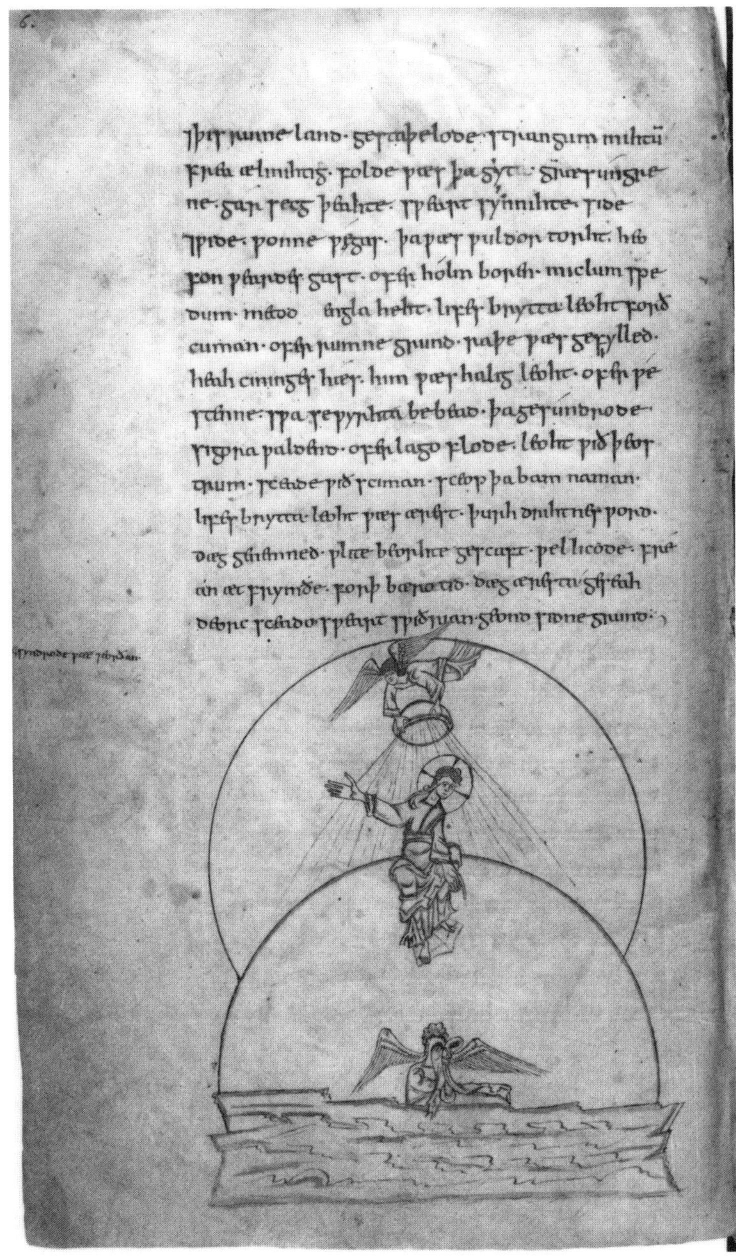

Figure 2. Oxford, Bodleian Library Junius 11, p. 6. By permission of the Bodleian Library, Oxford.

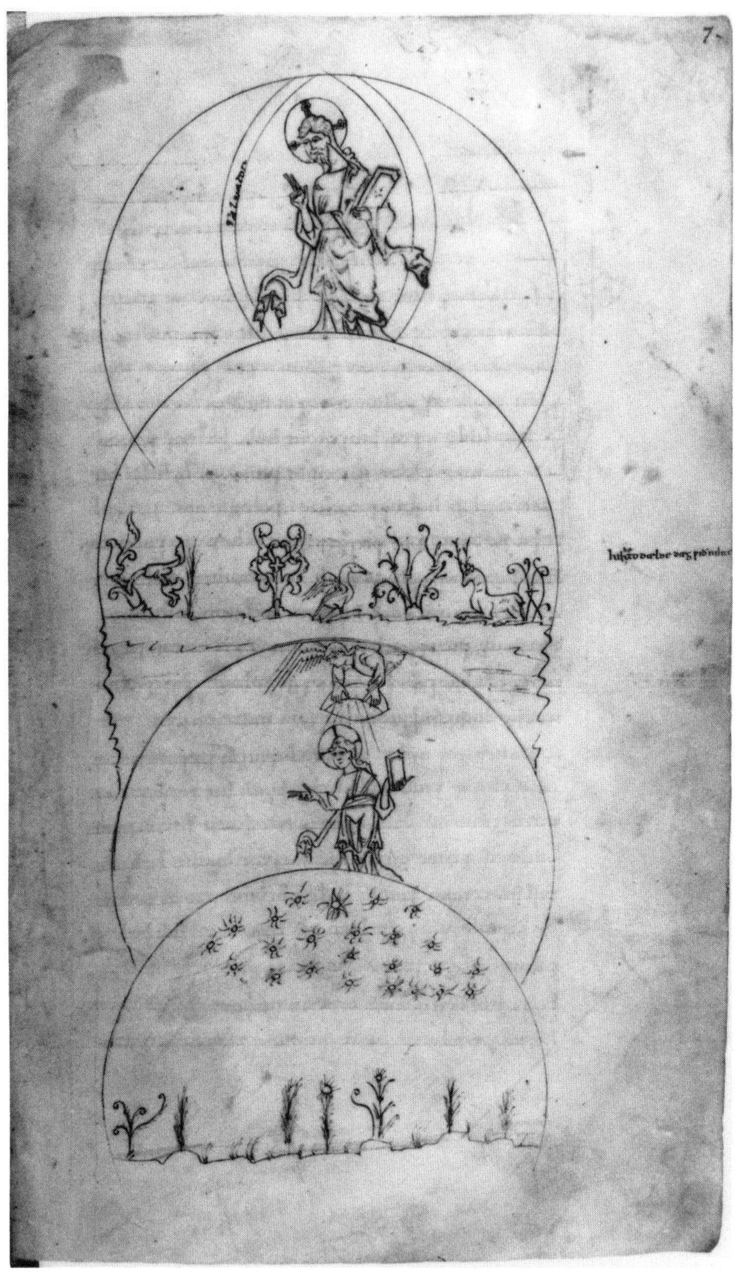

Figure 3. Oxford, Bodleian Library Junius 11, p. 7. By permission of the Bodleian Library, Oxford.

Figure 4. London, BL Cotton Claudius B.iv, fol. 2r. By permission of the British Library.

Figure 5. Oxford, Bodleian Library Junius 11, p. 3. By permission of the Bodleian Library, Oxford.

Figure 6. London, BL Royal 2 B.vii, fol. 1v. By permission of the British Library.

Figure 7. London, BL Cotton Tiberius C.vi, fol. 7v. By permission of the British Library.

Figure 8. Cambridge, Fitzwilliam Museum 330, leaf 1. By permission of the Fitzwilliam Museum.

Figure 9. London, BL Royal 2 B.vii, fol. 15v. By permission of the British Library.

Figure 10. London, BL Cotton Claudius B.iv, fol. 68v. By permission of the British Library.

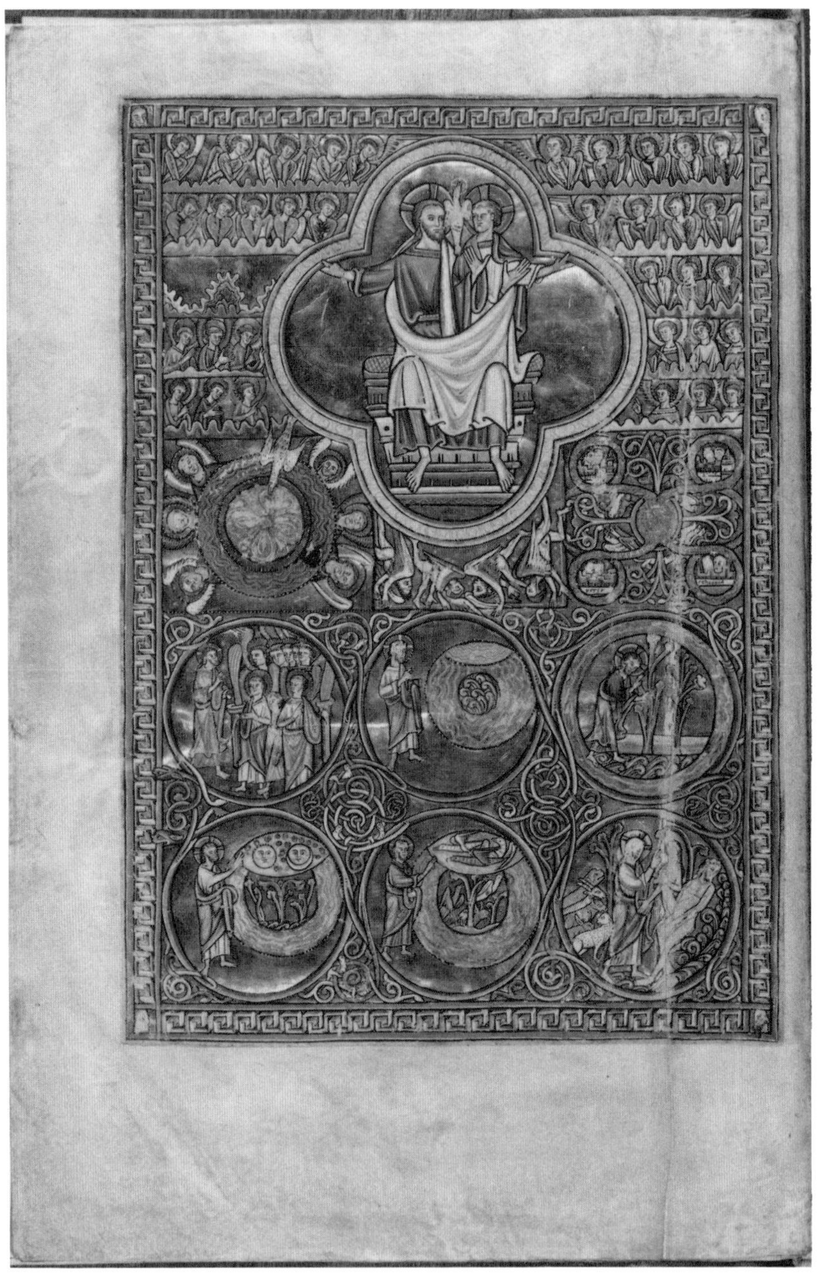

Figure 11. The Pierpont Morgan Library, New York, M. 791, fol. 4v. By permission of The Pierpont Morgan Library.

Figure 12. The Pierpont Morgan Library, New York, M. 791, fol. 4v (detail). By permission of The Pierpont Morgan Library.

Figure 13. London, BL Cotton Galba A.xviii, fol. 2v. By permission of the British Library.

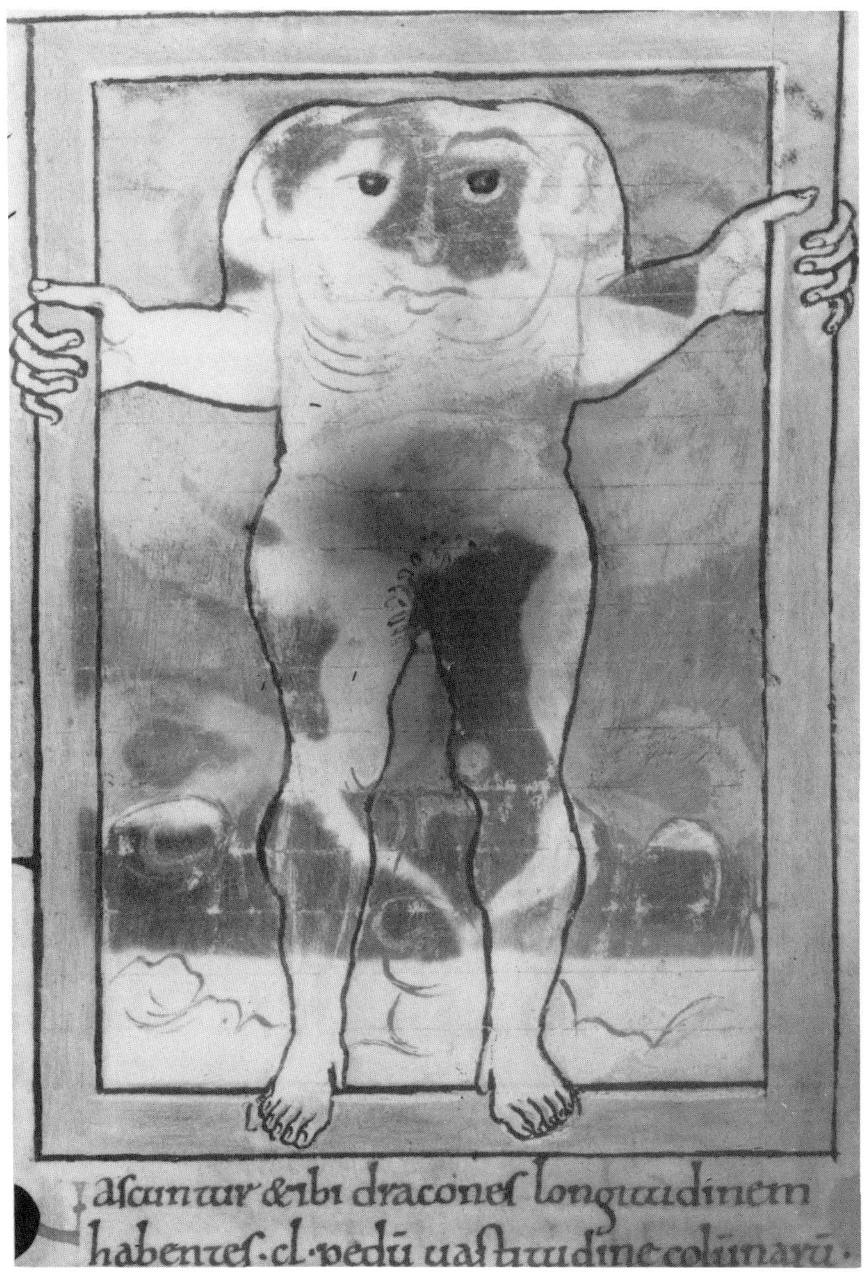

Figure 14. London, BL Cotton Tiberius B.v, fol. 82r. By permission of the British Library.

Figure 15. London, BL Cotton Galba A.xviii, fol. 21r. By permission of the British Library.

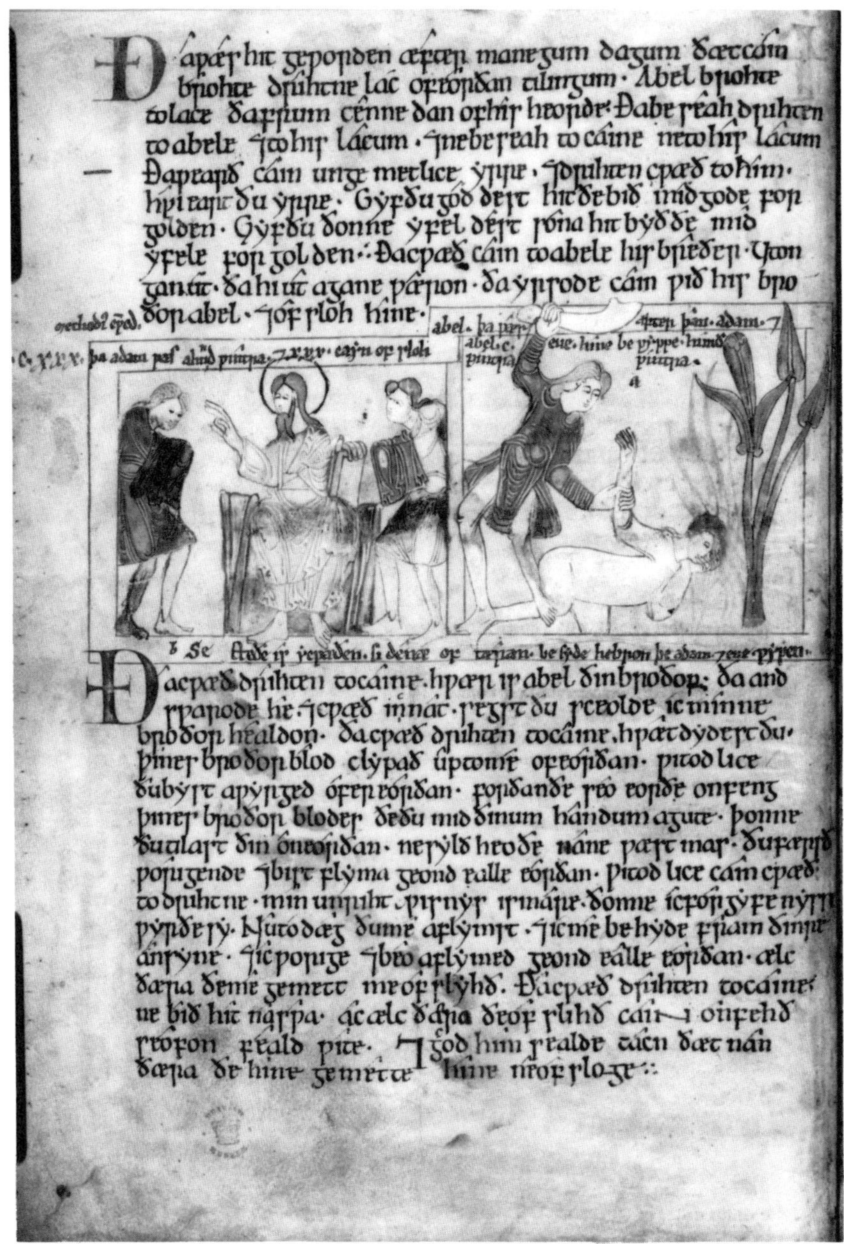

Figure 16. London, BL Cotton Claudius B.iv, fol. 8v. By permission of the British Library.

Figure 17. London, BL Add. 47682, fol. 5r. By permission of the British Library.

NOTES

1. Francis Wormald, "The Survival of Anglo-Saxon Illumination after the Norman Conquest," *Proceedings of the British Academy*, 30 (1944), 1–19.

2. Kristine Edmondson Haney, *The Winchester Psalter: An Iconographic Study* (Leicester, 1986).

3. The ideas presented in this paper come from research done for a book-length study I am completing entitled "Genesis Illustration in Medieval England: The Anglo-Saxon Achievement." This research was supported by a Fellowship for Independent Study and Research from the National Endowment for the Humanities, as well as three awards from the Research Foundation of the City Univ. of New York. In addition, an award from the George N. Shuster Fellowship Fund of Lehman College, CUNY, for which I am most grateful, helped defray photographic expenses for this publication.

4. See Nigel Morgan, *Early Gothic Manuscripts*, vol. 1, A Survey of Manuscripts Illuminated in the British Isles 4, ed. J. J. G. Alexander (London, 1982) (hereafter, Morgan I), #63, pp. 109–10. The initial is illustrated in color in J. J. G. Alexander, *The Decorated Letter* (New York, 1978), pl. 28.

5. For the manuscript as a whole see Don Denny, "The Historiated Initials of the Lobbes Bible," *Revue Belge d'Archéologie et d'Histoire de l'Art*, 45 (1976/77), 3–26. For the Genesis initial itself see pp. 3–4, and p. 17, where the author notes possible connections of the Lobbes image with Anglo-Saxon precedents. The Lobbes initial is also illustrated in Johannes Zahlten, *Creatio mundi: Darstellungen der sechs Schöpfungstage und naturwissenschaftliches Weltbilt im Mittelalter* (Stuttgart, 1979), fig. 74, and p. 58.

6. For an extended discussion of the images on these two pages of the manuscript, as well as relevant prior bibliography on the manuscript as a whole, see pp. 109–40 of my 1978 Columbia Univ. Diss., "The Iconographic and Compositional Sources of the Drawings in Oxford, Bodleian Library MS Junius 11" (hereafter, Broderick).

7. H. R. Broderick, "Observations on the Method of Illustration in MS Junius 11 and the Relationship of the Drawings to the Text," *Scriptorium*, 38 (1983), 161–77.

8. Conveniently illustrated in black and white in Kurt Weitzmann and Herbert L. Kessler, *The Cotton Genesis: British Library Codex Cotton Otho B.VI* (Princeton, 1986),

figs. 3–5, 12. For the entire sequence of the mosaics see Otto Demus, *The Mosaics of San Marco in Venice* (Chicago, 1984).

9. Morgan I, p. 110.

10. For a summary of the provenance question see Broderick, pp. 44–52; more recently, the articles by P. J. Lucas, "MS Junius 11 and Malmesbury, I," *Scriptorium*, 34 (1980), 212–20, and pt. 2, *Scriptorium*, 35 (1981), 3–15, where the author makes a case for Malmesbury as the manuscript's place of origin, an attribution questioned by A. N. Doane, *Genesis A: A New Edition* (Madison, 1978), p. 24.

11. See C. R. Dodwell and Peter Clemoes, *The Old English Illustrated Hexateuch*, EEMF 18 (1974), p. 17, where Dodwell does not claim that the Hexateuch image is the earliest extant illustration of these two events.

12. Broderick, pp. 91–108.

13. Reproduced in facsimile with descriptive notes and introduction by Sir George Warner, *Queen Mary's Psalter, Miniatures and Drawings by an English Artist of the 14th Century* (London, 1912). For description and bibliography see L. F. Sandler, *Gothic Manuscripts: 1285–1385*, vol. 2, A Survey of Manuscripts Illuminated in the British Isles 5 (London, 1986) (hereafter, Sandler II), #56, pp. 64–66.

14. Adelheid Heimann, "Three Illustrations from the Bury St. Edmunds Psalter and Their Prototypes," *Journal of the Warburg and Courtald Institutes*, 29 (1966), 39, 43ff.; Elżbieta Temple, *Anglo-Saxon Manuscripts, 900–1066*, A Survey of Manuscripts Illuminated in the British Isles 2 (London, 1976), #98, pp. 115–17.

15. See Morgan I, #72a, p. 118, for description and bibliography. The majority of Anglo-Saxon examples of the "animalized" jaws of Hell show them in a profile or three-quarter view. The upturned, symmetrical representation of these jaws of Hell opening directly upward appears to originate in the 12th-century version of the Utrecht Psalter manuscript known as the Eadwine Psalter (Cambridge, Trinity College Library R.17.1); see D. Tselos, "English Manuscript Illustration and the Utrecht Psalter," *Art Bulletin*, 41 (1959), fig. 2 (fol. 3v). The origins of the "animalized" Hell mouth in Anglo-Saxon art have been explored by Joyce Galpern, "The Shape of Hell in Anglo-Saxon England," Diss. Univ. of California, Berkeley, 1977, pp. 119–54.

The manner in which the four semicircles are linked together with the circle in the center framing the seated Creator in the Fitzwilliam leaf is reminiscent of the *schema* known as the "Harmony of the Elements," intended to accompany medieval texts of Bede's *De Natura Rerum*. This and other symbolic *schemata* are discussed by H. Bober, "An Illustrated Medieval School-Book of Bede's 'De Natura Rerum,'" in *The Journal of the Walters Art Gallery*, 19–20 (1956–57), esp. p. 84 and fig. 5. See also Zahlten, pp. 133–44, where the relationship of the Four Elements to the Creation of the World is discussed in some detail.

The format of the quatrefoil-like four circles of the Queen Mary Psalter image is even closer to a second image of the Fall of Lucifer from the deBrailes workshop, fol. 24r of Baltimore, Walters Art Gallery 106, reproduced as fig. 235 in Morgan I, catalogue #71. It is also probable that the four circles in the Queen Mary Psalter image signify the first four days of Creation, as the very next image in the Psalter on fol. 2r represents the work of the fifth and sixth days.

16. Kathryn A. Smith, "History, Typology and Homily: The Joseph Cycle in the Queen Mary Psalter," *Gesta*, 32.2 (1993), 147–59.

17. Ibid., p. 147.

18. In its various pictorial forms it is not altogether clear whether a dove is specifically represented.

19. Smith, p. 149.

20. See n. 11 above.

21. W. Kroll and K. Witte, eds., *Paulys Realencyclopädie der classischen Altertumswissenschaft* (Munich, 1921), article, "*Sceptrum*," 368–72. Smith, p. 157, n. 11, cites as well examples of bird-topped rods or scepter in Ottonian manuscript illustrations of the 10th and 11th centuries.

22. Morgan I, #32, pp. 79–81. Folio 4v is illustrated in color in W. von den Steinen, *Homo Caelestis*, vol. 2 (Munich, 1965), color pl. preceding pl. 239.

23. George Henderson, "Studies in English Manuscript Illumination, II," *Journal of the Warburg and Courtauld Institutes*, 30 (1966), 128–29.

24. John H. Plummer, "The Lothian Morgan Bible: A Study in English Illumination of the Early Thirteenth Century," Diss. Columbia Univ. 1953, p. 68. For an illustration of the *Hortus* illustration see Zahlten, fig. 342.

25. See Broderick, pp. 112–15, for an explanation of this motif and action.

26. Illustrated as fig. 3 in H. R. Broderick, "Observations on the Creation Cycle of the Sarajevo Haggadah," *Zeitschrift für Kunstgeschichte*, 48 (1984), 320–32.

27. Plummer, p. 68.

28. Barbara Raw, "The Drawing of an Angel in MS 28, St. John's College, Oxford," *Journal of the Warburg and Courtauld Institutes*, 18 (1955), 318–19.

29. See Temple, #5, pp. 36–37.

30. See Robert Deshman, "Anglo-Saxon Art after Alfred," *Art Bulletin*, 56 (1974), 181, n. 24, where the author identifies this figure in the topmost register of the image as an angel who "seems to offer a vessel, perhaps a misunderstanding of the model." That the vessel may be meant to contain "rays" of light, rather than "stalks" of grain as in the case of Cain, below at the right, finds possible corroboration in such images as that of *Lux* on the lower left of fol. 51r of the St. Bertin Gospels (New York, Pierpont Morgan Library 333) illustrated in color in Alexander (see n. 4 above), pl. 21. A similar confusion of "stalks" and "rays" occurs at the upper right of fol. 5v of the Ripoll Bible (Vatican, Bibl. Apost. Vat., Vat. lat. 5729), where a personification of Day or Light is shown holding what appear to be stalks or flowers in its right hand. These "flower stalks" were no doubt originally meant to be rays of light from a torch similar to that of a similar personification in the Vatican Octateuch, Codex graecus 747 (see n. 26 above). The Ripoll image is illustrated as fig. 54 in Zahlten.

31. See my remarks on this aspect of the Athelstan image in H. R. Broderick, "Some Attitudes toward the Frame in Anglo-Saxon Manuscripts of the Tenth and Eleventh Centuries," *Artibus et Historiae*, 5 (1982), 31–32.

32. Ibid., pp. 32–33.

33. Illustrated as fig. 101 in C. M. Kauffmann, *Romanesque Manuscripts, 1066–1190*, A Survey of Manuscripts Illuminated in the British Isles 3 (London, 1975), #35, pp. 74–75.

34. Illustrated as fig. 210 in Temple. See also Plummer, pp. 58–59.

35. Plummer, p. 61.

36. Ibid., p. 77.

37. Konrad Hoffmann, *The Year 1200*, vol. 1 (New York, 1970), p. 264.

38. See Deshman, p. 181.

39. For several Roman examples in mosaic as well as carved sarcophagi, see Lieselotte Kötzsche-Breitenbruch, *Die neue Katakombe an der Via Latina in Rom: Untersuchungen zur Ikonographie der alttestamentlichen Wandmalereien*, Jahrbuch für Antike und Christentum, Ergänzungsband 4 (Münster, 1976), p. 49, esp. nn. 295, 296.

40. See Sandler II, #97, pp. 105–06.

Present State and Future Directions: Art and Archaeology

Anglo-Saxon Art: So What's New?

†Robert Deshman

That the art of the Anglo-Saxons is one of their most brilliant and visible achievements is obvious. Illustrations of the icons of Anglo-Saxon art are all but obligatory in survey books, and Anglo-Saxon exhibitions attract large audiences, including many who know little of the culture that created it. In a volume devoted to the issues of the preservation and transmission of that culture, it is appropriate to take stock of what we know and want to know about Anglo-Saxon art, and to ask how that knowledge can contribute to our understanding of the larger culture.

A few words should be said at the outset about the preservation of the works themselves. We undoubtedly possess only a minute and random sampling of what once was. Virtually nothing remains of frescoes, textiles, and major precious metalwork, and even in better preserved media there are enormous gaps of preservation. We would give much to know about the manuscripts or, for that matter, anything else that Canterbury artists made in the century after Augustine. Archaeologists will continue to unearth some new Hiberno-Saxon sculpture and metalwork, and neglected or misattributed works such as the Brussels Cross[1] or the Nether Wallop frescoes[2] might be rediscovered. Nonetheless, we probably cannot hope for very much more than we already have.

To help fill this void there are the scattered, incidental mentions of Anglo-Saxon art in the written sources. Over 30 years ago Lehmann-Brockhaus[3] compiled a massive compendium of these sources, but only recently did C. R. Dodwell[4] systematically comb these in an effort to glean a new perspective on the art and artists. He found much useful information, though it is not always easy to distinguish between reality and rhetoric in the sources. As valuable as this enterprise is, the gulf between reading about and seeing a work of art is difficult to bridge: nothing written by the Anglo-Saxons registers the vast differences between the evangelist portraits in the eighth-century Lichfield Gospels and the eleventh-century Grimbald Gospels.[5] A picture is still worth a thousand words, and the surviving monuments will undoubtedly remain the primary source for the study of Anglo-Saxon art.

In the last few decades the task of research has been greatly facilitated by a trend to make these works more accessible through comprehensive publications. *A Survey of Manuscripts Illuminated in the British Isles*, edited and partly authored by Jonathan Alexander,[6] has given us convenient, reliable catalogues of almost all the miniature paintings, and Thomas Ohlgren's supplementary index of iconography and reproductions makes these volumes even more useful.[7] The continuing publication of facsimiles[8] has also done much to improve access to the material, though their ever-increasing expense limits their circulation. As far as ivory carvings are concerned, there is John Beckwith's corpus,[9] though its attributions and datings should always be weighed against those in the older catalogues of Longhurst[10] and Goldschmidt,[11] which have not lost their value. Rosemary Cramp's monumental corpus of pre-Conquest stone carving promises to revolutionize the study of this medium.[12] At long last we shall have ready access to good quality reproductions and up-to-date information and analysis of the enormous amount of surviving sculpture. The last decade has also seen a series of major exhibitions of Insular, Anglo-Saxon, and Viking art.[13] It goes without saying that these projects of systematic documentation and display have placed the study of Anglo-Saxon art on a much more solid footing. The more essential issue, however, is what kind of edifice is to be built on this foundation.

The traditional questions we have posed about a work of art are when and where it was made, and what were its sources. To answer them we have analyzed style, ornament, and iconography and correlated the results of these art-historical investigations with the complementary evidence of provenance, paleography, text, archaeology, and history. Our efforts have met with mixed success, especially in the case of the Hiberno-Saxon art.

No one needs to be reminded of just how unsure we are of exactly where and when most of the pre-Carolingian Insular illuminated manuscripts were produced. Of the great northern Gospel books, only Lindisfarne can be dated and localized with any confidence. There does seem to be a growing consensus that both Durrow and Kells are Iona products,[14] though we shall probably never be certain and there is still a wide latitude in dating. At least the sculpture has the advantage of being located where it was made, but then it also has the disadvantage that we can only arrange it in a loose relative chronology. And "wild cards" like the Reculver Cross, whose date oscillates between the seventh and tenth centuries,[15] continue to bedevil the game. The evidence for the dating and localization of Hiberno-Saxon art is at best fragmentary and difficult to interpret, and how much more so when the issues are inflamed by nationalistic concerns. The division of Insular art into Irish and Anglo-Saxon camps will probably continue to be a major scholarly preoccupation, though for what it is worth, this North American observer shares the view of Wilhelm Koehler[16] that the problem is of secondary importance.

If we turn to later Anglo-Saxon art, here too the traditional thrust of scholarship has been dating and localization. More abundant evidence of all sorts has allowed us to construct a more or less secure relative and absolute chronology for the illuminated manuscripts, and this in turn has paid dividends for other, stylistically related media. We are also fortunate to be able to place many of the manuscripts in major centers. As early as 1912, Otto Homburger[17] was able to write a book on the late tenth-century illuminations of a major scriptorium, Winchester. I would not want to hold my breath waiting for the first art-historical monograph on an Hiberno-Saxon scriptorium. We owe an incalculable debt to Francis Wormald, who with equal expertise in art history, paleography, and liturgy established an enduring framework for the study of later Anglo-Saxon art.[18] Subsequent advances in our knowledge of tenth- and eleventh-century paleography[19] have for the most part only validated the acuity of his judgments. Occasionally, however, his towering authority might have lulled us into complacency.

In one of his last papers, for instance, Wormald dated two evangelist portraits added to an eighth-century Irish pocket Gospels in the British Library to the first half of the tenth century (fig. 1), suggesting that they stood at the "cross-ways" between the styles of the first half and the second half of the century.[20] He evidently believed they were painted at the same time as a scribe, *Eduuardus* the deacon, added a page of text (fol. 66) in a reformed Insular minuscule. Subsequent scholarship has echoed Wormald, dating the pictures c. 950.[21] This is questionable on several grounds. As David Dumville[22] has pointed out, the recent considerations of the manuscript have overlooked the fact that there were two separate phases of textual additions: the first c. 890–c. 930 by *Eduuardus* and the second at a later, as yet undetermined, date by another scribe. In any case there is no reason why the miniatures have to have been done at the same time as either of the added texts. The only valid dating criterion is the internal evidence of the style and ornament of the pictures. Wormald rightly emphasized their stylistic distance from illuminations of the first half of the century in the Galba (Athelstan) Psalter and the Bede Life of St. Cuthbert in Cambridge.[23] He did not mention that they are equally distant from the drawings made in the period around the middle of the century, which are in a carefully executed, plastic style,[24] and this casts doubt on the traditional dating. By far the best comparisons for the sketchy, contorted drapery and bright palette of the evangelist portraits are in the Benedictional of Æthelwold,[25] and they must be approximately contemporary with or even a bit later than this Winchester manuscript, which can be dated c. 973.

Wormald also attributed an unfinished drawing and a painted miniature and initial in a Boethius manuscript in Paris (figs. 2, 3) to an English artist working in the last quarter of the tenth century, and once again later scholarship has routinely repeated his opinion.[26] Yet even when the differences in medium are taken into account, the stylistic discrepancy between the two is so vast that one hand could not have possibly done them both. In fact, the drawing, which shows Boethius with Philosophy and three Muses, predates the paintings by about a quarter of a century. The Muses closely resemble the Women at the Tomb in Æthelwold's Benedictional (fig. 4).[27] The drawing has guide marks and uninked stylus lines (difficult to see in the reproduction) that allow the unfinished parts of its frame to be reconstructed with some assurance (fig. 5).[28] The manner in which the borders would have been systematically integrated with the composition by overlapping and other devices is strikingly similar to the methods used in the Winchester manuscript. The misdating of the drawing has obscured its importance for the genesis of the Winchester style during Æthelwold's episcopate (963–84).

So far, newer methodological approaches such as deconstruction that have begun to influence other fields of art history have, for better or worse, had little impact on the study of Anglo-Saxon art. But one trend in art history has sought to integrate art into its broader cultural context, and in this case Anglo-Saxonists have also begun to frame new questions regarding the interpretation of art and its historical and intellectual significance.

George Henderson's important *From Durrow to Kells* (1987) was written with the specific intent of viewing insular Gospel books from the novel perspectives of patronage and function rather than the accustomed ones of ornament and style.[29] The result is a breath of fresh air in the field, but it has to be admitted that anyone attempting such a feat faces daunting obstacles. Since most of the manuscripts float in a geographic and chronological limbo, to anchor them to specific personalities and events inevitably involves a high degree of speculation. Then again, the very nature of Hiberno-Saxon art creates much uncertainty about the proper limits and methods of interpretation.

Twentieth-century viewers have learned to respect and appreciate the aesthetic value of the abstract Insular style. We all know the images look "terrific," but what, if anything, do they mean? The Insular culture that produced them was highly intellectual and profoundly learned, and so in the last few decades there has been a tendency to assume that there must be conceptual content, often arcane and erudite, in the imagery. In the case of monuments like the Ruthwell and Bewcastle Crosses, the diversity and quantity of narrative subject matter erases any doubt that there is an underlying learned program. It is no accident that these crosses were the object of some of the earliest attempts to relate Hiberno-Saxon art to its specific intellectual and religious milieu. I refer to the pioneering studies of Saxl and Schapiro,[30] who both used art historical approaches developed for Mediterranean art. But these crosses are the exception rather than the rule. Most often Insular artists restricted themselves to ornament and evangelist portraits and symbols, and it is much harder to know whether these kinds of images were intended to communicate complex, learned symbolism.

A few examples of the dilemmas this can cause are instructive. Carl Nordenfalk[31] first suggested that the fish-man in the genealogical list of Luke in the Book of Kells (fig. 6) singles out the line with the name of the prophet Jonah (*IONA*) to draw our attention to the manuscript's presumed place of origin, Iona. When it emerged that *IONA* was not a contemporary name of the island, the argument was shifted. According to Meyvaert,[32] the artist wanted to draw our attention to the monastery's founder, St. Columba, whose name was etymologically associated with the prophet Jonah and *columba* 'dove'. Given the visual wit so abundant in the Book of Kells, the argument is appealing. But we should look again. Was the artist really "pointing to Jonah's name?"[33] The figure grabs the *t* of "fuit" and turns away from the column with the names of the prophets. Surely the artist would have shown him in more direct contact with the name of Jonah if he had intended to call attention to it. It is questionable whether this fishy figure has any more significance than the birds above and below him—all of which also grab the final letter of "fuit" opposite them. Valid arguments have been advanced for the Iona provenance of the Book of Kells, but this is not one of them.

When one turns to carpet and initial pages, the problem of deciding whether ornament is decorative or symbolic is even more acute. Take the opening carpet page of the Book of Durrow: What one man considers an image of the relics of the cross on the altar of the church of Golgotha during the Good Friday Adoration of the Cross,[34] another regards as an ornamental exercise in the manner of a Roman floor mosaic or a shoulder clasp that might not even represent a cross.[35] Or there is the Chi-Rho page of the Book of Kells (fig. 7) with its famous carnival of the animals. One art historian sees the cats and mice at the foot of the Chi as charming but meaningless drolleries, no different than the ornamental text fillers elsewhere in the manuscript;[36] a second sees them as an allegory of demons menacing sinners who can be redeemed by the Eucharist;[37] and a third sees the cats catching the mice as analogous to the mousetrap of the cross that snared the Devil and in the same breath regards these presumably devilish mice as symbols of Christ's Incarnation and Resurrection.[38]

Even the narrative images are often so isolated, idiosyncratic, and ambiguous that we have difficulty determining what they mean. In the Temptation scene in the Book of Kells (fig. 8), for example, Christ emerges from the top of the temple instead of standing on its pinnacle, as specified in the Gospels (Matthew 4:5, Luke 4:5). This might be taken as the artistic license of a non-naturalistic style. Then again, Henderson[39] believes that Christ's Temptation is telescoped with his subsequent Preaching in the Synagogue, so that he is also represented preaching from a pulpit to the mysterious crowds whose presence is not explained by the narrative of the Temptation. Christ, however, turns away from one group and ignores the others below him, and his fusion with the temple can be paralleled in Ottonian scenes without any audience.[40] For these reasons Henderson's interpretation seems unlikely. Nordenfalk[41] proposed that Christ's integration into the temple pinnacle illustrates an interpretation of the event found in Prudentius' *Dittochaeum*.[42] In the Gospels (Matthew 21:42, Mark 12:10, Luke 20:17) Christ quoted Psalm 117:22, comparing himself to the stone rejected by the builders but become the head of the corner, and so Prudentius interpreted the Christ at the Temptation as the keystone elevated to the top of the new temple after the destruction of the old one. I might add that later Anglo-Saxon art substantiates this symbolic interpretation. The literal illustration of verse 22 of Psalm 117 in the Harley Psalter (fig. 9) shows Christ just as in the Kells scene. This particular Anglo-Saxon drawing does not depend on the Utrecht Psalter[43] and might very well reflect an older Insular iconography. Cornerstone symbolism might also have prompted the Kells artists to place the mysterious unidentified figures beneath the base of the temple. Ephesians 2:20–21 also termed Christ "the chief cornerstone" of a spiritual temple "built upon the foundation of the apostles and prophets."[44]

The example of this Kells miniature cautions that we should by no means dismiss the possibility of symbolism in Hiberno-Saxon art, but we ought to avoid elaborate symbolic interpretations based on little more than a daisy chain of largely unrelated exegetic texts, many of which have no direct connection to the specific context or content of the image. It is all too easy to turn Insular imagery into art historical Rorschach blots.

We are on firmer grounds for the interdisciplinary interpretation of tenth- and eleventh-century Anglo-Saxon art. There is a much wider range of subject matter rendered in a more naturalistic style, and by this time there also is a body of comparative visual material from the Continent. Increasingly, later Anglo-Saxon art has been seen as an integral part of the wider culture. Mary Clayton's excellent book on the cult of the Virgin Mary, for example, draws heavily on iconographic evidence.[45] But in our rush to relate the art to the historical and intellectual context, we ought not leave behind some of the more traditional approaches.

Source study, for instance, is sometimes considered old-fashioned and irrelevant to the understanding of the cultural role of a work of art (or literature). So Barbara Raw[46] in her book on Anglo-Saxon Crucifixion iconography acknowledges that she has de-emphasized questions of artistic sources and analogues to concentrate on cultural context. My own judgment, however, is that issues of sources and context are often intertwined.

Let us take the example of Crucifixion iconography. Raw properly stresses that the Anglo-Saxon images often had a devotional character that allowed viewers to re-experience the event as if they were really there. So in the Weingarten Gospels in New York, the donor Judith of Flanders kneels and embraces Christ's cross (fig. 10).[47] Raw finds evidence for this devotional attitude in the Carolingian liturgical commentary of Amalarius of Metz. Comparing his Good Friday veneration of the cross to the adoration of the relics of the True Cross in Jerusalem by the early Christian pilgrim Paula, Amalarius wrote that she was "'prostrate before the cross as though she saw the Lord hanging there,' and I, lying before the cross, have Christ suffering for me written on my heart. . . ."[48] Although Raw mentions in passing that there are Carolingian devotional miniatures such as the one of King Charles the Bald in his prayerbook in Munich (fig. 11) that also show a donor kneeling before Christ on the cross, she fails to say that this composition actually illustrates prayers for the Good Friday veneration of the cross.[49] Furthermore, the earliest extant images of proskynesis at the Crucifixion occur on early Christian Palestinian ampullae that pilgrims to the Holy Land acquired as relics of the *loca sancta*.[50] The figures kneeling and touching Christ or the cross on these are probably pilgrims like Paula who venerated the True Cross in Jerusalem.[51] It seems arbitrary, to say the least, to relate our Anglo-Saxon image to the earlier tradition of devotional texts but to isolate it from the closely associated, earlier representational tradition. Only in the light of this iconographic tradition does it become clear that there is nothing particulary original or unusual about the Anglo-Saxon use of Crucifixion iconography to evoke the real presence of Christ,[52] though perhaps one might argue that the Anglo-Saxons emphasized this approach more than their Continental counterparts. The true originality of the Anglo-Saxon miniature only emerges when it is measured against the earlier visual tradition, when we seek the ways in which it differs from its antecedents. In fact two features about the depiction of Judith stand out against this background: this is one of the earliest, perhaps the earliest image of a woman in proskynesis before the cross, and the fervor with which she embraces it is unprecedented.[53] This miniature has the potential to provide some interesting insights into the role of aristocratic women in Anglo-Saxon culture and into the emotional intensity of Anglo-Saxon devotion to the cross.

While serious difficulties hamper the integration of early Insular art into specific historical and intellectual contexts, the prospects are brighter for the later period. That the works of the tenth and eleventh centuries are no longer so isolated and can often be related to an antecedent iconographic tradition is a significant advantage that ought not be discarded. The evaluation of this relationship should be one of the means to highlight the creativity of Anglo-Saxon art, and in the apprehension of that creativity lies a more profound understanding of the unique character and qualities of Anglo-Saxon culture. To know what's new we sometimes need to know what's old.

UNIVERSITY OF TORONTO

Figure 1. London, BL Add. 40618, fol. 22v: Luke (photo: trustees of the British Library). By permission of the British Library.

Figure 2. Paris, BN, Lat. 6401, fol. 158v: Boethius (photo: Paris, Bibliothèque Nationale).

Figure 3. Paris, BN, Lat. 6401, fol. 5v: Boethius, Philosophy, and the Muses (photo: Paris, Bibliothèque Nationale).

Figure 4. London, BL Add. 49598, fol. 51v: Women at the Tomb (photo: London, Warburg Institute). By permission of the British Library.

Figure 5. Reconstruction of fig. 3 (drawing: Juliana Bianco, 1991).

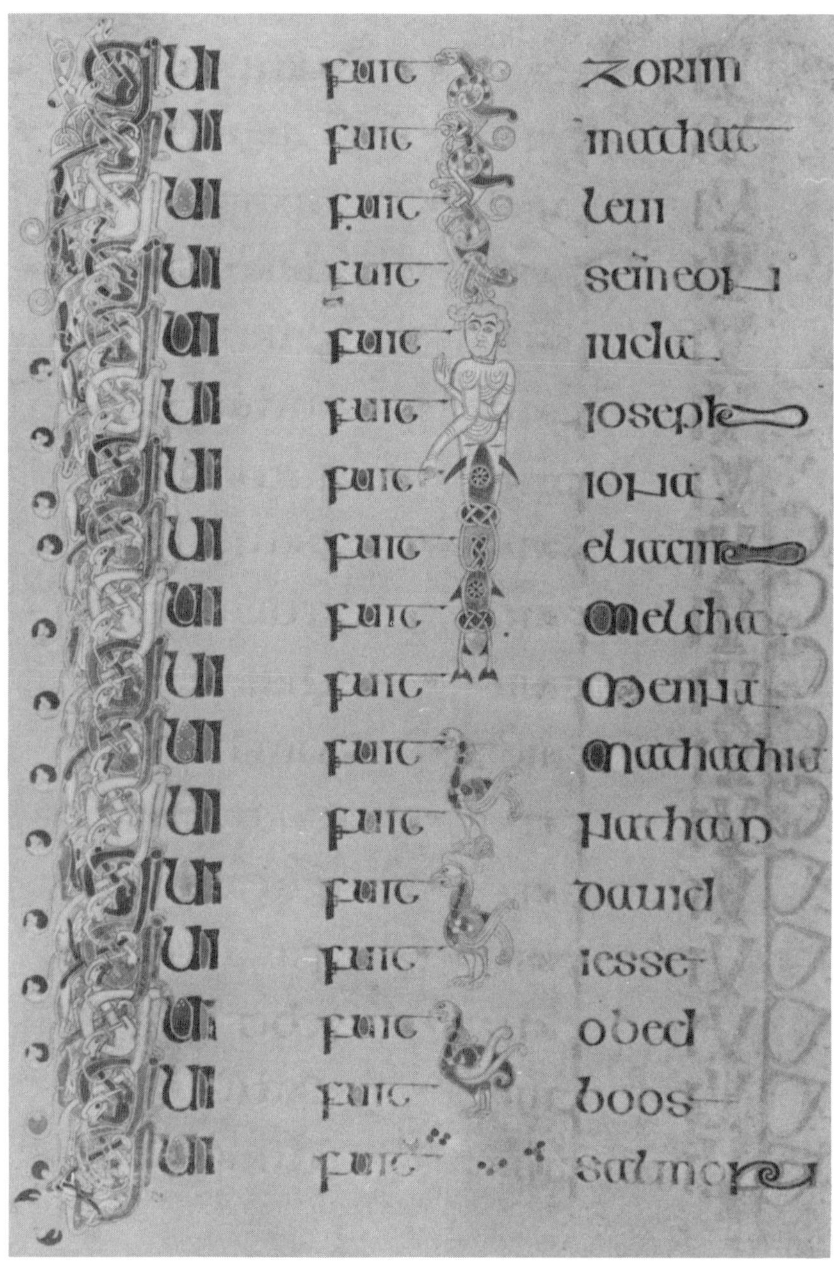
qui fuit zorim
qui fuit mathat
qui fuit leui
qui fuit semeon
qui fuit iuda
qui fuit ioseph
qui fuit iona
qui fuit eliacim
qui fuit melcha
qui fuit menna
qui fuit mathathia
qui fuit nathan
qui fuit dauid
qui fuit iesse
qui fuit obed
qui fuit boos
qui fuit salmon

Figure 6. Dublin, Trinity College 58, fol. 201r: genealogy of Christ (photo: The Board of Trinity College Dublin).

Figure 7. Dublin, Trinity College 58, fol. 34r: Chi Rho monogram (photo: The Board of Trinity College Dublin).

Figure 8. Dublin, Trinity College 58, fol. 202v: Temptation of Christ (photo: The Board of Trinity College Dublin).

Figure 9. London, BL Harley 603, fol. 60r: Ps. 117 (detail) (photo: London, The Conway Library, Courtauld Institute of Art). By permission of the British Library.

Figure 10. The Pierpont Morgan Library, New York, M.709, fol. 1v: Crucifixion with Judith of Flanders (photo: The Pierpont Morgan Library, New York).

Figure 11. Munich, Residenz, Schatzkammer, Prayerbook: fols. 38v–39: Crucifixion with Charles the Bald (photo: Munich, Bayer. Verwaltung der staatl. Schlösser, Gärten u. Seen Museumabteilung).

NOTES

1. *The Golden Age of Anglo-Saxon Art, 966–1066*, ed. Janet Backhouse, D. H. Turner, and Leslie Webster (London, 1984), pp. 90–92, no. 75, color pl. XXIII, fig. 75.

2. Pamela Tudor-Craig, "Nether Wallop Reconsidered," in *Early Medieval Wall Painting and Painted Sculpture in England*, ed. Sharon Cather, David Park, and Paul Williamson, British Archaeological Reports British Series, 216 (Oxford, 1990), pp. 89–104; Pamela Tudor-Craig and Richard Gem, "A 'Winchester School' Wall-Painting at Nether Wallop, Hampshire," ASE, 9 (1981), 115–36.

3. Otto Lehmann-Brockhaus, *Lateinische Schriftquellen zur Kunst in England, Wales, und Schottland von Jahre 901 bis zum Jahre 1307*, 5 vols. (Munich, 1955–60).

4. C. R. Dodwell, *Anglo-Saxon Art: A New Perspective* (Ithaca, NY, 1982).

5. Cf. J. J. G. Alexander, *Insular Manuscripts, 6th to the 9th Century*, A Survey of Manuscripts Illuminated in the British Isles 1, ed. J. J. G. Alexander (London, 1978), no. 21, figs. 80, 82; Elżbieta Temple, *Anglo-Saxon Manuscripts, 900–1066*, A Survey of Manuscripts Illuminated in the British Isles 2 (London, 1976), no. 68, fig. 215.

6. See the previous note.

7. Thomas H. Ohlgren, *Insular and Anglo-Saxon Illuminated Manuscripts: An Iconographic Catalogue, c. A.D. 625–1100* (New York, 1986), and *Anglo-Saxon Textual Illustration: Photographs of Sixteen Manuscripts with Descriptions and Index* (Kalamazoo, 1992).

8. *The York Gospels: A Facsimile with Introductory Essays*, ed. Nicolas Barker (London, 1986), and *The Book of Kells*, ed. Peter Fox, 2 vols. (Lucerne, 1990).

9. John Beckwith, *Ivory Carvings in Early Medieval England* (London, 1972).

10. Margaret H. Longhurst, *English Ivories* (London, 1926).

11. Adolf Goldschmidt, *Die Elfenbeinskulpturen aus der romanischen Zeit XI.–XIII. Jahrhundert*, vol. 4 (1926; rpt. Berlin, 1975).

12. *Corpus of Anglo-Saxon Stone Sculpture in England*, ed. Rosemary Cramp, vols. 1– (Oxford, 1984–).

13. *The Making of England*, ed. Janet Backhouse and Leslie Webster (London, 1991); *"The Work of Angels," Masterpieces of Celtic Metalwork 6th–9th Centuries* A.D. (London, 1989); *Golden Age*, ed. Backhouse, Turner, and Webster; *The Vikings in England*, ed. James Graham-Campbell et al. (London, 1981).

14. Carl Nordenfalk, "Another Look at the Book of Kells," in *Festschrift Wolfgang Braunfels*, ed. F. Piel and J. Traeger (Tübingen, 1977), pp. 275ff.; George Henderson, *From Durrow to Kells: The Insular Gospel-Books 650–800* (London, 1987), pp. 54ff., 179ff.; Paul Meyvaert, "The Book of Kells and Iona," *Art Bulletin*, 71 (1989), 6–19; Martin Werner, "The Cross-Carpet Page in the Book of Durrow: The Cult of the True Cross, Adomnan, and Iona," *Art Bulletin*, 72 (1990), 174–223.

15. Cf. *Golden Age*, ed. Backhouse, Turner, and Webster, pp. 40ff., no. 22 (late 9th/early 10th century); Ruth Kozody, "The Reculver Cross," *Archaeologia*, 108 (1986), 67ff. (7th century).

16. As reported by Carl Nordenfalk, "One Hundred and Fifty Years of Varying Views of Early Insular Gospel Books," in *Ireland and Insular Art* A.D. *500–1200*, ed. Michael Ryan (Dublin, 1987), p. 4.

17. Otto Homburger, *Die Anfänge der Malschule von Winchester im X. Jahrhundert*, Studien über christliche Denkmäler, NS 13 (Leipzig, 1912).

18. Many of his more important publications have been reprinted in Francis Wormald, *Collected Writings*, vol. 1, *Studies in Medieval Art from the Sixth to the Twelfth Centuries*, ed. J. J. G. Alexander, T. J. Brown, and Joan Gibbs (London, 1984).

19. T. A. M. Bishop, *English Caroline Minuscule* (Oxford, 1971); David N. Dumville, "English Square Minuscule Script: The Background and Earliest Phases," ASE, 17 (1987), 147–79.

20. Francis Wormald, "The 'Winchester School' before St Ethelwold," in *England before the Conquest: Studies in Primary Sources Presented to Dorothy Whitelock*, ed. Peter Clemoes and Kathleen Hughes (Cambridge, 1971), pp. 309ff., figs. 5 a, b, rpt. in Wormald, *Studies*, pp. 80f., figs. 89, 92–93.

21. Temple, pp. 43ff., no. 15, figs. 49, 51, 52; *Golden Age*, ed. Backhouse, Turner, and Webster, p. 27, no. 8, fig. 8.

22. Dumville, pp. 161, 168ff., pl. 3.

23. Temple, figs. 29–33. Wormald, "'Winchester School,'" pp. 309f., rpt. *Studies*, pp. 80ff., did see ornamental similarities to these earlier illuminations, but these carry little weight. He himself noted that the leaf-scroll in the border of the Luke miniature is also comparable to late 10th-century ornament, as are the gripping animal heads (cf. Temple, figs. 104–07, 110–14). The long, plastically projecting leaves in the bosses of the Luke portrait are more like the classicizing foliage in the rosettes in the Benedictional of Æthelwold (fig. 4) than earlier leaf-work, which usually curls parallel to the picture plane.

24. Cf. the drawings in Dunstan's "classbook" (Bodleian Library, Auct. F. 4. 32) and a copy of Gregory's *Pastoral Care* (Oxford, St. John's College, 28); Robert Deshman, "The Leofric Missal and Tenth-Century English Art," ASE, 6 (1977), 152–54, pls. 3a, 3b; Temple, figs. 41, 42.

25. Compare the curtains above the evangelists to the drapery of the saints and apostles on fols. 1v–4r of the Benedictional, reproduced in part by Francis Wormald, *The Benedictional of St. Ethelwold* (London, 1959), pls. 1, 2. The portraits of Luke and John in the two manuscripts are also iconographically related, as Wormald already observed.

26. Wormald, "'Winchester School,'" pp. 311ff., figs. 3d, 5c, 6, rpt. in Wormald, *Studies*, pp. 82–84, figs. 84, 109. Following him are Temple, p. 59, no. 32; *Golden Age*, ed. Backhouse, Turner, and Webster, p. 65, no. 44; and François Avril and Patricia Danz Stirnemann, *Manuscrits enluminés d'origine insulaire VIIe–XXe siècle* (Paris, 1987), pp. 15f., no. 19, pls. B, 5.

27. The drawing technique is also related to the Benedictional; see Deshman, "Leofric Missal," pp. 160ff.

28. Un-inked stylus lines delineate the upper corner rectangles, the upper horizontal border, and the inside edge of the right vertical border. The mark in the roundel next to Philosophy's leg was to indicate the inner edge of the left vertical border. The row of five marks level with the scepter's terminal were guides for the upper band of the horizontal border. The two marks to the left of the scepter were also to indicate the sides of the left rectangle, while the first of the three other marks on the right side of the page was a guide

for the left side of the right corner rectangle (the stylus sketch for this passes through the mark). The mark on the far right was probably to indicate the right side of this rectangle. The function of the middle of the three marks is unclear (the stylus sketch for the inside edge of the right vertical border passes a few millimeters to its right). My reconstruction shows the upper rectangles according to the marks and the sketches, even though they are not quite the same size and also are slightly larger than the lower rectangles. There are some irregularities in the completed parts of the frame below, e.g., the left vertical border is narrower than and not quite parallel to the right one. Erasure marks around the two lower rectangles, however, suggest that they were originally to have been the same size as the upper ones but were reduced in the final drawing (cf. also the erasures above the left roundel and the lower legs of the figure of Philosophy). Possibly the finished versions of the upper rectangles would have undergone a corresponding reduction.

29. Henderson (n. 14 above), p. 6.

30. Fritz Saxl, "The Ruthwell Cross," *Journal of the Warburg and Courtauld Institutes*, 6 (1943), 1–19; Meyer Schapiro, "The Religious Meaning of the Ruthwell Cross," *Art Bulletin*, 26 (1944), 232–45.

31. Nordenfalk, "Another Look at the Book of Kells," p. 278, fig. 3.

32. Mayvaert, pp. 6ff., fig. 1.

33. Suzanne Lewis, "Sacred Calligraphy: The Chi Rho Page in the Book of Kells," *Traditio*, 36 (1980), 139, n. 1.

34. Werner, pp. 174ff., fig. 1.

35. Meyer Schapiro and Seminar, "The Miniatures of the Florence Diatessaron (Laurentian MS Or. 81): Their Place in Late Medieval Art and Supposed Connection with Early Christian and Insular Art," *Art Bulletin*, 55 (1973), pp. 523ff., fig. 15.

36. Carl Nordenfalk, "Katz und Maus und andere Tiere im Book of Kells," in *Zum Problem der Deutung frühmittelalterlicher Bildinhalte*, ed. Helmut Kolh, Veröffentlichungen des vorgeschichtlichen Seminars der Philipps-Universität Marburg a.d. Lahn, Sonderband 4 (Sigmaringen, 1986), 21ff., figs. 1–5.

37. Sally Mussetter, "An Animal Miniature on the Monogram Page of *the Book of Kells*," *Mediaevalia*, 3 (1977), 19–30.

38. Lewis, pp. 139ff.

39. Henderson, pp. 168ff.

40. Nordenfalk, "Another Look at the Book of Kells," p. 277; cf. Ernst Günter Grimme, *Das Evangeliar Kaiser Ottos. III. im Domschatz zu Aachen* (Freiburg im Breisgau, 1984), p. 30.

41. See the previous note.

42. *Aurelii Prudentii Clementis Carmina*, ed. Maurice P. Cunningham, CCSL 126 (Turnhout, 1966), p. 396.

43. Judith Ellen Duffey, "The Inventive Group of Illustrations in the Harley Psalter (British Museum Ms. Harley 603)," 2 vols., Diss. Univ. of California, Berkeley, 1977, pp. 45, 122ff.; also Midori Tsuzumi, "Anglo-Saxon Creativity in the Illustrations of the Harley Psalter *(British Library, Ms. Harley 603)*," *Bulletin of Nagoya University of Arts* (in Japanese), 10 (1988), pp. 23ff., pl. 2.

44. Although not citing this text, Carol Ann Farr, "Lection and Interpretation: The Liturgical and Exegetical Background of the Illustrations in the 'Book of Kells,'" Diss. Univ. of Texas, Austin, 1989, pp. 60ff., 115, has also related these figures to the saints edified into the living church of Christ.

45. Mary Clayton, *The Cult of the Virgin Mary in Anglo-Saxon England* (Cambridge, 1990).

46. Barbara Catherine Raw, *Anglo-Saxon Crucifixion Iconography and the Art of the Monastic Revival* (Cambridge, 1990), p. 2.

47. Raw, pp. 24, 63f., pl. 16.; Temple, pp. 108f., no. 93, fig. 289.

48. Amalarius, *Liber Officialis*, I.14.7, ed. John Michael Hanssens, *Amalarii Episcopi Opera Liturgica Omnia*, Studi e testi, 139, II (Vatican City, 1949), p. 101: "'Prostrataque ante crucem, quasi pendentem Dominum cerneret;' et ego iacens ante crucem, passus Christus pro me proscriptus est in corde me. . . ." Quoted by Raw, p. 55.

49. Robert Deshman, "The Exalted Servant: The Ruler Theology of the Prayerbook of Charles the Bald," *Viator*, 11 (1980), 387ff., fig. 1, where also the idea of the donor

re-experiencing the event as a living reality is related to Amalarius' comments on the Good Friday ceremony. See also Percy Ernst Schramm, *Die deutschen Kaiser und Könige in Bildern ihrer Zeit 751–1190*, 2nd ed., ed. Florentine Mütherich (Munich, 1983), pp. 167f., 308f., no. 37.

50. André Grabar, *Ampoules de Terre Sainte* (Paris, 1958), no. 13, pl. 24, also pls. 5, 11–14, 16, 18, 22, etc.

51. Gary Vikan, *Byzantine Pilgrimage Art*, Dumbarton Oaks Byzantine Collection Publication, 5 (Washington DC, 1982), pp. 22ff., 40f., figs. 31, 32.

52. For this and other aspects of the widespread use of early Christian and medieval images as visualizations of the believers' participation in and presence at past sacred events, see Robert Deshman, "Servants of the Mother of God in Byzantine and Medieval Art," *Word and Image*, 5 (1989), 33–70; William Loerke, "'Real Presence' in Early Christian Art," in *Monasticism and the Arts*, ed. Timothy Gregory Verdon (Syracuse, NY, 1983), pp. 29–51.

53. Noting this, Raw, p. 160, suggests that Judith is depicted in the guise of Mary Magdalene, a notion previously advanced by Paul Thoby, *Le Crucifix des origines au Concile de Trente* (Nantes, 1959), p. 41, and Gertrud Schiller, *Ikonographie der christlichen Kunst*, vol. 2 (Gütersloh, 1968), p. 128. But no contemporary text describing the Magdalene in proskynesis before the cross is adduced, and the first examples of the Magdalene in this pose in narrative Crucifixion scenes are much later. See Frank O. Büttner, *Imitatio Pietas* (Berlin, 1983), pp. 142ff. The unique gesture of the Virgin, reaching up to Christ's side wound, apparently to staunch the bleeding, is another sign of the image's extraordinary emotionalism. Editors' postscript: readers should note the appearance of these important works since the late Prof. Deshman completed this essay: *The Ruthwell Cross*, ed. Brian Cassidy (Princeton, 1992); Richard Gameson, *The Role of Art in the Late Anglo-Saxon Period* (Oxford, 1995); and Robert Deshman, *The Benedictional of Aethelwold* (Princeton, 1995). The editors wish to thank Herbert L. Kessler (Johns Hopkins Univ.) for screening this essay.

Not Why But How: The Contribution of Archaeological Evidence to the Understanding of Anglo-Saxon England

Rosemary Cramp

In attempting to assess the nature and the utility of archaeological evidence for increasing our understanding of Anglo-Saxon England, I am very conscious of the fact that the archaeologists who work in this period as their primary interest are few and have never been widely represented in ISAS. I would therefore like first to consider the position of Early Medieval archaeologists within the general subject of archaeology, then to look at the nature of the evidence and the methodology of its interpretation, and finally to assess the current contribution of archaeology and the range of future possibilities.

For anyone who works as an archaeologist in a semi-historic period, the research agenda has in the past been set, almost automatically, by scholars in textual disciplines, whether historians or those concerned with the language or literature of the defined culture or cultures. The "period" itself is usually defined by political events, and the spatial limits of the research are often defined by linguistic boundaries; yet the cultures in which the archaeologists may be interested do not respect these same temporal or physical limits. For Anglo-Saxon Studies, this is clearly to be seen in pottery studies or in architectural history where terms such as *Saxo-Norman* have been coined to reflect Anglo-Saxon styles that continued into the period of the Norman hegemony. It is also reflected in the difficulties encountered in assessing the western limits of the Anglo-Saxon kingdoms, especially that of Bernicia.

These research parameters are, I suppose, the legacy of the primacy of Classics within the Arts curriculum, where classical civilization was seen as an entity and archaeological investigation was prompted very often by the desire to understand the context of a documented event, of a recorded place, or even of a person. The foundations of our study of Anglo-Saxon England, as defined annually in the periodical of that name, have been largely documentary, and the temporal and physical boundaries of the subject are defined by the currency of Old English, although a wider intellectual framework is provided by sources in Early Medieval Latin. The documents in both languages provide an indispensable insight into the individual and collective attitudes, the social organization and political events of Anglo-Saxon England, but they are nonetheless selective in their social and topographic reference, and they are an incalculable remnant of a larger body of evidence. They are spread over six hundred years, and there is sometimes the tendency to see their evidence as more coherent and continuous than it can possibly be.

Archaeological evidence is likewise patchy, incoherent, and non-selective (save in the materials which survive best in the ground). The increasing body of evidence, more skillfully retrieved over the last 25 years, has enabled archaeologists to consider more complex problems in the transmissions of cultures. The processes of renewal of societies after the collapse of a sophisticated political system; the assimilation of the Germanic and native populations; the coincidence or divergence of political and cultural groupings of peoples in Britain; urban renewal and development, cult and cultural conflicts, are all current research problems. Archaeologists today are concerned to make their evidence speak with its own voice, but one must in truth say that they themselves do not speak with one voice. Not all have accepted, but all have been affected, willy nilly, by the new theories and practices promulgated—most widely in the United States—in the 1960's and 1970's.

In those heady days archaeologists followed the path explored earlier by anthropologists in the search for predictive laws of human behavior, an approach which appears to accept the notion that human societies are natural systems which can be reduced to variables. They turned their backs on the models provided by history and applied the models of their anthropological colleagues. An empathetic study of the past was firmly rejected by leaders of fashion such as Binford,[1] and acceptance of the simple logic that to imagine the intentions, actions, and beliefs of people in former times is not the same as experiencing them in the present justifiably shut the door on certain types of enquiry. This may now seem self-evident, but how often have we discussed the past as though it were a territory we had actually visited, so cozily constructed that we really felt "at home" in it? No archaeologist can ever be the same after the wet-towel slapping provided by the New Archaeology. But the actual period of unquestioning acceptance was very brief. By the early 1980's many who had hoped to escape from historical particularism were returning to historical models and struggled to investigate material remains as if they were texts,[2] or fossilized ideas that could reveal individual motivation. I must confess that I cannot subscribe to the attempt to "read" artifacts in the same way as texts, and indeed believe that as archaeologists we can only see the random results of human intentions, not the intentions themselves. Nevertheless, I could still subscribe to Driscoll's view that "documents and artefacts are the products of similar mental processes, which are to be understood by using similar analytical frameworks."[3]

The failure of the New Archaeology to convert many medieval European archaeologists to its ways may well be due, as has been claimed, to the constant presence of documentary history; even Binford seems now to concede that there is a valid archaeological viewpoint in which,

> so long as we have historical documents which preserve observations, made by people actually present about the dynamics of places in the past, we have the option of excavating those places and, walking through history, as it were alongside an historical character trying to relate what we find in the ground to what he reports as having occurred there.[4]

I must say that I find that a very mushy statement. Occasionally textual sources have been successfully used as an excavation blueprint, such as Quirk's analysis of the records concerning the positioning of the pre-Conquest churches at Winchester,[5] which was extensively used by Martin Biddle in his excavation program. But how often do we find the garrulous mentor in the past who provides us with enough relevant information to guide an excavation program? More often than not, the two types of evidence do not converge at any point, and, though from excavation one may produce knowledge of a physical environment in which a known historical character could have existed (for example, the room in which Bede ate!), what has it added to our knowledge of him, or what has his past presence added to our knowledge of the excavated room? Perhaps there is an extra dimension provided by such contact which it is very difficult to define: for those who are interested in the period there is an added resonance, which is a matter for the heart rather than the head.

Medieval archaeologists have probably benefited from the conversions and reconversions of their colleagues in pre-history, since most of them have a proper respect for the complex problems that textual sources raise. In a perceptive paper, "The 'Proper Study' of Medieval Archaeology," David Austin discusses why archaeologists whose field of study is medieval Europe eschewed most of the theories of the New Archaeology but tried to find some common ground with prehistory while still accommodating the views of the medieval historian. He divides the matter for debate into three key elements: "humanity as individual, humanity as social being, and humanity as member of the biosphere."[6] I am glad to say that he concedes that the individual is more readily detected and defined in the written than in the material record. But I think that his claim that archaeologists rather than historians or students of literature are "better placed to see the creative mind and the individual will active within society"[7] is rather tendentious. I really do not believe that we can recognize the individual will in our type of data.

In Anglo-Saxon archaeology one can detect the same maker's hand on two pots or pieces of sculpture, one can even discover artifacts that are signed by a named person, but, since that person has no biography, he has no further context. We have, so far as I know, no corpus of evidence which can chart the development of an artistic career or even the results of the patronage of an individual, but does any body of Anglo-Saxon evidence provide this? It is true that we can see potential cultural interactions in the Germanic silver buckle discovered at South Cadbury[8] or the gilt disk decorated with interlace found on the Dalriadic site of the Dunadd hillfort.[9] We shall know more about the circumstances of production of artifacts as the recent excavations of so many production and productive centers are published, but the canons of training are apparently such that it is often difficult to isolate the individual. It is in Austin's second category (humanity as social being)—although not in the terms he suggests—that I would see the greatest possibilities for independent contribution by the Anglo-Saxon archaeologist. The insights provided by modern social theorists concerning social formations are of direct relevance to the type of evidence archaeology can provide. Here there is the genuine possibility of providing a continuum of evidence for the processes such as I mentioned previously, in relating the discontinuous evidence provided by the texts to better-defined contexts.

Perhaps we could take artifacts first. The understanding, in Austin's words, "that material things in addition to mere function have a meaning content and convey messages"[10] is surely true. Dress and jewelry most certainly conveyed clearer and more formal messages in the Early Medieval period than they do today, although whether we today can interpret the messages accurately is uncertain. The mere knowledge of the possibility, however, encourages the attempt. The association of certain types of jewelry not just with social groups and their aspirations but with ethnic or age groups has of course long been postulated. Julian Richards' work on the significance of the form and decoration of Anglo-Saxon cremation urns[11] has taken this much further and has demonstrated that certain types of decoration do seem to be related to specific age and status groups. It should be noted here that the old adage that the Anglo-Saxons were made in England has been continuously reinforced as larger areas of cemeteries are excavated, and also excavated better. Catherine Hills pointed out some time ago in a valuable article, "The Archaeology of Anglo-Saxon England in the Pagan Period,"[12] that it is in the sixth rather than the fifth century that one sees regional differentiation among grave goods. At the time of the migrations some "Anglo-Saxons" may have looked like Franks, some like Roman Britons, and others like Danes or Jutes, but the distinctive regional cultures exemplified in different burial styles or the fastenings of national or regional costume developed later. At the same time the Picts and the Scots also emphasized their different identities in their material cultures—including, of course, their funerary monuments. (The fact that by the late eighth/early ninth century everyone in Anglo-Saxon England, from Devon to Coldingham, in what is now Scotland, was wearing similar dress fastenings may speak volumes for the unity of the Anglo-Saxon kingdoms.)

Also perceptible in the seventh-century graves throughout Anglo-Saxon England is an increasing differentiation between rich and poor grave deposits, which has been given various explanations: greater social stratification and a response to the growing power of Christianity are two of the most popular. The contribution of archaeological evidence to the understanding of social interactions among the Anglo-Saxons, particularly the early settlers, has been considerable. Here there are important differences between what the surviving texts and what the material evidence suggest. As indicated above, it has become clear that the linguistic model of ethnic origins is too simple to fit the complexity of the material evidence. A dominant group may have given its name to a region, but within that region there were clearly many different social practices. *The Origins of the Anglo-Saxon Kingdoms*, edited by Steven Bassett,[13] considers under the headings of the major kingdoms how the mixed groups of peoples who called themselves by a variety of names were formed into states. For me, the chapter by Martin Carver, "Kingship and Material Culture in Early Anglo-Saxon East Anglia," is the only one that exploits to the full the new evidence which archaeology has provided for the study of this topic.[14] Of course, East Anglia has been the subject of intensive fieldwork for some time, and the important burial ground at Sutton Hoo has focused attention and yielded very surprising results. The sixteen bodies that surrounded Mound 5 may be prisoners of war or penal sacrifices, but they throw an interesting light on the savagery of the early Anglo-Saxon burial practices.[15]

The most recent excavations at Sutton Hoo have revealed not only earlier prehistoric burials on the site but also Roman barrows within sight of the burial ground, across the river. This conjunction of pagan Anglo-Saxon burial grounds with earlier burials or religious sites is now known to be a common phenomenon. What were the intentions of the Anglo-Saxons in so locating their burial grounds is still a matter for debate; it may be because they wished to legitimize their land claims by spurious links with local "ancestors"; it may be that these monuments seemed to them consonant with a religious place.

We also can note the phenomenon of increased wealth for some individuals and greater social stratification in burials by the seventh century, but we cannot say why. When we have early Laws, we do not need to be told that this was a ranked society, but the processes whereby this came about, and the regions in which it first appeared, are of interest. We can also see by the late seventh century all over Anglo-Saxon England, right into the newly won territories of northern Northumbria, the tendency to divide off one's house and yard from those of others. Is this an increase in the desire for privacy, a status sign, or a legal enforcement? Certainly it provides concrete examples of the barriers that, if broken, would be subjected to the penalties of law, according to the status of their owners.

Archaeological sites are still the nuts and bolts of the subject, and here, over the last twenty or so years, archaeologists of all periods have dramatically enhanced their skills. Understanding how deposits are formed is one of the necessary but tedious problems that has exercised archeological practitioners to very good effect, as they try to see behind these physical entities the events which have formed them. Sometimes these are the result of man's activities, sometimes the results of beasts' or biological activities. It is important for those outside the discipline who use the evidence from archaeological reports to be at least aware of whether or not such an assessment has been made in a given report, since it would enhance the validity of the archaeological conclusions.

The increased importance given to an understanding of the physical environment of individuals and groups has also increased our knowledge of the changing Anglo-Saxon landscape, sometimes with surprising results. We know, for example in Northumbria, that the withdrawal of the Roman army did not always signal great changes in the pattern of rural land use, although there was a tendency for pasture to increase in the sixth century.[16] The record of changes in settlement types and patterns that took place before the documentary evidence for their social and legal structure is potentially of great value for the student of this period, as is the examination of the lifestyles of those groups in society whose doings are not well represented in the literature.[17] The production of a data base for all types of ecological evidence—seeds and pollen, animal, bird, and fish bones, remains of insects, parasites, copralites—will one day provide us with a changing picture of life in Anglo-Saxon England which will be socially, temporally, and regionally diverse. At the moment the results are too site-specific to be useful, although regional pictures are building up. One day we may be able to distinguish between the eating habits of the West Saxons and the Northumbrians in the way that modern politicians distinguish the healthy eating of the southern English from the chips and butties of the northerners. In addition, the postwar excavations in European towns have not only increased our knowledge of urban planning and the way in which the town and countryside interact[18] but they also have provided in their deep deposits intact organic artifacts such as textiles, wooden utensils and tools, and, most exciting for me at least, wooden structures. We have now the possibility of seeing in northwest Europe changes of fashion in those things that most identify the groupings of peoples: dress, eating habits, and domestic architecture (would, alas, I could add speech!). There is no substitute for the hard slog of collection, identification, classification, and interpretation of artifacts and ecofacts, and it is lucky that computerization of data has arrived just at the time when archaeological data threaten to overwhelm us all.

It is a cheering thought that in my working life as an Anglo-Saxon specialist, the Anglo-Saxon peoples have emerged from being visible only in death to visible in life. Their material culture, which appeared once as a void between the Roman and High Medieval periods, is every day further identified. It is the Britons who are almost invisible. I hope that when the results of British and English excavations are compared with those in Scandinavia and the North Sea littoral, we shall be able to see the spread and change of architectural fashions as now we are able to see, through careful excavations such as Whithorn,[19] the translation and transmutation of Northumbrian architectural styles to the far west of Britain.

One of the most interesting problems that more extensive excavation has posed is the nature of sites which are first identified in one category and then do not seem to fit our accepted criteria for such sites, so that they are difficult to categorize in the nomenclature to which we are accustomed. Alternatively, they appear to change their function and organization through time. One should hardly be surprised that one cannot categorize every site according to textual criteria, nor that there should be social and economic changes reflected in sites. This is to fall into the trap which I noted at the beginning of this paper, viz., considering Anglo-Saxon England as too monolithic an entity. The debate as to what constituted a town—whether the functions or the formal organization, or both—is an old one, and the problems of what are proto-towns—monasteries, royal estates, or riverbank trading posts—are given a new emphasis in the excavation of sites such as Flixborough in Lincolnshire and Whithorn in Galloway. In the former, nine thousand artifacts have been discovered, many of which have their parallels in the presumable monastic site of Whitby.[20] What has been excavated is a large industrial area which has yielded styli (some of silver) and two inscribed metal objects, as well as a great deal of ornamental metal-work. But are we here looking at a *vicus* of a monastery that we cannot identify or at a production center organized by a secular lord? The same sort of problem is to be found at Brandon or Burrow Hill in Suffolk, which appear to be respectively monastic and secular but could have changed their functions.[21]

We must allow for the fact that we usually argue from incomplete site excavation. A recent excavation at the site of Hoddom near to Ruthwell, where many early crosses have been found, is a case in point. The scale of rescue excavation here enabled one to see not just the ceremonial center of the monastery as at Wearmouth and Jarrow but also the outer enclosure with its associated large-scale domestic buildings.[22] At Whithorn the longer research excavation has revealed an area of the site that is not only in its "Northumbrian phase" very similar in layout to Jarrow but has many different phases of activity and emphasis; so, for example, it seems to revert to a secular type of trading center after the "Northumbrian phase."[23]

The late ninth century is a watershed in the increase of production and scale of internal distribution throughout Anglo-Saxon England: it is, for example, the period when one has evidence for quarry production of sculpture as well as the development of urban industries. The smaller-scale industries of the period before are much harder to define, and indeed to understand in an economic network. I believe that the value of the archaeological evidence for the study of Anglo-Saxon England will become fully apparent only when the massive bodies of evidence with which practitioners are now struggling are fully digested. It will then be seen that new contexts of activity have been discovered which are not identified in texts, and that the processes of change and development over six hundred years can be so identified that it will be as possible to think of the difference in lifestyle between the mid-seventh and the mid-eighth or the mid-ninth centuries in the same fashion as one can for the fourteenth, fifteenth, or sixteenth centuries. We can already, of course, see that temporal change will be modified by social and regional differences. I am not sure how much this will interest or enlighten the student of literature or the textual critic, but it should provide a wider and firmer context for their enquiries.

As I said earlier, I do not feel that we can reconstruct individual lives through archaeological evidence, and though archaeologists constantly interrogate their evidence as to why it is so, I do not believe that they can offer more than an opinion as to *why* events in the past which produced their evidence took place. Their opinions here have no more validity than those from any other discipline. What they can offer is an increasingly informative account of *how* events took place and an increasingly clear account of what those events were. These events at the moment are very much localized, but as I have attempted to demonstrate, there are already hints that some events can be seen as coexistent over a wide area. They may soon be seen as trends, temporal or social fashions, which can define new contexts for textual studies.

Anglo-Saxon archaeologists, having refined their own skills and set their own agendas, are clearly no longer too insecure to consider the agendas of their fellow professionals in the same period of study. I would like to think that in the future ISAS will offer some questions which it corporately would like to see answered within the constraints of the archaeological endeavor.

DURHAM, ENGLAND

NOTES

I would like to thank Paul Szarmach and Joel Rosenthal for their generous hospitality during the Fifth ISAS Conference, and for their patience in awaiting the written paper.

1. See Lewis R. Binford, "Archaeology as Anthropology," *American Antiquity*, 28 (1962), 217–25; Binford, "Meaning, Inference and the Material Record," in *Ranking, Resource and Exchange*, ed. A. C. Renfrew and S. Shennan (Cambridge, 1982), pp. 160–63. Binford's work over the last 30 years has been exceptionally influential among British archaeologists, although obviously there were many schools of "New Archaeology" in the U.S.A.

2. Ian Hodder, *Reading the Past: Current Approaches to Interpretation in Archaeology* (Cambridge, 1986), pp. 147–71.

3. Stephen T. Driscoll, "The Relationship between History and Archaeology: Artifacts, Documents and Power," in *Power and Politics in Early Medieval Britain and Ireland*, ed. S. T. Driscoll and M. R. Nieke (Edinburgh, 1988), p. 166.

4. Lewis R. Binford, *In Pursuit of the Past* (London, 1983), pp. 25–26.

5. R. N. Quirk, "Winchester Cathedral in the Tenth Century," *Archaeological Journal*, 114 (1957), 28–68.

6. David Austin, "The 'Proper Study' of Medieval Archaeology," in *From the Baltic to the Black Sea: Studies in Medieval Archaeology*, ed. D. Austin and L. Alcock (London, 1990), p. 32.

7. Austin, p. 33.

8. Leslie Alcock, *'By South Cadbury is that Camelot . . .' Excavations at Cadbury Castle 1966–1970* (London, 1972), pl. 78.

9. Margaret R. Nieke and Holly B. Duncan, "Dalriada: The Establishment and Maintenance of an Early Historic Kingdom in Northern Britain," in Driscoll and Nieke, eds., p. 15.

10. David Austin and Julian Thomas, "The 'Proper Study' of Medieval Archaeology: A Case Study," in Austin and Alcock, eds., p. 44.

11. Julian D. Richards, *The Significance of Form and Decoration of Anglo-Saxon Cremation Urns*, British Archaeological Reports British Series 166 (Oxford, 1987); J. D. Richards, "Style and Symbol: Explaining Variability in Anglo-Saxon Cremation Burials," in Driscoll and Nieke, eds., pp. 145–61.

12. Catherine Hills, "The Archaeology of Anglo-Saxon England in the Pagan Period: A Review," ASE, 8 (1979), 297–329.

13. Steven Bassett, ed., *The Origins of Anglo-Saxon Kingdoms* (London, 1989).

14. Martin Carver, "Kingship and Material Culture in Early Anglo-Saxon East Anglia," in Bassett, ed., pp. 141–58.

15. Martin Carver, "The Anglo-Saxon Cemetery at Sutton Hoo: An Interim Report," in *The Age of Sutton Hoo*, ed. M. O. H. Carver (Woodbridge, 1992), fig. 69. Since I gave the paper at ISAS this important volume has been published, and this contains not only the most recent studies on the burial ground and its context but also several other papers which are directly relevant to the subject of my paper, but which I could not take into account.

16. Nick Higham, *The Northern Counties to* AD *1000* (London, 1986), pp. 248–49.

17. An important collection of essays that usefully brings together much of the ecological and landscape evidence is *Archaeological Approaches to Medieval Europe*, ed. Kathleen Biddick (Kalamazoo, 1984). For a more recent view see S. P. Dark (née Day), "Palaeoecological Evidence for Landscape Continuity and Change in Britain, ca A.D. 400–800," in K. R. Dark, ed., *External Contacts and the Economy of Late Roman and Post-Roman Britain* (Woodbridge, 1996).

18. Hodges' work on the mechanics of trade and exchange of goods before the Viking Age has been particularly stimulating. See Richard Hodges, *Dark Age Economics* (London, 1982), and "North Sea Trade Before the Vikings," in Biddick, ed., pp. 193–201.

19. Peter Hill, *Whithorn 4. Excavations 1990–1991* (Whithorn, 1992); and Peter Hill, *Whithorn and St Ninian: The Excavation of a Monastic Town 1984–91*, forthcoming.

20. Leslie Webster and Janet Backhouse, eds., *The Making of England: Anglo-Saxon Art and Culture,* AD *600–900* (London, 1991), pp. 94–101, 141–46; B. Whitwell, "Flixborough," *Current Archaeology*, 126 (1991), 244–47; R. J. Cramp, "A Reconsideration of the Monastic Site of Whitby," in *The Age of Migrating Ideas*, ed. R. M. Spearman and J. Higgitt (Edinburgh, 1993), pp. 64–73.

21. Webster and Backhouse, eds., pp. 81–88; R. D. Carr, A. Tester, and P. Murphy, "The Middle Saxon Settlement at Staunch Meadow, Brandon," *Antiquity*, 62 (1988), 371–77; V. Fenwick, "Insula de Burgh. Excavations at Burrow Hill, Butley, Suffolk 1978–1981," in *Anglo-Saxon Studies in Archaeology and History*, 3 (1984), ed. S. Chadwick Hawkes, J. Campbell, and D. Brown, pp. 35–54.

22. Christopher E. Lowe, "New Light on the Anglian 'Minster' at Hoddom," *Transactions of the Dumfriesshire and Galloway Natural History and Antiquarian Society*, 66 (1991), 11–35; idem, "Hoddom," *Current Archaeology*, 135 (1993), 88–92.

23. Hill, *Whithorn 4*; and Hill, *Whithorn and St Ninian.*

Literary Approaches

CETERIS IMPARIBUS: ORALITY/LITERACY AND THE ESTABLISHMENT OF ANGLO-SAXON LITERATE CULTURE

URSULA SCHAEFER

Our orientation in everyday life to a large extent functions on the recognition of phenomena as identical or unidentical to phenomena we have previously experienced. In scholarly research we proceed similarly. My purpose in the present essay is to draw the attention of Anglo-Saxonists to two points at which such a process may lead us into "a fallacy of analogy." One point concerns the question of how to assess the anthropological and cultural impacts of the transition from orality to literacy in Anglo-Saxon England; the second thematizes the place of writing and of the written in this culture. With regard to this second point, I will show that in early medieval culture in general, and in Anglo-Saxon England in particular, this place differed significantly from the one that writing and the written assume in our own highly literate culture. The question "How to assess the impacts of the transition from orality to literacy?" is, of course, closely linked to the question of locating writing and the written. Here the impending "fallacy" is not that of a tacit inference of sameness between the early medieval and our own cultural conditions but rather the fallacy of too rashly transferring deep-structure findings from one surface development to another, analogous, development.

In the last 30 years or so we have learnt much about the consequences of a culture's transition from orality to literacy; we have also become increasingly aware that conclusions that suggest themselves by analogy to modern observations must be drawn with utmost care. To be sure, the access to writing and the degree to which writing is used for verbal communication and conservation have a decisive influence on the modes of human conceptualization. Walter Ong has put this insight into the poignant sentence "Writing is a technology that restructures thought" (the title of an article in which he recapitulates the most important points of this restructuring).[1] Our growing awareness of the impact of literacy (of course, always also of orality) is primarily based on findings by psychologists, anthropologists, and linguists from contemporary research in illiterate or barely literate cultures.[2] A steadily increasing number of publications on historical cultures corroborates and complements the modern findings.[3]

One area that lends itself to contemporary research on the effects of literacy is Black Africa. Since the nineteenth century, European colonial politics has brought the use of writing to African cultures that had previously been purely oral. There we still may closely witness what is happening in the transition from pure, primary orality to fully-developed literacy. To date, those cultures have by no means attained full literacy, although some outstanding figures have (e.g., Léopold Sédar Senghor, former President of Senegal, entered the sacred circle of the *immortels* in the *Académie française*). The contemporary observations show that "oral modes" are not eradicated at once, even though the part of the population that has remained illiterate is indirectly affected by the effects of spreading literacy. The extent to which modes of thinking (in the widest sense) rooted in the native, oral culture are shed may be a more or less conscious decision in the cases of those who have experienced schooling; and this shedding of orality very much depends on the extent to which people are willing—or forced—to merge with the culture of the colonial power. This is a very complex problem that may only be touched upon here. However, there can be no doubt that what on the surface appears as "innocent alphabetization" deeply affects the sphere of individual and/or ethnic identity.

Within the historical disciplines, the need to assess certain cultures within the parameters *orality/literacy* is increasingly acknowledged.

The idea has now been well established that the cultural history of the European Middle Ages should/must be seen as that of the transition from orality to literacy, and that consequently medieval research needs to integrate the insights of modern psychology, linguistics, and anthropology into its considerations. As the historian Hanna Vollrath put it more than a decade ago, ". . . der methodische Ausgang vom kulturprägenden Charakter der Oralität [erlaubt es], grundlegende Probleme des Mittelalters klarer zu fassen."[4]

Before I turn to more concrete deliberations vis-à-vis Anglo-Saxon culture and to what Katherine O'Brien O'Keeffe has recently characterized as a period of "transitional literacy,"[5] I want to address a terminological problem. It is noteworthy that in her 1981 article Vollrath uses the term *Oralität*, a Latino-German loan creation on the model of the (Latino-)English *orality*. Meanwhile, German scholars use the Germanic *Mündlichkeit* and oppose it to *Schriftlichkeit*, for which the English *literacy* may (partly) be a terminological equivalent. The interesting point is that German *Schriftlichkeit* is the abstract noun derived from the adjective *schriftlich*, which simply means 'in writing' or 'written'. While the German *Schriftlichkeit* thus always primarily conjures up the written medium and is hence often equated with 'something in writing' or adverbially simply with 'doing something in writing', *literacy* is heavily charged with culture-specific connotations, which only indirectly have to do with the medium. In German no human being may be **schriftlich* if the intended meaning is 'he or she is *literate*' in the sense of 'being able to read and write'. Even more strangely: German does not even have an adjective for *literate* in this sense; it paraphrases this capacity: *jemand kann lesen und schreiben*. The secondary meaning of *literate* as 'educated, cultured' has the (very German) translation *gebildet* (literally [!] 'formed').[6] This terminological problem illustrates the fact that these notions lack what some hold to be the basic demand with which academic, scholarly discourse should comply: one-to-one translatability.[7] Furthermore, the terminological problem is just the tip of the iceberg of our own heuristic and hermeneutic difficulties in dealing with the "orality/literacy problem."

What exists in writing cannot but be a product of literacy, in the sense of 'use of the written medium'. We have gained a better understanding of what this use of the medium actually implies. Hence, we probably agree that we should not expect any historical written text to comply entirely with all the conditioning factors of literacy—this time in the sense of 'a cultural state with its specific conceptualizations'. Vollrath has dealt with impressive examples from the late eleventh century in which some specific legal conflict had been handled from different angles. She demonstrates how Odo of Ostia (later Pope Urban II), who "undoubtedly belonged to the intellectual elite of his Ages," was able to deal with this conflict by "discern[ing] the meaning, the sense, and the underlying principle of a text and discuss-[ing] it rationally."[8] Vollrath's counter-example is Odo's contemporary Frutolf von Michelsberg, who, reporting in a chronicle the same conflict, can be seen clearly as roaming in a world that "functioned according to the rules of an oral legal system in which a text remained a stranger. It [the text] was accepted when it corroborated what everyone already knew, and it was eliminated when it disturbed prevalent convictions."[9] Thus Vollrath's study of her sources succeeds in furnishing evidence that we can find both men like Odo who were able to argue textually, and at the very same time, men like this "learned monk at the end of the [eleventh] century [who] was unable to integrate a text into his world."[10]

Findings such as those produced by Vollrath are immensely valuable because they help us find a better *historical* insight into the specificity of literate "mental operation[s]" vs. operations that are more "orally oriented."[11] Such insights are needed to gain a clearer picture of landmarks within this transitional continuum. In Vollrath's examples we may see "transition in progress," as it were, because men such as Odo and Frutolf display two mental modes that we, from our historical stance, identify as "the old" vs. "the new."

It is methodically convenient to conceive of this transition as a linear and gradual development from orality to literacy, and thus we are wont to look for traces of the first within the second. Katherine

O'Brien O'Keeffe demonstrates how fertile this approach can be. In the preface to her book *Visible Song* she states,

> It would be mistaken, I believe, to ascribe to the Anglo-Saxons the presuppositions and practices of our own literacy. Further, my argument assumes the possibility of one or more transitional states between pure 'orality' and pure 'literacy' and seeks to describe some of the features of an early transitional state characterized by what I shall call 'residual orality'.[12]

While I too concentrate here on Anglo-Saxon England, I do *not* deal so much with the question of to what extent we may retrieve "traces of orality" in written material of the earlier Middle Ages. My aim is to recognize factors that should *precede* any such "archaeology."

For one thing, I suggest we keep well in mind how literacy came to England. Much of what I present here on this matter has already been expounded by Patrick Wormald in his article "The Uses of Literacy in Anglo-Saxon England."[13] The reason I resume this problem at this point is a heuristic one. As I have just pointed out, a considerable part of what we know about the "implications of literacy" is drawn from findings from cultures that have become literate due to modern colonialization. I think it is indispensable to become aware of the differences between this kind of literarization and the kind that occurred in the early Middle Ages. There is no question here of the legitimacy of transferring modern findings to historical research—to the contrary, it is a matter of pointing out where we have to look for the *ceteris imparibus*. For the same reason I present the second point, namely, the search for a better historical understanding of the value and use of written material in those times. As has been said, we should not assume that anything existing in writing complies in full with the exigiencies of our modern, completely developed, literacy. Conversely, we should not expect anything existing in writing to have served the same purposes that written material does today.

A very cursory glance at the establishment and (restricted) spread of literacy in Anglo-Saxon England draws our attention to the pertinent differences between this historical phenomenon and that of its modern, colonializing counterpart. Even when it spreads slowly and gradually, the colonializing import of literacy must come as a shock to such cultures, since something more than a technology is superimposed on autochthonously developed social and cultural habits and traditions. Even where the alien intellectual overpowering is performed without malicious intent, its effects are that of a more or less latent, continuous repression, particularly of the orally inherited culture. In Anglo-Saxon England, as much as in other early medieval Germanic societies, literacy did not come with a colonializing power in the sense that it interfered immediately with the native social and cultural organization. Literacy, rather, was closely attached to the missionaries of the Christian religion, and it thus remained closely tied to religion up to the High Middle Ages. Furthermore, we should see that in early medieval Europe literacy existed mainly as the literacy of (part of) the clerical and monastic population, and that it mainly served their religious purposes.[14] Until the tenth century "pragmatic literacy" played a very minor role, at best.[15] Along with Talcott Parsons, one may call this a "craft literacy."[16]

Still further—and this second point is the basic condition for the first—literacy, or, more specifically, literateness, was not established merely as a "by-product" of the new religion. This religion was very closely connected with literacy, as the Christian faith has always been a "religion of the written word." As much as the Mosaic religion and Islam,[17] the Christian religion is a *book religion* in various respects. For one thing, the Christian belief appeals to the Bible as the Scripture of Revelation. Within the New Testament the prophecies and promises of the Old Testament are fulfilled: "Filius . . . hominis vadit, sicut scriptum est de illo" 'The Son of man goes as it is written of him' (Matthew 26:24). The Bible (in the original Greek, a plural: *tà biblía*) is a considerably auto-referential book: 'as it is written' ("sicut scriptum est")[18] or 'according to the Scriptures' ("secundum Scripturas"),[19] run the formulae. Literacy itself is a biblical topic, and as such literacy is tacitly presupposed: God himself 'wrote [the Ten Commandments] in two tablets of stone' (Deuteronomy 5:22; "scripsit ea in duabus tabulis lapideis"). In Revelation, God is 'Alpha and Omega' (Revelation 21:6; 22:13; "ego sum alpha et omega").[20]

For the Germanic tribes that had settled in Britain the new religion was thus centered on literacy, and for the keepers of this belief literacy mainly centered on religion. This is to say: to begin with, competence in reading (and, to a lesser degree, writing) enabled one to grasp and deal with the religious teaching.[21] Conversely, in order to gain this competence one had to use the media that conveyed the teaching, in particular the canonical Scriptures.

In Anglo-Saxon England the "transition from orality to literacy" was thus a process completely different from alphabetization in the colonies of the nineteenth and twentieth centuries, and it was also very different from the process that we may, for instance, reconstruct for Greek Antiquity.[22] In Anglo-Saxon England the import of literacy or literateness mainly concerned the mediators themselves. These mediators were—in a monastically-religious sense—submitted to the provision that Dom Leclercq has phrased ". . . puisque l'Écriture est un livre, il faut savoir le lire" ['as Scripture is a book, it is necessary to know how to read it'].[23]

Here is the point: the tight and inextricable intertwining of religion and literacy manifests itself—at least until the High Middle Ages (until the rise of the universities)—in the fact that the men and women of religion remained the people who had the capacity to deal with what existed in writing and who passed this capacity on. We find evidence of this double tie, for instance, in one of Aldhelm's riddles:

> Me dudum genuit candens onocrotalus albam,
> Gutture qui patulo sorbet de gurgite limphas.
> Pergo per albentes directo tramite campos
> Candentique viae vestigia caerula linquo,
> Lucida nigratis fuscans anfractibus arva.
> Nec satis est unum per campos pandere callem,
> Semita quin potius milleno tramite tendit,
> Quae non errantes ad caeli culmina vexit.[24]

The riddle's solution is *penna*, the quill, a tool—in all senses of the word—with which one is enabled to attain the celestial realm.

As is well known, Aldhelm's riddle has a parallel in the riddles of the *Exeter Book*. Riddle 51 uses the same image of the dark tracks on light ground:

> Ic seah wrætlice   wuhte feower
> samod siðian;   swearte wæron lastas,
> swaþu swiþe blacu. . . .
>
> (*Riddle* 51, 1–3a)[25]

This Old English riddle does not mention any religious aims to which those tracks could lead, while in Aldhelm's *penna* riddle the skill of writing is unequivocally linked to the religious function that, for Aldhelm, has to do not only with what the writing is about but also with the act of writing itself.[26] Another of the *Exeter* riddles, Riddle 26, takes up the image of the 'black tracks', the *sweartlast* (11a), on which the quill, the 'bird's joy' (*fugles wyn*, 7b) travels. In the last eleven (of altogether 28) verses the effect of "using" *the* book, the Bible, is depicted most appealingly:

> Gif min bearn wera   brucan willað,
> hy beoð þy gesundran   ond þy sigefæstran,
> heortum þy hwætran   ond þy hygebliþran,
> ferþe þy frodran   habbaþ freonda þy ma,
> swæsra ond gesibbra,   soþra ond godra,
> tilra ond getreowra,   þa hyra tyr ond ead
> estum ycað   ond hy arstafum
> lissum bilecgað   ond hi lufaþ fæþmum
> fæste clyppað.   Frige hwæt ic hatte
> niþum to nytte   nama min is mære
> hæleþum gifre   ond halig sylf.
>
> (*Riddle* 26, 18–28)[27]

Again: not just any kind of book may have this effect: it is the *halig* one that does.

To sum up briefly: When the Anglo-Saxons came into contact with the (Christian) culture of literacy, this was by no means a (more or less) forceful acculturation, it was *not* the kind of acculturation through a political power as were the modern, "colonializing" transitions from orality to literacy. Obviously, literacy was (in a way) superimposed on the Anglo-Saxons, but, on the one hand, nobody was forced into learning to read (and write)—not to mention learn Latin—except those consigned to a monastery at an early age; on the other, as far as we know no attempt was made to prevent anybody from learning to read. One must agree fully with Wormald, who has refuted a claim that Jack Goody advanced several times,[28] namely that the medieval kind of literacy was "confined to a particular group" (so far, he is correct) that excluded others *consciously* (the misconception) from immediate access to the written texts. Goody contends that "the scribal culture continues; the *literati* hold onto their monopoly, the mandarinate maintains control."[29] Goody here works on the inappropriate equation of the medieval monastic and clerical community with a priesthood that forms a caste (such as the mandarins). Castes are characterized by being impermeable from outside, from above, from below. Yet within the history of the Roman Church both the priesthood and the monastic orders have always been open for members of virtually any class of society. That literacy itself was also open to the laity is illustrated by the prominent example of King Alfred. Alfred had the urge to acquire the skills of reading and writing, and it took him a long time to arrive at his aim, as the testimony of his teacher and biographer, Asser, so vividly (and confusingly) tells us. It may very well be that the Latin language made things that difficult for the studious young prince (and later, the king).

The learning of Latin was—we must not forget this—always inseparable from learning to read (and write) and vice versa.[30] In this we may see a similarity with the "colonializing" acquisition of literacy: in the modern colonies, schooling invariably implied learning the language of the colonializer. However, there is once again a fundamental difference between this and the medieval situation. In the colonies the foreign language was that of the alien dominating power; in the Middle Ages, Latin was the Language of Revelation and Salvation, "God's Language," as it were. Thus, while in the modern colonies the forced acquisition of that foreign language may be identified with the "oppressors," in the Middle Ages the acquisition of Latin was automatically identified with the (relatively) safe way to Salvation. This latter point may account for the fact that, as far as Anglo-Saxon England is concerned, we know of no source that speaks critically about literacy. With the Ostrogoths—to name another, earlier Germanic example—things were obviously different.

When the Ostrogoths under the leadership of Theoderic intruded into the Western Roman realm they were already Christianized (although adhering to the "wrong," Arian, belief). One may say that they (partly) acculturated themselves in the surrounding of a literate culture (cf. Boethius), but a culture that was on the decline. The Byzantine historian Procopius tells us about Theoderic's daughter Amalasuntha, who "wished to make her son resemble the Roman princes in his manner of life, and was already compelling him to attend the school of a teacher of letters,"[31] whereupon Gothic "notable men" gathered and objected that letters "are far removed from manliness, and the teaching of old men results for the most part in a cowardly and submissive spirit."[32] Some 350 years later no such objections were made in view of the education of the West Saxon prince Alfred.

What is remarkable about the expansion and development of literacy in Anglo-Saxon England is that fairly soon it took hold of the vernacular. The fact that the Germanic languages, and in particular Anglo-Saxon, were scripted much earlier than the Romance vernaculars is commonly explained as follows: while in the Romance cultures the *vernacular* that one *spoke* was considered a deteriorated version of the *Latin* one *wrote*, no such barrier existed in Germanic cultures.[33] Herbert Grundmann states, "Das Angelsächsische war fremd und andersartig genug, dass man es unbedenklich schreiben konnte ohne Sorge, es könnte das aus guten alten Texten erlernte Latein verderben statt ergänzen."[34]

In this context Grundmann credits Bede with a special benevolence toward and special support of the vernacular in relation to the literate (Latin) culture. He cites Cuthbert's report that Bede planned to translate the Gospel of St. John for the *idiotae* and that Bede himself recited the vernacular *Deathsong* in the hour of his death.[35] Then there is the well-known Cædmon story that Bede relates in *Historia Ecclesiastica Gentis Anglorum* IV.22. Cædmon, an illiterate farmhand, was enabled by divine inspiration not only to produce a *Hymn on Creation* but also to versify renderings of all major parts of the Bible "in sua, id est Anglorum, lingua" ['in his, i.e., English, language']. What Grundmann does not say is that we may well infer this detailed story of Cædmon to be (probably) less a "literally true story" than an attempt on Bede's part to legitimize religious poetry in the vernacular.[36] Curiously enough, Grundmann paraphrases the Cædmon story by saying that Cædmon was a Christian poet, "der seine angelsächsischen Bibeldichtungen den doctores vortrug, denen er den Stoff verdankte und die ihn aufschreiben konnten."[37] Let us turn to Bede himself. In Latin the passage paraphrased by Grundmann reads: "At ipse cuncta, quae audiendo discere poterat. Rememorando secum et quasi mundum animal ruminando, in carmen dulcissimum convertebat suauiusque resonando doctores suos uicissim auditores faciebat."[38] There is not the slightest hint in the original Latin version that anybody wrote anything down. However, if we look into the Old English translation of the *Historia Ecclesiastica*, the equivalent of the end of the quote just given runs thus: ". . . 7 his song 7 his leoð wæron swa wynsumu to gehyranne, þætte seolfan þa his lareowas æt his muðe wreoton and leornodon."[39] The Latin *doctores* who were turned by Cædmon into *auditores* have become "teachers" who "wrote from his mouth and learnt." The Old English translator must have felt compelled to be a little more explicit about what happened when those "teachers" were taking over the part of "listeners." The translator specifies the situation of listening as one of "writing down (what is heard)" and also of "learning," which must mean 'learn by heart, memorize'. The translator thus magnifies the process of mere listening into two subsequent types of preservation, those of writing down and of memorization.

Our modern minds think of those two types of preservation as alternative, and we certainly hold the act of writing down the material to be the safer. The translator must have thought otherwise; he lets the *doctores* make a "backup copy," as it were, the memorizing storage in the human brain. This leads us to the other point on which I want to elaborate: how written material was evaluated and used in those days of "transitional literacy."

In our twentieth-century literacy we conceive of the technology of writing as one means by which our minds are freed from having to retain something in our memory: what is written down, whether we do it ourselves or whether somebody has done it for us, can be deleted, as it were, from our "ready access memory." This is what Jack Goody sees as the main achievement of the introduction of alphabetic writing in ancient times:

> the human mind was freed to study static 'text' (rather than be limited by participation in the dynamic 'utterance'), a process that enabled man to stand back from his creation and examine it in a more abstract, generalised, and 'rational' way.[40]

While this may hold true for the ancient world, it most certainly does not hold—at least not in this absolute way—for the early Middle Ages.

Yet again, let us abstain from over-generalization. I have pointed out elsewhere[41] that the Anglo-Saxon poet Cynewulf does indeed give us evidence of such a "standing back from his own creation" when, for instance, he—with some authorial pride—leads up to his "runic signature" at the end of his *Fates of the Apostles* by saying,

> Her mæg findan forþances gleaw,
> se ðe hine lysteð leoðgiddunga,
> hwa þas fitte fegde. . . .
> (*Fates of the Apostles*, 96–98a)[42]

or when he entreats his audience towards the end of *Juliana*:

Bidde ic monna gewhone
gumena cynne, þe þis gied wræce,
þæt he mec neodful bi monan minum
gemyne modig. . . .
(*Juliana*, 718b–21a)[43]

Cynewulf, however, is a rare exception. Other Anglo-Saxon poets—and also Cynewulf himself at some point (though half-heartedly)—even take away the "static" quality of material that already exists in writing, at least when they transpose it into their own epic language. Thus, the opening of the Old English *Exodus* does not refer to the deeds of Moses as "hit/þus ys awriten"[44] but rather as

Hwæt! We feor and neah gefrigen habbað
ofer middangeard Moyses domas . . .
(*Exodus*, 1–2).[45]

The poet of *Andreas* also chooses not to refer to the venerable written source:

Hwæt! We gefrugnan on fyrndagum
twelfe under tunglum tireadige hæleð . . .
(*Andreas*, 1–2).[46]

These poets thus integrate their religious poems into what we, along with Maurice Halbwachs, may call the "collective memory."[47] The transposition of this biblical material into the vernacular language and indigenous narrative form seems also to have necessitated its integration into the chain of tradition in order to endow these narratives with relevance for the English audience. The reference to a *written* source—even if this source never existed—is a matter for the later Middle Ages.

But not only memory guaranteed relevance through its collectivity. Storing something within one's own memory—memorization—was obviously also considered the way to deal appropriately with writings. It was a hermeneutic technique.[48] As late as the twelfth century we hear from Petrus Venerabilis about a monk whose mouth incessantly ruminates the holy words ("os sine requie sacra verba ruminans").[49] Dom Leclercq characterized the consequences of this kind of appropriation of the written thus:

> . . . il en résulte une mémoire musculaire des mots prononcés, une mémoire auditive des mots entendus. La *meditatio* consiste à s'appliquer avec attention à cet exercice de mémoire totale; elle est donc inséparable de la *lectio*. C'est elle qui, pour ainsi dire, inscrit le texte sacré dans le corps et l'esprit.[50]

It is noteworthy that Bede attributed the same kind of appropriating process to the illiterate Cædmon who also "ruminated" the biblical narratives before he turned them into vernacular verse.

Memorization was not only the means by which religious people tried to gain a better understanding of texts; it also allowed illiterate people to avail themselves of written material. Our prime example is young Alfred, of whom Asser tells the following well-known episode.[51] Alfred's mother one day showed to him and his brothers "quemdam Saxonicum poematicae artis librum" ["a book of English poetry"] and promised that she would give it to that one of her children who "discere citius istum codicem possit" ["can learn it [this book] the fastest"].[52] Young Alfred took the book, "magistrum adiit et legit" ["went to his teacher and learnt it [/read it]"[53]]. Whatever Asser may have meant by *legit*—according to Asser himself, Alfred at this point in time was still illiterate—the result was that Alfred, after "reading" the book, then "matri retulit et recitavit" ["took it back to his mother and recited it"]. One hopes that Alfred's mother stuck to her promise to give the book to the diligent boy!

An interesting detail is the motivation that Asser gives for the child Alfred to undergo the toil of learning a whole book by heart. Alfred was "pulchritudine principalis litterae illius libri illectus" ["attracted by the beauty of the initial letter in the book"]. We may well suppose that writing itself must have an almost magic attraction for people who cannot read (or write).[54] There is evidence that for missionary purposes script was used to manifest the *value* of the written word. In a letter dated to the year 735, Boniface asks Eadburga, the Abbess of Thanet, ". . . ut mihi cum auro conscribas epistolas domini mei sancti Petri apostoli ad honorem et reverentiam sanctarum scripturarum ante occulos carnalium in praedicando. . . ."[55] The underscoring that the copy be made in golden letters (for which he himself provided the material) illustrates this other possible use of the written: to impress the heathens—those "carnally minded"—whom Boniface wants to convert to the Christian belief. He certainly did not show the manuscript so that his audience should read the wording of the Letter of St. Peter. Here the golden writing becomes a symbol of a different kind. The sign value of what is written is reversed, as it were: it is not the medial representative of something else—a sequence of sounds—but rather a sign for itself. Divine Revelation in its manifestation as golden letters does not only *mean* something valuable, it *is* in itself valuable.

The one purpose that books, codices, hardly ever had in the Middle Ages was that of everyday use. Most of the content was available, word by word, in the memory of individuals. Even in the pursuit of a better understanding of what the books contained, one did not read and re-read the written words but ruminated them by repetition—memorized repetition, that is! Memorization, we know from many medieval contemporary sources, was the basic part of schooling.[56] Thus in his *Colloquy* Ælfric Bata, a pupil of the tenth-century scholar (and archbishop) Ælfric, has the master give the following assignment to his students: ". . . petite libros uestros cito, et in scamnis uestris sedentes legite, et firmate acceptos uestros, ut properanter reddere ualeatis cras in primo mane. . . ."[57] Although skeptics may doubt whether *firmare* here really means 'to learn by heart' and whether *reddere* could not refer simply to the returning of the books, the remainder of this sentence clearly refers to memorization as the appropriate way of understanding a book. Moreover, it also underscores a practical side of memorization in times that did not yet know of reading glasses:

> . . . [ut ualetis] deinde plus discere a nostro instructore, ut quando senes eritis, tunc memoriter in cunctis libris Latinis legere possitis et aliquid intellegere in illis . . . quia legere libros et non intellegere neglegere est secundum Catonis sententiam.[58]

In view of the specific dealing with the written in (early) medieval literate culture, we should not take the codices for what they were *not* meant to be for contemporaries. Goody's idea that alphabetization had an emancipating effect in that it enabled man to "stand back from his creation and examine it in a more abstract, generalised, and 'rational' way"[59] may only be valid in a restricted sense for the medieval way of dealing with what one found in the codices, the venerable scriptures one would not dare "stand back from" but rather upon which one would expend effort to appropriate, by "ruminating," "mulling over," them. The modern notion of "internalization," introduced by Behaviorist psychology, might rather aptly reflect how written material was dealt with.

Here I have given some details about the introduction of and contemporary attitude toward early medieval literacy in order to illustrate two things that must be kept in mind. First: literacy, at least to begin with, was *not meant for pragmatic purposes*. Its close ties with the dominant religion do not necessarily imply that literacy was a privilege over which a closed caste assiduously watched. While this tie was always present, the "consequences of literacy," its impacts on human conceptualization, may have taken quite a long time to emerge. Literacy did not necessarily interfere with other forms of social and cultural organization (as it has done in modern "colonializing").[60] On the contrary: if, for instance, the poet of the Old English *Exodus* lets the epic begin in such a way that it signals the traditionality of the "collective memory," the new religion subordinates itself to those hermeneutic conditions that are inherited from orality.

Second: if we consider the ample evidence of how medieval literate learning dealt with what existed in writing, what notion this culture had of "understanding" what is written, we should regard this as a warning as to how *we* deal with what has come down in writing from this period. Our advanced literacy takes a piece of writing as a "text," something one may and in fact *has to* perceive as a unit of meaning, and which is organized in such a way that this very meaning may be retrieved from the text itself.[61] In early medieval culture hardly anyone would have conceived of looking for the meaning of sentences or words by examining the immediate *linguistic* context of the sentence or word under consideration. This is the fully-fledged literate way, and obviously alien to earlier cultural stages. The fact that for the early Middle Ages the meaning of something in writing was *not* constituted by the immediate *linguistic* context is amply substantiated by what we would call "quotations" from other writings. The large number of "decontextualized" quotations from the Bible and other canonical writings gives evidence that the "texture" of something written was not necessarily untouchable.[62]

Obviously Anglo-Saxon culture had a sense for the "wrong" kind of consumption of what existed in writing: "legere libros et non intellegere neglegere est," as Ælfric Bata quotes.[63] Let us take heed that, as we converse with written evidence from that culture, we do not in the end find ourselves in the same state as the agent of Riddle 47 in the *Exeter Book*:

> Moððe word fræt. Me þæt þuhte
> wrætlicu wyrd, þa ic þæt wundor gefrægn,
> þæt se wyrm forswealg wera gied sumes,
> þeof in þystro, þrymfæstne cwide
> ond þæs strangan staþol. Stælgiest ne wæs
> wihte þy gleawra, þe he þam wordum swealg.[64]

HUMBOLDT-UNIVERSITÄT ZU BERLIN

NOTES

1. Walter Ong, "Writing Is a Technology That Restructures Thought," in *The Written Word: Literacy in Transition*, ed. Gerd Baumann (Oxford, 1986), pp. 22–50.

2. For a bibliography see Walter Ong, *Orality and Literacy: The Technologizing of the Word* (London, 1982), and Eric Havelock, *The Muse Learns to Write: Reflections on Orality and Literacy from Antiquity to the Present* (New Haven, 1986); for linguistics see also the basic article by Peter Koch and Wulf Oesterreicher, "Sprache der Nähe—Sprache der Distanz: Mündlichkeit und Schriftlichkeit im Spannungsfeld von Sprachtheorie und Sprachgeschichte," *Romanistisches Jahrbuch*, 36 (1985), 15–43.

3. For Greek Antiquity see Eric Havelock, *Preface to Plato* (Cambridge, MA, 1963), *Origins of Western Literacy* (Toronto, 1976), and *The Muse Learns to Write*; Wolfgang Rösler, "Die Entdeckung der Fiktionalität in der Antike," *Poetica*, 12 (1980), 283–319, and "Schriftkultur und Fiktionalität. Zum Funktionswandel der griechischen Literatur von Homer bis Aristoteles," in *Schrift und Gedächtnis: Beiträge zur Archäologie der literarischen Kommunikation*, vol. 1, ed. A. Assmann, J. Assmann, and Ch. Hardmeier (Munich, 1983), pp. 109–22. For the Middle Ages see, among others, T. M. Clanchy, "Remembering the Past and the Good Old Law," *History*, 55 (1970), 165–76, and *From Memory to Written Record: England 1066–1307* (London, 1979); Elizabeth Eisenstein, "Clio and Chronos: An Essay on the Making and Breaking of History-Book Time," *History and Theory*, Beiheft 6 (1966), 36–64; Brian Stock, *The Implications of Literacy: Written Language and Models of Interpretation in the Eleventh and Twelfth Centuries* (Princeton, 1983) and "Medieval Literacy, Linguistic Theory, and Social Organization," *New Literary History*, 16 (1984/85), 14–29, and "History, Literature, Medieval Textuality," *Yale French Studies*, 70 (1986), 7–17; Hanna Vollrath, "Das Mittelalter in der Typik oraler Gesellschaften," *Historische Zeitschrift*, 233 (1981), 571–94, and "Bücher—nein danke! Die mündliche Welt des Mittelalters," *Journal für Geschichte* (1984,3), 24–29.

4. Vollrath, "Das Mittelalter," p. 588; tr.: '. . . [the] basic problems of the Middle Ages may more clearly be conceived of if we approach them by taking into account orality as a culture-dominating factor'.

5. Katherine O'Brien O'Keeffe, *Visible Song: Transitional Literacy in Old English Verse* (Cambridge, 1990), p. 21.

6. Note that *Webster's Dictionary* lists the (etymologically) secondary meaning first!

7. It is not my aim here to investigate further into the cultural specificity of the terminology, let alone of the research done under these headings. For the comparison of English and German terminology see also Ursula Schaefer, "Zum Problem der Mündlichkeit," in *Modernes Mittelalter. Neue Bilder einer populären Epoche*, ed. Joachim Heinzle (Frankfurt/M., 1994), pp. 357–75, esp. 358–61; see Adam B. Davis "Übergänge und Spannungsfelder zwischen amerikanischen und deutschen Studien zur Mündlichkeit," in *Kulturelle Perspektiven auf Schrift und Schreibprozesse*, ed. Wolfgang Raible, ScriptOralia 72 (Tübingen, 1995), pp. 215–32.

8. Vollrath, "Oral Modes of Perception in Eleventh-Century Chronicles," in *Vox Intexta: Orality and Textuality in the Middle Ages*, ed. A. N. Doane and Carol Braun Pasternack (Madison, 1991), pp. 104, 111.

9. Ibid., p. 110.

10. Ibid., p. 111.

11. Vollrath adapts some of Brian Stock's ideas on the "implications of literacy" and connects them to more general observations advanced by Jack Goody. By picking up Goody's dictum that "written formulations encourage the decontextualization or generalization of norms" (*The Logic of Writing and the Organization of Society: Studies in Literacy, Family, Culture and the States* [Cambridge, 1986], p. 12), she approaches her sources with the question "But exactly what kind of mental operation is necessary for decontextualization on the one hand and for the fitting of general norms into a given context on the other?" ("Oral Modes," p. 103).

12. O'Keeffe, p. x.

13. Wormald's "The Uses of Literacy in Anglo-Saxon England" appears in *Transactions of the Royal Historical Society*, 5th ser., 27 (1977), 95–114.

14. This is, of course, the etymological origin for what has finally wound up in present-day English as *clerk* with its various denotations down to AmE, "one who works at a sales or service counter" (*Webster*). It is interesting to note that—at least in literary (and/or ironic [!]) usage—the French *clerc* has retained the meaning "*lettré* [!], *savant*" (*Larousse*). *Lettré*, in its turn, is the—somewhat stronger—correspondent of English *literate* in the sense of '(very) educated'. French *savant* seems untranslatable.

15. See Wormald, pp. 111ff.

16. Talcott Parsons, *Societies: Evolutionary and Comparative Perspectives* (Englewood Cliffs, NJ, 1966), pp. 51–52; he speaks about the "archaic . . . intermediate society," whose "cultural elaboration is linked with the literacy of priesthoods and their capacity to maintain a stable written tradition. The literacy is, however, still esoteric and limited to specialized groups—hence, it is craft literacy." According to Parsons this "archaic intermediate society" is followed by an "advanced intermediate society," which is characterized by a "full upper-class literacy" (ibid., p. 51). At best this state of affairs is attained in the later Middle Ages. One characteristic of the European Middle Ages is the fact that it may be assigned completely to neither the one nor the other type of society.

17. Islam collectively calls those of the Mosaic, Christian, and Islamic belief the "peoples of the Book."

18. Twelve times, e.g., in Paul's Epistle to the Romans alone: 1:17, 2:23, 3:4, 3:10, 4:17, 8:36, 9:13, 9:33, 11:8, 15:3, 15:9, 15:20.

19. See I Corinthians 15:3–4 where the formula is used twice in the so-called "ur-Creed." As introduction Paul says: "Tradidi enim vobis in primis quod et accepi" ('For I delivered unto you first of all that which I also received'). Then he obviously quotes what may, in his time, have been orally spread but nevertheless was deeply relying on literacy: "quoniam Christus mortuus est pro peccatis nostris secundum Scripturas: et quia sepultus est, et quia resurrexit tertia die secundum Scripturas" ('how that Christ died for our sins according to the Scriptures; And that he was buried, and that he rose again the third day according to the Scriptures'). In itself this phrasing—in order to preserve its sacred validity—has hence to remain untouched as Paul says when he stresses that "sic praedicamus, et sic credistis" (15:11) ('so we preach and so ye believed'). The latter is, of course, the "legislative" power of the unchanged wording, the *verbatim* passing on which, for this matter, guarantees validity in both oral and literate tradition.

20. See Hans-Martin Gauger, "Nietzsche: Zur Genealogie der Sprache," in *Theorien vom Ursprung der Sprache*, ed. J. Gessinger and W. von Rahden, 2 vols. (Berlin, 1989), vol. 1, pp. 585–606, here 589–90.

21. See Jean Leclercq, *L'Amour des lettres et le désir de Dieu. Initiation aux auteurs monastiques du moyen âge* (Paris, 1957), pp. 71–72.

22. See in particular Havelock, *Preface to Plato*, and *The Muse Learns to Write*, pp. 79–126; Jack Watt and Ian Watt, "The Consequences of Literacy," in *Literacy in Traditional Societies*, ed. J. Goody (Cambridge, 1968), pp. 27–69 (first publ. 1962–63); Ong, *Orality and Literacy*, passim.

23. Leclercq, p. 71.

24. Ed. Rudolph Ehwald, MGH, *Auctores Antiquissimi* 15, p. 15 (Riddle LIX); tr. Michael Lapidge and James Rosier, *Aldhelm: The Poetic Works* (Cambridge, 1985), p. 82: "The bright pelican, which swallows the waters of the sea in its gaping throat, once begot me (such that I was) white. I move through whitened fields in a straight line and leave dark-coloured traces on the glistening path, darkening the shining fields with my blackened meanderings. It is not sufficient to open up a single pathway through these fields—rather, the trail proceeds in a thousand directions and takes those who do not stray from it to the summits of heaven."

25. Unless stated otherwise, the Old English quotations are taken from *Anglo-Saxon Poetic Records* [ASPR], ed. George Philip Krapp and Elliott Van Kirk Dobbie, 6 vols. (London, 1931–52); here: ASPR 3 (1936), p. 207; tr.: 'I saw four strange creatures travel together; dark were their tracks, their trail very black. . . .'

26. See also the *Indovinello Veronese*, a *probatio pennae* from the 8th/9th century considered the first written evidence of the Italian vernacular: "Se pareba boves, alba pratalia araba / albo versorio teneba, negro semen seminaba" (approximately, the ultimate meaning is still being discussed): 'One drove oxen, one plowed white pastures / one held a white plough, one sowed black seeds'; see P. Rajna, "Un' indovinello volgare scritto alla fine del secolo VIII a al principio del IX," *Speculum*, 3 (1928), 291–313.

27. ASPR 3, p. 194; tr.: 'If the children of men will use me they will be the safer and the more triumphant, [their] hearts the bolder, and happier in mind, their spirit the wiser; they will have the more friends, more intimate and closer, truer and better, more useful and loyal, who augment their glory and happiness gladly, and they lay around [them] support and kindness, and they embrace them fast with love. Learn what I am called, in affliction I am useful. My name is famous, of help for men, and myself [is] holy'.

28. Wormald (p. 97) refers to Goody, ed., *Literacy in Traditional Societies* (Cambridge, 1968); I subsequently quote from Goody, *Domestication of the Savage Mind* (Cambridge, 1977).

29. Goody, *Domestication*, pp. 151–52.

30. For the important part the vernacular played for the acquisition of Latin in 10th-century England, see now George Hardin Brown, "Latin Writing and the Old English Vernacular," in *Schriftlichkeit im frühen Mittelalter*, ed. Ursula Schaefer, ScriptOralia 53 (Tübingen, 1993), pp. 36–57.

31. Procopius, *History of the Wars*, V.ii; tr. H. B. Dewing, *Procopius*, 7 vols. (London, 1908), vol. 3, *History of the Wars, Books V and VI*, p. 19.

32. Ibid.; for an appreciation of this see Vollrath, "Bücher—nein, danke."

33. Note that Wulfila's (Ostro-)Gothic translation of the Bible from the 4th century is the oldest evidence of a Germanic language; a closer scrutinization of Wulfila's achievement within the context of orality/literacy research is still lacking.

34. Herbert Grundmann, "Litteratus—illitteratus. Der Wandel einer Bildungsnorm vom Altertum zum Mittelalter," *Archiv für Kulturgeschichte*, 40 (1958), 1–65, here p. 35; tr.: 'Anglo-Saxon was alien and different enough, in order to be written without the fear of corrupting the Latin that one had acquired from good old texts'.

35. Ibid.

36. The possible legitimizing purpose of Bede's Cædmon story is addressed for instance by G. W. Weber, "Altenglische Literatur: volkssprachliche Renaissance einer frühmittelalterlichen christlichen Latinität," in *Neues Handbuch der Literaturwissenschaft*, vol. 4, *Europäisches Frühmittelalter*, gen. ed. Klaus von See (Wiesbaden, 1985), pp. 277–316, here 296, and Dwight Conquergood, "Literacy and Oral Performance in Anglo-Saxon England: Conflict and Confluence of Traditions," in *Performance of Literature in Historical Perspectives*, ed. D. W. Thompson et al. (Lanham, MD, 1983), pp. 107–45.

37. Grundmann, p. 35; tr.: '. . . who recited his biblical poetry to the *doctores* to whom he owed the [narrative] material and who were also able to write it down'.

38. *Bede's Ecclesiastical History of the English Nation*, ed. and tr. Bertram Colgrave and R. A. B. Mynors (Oxford, 1969), p. 418; tr.: "He learned all he could by listening to them and then, memorizing it and ruminating over it, like some clean animal chewing the

cud, he turned it into the most melodious verse: and it sounded so sweet as he recited it that his teachers became in turn his audience" (p. 419).

39. *The Old English Version of Bede's Ecclesiastical History of The English People*, ed. with tr. and introd. by Thomas Miller, EETS OS 96 (1891), p. 346; tr.: "And his song and his music were so delightful to hear, that even his teachers wrote down the words from his lips and learnt them" (p. 374).

40. Goody, *Domestication*, p. 37.

41. See Ursula Schaefer, "Hearing from Books: The Rise of Fictionality in Old English Poetry," in *Vox Intexta*, ed. Doane and Pasternack, pp. 117–36, here 125–34, and Schaefer, *Vokalität: Altenglische Dichtung zwischen Mündlichkeit und Schriftlichkeit*, ScriptOralia 39 (Tübingen, 1992), pp. 166–77.

42. ASPR 2, pp. 53–54; tr.: 'Here may the one who is wise of thoughts / who likes this song, find / who made this song. . . .'

43. ASPR 3, p. 133; tr.: 'I pray every man / of human kind, who may recite this song, / that he earnestly and fervently remember me, / the needful, by my name. . . .'

44. This is how the Old English Bible translation renders *scriptum est enim*; see, e.g., Matthew 4:4, 6, 7, 10 (*The Old English Version of the Gospels*, ed. Roy M. Liuzza, EETS OS 304 [1994], p. 7).

45. ASPR 1, p. 91; tr.: 'Lo! We have—far and near—heard throughout the world Moses' decrees. . . .'

46. ASPR 2, p. 3; tr.: 'Lo! We heard in days past [how] twelve under the stars, famous men. . . .'

47. See Maurice Halbwachs, *La mémoire collective* (Paris, 1968; first, smaller ed. 1950); Cynewulf tries the same kind of exordium in *Juliana* (ASPR 3, p. 113): "Hwæt! We ðæt hyrdon hæleð eahtian, / deman dædhwate, þætte in dagum gelamp / Maximianes" (lines 1–3a).

48. See for this most recently Ivan Illich's essay "*Lectio Divina*" in *Schriftlichkeit*, ed. Schaefer, pp. 19–35.

49. Petrus Venerabilis, *De Miraculis*, I.20, PL 189, 887; the passage is quoted by Leclercq in *L'Amour des lettres*, p. 71.

50. Leclercq, p. 72; tr.: '. . . the result is a muscular memory of the words pronounced, an aural memory of the words heard. The *meditatio* consists of lending oneself with [complete] attention to this exercise of total memory (/memorization); it is hence inseparable from the *lectio*. It is [this memorization] which, as it were, inscribes the sacred text in the body and the mind'.

51. The following Latin quotations are taken from William H. Stevenson's edition of *Asser's Life of King Alfred* (Oxford, 1904), ch. 23, p. 20; the English translation is taken from *Alfred the Great: Asser's "Life of King Alfred" and Other Contemporary Sources*, tr. with introd. and notes by Simon Keynes and Michael Lapidge (Harmondsworth, 1983), p. 75.

52. Note that Alfred's mother (in Asser's rendering) here uses the Latin verb *discere* to mean 'learn by heart, memorize'. The Old English translator of Bede's *Historia* uses the OE *leornian* (with no equivalent in the Latin original) also to mean 'memorize'.

53. Keynes and Lapidge translate *legit* as "learnt it," commenting that in the phrase *magistrum adiit et legit* "either *et* is an error for *qui* (in which case the master 'read the book to Alfred') or *legit* means 'absorbed its contents' or 'learnt' [. . .]" (p. 239, n. 48).

54. See most recently Wolfgang Hartung, "Die Magie des Geschriebenen," in *Schriftlichkeit*, ed. Schaefer, pp. 109–26.

55. *Bonifatii Epistulae—Willibaldi Vita Bonifatii/Briefe des Bonifatius—Willibalds Leben des Bonifatius*, ed. and tr. R. Rau, Freiherr-vom-Stein-Gedächtnisausgabe vol. IVb (Darmstadt, 1968), Ep. 35, p. 114; tr. Ephraim Emerton, *The Letters of Saint Boniface* (New York, 1976), p. 76: "that you make a copy written in gold of the Epistles of my master, St. Peter the Apostle, to impress honor and reverence for the Sacred Scriptures visibly upon the carnally minded to whom I preach. . . ."

56. See Pierre Riché, "Le Rôle de la mémoire dans l'enseignement médiéval," in *Jeux de mémoire: Aspects de mnémotechnie médiévale*, ed. B. Roy and P. Zumthor (Montreal, 1985), pp. 133–48, and *Écoles et enseignement dans le Haut Moyen Âge. Fin du Ve siècle–milieu du XIe siècle*, 2nd ed. (Paris, 1989), pp. 187–266 (pt. 3, chs. 1–3).

57. William H. Stevenson, ed., *Early Scholastic Colloquies* (Oxford, 1929), p. 29; tr.: '. . . ask quickly for your books, and read while you are sitting on your stools, and consolidate what you have received [i.e., learnt], so that you are able to render [it/them?] first thing in the morning. . . .'

58. Ibid.; tr.: '. . . [so that you are able] subsequently to learn more from our instructor, so that, when you will be old, you may then read in all Latin books from your memory and understand anything in them . . . because—according to the sentence of Cato —to read books and not understand [them] is to neglect [them]'. The Cato mentioned here is the Roman poet of the 3rd century A.D. who belonged to the medieval "school authors".

59. Goody, *Domestication*, p. 37.

60. Things seem to be changing in England in the 10th century, for which Wilhelm Busse has diagnosed an emerging conflict between oral and written tradition in the wake of the Benedictine reform: ". . . the real impetus towards learning and booklore on a more general scale began only with the Benedictine reform movement. This leads to a cultural clash of social norms of behaviour in which traditions based on oral transmission and those based on the written, especially on biblical history, came into conflict, were discussed, and digested in literature" ("Boceras. Written and Oral Traditions in the Late Tenth Century," in *Mündlichkeit und Schriftlichkeit im englischen Mittelalter*, ed. Willi Erzgräber and Sabine Volk, ScriptOralia 5 [Tübingen, 1988], pp. 27–37, here 37).

61. See David Olson, "From Utterance to Text: The Bias of Language in Speech and Writing," *Harvard Educational Review*, 47 (1977), 257–81; for this also the chapter "Poetische Kommunikation in der Vokalität," in Schaefer *Vokalität*, pp. 11–14; see also Schaefer, "Hearing from Books," pp. 119–25.

62. See for this the chapter "Das Zitieren," in Schaefer, *Vokalität* (pp. 37–41); the difficulty with contextual interpretation is also vividly illustrated in Vollrath, "Oral Modes."

63. I suggest that the solution to *Riddle* 47 may well not be merely the—all too obvious—'bookworm' or 'book moth' but a senselessly ruminating monk.

64. Tr.: 'A moth ate words; methought this was a strange fate when I heard of the wondrous thing, that the worm swallowed the song / poem of some man, [like a] thief in the darkness, this glorious saying, and the strong binding. The thieving spirit was none the wiser, that had swallowed the words'.

Subjectivity/Orality: How Relevant Are Modern Literary Theories to the Study of Old English Poetry? What Light Can the Study of Old English Poetry Cast on Modern Literary Theory?

Rosemary Huisman

One of the most consistent concerns of recent literary theory, whether explicitly or implicitly, has been the problem of the construction of the subject position or subjectivity, that is, that social and historical positioning of the individual through which production and interpretation of texts are possible. For modern critics, the notion of "the meaning" of the text, a meaning identified with the authorial voice, has been undermined because of its reliance on a simplistic "conduit model" of language.[1] Where now does authority reside? A functional linguist, like Michael Halliday, sees meaning as culturally constructed; such views have been elaborated in the work of British scholars like Norman Fairclough, who see the interpretation and production of a text taking place through the individual's internalized resources, these resources deriving from the individual's experiences of social conditions, including the experience of text.[2] A commentator like Jacques Derrida, writing from a primarily philosophical background, can deny the possibility of present meaning, meaning as presence, altogether,[3] and a theoretical semiotician, like Umberto Eco, sees metaphor as the "cognitive tool" for moving through the similarities of the culture, so that ultimately any linguistic item can be linked to any other.[4] Eco calls this interpretative drift "unlimited semiosis";

its constant displacement of ultimate or absolute signification is the *différance* of which Derrida writes. Feminist writing has made particular use of Derridean notions of "deconstruction," where conventional or traditional readings of texts can be "decentered" so that marginalized positions of subjectivity, like that associated with feminist readings, can be (re)instated as interpretative positions.[5] And so on.

Why should one talk about these matters at a conference on Old English? I want to suggest that, while talking about Old English texts in the context of these recent writings on literary theory may enable one to say new or different kinds of things about much-discussed Old English works, such talk also throws some light on recent theory itself. It is not irrelevant to the theme of this volume to suggest that the study of Old English is not merely of interest to those focused on that historical period but that it also has wider relevance for those whose primary concern is later literature, or literary theory generally.

In particular, I want to suggest that there are unrecognized limitations in the usual accounts of subjectivity because such accounts typically focus on texts in Modern English, and especially on nineteenth- and twentieth-century writing. A focus instead on Old English texts reveals, I suggest, that what have been put forward as philosophically general theories are in practice context-dependent theories, in particular that these theories take as natural or transparently obvious what is contingent, that is, the social conditions associated with text production and interpretation in recent Western culture. Making particular use of Walter Ong's views of "the psychodynamics of orality" in his book *Orality and Literacy*,[6] I want to argue that, according to Ong's criteria, Anglo-Saxon culture is a culture of high residual orality.[7] And because surviving Old English poetry, however literate the source of much of its subject-matter, is still composed in Germanic versification based on pre-literate oral traditions, this paper will particularly consider subjectivity in Old English poetry.[8]

I wish to talk about subjectivity in a way associated with the French linguist Benveniste, and as expanded in film criticism by, among others, Kaja Silverman. In this approach, subjectivity is constituted simultaneously by three subject positions, that of the speaking subject, that of the subject of speech, and that of the spoken subject.[9] To give an over-simplified example of what I mean by these three types of subject: *from the point of view of production*, the speaking subject of *Beowulf* is the *scop*, the subject of speech is the participant, whether narrator or poetic character, of whom the first-person pronoun is used in the text, and the spoken subject is that position prepared for us, the listeners, to identify with to the extent that we "make sense" of or "construct an interpretation" of the poem. Yet *from the point of view of interpretation*, the spoken subject position is that which the reader actually occupies in order to make sense of the text (or in order to reject it as senseless), the subject of speech is again the position of whatever participant is indicated by the first-person pronoun in the text, and the speaking subject is the implied poet, that is, the poetic persona or speaking presence the reader constructs while making sense of the poem.[10]

Now in uncritically applying this tri-part subjectivity I beg a large question in relation to the speaking subject—the very question of subjectivity and orality. It is an axiom of much modern literary theory that, from about the seventeenth century on, the modern individual, psychologically internal, humanistically and logocentrically centered speaking subject, came to be constructed. This is the self-knowing subject of scientific discourse.[11] The trace of its textual presence is a sustained positioning of narrative point of view in spatio-temporal terms. Unless we read an ideological difference between implied author and narrator, as in satire, parody, and so on, we co-operatively read an implied speaking subject positioned as the narrator; in modern texts the narrator is typically located by the spatio-temporal point of view from which events are told.[12] But how relevant is this account to Old English texts? The poem *Judith*, in earlier critical opinion cited by Alain Renoir (in 1962),[13] had received glowing praise because of its apparent narrative consistency: it is "a narrative poem of great energy and fiery story-telling . . . devoid of the superfluity of homiletic elements which so often mar its companion

Beowulf" (George K. Anderson in 1949). In his discussion Renoir certainly assumes a "knowing subject" choosing spatio-temporal positioning, as in, for example, "the method whereby the poet moves through space and time, and shifts the point of view of his narrative, is one that . . ." (p. 150) and "we must note a master-stroke of narrative perspicuity when he [the poet] delays the discovery of Holofernes' death until . . ." (p. 154). A critical principle that obliges one to find *Beowulf* "marred" needs close examination. Consider the drowning of the Egyptians in the Old English poem *Exodus* at lines 447–515. One recalls the tumbling repetition of destruction in the water, with events appearing to progress chronologically only for the telling to return to the same matter. An immediate modern response could be, "obviously here we have syntactic symbolism: the tumbling of water, the tumbling of syntax," but how coherently can one construct a speaking subject, positioned in the narrative? Spatially, one reads now with the Egyptians, psychologically internal to them, "being terrified," now with the Israelites, psychologically internal to them, "blood-terror," or even with the sea, which is personified, "threatened death." And a speaking subject is certainly not positioned in human time, with event chronologically succeeding event, but in what one might call historical time. The whole conglomerate of events can be read as one historical event which can then be placed outside of time, in exegetical equivalents of type and anti-type. In summary, rather than the subjectivity of the knowing individual we read here a communal, externalized subjectivity, omnipresent, outside individual human positioning and copiously inclusive. Ong makes several observations relevant to this positioning of the speaking subject in his chapter "Some Psychodynamics of Orality."[14] In discussing the characteristic redundancy of oral expression he comments, "oral cultures encourage fluency, fulsomeness, volubility."[15] One instantly recalls that variation, the characteristic Old English poetic device, has this redundant function. And, again for Ong, "primary orality fosters personality structures that in certain ways are more communal and externalized, and less introspective than those common among literates."[16] By "less introspective" I take Ong to mean not that such cultures are uninterested in mental states—one kind of interpretation of *The Wanderer* has taken the poem to be centrally concerned with such interest[17]—but that they are less interested in the individual response, more interested in the common or general human condition. Peter Clemoes has attributed just such generality to the narrator of *Beowulf*:

> The Beowulf narrator's relationship with us is more impersonal and distant . . . it [the voice of the *Beowulf* narrator] remains the voice of traditional corporate wisdom, indistinguishable from the kind the protagonists utter themselves—"þæt wæs god cyning"—and claims only to share in collective indirect knowledge.[18]

If you immediately counter that poems such as *Exodus*, of Christian subject-matter, necessarily arise in a culture using written models, then I suggest that we take seriously information the Anglo-Saxon poets give us about the relation between orality and literacy in Anglo-Saxon culture.

The so-called "Poems of Common Wisdom" particularly describe these matters.[19] *Vainglory* begins with a description of oral learning of literate knowledge (which itself has oral antecedents):

> Hwæt, me frod wita on fyrndagum
> sægde, snottor ar, sundorwundra fela!
> Wordhord onwreah witgan larum
> beorn boca gleaw, bodan ærcwide,
> þæt ic soðlice siþþan meahte
> ongitan bi þam gealdre godes agen bearn, . . .[20]

> Listen! Long ago I was told many extraordinary and astonishing things by someone both learned and experienced, a wise man with a message. Through the prophet's teaching this man, expert with books, brought to light a treasure of words, spoken in the past by a preacher, so that as a result of his solemn song I could afterwards recognize properly God's own son, . . .[21]

And the Old English poem *The Order of the World* begins by describing the oral acquisition of religious knowledge, its transmission by poetry, and the copiousness of this divine message, too great for any individual human mind to encompass:

Wilt þu, fus hæle, fremdne monnan,
wisne woðboran wordum gretan,[22]
fricgan fealgeongne ymb forð gesceaft,
biddan þe gesecge sidra gesceafta
cræftas cyndelice cwichrerende,
þa þe dogra gehwam þurh dom godes
bringe wundra fela wera cneorissum!
Is þara anra gehwam orgeate tacen,
þam þurh wisdom woruld ealle con
behabban on hreþre, hycgende mon,
þæt gearu iu, gliwes cræfte,
mid gieddingum guman oft wrecan,
rincas rædfæste; cuþon ryht sprecan,
þæt a fricgende fira cynnes
ond secgende searoruna gespon
a gemyndge mæst monna wiston.
Forþon scyle ascian, se þe on elne leofað,
deophydig mon, dygelra gesceafta,
bewritan in gewitte wordhordes cræft,
fæstnian ferðsefan, þencan forð teala;
ne sceal þæs aþreotan þegn modigne,
þæt he wislice woruld fulgonge.
Leorna þas lare. Ic þe lungre sceal
meotudes mægensped maran gesecgan,
þonne þu hygecræftig in hreþre mæge
mode gegripan. . . .[23]

Will you, onward-going man, speak with a stranger, a learned singer, will you ask a much-travelled person about the created world, pray that he should declare to you the natural and dynamic abilities of the great created beings, those which every day through God's authority bring[24] many marvels to the generations of men! To each of those who through wisdom can comprehend it in his mind, it is a manifest sign, thinking man, that once formerly men, resolute men, often made pronouncements in the art of music with songs; they could

> speak the truth so that most men of the race of human beings, by always asking and reciting and being always mindful (of these matters) understood a measure of secret things. Therefore, let one who lives boldly learn by inquiry, deeply meditating, of the mysteries of created beings, let him inscribe in his understanding[25] the power of the word-treasury, fasten it in his mind and meditate continually and properly; an active man must not tire of that, that he should wisely complete his journey on the earthly way. Learn this teaching. I must forthwith declare to you the power of the Creator, greater than you, though wise, can apprehend in your heart, in your mind.[26]

The lexical stem *bewrit-* of line 19, which, I, like W. S. Mackie, translate 'to inscribe', does not have a necessarily literate implication but appears as appropriately to be translated as 'mark'; its five other occurrences in Old English, all in the Pseudo-Apuleius Herbarius, all appear in the context of 'marking about' with ice, with gold, and so on.[27] Note the emphasis in this account on the role of verbal exchange, of dialogue, in asking and inquiring, in the acquisition and retention of knowledge. Ong discusses the preservation of knowledge in oral cultures through just such exchanges and comments: "Oral cultures tend to use concepts in situational, operational frames of reference that are minimally abstract in the sense that they remain close to the living human life-world."[28] The functional and situational definitions and assertions of sententious utterances in Old English poetry have just this feature. It is unsurprising, then, that the gnomic verses of the Exeter Book, referred to as *Maxims I*, open with an injunction to learn through dialogue:

> Frige mec frodum wordum! Ne læt þinne ferð onhælne,
> degol þæt þu deopost cunne! Nelle ic þe min dyrne gesecgan,
> gif þu me þinne hygecræft hylest ond þine heortan geþohtas.
> Gleawe men sceolon gieddum wrixlan. . . .[29]

> Question me with wise words. Do not let your mind be hidden,
> or the mystery that you know most deeply. I will not tell you my secret
> if you conceal from me your wisdom and your heart's thoughts.
> Wise men shall exchange sayings.[30]

The word *gid*(*d*) Klaeber glossed as 'formal speech' for *Beowulf*.[31] In its dictionary citations the word appears to be a generic carry-all but common to the lexical stem is an "oral" semantic component.[32]

Now, to claim that in the production of Old English poetry the speaking subject was diffusely positioned, that is, externally and communally positioned, is not to deny the possibility of an individual speaking presence—in fact, quite the contrary. As a discussion of the subject of speech will make clear, in Old English poems a speaking presence is often insistently presented, as a character or as a first-person speaker/persona/narrator. We see this in *The Order of the World*, with its first-person "speaker," and conversational questions and commands to the second-person "listener." What is lacking, however, is the effaced but nonetheless consistently positioned "individual author" of the modern era, of whom the quintessential example would be that of the third-person narrator of the nineteenth-century novel.[33] With such a lack the "deconstructive strategy" of post-structuralist literary criticism just is not relevant, that is, there is no psychologically centered "knowing subject" to be displaced. Ong comments that "the work of the deconstructionists and other textualists" (as he chooses to call [post-]structuralists) "derives its appeal in part from historically unreflective, uncritical literacy"[34] and "the 'deconstruction' of literature . . . remains a literary activity."[35] These considerations also explain how a modern reader may read Old English poetry anachronistically. The post-Romantic spoken subject position, from which a reader, assuming thematic and structural unity, reads for "unifying images/themes" and so on, is one which assumes just such an implied author as a deconstructive reading seeks to dethrone, that is, one whose self-conscious presence underwrites the unity of the text. Think of the articles with titles like "The Structural Unity of the . . ." *Wanderer*, *Seafarer*, or what have you, which were particularly common from the 1940's to the 1960's in Old English literary criticism. The very problems a modern reader can have in reading Old English poetry—that it resists the neat coherent narrative and thematic summary—give insights into our assumptions about "natural" reading practices.

Since the situation of conversational exchange is so important in Anglo-Saxon epistemology, as I have suggested with quotations from the Wisdom texts, it is unsurprising that the written texts which we have appropriate this validity for themselves, that is, they appear to favor the language of dialogue, with the use of first- and second-person pronouns. I wrote above that in Old English poems a speaking presence is often insistently presented, as a character or as a first-person speaker/persona/ narrator, through the use of the subject of speech, that is, the use of the first-person pronoun. As prolegomena to further work on this topic, I give in the remainder of this paper a summary account of the subject of speech in different Old English poems.[36] (I exclude any discussion of the speech of characters, such as Beowulf or Hrothgar, who do not narrate the poem "to the reader," though they may well "narrate" to other characters within the poem.)

The first-person narrator, or poetic persona, is common. The first-person pronoun may refer to a non-human subject of speech or to a human subject of speech. Of the first kind, the non-human subject of speech is the "I" of a speaking object, often referred to as *prosopopoeia*, as is found in all but one (number 22) of the first 27 Riddles in the Exeter Book.[37] Similar but not identical to this is the "I" used of a speaking object which not only speaks but also is given a more extended social role, is personified, if you like, as character in the narrative of which it is also narrator, like the message stick in *The Husband's Message* and the cross in *The Dream of the Rood*. Thus the literate visual object, such as a marked stick or engraved cross, is reconstituted as a speaking presence, through which oral language a situation of conversational exchange can be understood.

Second, the first-person pronoun may refer to a human subject of speech as narrator or poetic persona. One needs to distinguish between the use of the singular and plural pronoun. First, the singular pronoun: a primary division here is between those who are characters in their own telling and those whose function is limited to that of narrator/ speaker. The first type (a character in its own telling) is common; most of the occurrences are in the Exeter Book: *The Seafarer*, *Widsith* (with a few lines of third-person narration at beginning and end), *The Wife's Lament*, *Resignation*, *The Rhymed Poem*, *Deor*, *Wulf and Eadwacer*, and, in the Vercelli codex, the dreamer of *The Dream of the Rood*, the persona of the *Fates of the Apostles*.[38]

Contrasted with the narrator/character is the narrator/speaker, that is, the use of "I" to represent a participant whose function is limited to that of narrator/speaker. First, such an "I" is used with verbal processes, that is, processes of talking, telling,[39] as in lines 1–4 of *Maxims I*, already quoted, lines 1–3 of *The Whale*, line 46 of *The Day of Judgment*.

Second, such an "I" is also used with various mental processes, as in *The Wanderer* ("ic geþencan ne mæg . . . ," line 58), and in many riddles ("ic geseah, ic wat").[40] For the purposes of this discussion, the most significant use of the "I" who is a narrator/speaker is that associated only with mental processes of hearing, or learning by hearing; such a use displaces authority for the narrative to an oral antecedent. The notable example here is *Beowulf*: the verbs *hyran* (five occurrences) and *gefrignan* and its derived noun *gefræge* (twelve occurrences) are the only lexical items associated with first-person pronouns for the *Beowulf* narrator.[41] This use also occurs six times in *Genesis A*,[42] once in *Exodus* (line 98), twice in *Christ and Satan* (223, 524) and in *Judith* (7, 246), three times in *Widsith* (Widsith is speaking as narrator, 10, 17, 71), once in *The Panther* (8) and *The Partridge* (1–2), in some Riddles (for example, Exeter Book numbers 45, 47, 48), three times in *Andreas* (lines 1093, 1706, 1626), and once in the *Finnsburh Fragment* (37). It is tempting to relate this use to earlier textual practices. *The Phoenix* begins with a similar lexical use but is grammatically different—with a perfect construction, *Hæbbe ic gefrugnen*, instead of the simple preterite, and a *þæt* clause following rather than the simple accusative plus infinitive.

The use of the plural first-person pronoun complicates the subjectivity positioning. If one reads the "we" exclusively, as not including you the reader, then the subject of speech is being read as not including the spoken subject position. If one reads the "we" inclusively, then one is, in the process of interpretation, accepting a spoken subject position located as the subject of speech and possibly also the implied speaking subject. Such an identification of the various positions of subjectivity, to the extent that it seems "natural," promotes the reader's acceptance and (re)endorsement of the values/attitudes/practices being read in the text. Given what I have said earlier about the externalized, communal speaking subject, one would expect considerable use to be made of the plural pronoun for these communal identifications. What one finds, rather, is its use as narrator "we" at the beginning of poems or sections. In such positions it promotes a reading practice in which the listener/reader takes up the prepared spoken-subject position; subsequently, a compliant listener/reader will continue with this positioning without explicit encouragement: so, line 1 *Beowulf* (its only use in that poem), lines 1–2 *Exodus* (its only use), line 1 *Juliana*. It occurs in *Genesis B* (939), *Christ A* (78, 301) and *Christ B* (586), *The Fates of the Apostles* (23, 63), *Deor* (14). All these examples use the two lexical verbs of the *Beowulf* singular examples, *hyran* and *gefrignan*. Again *The Phoenix* is like but unlike the previous examples at line 393: ". . . habbaþ we geascad þæt ælmihtiga"[43]—with a different verb, and the *þæt* clause following. *Guthlac A* makes the traditional oral claims, but there is a suggestion that these refer to recent exchanges: the "lately" of *Guthlac A*: "Magun we nu nemnan þæt us neah gewearð / þurh haligne had gecyþed, / hu . . ." ('Now may we declare what lately was made known to us by men of holy state, how . . . ,' lines 93–95) is followed by the quite conventional *Guthlac A*: "Hwæt, we hyrdon oft þæt se halga wer . . ." ('Lo! we have often heard that the holy man . . . ,' line 108), but the third and final example makes an unambiguous claim to an eyewitness account: *Guthlac A*: "Hwæt we þissa wundra gewitan sindon! / Eall þas geeodon in ussera / tida timan . . ." ('Lo! of these wonders we are witnesses; all these things happened in the time of our own life-tides . . . ,' lines 752–54). Perhaps I am naive to take this claim as any more than a generic convention.[44] Nevertheless, these details do incline me to take seriously what the poets tell us about their sources of information. Thus *Guthlac B,* credited with a literary source, the *Vita Sancti Guthlaci* of Felix,[45] has ". . . Us secgað bec / hu . . ." (878), and none of the oral references of *Guthlac A*. Poems of Christian subject-matter unsurprisingly make reference to written sources (the most frequent expression being *us gewriten secgað*[46]). One notes how frequently writings and books themselves are grammatically given an oral semantic role, as speakers of verbal processes of saying, an assimilation of the visual object to the speaking presence previously mentioned in relation to the message stick and cross in *The Husband's Message* and *The Dream of the Rood*.[47]

I have excluded from this discussion what I think of as the homiletic first-person plural, that is, the use of "we/us" for inclusive admonitory remarks, typically towards the end of poems, as from line 146 in *The Dream of the Rood.* The homiletic first person occurs more frequently in oblique forms of the paradigm ("us," "our") and occurs with many different processes, that is, verbal meanings, whereas the "we" with narrator function occurs with verbal and mental processes. I suspect the former, the homiletic use, developed from classical (literary) models whereas the latter, the narratorial use, developed from Germanic (oral) traditions.

Anglo-Saxon studies from the nineteenth century on have always been influenced by current theories of language and literature and the relation of language to literature,[48] and, whether we like it or not, our object of study not only will be studied by new methods and from the perspectives of new theories but also will transmute into a different object through that new regard. In this paper I have tried to indicate more positively the reverse direction: that our practices in relation to Anglo-Saxon Studies can help enlarge/redefine/recontextualize literary theories which have ignored their own axioms, that is, which have neglected to take into account the subjectivity of their own social and historical positioning.

UNIVERSITY OF SYDNEY

NOTES

1. M. J. Reddy, "The Conduit Metaphor: A Case of Frame Conflict in Our Language about Language," in *Metaphor and Thought*, ed. A. Ortony (Cambridge, 1979), pp. 284–324.

2. M. A. K. Halliday, *Language as Social Semiotic: The Social Interpretation of Language and Meaning* (London, 1978); Norman Fairclough, *Language and Power* (London, 1989).

3. Jacques Derrida, *Of Grammatology*, tr. Gayatri Chakravorty Spivak (Baltimore, 1974). See esp. ch. 2, "Linguistics and Grammatology."

4. Umberto Eco, *Semiotics and the Philosophy of Language* (London, 1984). See esp. chs. 3 and 4, "Metaphor" and "Symbol."

5. For example, Michelle Royer, "Deconstructions of Masculinity and Femininity in the Films of Marguerite Dumas," in *Feminine, Masculine and Representation*, ed. Terry Threadgold and Anne Cranny-Francis (Sydney, 1990), pp. 128–39. Feminists are not necessarily happy about the contributions of male writers like Derrida: see Rosi Braidotti, "The Problematic of 'the Feminine' in Contemporary French Philosophy: Foucault and Irigaray," in *Feminine, Masculine and Representation*, pp. 36–47.

6. Walter Ong, *Orality and Literacy* (London, 1982),

7. Since first writing this paper, I have read the profoundly interesting study of memory in medieval culture by Mary Carruthers, *The Book of Memory* (Cambridge, 1990). Carruthers queries the usefulness of the distinction between "oral" and "literate" societies. She describes the ancient equating of remembering with writing on the mind (p. 31), though the greater reliance on memory has usually been seen by modern scholars as the mark of a less literate society (p. 10). Further, she argues that "the idea that language is oral, that writing is not a fundamental part of it, is a modern one. . . . My study will make it clear that from the earliest times medieval educators had as visual and spatial an idea of *locus* as any Ramist had, which they inherited continuously from antiquity, and indeed that concern for the lay-out of memory governed much in medieval education designed to aid the mind in forming and maintaining heuristic formats that are both spatial and visualizable" (p. 32). Nevertheless, I think Carruthers' conclusions support rather than undermine the suggestions made in this paper; I comment further where appropriate in the notes.

8. Phrases like Ong's *high residual orality*, or Katherine O'Brien O'Keefe's *transitional literacy* (as used in *Visible Song: Transitional Literacy in Old English Verse* [Cambridge, 1990]), may suggest a single continuum of cultural possibilities between two extreme points of orality and literacy. Such a simple opposition of two terms is misleading. A more accurate description of the productive and interpretative linguistic practices in a culture must at least employ the four terms *speaking*, *listening*, *writing*, *reading*, for the relation between any two of these can vary historically. O'Keeffe implies as much in her discussion of anachronistic interpretations of "literacy" and "reading" ("Introduction," pp. 6–21). This paper does not concern itself with the written poem in Old English; elsewhere I will argue that *transferred literacy* rather than *transitional literacy* is my preferred term for describing the graphic display of English poetry from the Old to the Middle English period. Irrespective of the terms used, however, this paper considers the characteristics of a culture which Ong chooses to call one of "high residual orality" and concludes that subjectivity positioning in Old English poetry does indeed exhibit many of those characteristics. Consciousness, if you like, lags behind graphic display in the movement from orality to literacy. We are on the brink of a much larger area than this paper can encompass, the chicken-and-egg relation of the influence of changing technology on consciousness vs. the influence of changing consciousness on the utilization of new technology. The latter is a major concern of M. T. Clanchy's book *From Memory to Written Record: England 1066–1307* (Oxford, 1979; 2nd ed., 1993).

9. The first two phrases derive from the work of the French linguist Émile Benveniste in *Problems in General Linguistics*, tr. Mary Elizabeth Meek (1966; Coral Gables, 1971). An introductory account appears in Kaja Silverman, *The Subject of Semiotics* (New York, 1983), pp. 43–53. An article in which I use this approach in relation to modern poetry is "Who Speaks and for Whom? The Search for Subjectivity in Browning's Poetry," *Journal of the Australasian Universities Language and Literature Association*, 71 (1989), 64–87.

10. The concern of post-structuralist literary theory has primarily been with the "speaking subject," the "subject of the enunciation." Changes in the positioning of the speaking subject will effect changes in the interpretation of the subject of speech (the "enounced" subject) and the spoken subject. Most notably used has been the later "genealogical" work of Michel Foucault on the "history of the different modes by which, in our culture, human beings are made subjects." (Foucault claims this has been the goal of his work "during the last twenty years" in his "Afterward: The Subject and Power," in *Michel Foucault: Beyond Structuralism and Hermeneutics*, Hubert L. Dreyfus and Paul Rabinow [Chicago, 1982], p. 208). This paper attempts some initial contribution to the study of the modes of subject construction in Anglo-Saxon culture.

11. See, e.g., Terry Threadgold, "Changing the Subject," in *Language Topics: Essays in Honour of Michael Halliday*, ed. Ross Steele and Terry Threadgold, vol. 2 (Amsterdam, 1987), pp. 549–97.

12. See Boris Uspensky, *A Poetics of Composition: The Structure of the Artistic Text and Typology of a Compositional Form*, tr. Valentina Zavarin and Susan Wittig (Berkeley, 1973).

13. Alain Renoir, "Judith and the Limits of Poetry," *English Studies*, 43 (1962), 145–55.

14. Ong, pp. 30–77.

15. Ibid., pp. 40–41.

16. Ibid., p. 69. In *The Book of Memory*, Carruthers describes the culture of the Middle Ages as more appropriately called a memorial culture than an oral (or residually oral) culture (p. 260), but she also comments on the communal understanding of meaning: "Where classical and medieval rhetorical pragmatism diverges from modern, I think, is in assigning a crucial role to a notion of comunal [*sic*] memory, accessed by an individual through education, which acts to 'complete' uninformed individual experience" (p. 24).

17. I am thinking of the edition by T. P. Dunning and A. J. Bliss in Methuen's Old English Library (London, 1969).

18. Peter Clemoes, "Action in *Beowulf* and Our Perception of It," in *Old English Poetry: Essays on Style*, ed. Daniel G. Calder (Berkeley, 1979), pp. 147–68. The quotation is from p. 150.

19. D. G. Calder and M. J. B. Allen in *Sources and Analogues of Old English Poetry*, vol. 1: *The Major Latin Sources in Translation* (Cambridge, 1976), p. 223, include under this heading *The Gifts of Men*, *The Fortunes of Men*, *Precepts*, *Vainglory*, *Maxims I* and *II*, *The Order of the World*, and *Instructions for Christians*, but comment that "the eight poems are no more than a sample of the wisdom literature represented in many Anglo-Saxon poems."

20. ASPR 3, *The Exeter Book*, ed. George Philip Krapp and Elliott van Kirk Dobbie, p. 147.

21. Translation from T. A. Shippey, *Poems of Wisdom and Learning in Old English* (Cambridge, 1976), p. 55.

22. Lexical items relevant to language use are underlined.

23. The Old English text is from ASPR 3, pp. 163–64.

24. To justify a similar plural translation of the verb, W. S. Mackie emends *bringe* to *bringe*[*n*] in his edition of the poem, titled as "The Wonders of Creation"; see the EETS edition of *The Exeter Book*, vol. 2 (1934; rpt. 1958), p. 49.

25. In the context of Carruthers' discussion in *The Book of Memory* that the memory is typically "inscribed" (as, e.g., on p. 31), 'memory' would be the more appropriate translation for *gewitte* here.

26. The prosaic translation given is my own. A highy wrought translation is given by Bernard F. Huppé in *The Web of Words* (Albany, 1970), in which he discusses four Old English poems including *The Wonder of Creation*. Huppé's understanding of the poem is criticized by J. E. Cross in "The Literate Anglo-Saxon—on Sources and Disseminations," the Sir Israel Gollancz Memorial Lecture, Proceedings of the British Academy 58 (1972), pp. 67–100.

27. This information is gleaned from the *Microfiche Concordance to Old English*, comp. Antonette Di Paolo Healey and Richard L. Venezky, published by the Dictionary of Old English Project (Toronto, 1980). In apparent contradiction to my point, Carruthers comments that "the metaphor of memory as a written surface is so ancient and so persistent in all Western cultures that it must, I think, be seen as a governing model or 'cognitive archetype,' in Max Black's phrase" (p. 16). However, elsewhere she writes, "Thus far, I have discussed this ancient metaphor of the waxed tablets as though its explanation of memory processes were modeled upon a previously familiar process of writing on a physical surface. In fact, however, both ancient and medieval authors reverse the direction of this metaphor" (she gives Greek and Latin examples) (p. 30). I suggest that Carruthers is here equating the visual and writing, that is, using *writing* in a looser or more inclusive sense including 'marking' rather than the more limited sense of marks which record language.

28. Ong, p. 49.

29. ASPR 3, pp. 156–57.

30. This is Mackie's translation in the EETS edition of the *Exeter Book.*

31. F. Klaeber, *Beowulf and The Fight at Finnesburg,* 3rd ed. (Boston, 1950).

32. Thus for Bosworth-Toller, gid: I *song, lay, poem,* II *speech, tale, sermon, proverb, riddle*; giddian: *to sing, recite, speak*; giddung: *song, saying, discourse*; gied: *song, lay, riddle.* Joseph Bosworth and T. Northcote Toller, *An Anglo-Saxon Dictionary* (Oxford, 1898; rpt. 1976). The Supplement particularly adds new citations and glosses for gid II, *formal speech* (Oxford, 1921).

33. So-called post-modernist texts self-consciously attempt to evade such centered positioning, as in textual pastiche.

34. Ong, p. 169.

35. Ibid., p. 77. Carruthers comes to a similar conclusion—though avoiding the label of "literacy"—about the ahistoricity of some uses of modern literary theory: "Students of medieval literature have for some time now realized that modern literary theory has intriguing parallels to the concerns and assumptions of medieval poets and readers. . . . Yet modern literary theory, when applied directly to medieval literature, has tended to obscure the very medievalness of that literature" (p. 259). Her point here is that "indeterminancy of meaning is the very character of recollective gathering" in the Middle Ages and so—as I have suggested above—deconstructive strategies do not reveal anything that was concealed by the medieval tradition of interpretation.

36. Ward Parkes gives, in an Appendix, "The Distribution of the 'I heard' Formulas," in "'I heard' Formulas in Old English Poetry," ASE, 16 (1987), 45–66. I do not discuss his approach, as his criteria for inclusion are different from mine, and his study of "the narrator" is located within accounts of narrativity dominant in French structuralism of the 1960's, in which subjectivity is unproblematic (see his references in n. 1).

37. Aldhelm, in the coda to a Latin riddle, changes from a subject of speech ("nature") patently *not* positioned as a human speaking subject to a subject of speech which can be so read, that is, the "I" pronoun can be read as referring to Aldhelm: "Listen and believe what I say, they are things a learned teacher could scarcely expound in words. Yet, in rejecting [these paradoxes], the reader still does not consider them frivolous. I ask

conceited professors what name I am dealing with" (tr. Calder and Allen, p. 170). The competitive use of the riddle in oral culture, which Ong discusses (pp. 53, 55), is nicely captured here.

38. The characterization of the implied poet/narrator in *Fates* and in the other three passages signed by Cynewulf, the "epilogues" to the Vercelli Book *Elene* and the Exeter Book *Juliana* and *Christ II*, requires more detailed study. More accurately, one could speak of the "dramatization" of the situation of exchange, so that the displaced literate situations of writer and reader are dramatized as one oral situation of speaker and listener, not the Derridean absence of writing but the bodily presence of speech. Thus in *Fates* and *Juliana*, the poet's projected listener (a character in the third person except for a brief "you" in *Fates* line 105) is one who prays, in *Christ II*, third-person "friends" who accept teaching. Only in *Elene* is the poet's own spiritual experience told without explicit reference to those who will hear/read the telling. I have begun a discussion of the use of didactic projection in Old English poetry in "Anglo-Saxon Interpretative Practices and the First Seven Lines of the Old English Poem *Exodus*: The Benefits of Close Reading," in *Parergon*, NS 10.2 (1992), 51–57.

39. I use the description of verb meanings as processes as described by M. A. K. Halliday, *An Introduction to Functional Grammar* (London, 1985), pp. 129–30.

40. A passing comment: going by the distribution of first-person pronouns, I read *The Wanderer* as having two characters, the wanderer who speaks from line 8 to line 28a and the wise man who speaks from line 92 to line 110, and I attribute the remaining lines to a first-person narrator, inferred from line 58. Certainly the accumulation of examples in this paper suggests to me that a first-person narrator is highly likely, though the diffuseness/communality of subjectivity is a textual environment tolerating more slippage between third- and first-person narration than our contemporary practices.

41. Only these two lexical stems, *hyr-* (lines 38, 62, 1197, 2163, 2172) and *gefræge*/*gefrign-* (74, 776, 837, 1011, 1027, 1196, 1955, 2685, 2694, 2752, 2773, 2837) occur with the "I" narrator in *Beowulf*. See my unpublished doctoral thesis, "A Computer Study Of Lexical Patterns in *Beowulf* and *Andreas*," Univ. of Sydney 1978.

42. *Genesis A*, lines 173, 1960, 2060, 2244, 2484, 2542.

43. All the brief examples following are from the ASPR. The translations are Mackie's in the EETS edition of the *Exeter Book*.

44. In contrast, I am inclined to take the claims to true personal experience in the opening lines of *The Seafarer* and *The Wife's Lament* as generic convention.

45. See Calder and Allen, pp. 108–12.

46. For example, *Genesis*, lines 1121, 1628, 2565, 2611; *Christ B*, 547; *Phoenix*, 311, 655.

47. So conventionally persistent is this assimilation that it survives in Modern English as the "normal" way to represent visual information, as in "the clock says three o'clock."

48. I discuss this in "Old English and Its Scholars: An Historical Study of Self-Perception," in *Semiotics, Ideology, Language*, ed. Terry Threadgold, E. A. Grosz, Gunther Kress, and M. A. K. Halliday (Sydney, 1986), pp. 147–63.

Manuscript Studies

VARIANT TEXTS OF AN OLD ENGLISH HOMILY: VERCELLI X AND STYLISTIC READERS

JONATHAN WILCOX

The process of transmission in a scribal culture is often considered antithetical to that of preservation: a text falls from prelapsarian perfection as it is (mis)copied by scribes. One editorial tactic to cope with such corrupted texts is an attempt to re-create an "original" true to the author's intent. In Old English studies that is usually viewed as an impossible ideal and stress is placed upon a single surviving manuscript, a "base text," with the danger of giving excessive respect to a single random survival.[1] I want to celebrate the process of transmission as a source of valuable information rather than bewail it as a cause for consternation.

This study will consider issues of transmission of Old English prose by focusing on the example of a single homily. I will show that scribes recorded significant editorial activity in the transmission of Old English texts and that this editorial activity preserves valuable insights into Old English perceptions of Anglo-Saxon prose style. In passing, I will demonstrate that this editorial activity was not always the work of scribes but rather sometimes that of the users of these homilies.

Some scribal interventions in homiletic manuscripts are particularly blatant: the scribe sometimes enters into a dialogue with his text. For example, Ælfric inserted a note in the second series of *Catholic Homilies* on the occasion of the festival of the Nativity of the Virgin Mary to the effect that Mary was conceived by human parents just like other mortals:

> ac we nellað be ðam na swiðor awritan þy læs ðe we on ænigum gedwylde befeallon; Eac þæs dæges godspel is swiðe earfoðe læwedum mannum to understandenne. hit is eal mæst mid haligra manna naman geset. and hi habbað swiðe langsume trahtnunge. æfter ðam gastlicum andgite. ði we hit lætað unsæd.[2]

In one manuscript (Oxford, Bodleian Library, Bodley 342), this statement has received the addition in an eleventh-century hand "ne geberaþ ðys naht þærto, buton for ydelnysse."[3]

Most scribal contributions are not so obvious, and they have generally been considered all the more objectionable as a consequence. A fundamental study on the scribal transmission of Old English was published by Sisam in 1946, who examined the text of poems which survive in more than one copy and concluded that the manuscripts could not be relied on to "faithfully reproduce the words of much older originals."[4] More recent work has focused upon some of the valuable information preserved through that faithlessness. Ashley Amos and Dorothy Horgan, in separate studies, have provided painstaking analyses of the different manuscript texts of Alfred's *Cura Pastoralis* and of excerpts from Ælfric's first homily in the first series of *Catholic Homilies*. The emphasis of both commentators is on changes in linguistic minutiae. They have demonstrated that each manuscript contains a text which has been subject to considerable revision, revealing "major, if not systematic, modernization of language" through a large number of minute linguistic variations.[5] In the case of the transmission of poetry, O'Keeffe has described the active roles played by some scribes in a tradition of copying which she calls "'formulaic' reading," "where the scribes' participation in the texts made them literate analogues to oral performers." She sees such transmission even in some poems that were clearly composed in writing.[6]

I will advance the consideration of variant versions of Old English prose texts by taking for granted linguistic alterations of the kind described by Amos and Horgan. I will examine, instead, other kinds of revisions which were made to an Old English prose text over time. O'Keeffe's study serves as a good model for considering verse texts; in the absence of the constraints of meter, however, the present study will center on questions of prose rhythm and prose style.

The large body of homiletic literature in Old English is particularly rich for a study of transmission because homilies were used and copied so extensively. I will focus my discussion on the tenth homily in the Vercelli Book, also known in editions as Blickling IX or Napier XLIX.[7] This homily is differently titled in different manuscripts; in the Vercelli Book it has no title. It provides a good case study on account of the number of manuscripts in which it survives and the work already done on its textual relations and sources.

The complete homily is extant in three manuscripts:

1. Vercelli, Biblioteca Capitolare CXVII, The Vercelli Book (s. x^2; A)
2. CCCC 421 (s. xi^1; N)
3. CCCC 302 (s. xi/xii; K)[8]

The second part of the homily exists as a separate entity in two manuscripts:

4. Elsewhere in CCCC 302 (K_2)
5. London, BL Cotton Faustina A. ix (s. xii^1; J)

A substantial excerpt from the homily occurs as part of a different homily (published as Belfour XII) in a single manuscript:

6. Oxford, Bodleian Library, Bodley 343 (s. xii^2; I)

A shorter excerpt occurs in another homily (published as Napier XXX) also contained in a single manuscript:

7. Oxford, Bodleian Library, Hatton 113 (s. $xi^{3/4}$; O)

Fragments of this homily occur in two other manuscripts:

8. Princeton University Library, W. H. Scheide Collection, The Blickling Homilies (s. x/xi; B)
9. Oxford, Bodleian Library, Junius 85 (s. xi^{med}; C)

Before it is possible to examine the changes which were introduced into the text, it is necessary to have a picture of the original homily.[9] The homilist begins with a brief account of the coming of Christ but is primarily concerned with judgment and Judgment Day. The homilist considers the fate of each soul at Judgment Day, centering on a speech by the Devil claiming a soul whose evil deeds outweighed his good. The Devil appeals for justice; God accepts his claim and consigns the sinner to hell-fire. The manuscripts of the shorter version (J and K_2) enter as the homilist describes an ungrateful rich man. The short-sighted rich man does not think about the end of his life and believes only in his riches, even though, as Christ tells him, he will lose them when he dies that night. This turns out to be the case: the man dies and his wealth goes to strangers and enemies. The more God gives, the more thanks he expects. The homilist warns that all the splendor of the earth is transitory, a reflection which leads him to a series of *ubi sunt* questions. Earthly joys are as fleeting as a passing shower. The homilist ends by exhorting the reader to turn to joy with the Lord in heaven.

The homily proceeds (like most anonymous Old English homilies) in an associative and discursive manner rather than by pursuing a rigorously-structured argument. Certain themes are stressed throughout the work: the power of God; man's need to repent and be obedient to him; and the inevitability of death and judgment. The absence of a single cohesive narrative running throughout the homily explains the ease with which passages were excerpted and taken into other homilies, as in the versions contained in MSS I and O.

The whole homily is written in a strikingly heightened prose style characterized by balance, which is often achieved through the use of tautologies. The rhythm is not consistently metrical although there is occasional use of two-stress rhythmical units.[10] One short passage (256/11–15, part of a translation of Matthew 25:41) has been viewed as a fragment of "'classical' Old English verse."[11] The homily's stylistic characteristics will be illustrated in the subsequent discussion.

The sources of this homily have been identified. The homilist draws on three different texts—Paulinus of Aquileia's *Liber Exhortationis*; an anonymous (pseudo-Augustine) sermon, *Remedia Peccatorum*; and Isidore's *Synonyma*.[12] Each source is used for a distinct part of the homily as follows:

> 253/13–257/9 < Paulinus of Aquileia, *Liber Exhortationis ad Henricum Comitem*, chapter 62 (PL 99, 271–72);
>
> 257/20–261/14 < *Remedia Peccatorum* ("Pseudo-Augustine" 310, PL 39, 2340–42);
>
> 261/15–264/5 < Isidore of Seville, *Synonyma de Lamentatione Animae Peccatoris*, Book II, 89–91 (PL 83, 865).

No sources have been identified for the introduction or conclusion of the homily, or for the link-passages.

Identification of the sources helps in establishing the textual relations of the manuscripts of the homily. A knowledge of these textual relations is crucial for the subsequent discussion of revisions to the homily. The manuscripts can be grouped through their incidence of shared errors. The five versions which contain more than half of the full homily (MSS N, K, A, J, K_2) will be the focus of the subsequent discussion. I will briefly present the evidence for relating these manuscripts. These textual affiliations have been discussed by numerous commentators: I will indicate where my discussion differs from earlier ones.[13]

MS A shares errors with K. A and K both omit a phrase which is present in N and which translates the source: "þæs hean deman" (254/6) is a translation of "piissimi judicis" (*Liber Exhortationis*, PL 99, 272). Likewise, A and K lack the phrase "afyrred fram þe," present in N at 261/5, which translates "a te" from the source at this point (*Remedia Peccatorum*, PL 39, 2342B, drawn from Luke 12:20). Scragg, however, disagrees with this affiliation. He suggests "that A is from an independent line of transmission," pointing to its "unique introductory paragraph and numerous verbal differences from BKN."[14]

NJK_2 share errors. A and K accurately translate Isidore's "in angustia" (§ 90) as "on nearonysse," whereas NJK_2 have "on eorðan" (263/1). NJK_2 also share a revision in the recasting of a question taken from Matthew 16:26 as an affirmation (264/22–265/1), where AK retain the form of a question.

Within the two groups of manuscripts, J and K_2 clearly share a common exemplar against N: J and K_2 contain only the last three-fifths of the homily and, even within this part, share many omissions from the other versions. Each of the five versions under consideration contains independent errors: none was copied from another and none represents intact the original homily.

The relationship of these five versions can be summarized in a stemma:

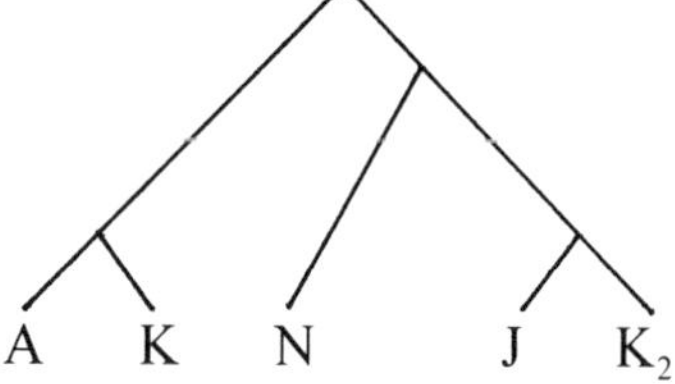

Using the information contained in this stemma, it is possible to pinpoint alterations that were introduced in the course of the transmission of the homily.

The A-text

Revisions made in MS A (or in lost predecessors to A) can be pinpointed with ease: as the stemma shows, a reading shared by N and K against A is original.[15]

The homily has been revised in A through the addition of a new introduction on the importance of teaching the gospel. Of more importance for this study are alterations in the rest of the homily which conform to a discernable pattern. There is a consistent tendency to lessen repetition. For example, ". . . þurh þa gesamnunge we wæron gefriðode feonda gafoles, and þurh þone tocyme we wæron geweorðade and gewelegade and gearade" becomes in A simply "þurh ða gesamnunge we wæron gefrioðode 7 gewelgode."[16] The expansive balance of the original is lost through the compression in A: the three rhyming verbs, two of which alliterate ("geweorðade and gewelegade and gearade") are replaced by just one ("gewelgode"). Similarly, "and þu hy forhogedest and geunrettest and þinne andwlitan fram hym awendest" becomes in A simply "7 þu hie oferhogodest."[17]

The same stylistic tendency is evident throughout the text in A. Tautologies are eliminated at the expense of the balanced style of the original. "Gelæste and gefyllede" (261/11) is reduced to simply "gelæste" (147). MS A misses the alliterative balance of "hwa him to hæle and to helpe . . . astah" (252/6–7), which is simplified to "hwa him to helpe . . . astah" (24–5); "to welan and to wiste" (259/16–17) is reduced to "to welan" (121–2); and MS A loses the grammatical rhyme of the tautologous "gelæstað and gehealdað" (257/6) which is reduced to simply "gelæstað" (89).[18]

These changes do not alter the substance of the homily in any very significant way: they are primarily changes to the rhythmical structure of the prose. The alterations described here could have been introduced at any time in the transmission from the hypothetical original to A. They are of interest because they reveal the active stylistic judgments of someone in the Anglo-Saxon period. The homily as it exists in A is by no means devoid of balanced structures and two-stress rhythms. Nevertheless, the elimination of some of the balanced tautological style of the original indicates that the homily has passed through a transmitter who did not especially prize this feature.

The N-text

For the two-fifths of the text which J and K_2 report, revisions in the text of N can be established through the agreement of AK with JK_2.[19] Revisions in N fall into three broad categories: they increase tautology, make a display of learning, and stress the role of a priest.

There is a small number of unequivocal increases in tautology in N. "Gecweden" (in JK_2 and supported by A) is expanded in N to "gecweden and gesæd" (258/19). N contains an additional clause in a passage attested by NJK$_2$AKIO: "forðam nis naht þyses middaneardes wlite [ac he is tweogendlic *in N only*], þysse worulde wela, he is hwylwendlic and feallendlic. . . ."[20] There are many other cases where it is unclear whether N contains an expansion or AK share a compression, e.g., "ymbhydige [and gemyndige *in N only*]" (253/16–17), "rihtne dom [and emne dom *N*]" (253/20), "[tæcan and *N*] cyðan" (255/6 and n.). Once again, the alterations do not substantially alter the content of the homily but demonstrate an acute concern with prose rhythm.

The show of learning is apparent in the case of two Latin quotations which have been added to N's version of the homily. Before the "verse paraphrase" of Matthew 25:41 there is a biblical quotation in N alone: "non noui uos, discedite a me, maledicti, qui operamini iniquitatem."[21] The manuscripts which contain this part of the homily are N and AK, so there is no textual evidence to establish whether the Latin is an addition in N or omission from AK. The question can be resolved on account of the wording of the quotation. The Old English text (256/10–15) is drawn from Matthew 25:41: "discedite a me, maledicti, in ignem aeternum."[22] N's reviser has provided the wrong scriptural passage: he has taken "maledicti" from Matthew 25:41 and inserted it in the context of a similar verse, Matthew 7:23, "nunquam novi vos: discedite a me, qui operamini iniquitatem."[23] It is inadequate as a source of the subsequent Old English passage, as it fails to mention the "everlasting fire" which is dwelt on at length in the homily (256/12–15).

The second Latin quotation is appropriate to the following Old English: "quid non possumus, fratres, de hoc cognoscere et ignoscere . . ." (261/14n), which corresponds to "hwæt, we nu magon, men þa leofestan [m. þ. l. *om. AKI*], be þyssum ongitan and oncnawan. . . ."[24] The manuscript witnesses are N, AK, JK$_2$, and I, which enters at this point. The Latin is not in any other manuscript. The following passage is a translation of Isidore, but the Latin sentence is not taken from there. It is possible that it comes from a lost intermediate source and was then lost independently from AK(I) and JK$_2$; it is far more likely that the reviser of N translated a short extract of his Old English homily into Latin.

These two changes provide an interesting reflection on the preoccupations of a reviser. It seems that he felt the need to give added authority to his preaching by weighting his homily with the authority of the sound of the language of the Church.

Two other changes in N's text are characteristic of other texts contained in this manuscript and provide a useful clue as to the author of some of the revisions. The homilist states (in versions other than N) that, as one might quench a raging flame with water, "swa man mid ælmessan ealle alyseð his gyltas 7 his synna gehæleð."[25] This is expanded in N: "swa man mid ælmessan synna ealle alyseð, gif hy habbað geandet hyra scriftan heora misdæda and on bote befangen."[26] The same point is added earlier in the homily in N: "and hy geandettað on minum naman [heora scriftan *in N only*] mid fæstenum. . . ."[27] In five of N's other homilies which also occur in other manuscripts, N is alone in adding "his scrifte" 'to his priest or confessor' to the requirement to "andettan synna," while two other longer changes make the same point.[28] Most of these unique readings are part of N's main text, but one of these alterations is made above the line in a hand which makes alterations only in this homily (Pope XI, 196).[29] Stressing the role of the priest in confession is a likely addition for a priest to make, perhaps while looking over a homily before delivering it. The instances of this addition in the main text were probably added by users of the homily to an antecedent copy of the manuscript. In making a new copy, the scribe would simply have incorporated glosses or marginalia into his text, a practice which is commonly attested for other Old English texts.[30]

The K-text

Revisions in K can be inferred from the agreement of A with N (and JK_2, where available). Alterations to the text in K form a consistent pattern, namely the addition of a defining or clarifying word, phrase, or clause. There are sixteen such additions in the course of the homily. Examples include the following:

1. þone dom, þe we to gelaðode syndan [on domes dæge *in K only*];[31]
2. þam anum, þe ofer ealle rixað [on heofonum *K*];[32]
3. to þam heah deman [þæt is ure drihten *K*].[33]

Some of these additions help define an idea more closely; their cumulative weight, however, indicates a preoccupation with the prose rhythms of the homily.

AND SO ON

It would be possible to continue looking at the readings peculiar to the remaining manuscripts and to each hypothesized text. MS I, for example, contains a compressed version of the image of a tree, which, in other manuscripts, "wexeð . . . þæt hit hlifað upp ofer eall þa oðre treowu and brædeð hit," but in MS I simply "weaxað . . . úp ofer alle þa oðre treón."[34] An interesting hypothetical text is the common ancestor of J and K_2. This common ancestor is characterized by clarifying additions, e.g., the rich man is "swær(mod)" in NAK, "swærmod to godan þingan" in JK_2;[35] while the exhortation "þu man" (259/1, 113) is provided with a verb, "gehyrest þu man."

Not all manuscript versions show the degree of stylistic divergence described here. The text in J, for example, is very similar to that in K_2. These two versions have not been subject to any significant process of stylistic revision between the time of composition of their common ancestor and the copying out of the surviving manuscripts.

CONCLUSION

Stylistic revisions can be seen in most surviving versions of the text of Napier XLIX. These revisions tend to follow consistent patterns, notably of expansion or abbreviation. The texts in N, K, and JK_2 have been subject to independent processes of expansion, that in A (and, to a lesser extent, I) to compression.[36] The consistent pattern of such revisions within each version suggests that they result from a deliberate and conscious campaign of revision.

The revisions described here have a negligible impact on the content of the homily. Their impact is primarily on the rhythm of the prose, which suggests that the revisions were motivated by considerations of prose style.

It is hard to establish who is responsible for such revisions, although some are demonstrably the work of the users of these texts, the *scriftan* who preached the homilies. One such user of MS N apparently felt a need for some learned Latin to reinforce the authority of his preaching. Other revisions may have been made systematically by the scribe or someone else working through the text prior to its recopying.

Pinpointing these scribal *usus scribendi* can be valuable for approaching other texts copied by the same scribe, even if they are unique copies. For example, the compression of Vercelli X in MS A suggests the possibility that other homilies in A have been subject to compression, especially if they share a probable history of transmission with Vercelli X. Uncertainty about how much the revisions are the work of previous users as opposed to scribes, however, should encourage caution in pursuing this approach.

A more useful line of enquiry is to consider the implications of such transmission for the study of Old English prose style. In a valuable study from 1962, Funke catalogued passages of heightened, rhythmical prose in anonymous Old English homilies.[37] By examining the treatment of these passages in the course of the transmission of a homily, it is possible to discover contemporary Anglo-Saxon attitudes to such heightened prose. Whoever made the revisions here has preserved evidence for a contemporary concern with and delight in Old English prose style.

The care devoted to rhythm and style detected in this homily is striking and raises the question whether this is typical of the transmission of other homilies. The detection of such extensive revision is dependent upon the survival of multiple manuscripts of the same text, which is rarely the case for anonymous homilies.[38] Ælfric's homilies do survive in sufficient multiple copies to provide the necessary evidence: it is clear that his texts were not usually revised stylistically to the extent described here.[39] The homily considered here is particularly loosely structured and rhetorically heightened, and this may have made it a favorite target for stylistic revision. Nevertheless, comparable degrees of stylistic revision can be seen in some other anonymous homilies where they survive in sufficient multiple copies to tell.[40]

Writers of Old English have left us no extended accounts of appropriate styles for writing in the vernacular. The metrical "rules" of Old English poetry have long been inferred by modern scholars. Close scrutiny of stylistic changes introduced in the course of transmission of Old English prose texts may enable us to tease out Anglo-Saxon attitudes to appropriate styles of vernacular prose. Those responsible for the changes to the style of the prose outlined here might be labeled "stylistic readers" on the model of O'Keeffe's "'formulaic' readers" of poetry. Careful scrutiny of such stylistic readers is worthwhile in order to pinpoint an Anglo-Saxon aesthetic of prose.

UNIVERSITY OF IOWA

NOTES

1. For discussions of the practice of textual criticism with respect to medieval texts see Lee Patterson, *Negotiating the Past* (Madison, 1987), ch. 3; Suzanne Fleishman, "Philology, Linguistics, and the Discourse of the Medieval Text," *Speculum*, 55 (1990), 19–37.

2. *Ælfric's Catholic Homilies: The Second Series: Text*, ed. Malcolm Godden, EETS SS 5 (1979), p. 271: 'but we will not write down more concerning that lest we fall into any error. Also, the gospel for that day is very difficult for lay men to understand: it is

almost completely filled with the names of holy men and they have a very long exposition according to the spiritual sense; therefore we leave it unsaid'. Unless otherwise indicated, all translations are mine.

3. 'It's not for that reason at all, but on account of idleness'. The comment is copied into the text of a derivative manuscript, CCCC 303. Ælfric's own note only circulated in manuscripts of the first recension of *Catholic Homilies II*; presumably he canceled it when he wrote his homily on the Nativity of the Virgin (Assmann III). For a similar scribal intervention *contra* Ælfric see the response to his note forbidding preaching on the "silent-days" of Holy Week in Oxford, Bodleian Library, Hatton 114 and in CCCC 178, discussed further by Joyce Hill, "Ælfric's 'Silent Days,'" *Leeds Studies in English*, NS 16 (1985), 118–31, esp. pp. 120–22, and Roberta Frank, "A Note on OE Swigdagas 'Silent Days,'" in *Studies in Honour of René Derolez*, ed. A. M. Simon-Vandenbergen (Ghent, 1987), pp. 180–89.

4. Kenneth Sisam, "The Authority of Old English Poetical Manuscripts," *Review of English Studies*, 22 (1946), 257–68, rpt. in *Studies in the History of Old English Literature* (Oxford, 1953), pp. 29–44. The quotation is from pp. 38–39.

5. Ashley Crandell Amos, *Linguistic Means of Determining the Dates of Old English Literary Texts* (Cambridge, MA, 1980), Appendix, pp. 171–96, and Dorothy M. Horgan, "The Lexical and Syntactic Variants Shared by Two of the Later Manuscripts of King Alfred's Translation of Gregory's Cura Pastoralis," ASE, 9 (1981), 213–21. The quotation is from Amos, p. 173. Horgan includes a brief account of some "stylistic variants," pp. 210–11.

6. Katherine O'Brien O'Keeffe, *Visible Song: Transitional Literacy in Old English Verse* (Cambridge, 1990), p. 192.

7. Citations are to the edition by Arthur Napier, *Wulfstan: Sammlung der ihm zugeschriebenen Homilien* (Berlin, 1883; rpt. with bibliographical supplement by Klaus Ostheeren, Dublin, 1967), homily XLIX, pp. 250–65, because this edition provides a full collation of N, K, and B. A's text is available ed. Paul E. Szarmach, *Vercelli Homilies IX–XXIII* (Toronto, 1981), pp. 11–18, which is cited in the case of references to A. I's text is edited by Arthur O. Belfour, *Twelfth-Century Homilies in MS Bodley 343*, EETS OS 137 (1909), as homily XII, pp. 124–35. The shortened versions in J and K_2 are available only in an unpublished Ph.D. diss. by Tolliver C. Callison, III, "An Edition of Previously Unpublished Anglo-Saxon Homilies in Mss. CCCC 302 and Cotton Faustina

A. ix," Univ. of Wisconsin-Madison 1973. See further, now, *The Vercelli Homilies and Related Texts*, ed. D. G. Scragg, EETS OS 300 (1992), pp. 191–218, for a complete edition incorporating all versions along with textual discussion.

8. On the distribution of the text in the various manuscripts see D. G. Scragg, "The Corpus of Vernacular Homilies and Prose Saints' Lives before Ælfric," ASE, 8 (1979), 223–77, at p. 230. Sigla are taken from Scragg.

9. For a fuller account of the content and effectiveness of this homily see Paul E. Szarmach, "The Vercelli Homilies: Style and Structure," in *The Old English Homily and Its Backgrounds*, ed. Paul E. Szarmach and Bernard F. Huppé (Albany, 1978), pp. 241–67 at 244–48.

10. See Otto Funke, "Studien zur alliterierenden und rhythmisierenden Prosa in der älteren altenglischen Homiletik," *Anglia,* 80 (1962), 9–36 at pp. 22–23.

11. See Joseph B. Trahern, Jr., "An Old English Verse Paraphrase of Matthew 25:41," *Mediaevalia* 1.2 (1977 for Fall 1975), 109–14.

12. The sources were established in the following studies: Karl Jost, *Wulfstanstudien*, Swiss Studies in English 23 (Bern, 1950), pp. 245–49; J. E. Cross, "'Ubi Sunt' Passages in Old English—Sources and Relationships," *Vetenskaps-societeten i Lund Årsbok* (1956), 25–44 at pp. 30–33; Lynn L. R. McCabe, "An Edition and Translation of a Tenth-Century Anglo-Saxon Homily, Vercelli X (Codex CXVII)," Diss. Univ. of Minnesota 1968, pp. 6–16; Callison, pp. 69–84; Wolfgang Becker, "The Latin Manuscript Sources of the Old English Translation of the Sermon *Remedia Peccatorum*," *Medium Aevum*, 45 (1976), 145–52.

13. Callison, pp. 153–98; D. G. Scragg, "Napier's 'Wulfstan' Homily XXX: Its Sources, Its Relationship to the Vercelli Book and Its Style," ASE, 6 (1977), 197–211 at pp. 200–01 and 205; Paul E. Szarmach, "MS. Junius 85 f. 2r and Napier 49," *English Language Notes,* 14 (1977), 241–46; Scragg, "Corpus," p. 230; Scragg, "The Homilies of the Blickling Manuscript," in *Learning and Literature in Anglo-Saxon England: Studies Presented to Peter Clemoes*, ed. Michael Lapidge and Helmut Gneuss (Cambridge, 1985), pp. 299–316 at 305–07. I have discussed the relationship of all the manuscripts in full in Wilcox, "The Compilation of Old English Homilies in MSS CCCC 419 and 421," Diss. Univ. of Cambridge 1987, pp. 149–58.

14. Scragg, "Homilies of the Blickling Manuscript," pp. 305–06. The specific readings which Scragg cites in this discussion are readings where A and K preserve the likely original and B and N share a revised reading. He is concerned in this discussion with the textual relations of the fragmentary B. See also Scragg, *The Vercelli Homilies*, pp. 191–95.

15. Scragg's alternative textual affiliation gives equal status to readings of A or those of K supported by the other manuscripts: either textual tradition has an equal claim to represent the original.

16. Napier XLIX, 251/15–17 (the reading of N and K): 'through that union [of the Holy Ghost and Mary] we were protected from the tribute of the devils and through that advent we were esteemed and enriched and spared'; Vercelli X, line 19: 'through that marriage we were protected and enriched'.

17. Napier XLIX, 258/6–8: 'and you despised them (the poor) and neglected them and turned your countenance from them'; Vercelli X, 103–04: 'and you despised them'.

18. MS A differs from the style of the original in a different way, too: the image "se goldbloma" 'the golden bloom' (251/11) is replaced by the more prosaic "se ælmihtiga Dryhten" (12).

19. Scragg's alternative stemma would provide evidence for revisions in N throughout the homily: any reading shared by A and K against N is evidence of revision to the text in N.

20. Napier XLIX, 263/10–12 (Vercelli X, 173–74): 'therefore the beauty of this world, the prosperity of this world, is nothing [but it is uncertain *in N only*], it is transitory and perishable. . . .'

21. Napier XLIX, 256/10n: 'I did not know you: depart from me, ye cursed, ye that worked iniquity'.

22. 'Depart from me, ye cursed, into everlasting fire'.

23. 'I never knew you: depart from me, ye that worked iniquity'.

24. Napier XLIX, 261/15–16: 'Lo, we may now, dearly beloved, concerning this know and perceive. . . .'

25. JK_2 at the equivalent of 257/22, broadly supported by A (Vercelli X, 99–100): 'so one with alms may completely redeem his sins and heal his trespasses'.

26. Napier XLIX, 257/22 and n.: 'so one with alms may completely redeem his sins, if they have confessed their misdeeds to their priest and received atonement'.

27. Napier XLIX, 264/11–13, Vercelli X, 188: 'and confess them in my name [to their priest *N*] [and make atonement] with fasting. . . .'

28. The five additions occur in the following texts: *The Homilies of Wulfstan*, ed. Dorothy Bethurum (Oxford, 1957), homily Xc, line 112; Bethurum XIII, lines 104–05; Belfour VI, 50/27; *Catholic Homilies I*, ed. Benjamin Thorpe, homily XIX, 266/13–14; *Homilies of Ælfric: a Supplementary Collection*, ed. John C. Pope, EETS OS 259–60 (1967–68), homily XI, line 196. The two longer additions occur in: *Angelsächsische Homilien und Heiligenleben*, ed. Bruno Assmann, Bibliothek der angelächsischen Prosa 3 (Kassel, 1889; rpt. with suppl. intro. by Peter Clemoes, Darmstadt, 1964), homily XI, lines 68–72; and *Catholic Homilies I*, XIX, 272/5–6.

29. CCCC 421, page 117, line 12. The same reviser makes one other addition: he adds *á* to create the tautologous tag "á on ecnysse" (Pope XI, line 507).

30. A revealingly intrusive example is provided by line 5 of Riddle 36 in the Exeter Book; see the comment on the line by Krapp and Dobbie, eds., *The Exeter Book*, ASPR 3 (1936), p. 341.

31. Napier XLIX, 253/18–19: 'the judgment which we are summoned to [on the Day of Judgment]', K.

32. Napier XLIX, 253/22–23: 'the one who rules over everything [in the heavens]', K.

33. Napier XLIX, 254/7–8: 'to that high judge [who is our lord]', K.

34. Napier XLIX, 262/5–7 (Vercelli X, 157): 'grows so that it towers up over all the trees and spreads out'; Belfour XII, 130/7–8: 'grows above all the other trees'.

35. 'Indolent (about good things)'.

36. If the textual affiliations described by Scragg are accepted, the version in A could be original and the other manuscripts could share more expansion. In that case, there would be only rarely attested examples of compression.

37. See n. 10 above.

38. See Scragg, "Corpus."

39. See, e.g., Godden's fully collated edition of *Catholic Homilies II*.

40. I have described the case for two other anonymous homilies, Wilcox, "Napier's 'Wulfstan' Homilies XL and XLII: Two Anonymous Works from Winchester?" *Journal of English and Germanic Philology*, 90 (1991), 1–19. A passage in "rhythmical prose" in one of these homilies provides an interesting example of careful and stylistically-conscious revision: four rhythmical lines in one version are equivalent to five in the other and yet both versions obey the loose "rules" of rhythmical prose.

The Hatton MS of the West Saxon Gospels: The Preservation and Transmission of Old English

Andreas Fischer

I: Introduction

The translation of the four gospels into West Saxon is extant in altogether six manuscripts:

CUL Ii.2 (Cambridge, Ker No. 20)
CCCC 140 (Corpus, Ker 35)
BL, Cotton Otho C.i (Cotton, Ker 181)
BL, Royal I A.xiv (Royal, Ker 245)
Bodleian, Bodley 441 (Bodley, Ker 312)
Bodleian, Hatton 38 (Hatton, Ker 325)

Four of these, namely Cambridge, Corpus, Cotton, and Bodley, are roughly contemporaneous, eleventh-century versions, whereas Royal and Hatton are considerably later, dated, respectively, to the latter half of the twelfth and to the late twelfth or early thirteenth centuries. Both of these manuscripts contain nothing but the four gospels, and according to Ker 387, Hatton is probably "a copy of Royal I A. xiv, which is itself a copy of Bodley 441." The overview below, which combines Skeat's stemma (1874 edition, p. x, and 1878, p. vii) with Ker's dating, may help to visualize the situation.

My interest in this paper is in the Royal and especially the Hatton manuscripts: they were written at least a century after the Norman Conquest and thus provide one of the few pieces of evidence we have of the continued life of an Old English text in the early Middle English period.[1] The Royal and Hatton versions of the West Saxon Gospels thus raise some intriguing questions: why would someone before and around 1200 copy an Old English text written some two centuries before, and how—that is, how faithfully—would he transcribe it?

THE WEST SAXON GOSPELS

Original MS (now lost)

CCCC 140 Ker 35 s. xi^{1}–xii	=	Bodleian, Bodley 441 Ker 312 s. xi^{1}	=	BL Cotton Otho C.i Ker 181 s. xi^{1}–xi^{med}	CUL Ii.2 Ker 20 s. xi$^{3rd\ quarter}$–xii^{1}
		BL Royal I A.xiv Ker 245 s. xii^{2}			
		Bodleian, Hatton 38 Ker 325 s. xii/xiii			

Since we have no detailed knowledge about the making of the Royal and Hatton manuscripts, the first question can only be answered in general terms. English ceased to be the official language of England after the Norman Conquest, and the tradition of official, that is institutionally supported, Anglo-Saxon literacy came to an end within about a hundred years after the Conquest. The clearest illustration of this process, of course, is the E-version of the Anglo-Saxon Chronicle and its continuation, the Peterborough Chronicle, which was discontinued in 1154. This interruption of the vernacular tradition also affected the English Bible, and in this context it is important to remember one striking difference between late Anglo-Saxon and early Norman England: while there are no fewer than three different versions of the New Testament in late Old English (the West Saxon translation plus the Mercian and Northumbrian glosses), there are none at all in early Middle English, and the first new translation of the Bible (the Wycliffite Bible) dates from as late as the fourteenth century. For about three hundred years after the Conquest, therefore, England had no "modern" Bible in the vernacular, although on the level of the lower clergy there must have been a need for one. I would like to suggest here that we have to see the Royal and the Hatton Gospels in this context, namely as vernacular Bibles that were copied and updated for practical purposes at a time when no really modern version was available. This conjecture is supported by at least one piece of tangible evidence: both manuscripts contain nothing but the translation of the four gospels, which may indicate that they were produced for practical rather than, say, antiquarian purposes.

This suggested reason for producing the Royal and Hatton manuscripts also goes some way towards answering the second question, namely how late twelfth- or early thirteenth-century scribes would copy an eleventh-century manuscript of the gospels. They were faced with two conflicting tasks. As copyists of an English text rather than as translators from Latin they would want to reproduce their exemplars as faithfully as possible, especially since they were copying a "sacred" text. In view of the intended practical purpose of their manuscripts, however, they would want to change, that is, modernize, them as much as necessary and as possible. In his book *The English Bible*, Bruce expresses this conflict as follows:

> A British Museum manuscript of the Wessex Gospels, copied in the early part of the twelfth century [obviously the Royal MS; A.F.], indicates that Old English biblical texts continued to be read by some people at least after the Conquest. But the impact of the Conquest, carried as it was by a new ruling class speaking Norman French, brought about such radical changes in spoken English that before long the Old English versions of the tenth century must have been unintelligible to the great mass of the English people.[2]

This is more than mere conjecture: from the beginning of the thirteenth century onwards catalogs of Old English manuscripts and the manuscripts themselves sometimes contain remarks like "vetustus et inutilis" or "non apreciatum propter ydioma incognita,"[3] which clearly indicate that they were not readily intelligible any longer. The two conflicting tasks facing the scribes favor two different methods of copying. The faithful rendering of a sacred text could be achieved by *literatim* transcription, that is, by copying on a letter-by-letter basis, for which comprehension was not necessary. Its modernization, on the other hand, would necessitate a form of "aural" transcription, which Roy Liuzza characterizes as follows:

> In such a transcription a scribe may alter the spelling of his exemplar according to more recent or more local usage; aural transcription will produce, in effect, a partial or thorough translation into the orthography of the scribe's own dialect, reflecting phonological changes or dialectal variation which rendered the spellings of the exemplar ambiguous, inadequate, or simply undesirable. In more extreme cases, the scribe may replace an obsolete word, correct a passage which he deems faulty, or alter for better or worse a phrase which does not survive the transition from his mind to his page.[4]

My main purpose in this paper will be to study some aspects of the modernization of the West Saxon Gospels and thus to contribute to our understanding of how Old English was transmitted, in however reduced a fashion, into the Middle English period. It is based on Skeat's edition (1871–87) and not, like Liuzza's paper, on a new collation of the various manuscripts.[5] The changes made in the Hatton MS concern all levels of linguistic description, though in varying degrees. In her edition and study of the Gospel of Matthew, Grünberg remarks on *phonological/graphological* and *morphological* changes,[6] although her main emphasis is on the eleventh-century Cambridge MS and not on the later ones. As far as I can see, *syntactic* changes are restricted to some minor changes in word order and are probably not worth a separate study. What remains to be investigated in greater detail are changes in the *lexicon*.[7] They will be the focus of this paper (a pilot study), and I shall differentiate among what I call cases of *modernization* (section II), *variation* (III), and *misunderstanding* (IV).

II: Modernization

A study of the lexical changes made by the Hatton and Royal scribes in the process of copying reveals that they often replaced certain words by their more "modern" equivalents, a process which here will be called *modernization*. To prevent possible misunderstandings at this point, it is necessary to say a few words concerning the terms *modern* and *modernization* as they are used here. It will be seen that the eleventh-century translation of the gospels does not always translate one Latin word by one Old English one but may make use of two (or more) available synonyms at different points in the text. In Corpus, for example, *gaudium* is rendered by *bliss* at Matthew 25:21, but by *gefēa* at Matthew 25:23. In cases of almost complete synonymy such as this one, it is difficult if not impossible to judge on what basis a speaker of English c. 1000 or 1200 would choose one or the other word, but the history of the language (as recorded in its historical dictionaries) reveals that *gefēa* became obsolete at the end of the Old English period, while *bliss* has remained in use until the present day. It is words like *bliss* that in the following will be called more modern by comparison with others that were current in the eleventh and twelfth centuries but disappeared soon after.[8] I shall discuss a few selected examples of such apparent modernization by comparing the evidence we get from the texts with that found in the dictionaries (mainly the OED and the MED). My starting point in each case is a Latin lemma, and I will study how it is represented in Corpus (C), Royal (R), and Hatton (H).[9]

My first group concerns words not attested in the post-Conquest period, that is, words listed neither in the OED nor in the MED. My examples are *gefēa* 'joy', *ðwēan* 'to wash', and *hana* 'cock, rooster'.

		C	R	H
gaudium[10]	*gefēa*	18	17	13
	bliss	6	7	11

As the example given above and the table show, Corpus has both *gefēa* and *bliss* as translation equivalents of *gaudium*, but the balance of 18/6 is shifted slowly towards the more modern word *bliss* in R (17/7) and H (13/11). This situation is typical of many other cases in the gospels: C frequently has two translation equivalents for one Latin word, the more modern of which is used progressively more frequently in R and H. The following is a parallel example, except that modernization is evident only in H:

		C	R	H
lavare, rigare[11]	*(ā)ðwēan*	20	20	18
	wascan	1	1	3

While these may be called examples of *partial modernization*, there are also some cases of *complete modernization*, where the modern word replaces the "old" one in all passages in question:[12]

		C	R	H
gallus	*hana*	7	7	0
	cocc	5	5	12

As mentioned above, neither the OED nor the MED records any examples of *gefēa*, *ðwēan*, or *hana*. Unless our records are defective (a possibility one always has to bear in mind, especially in this period), these words must have been nearly or even completely obsolete by the time the Hatton manuscript was produced, and we are dealing with obvious and—it seems—very necessary modernizations. In view of this it is rather difficult to interpret the many cases of partial modernization. Did the scribes sometimes retain the old word because they were still familiar with it,[13] or are we dealing with cases of *literatim* transcription? This further raises the question, unanswerable at this point, of whether the modernization we observe was fully or partly conscious.[14]

A second, probably larger group of modernizations consists of words that went out of use later, that is, in the course of the Middle English period. These may therefore be regarded as obsolescent at the time when the Royal and Hatton MSS were produced. Below I only include words that according to the dictionaries are last attested in the course of the thirteenth century, although words that went out of use in the fourteenth and even fifteenth centuries could be quoted as well.[15] It is doubtful in all these cases whether the Royal and Hatton scribes felt them to be obsolescent around 1200. However, the fact is that they did replace them, and the *post hoc* explanation offered here is that they did so with the intention of keeping their texts up-to-date. Another explanation, namely variation, will be discussed later. The examples that follow are arranged approximately in the order of their last attestation, from the earliest to the latest.

According to the OED (s.v. *andwurde*, *-wyrde*) and the MED (s.v. *andwurden*), Old English *andwyrdan*, one of the translation equivalents of *respondere*, is last attested in the *Lambeth Homilies* (c. 1175/ a. 1225). The table below, illustrating another case of complete modernization, confirms the obsolescence of *andwyrdan*:

		C	R	H
respondere	*andwyrdan*	14	2	0
	andswarian	184	196	198

Old English *ǣ* is another word last attested in the *Lambeth Homilies* (MED s.v. *e*, not in the OED). Its more modern competitor is the Old Norse loanword *lagu*.[16]

		C	R	H
lex	*ǣ*	42	40	8
	lagu	0	0	32
traditio	*lagu*	6	6	6

According to the dictionaries (OED s.v. *glew*, MED s.v. *gleu*), *glēaw* 'wise' is last attested c. 1290/1300 from the *South English Legendary*, its rival and eventual replacement being *wīs*.[17]

		C	R	H
prudens, peritus	*glēaw*	16	16	13
	wīs	0	0	3
sapiens	*wīs*	5	5	5

In the sense 'to give' (rather than the current sense 'to sell') *sellan* is last attested before 1300 (OED: *Cursor Mundi*, MED: *Bestiary*). A faint trace of this process, that is, the gradual obsolescence of *sellan* meaning 'to give', is to be seen in the Hatton MS, where some examples of *sellan* are replaced by *giefan*:

		C	R	H
dare	*(ge)sellan*	222	221	211
	giefan	0	0	9
	[others]	18	18	19

Very occasionally the Royal and Hatton copyists even emerge as lexical or semantic innovators. Royal, for example, may provide some of the earliest instances of the Scandinavian loanword *bāðe* ('both'; see IV below for details). Hatton first uses *smītan* rather than *slēan* in the sense 'to strike, beat' (Matthew 5:39 and 26:68, Luke 22:64; the Latin word rendered is always *percutere*). In Old English *smītan* is attested only in the sense 'to daub, smear, soil, pollute, defile',[18] while according to the OED (s.v. *smite*) the sense 'to strike' is a Middle English development first documented in Hatton. According to the OED (s.v. *slay*), *slēan* is last attested in this sense (rather than in the sense 'to kill') before 1300, namely in *Havelok*, whereas the MED (s.v. *slen*) quotes examples from as late as the latter part of the fifteenth century. Hatton, according to the OED (s.v. *eisell*), may also be the first English text to contain the French loanword *aisel, eisel* ('vinegar'; see also MED s.v. *aisel*).

		C	R	H
acetum	*eced*	6	6	2
	aisel	0	0	4

Like *bāðe* in Royal, this is one of the few cases in these late gospel versions where lexical modernization happened not through a shift towards a word already found in the text but through the introduction of a completely new word.

III: Variation

All these examples give evidence of lexical modernization (although in varying degrees), and they might conjure up the picture of the Royal and Hatton copyists as language-conscious persons, perhaps even as linguistic trend-setters. However, a closer look at the text reveals a rather more murky picture for at least two reasons. First, as the above examples show, lexical modernization in Royal and Hatton is often inconsistent and rarely complete. The shifts towards a more modern word are often slight, and it may be only in hindsight that we can interpret them as evidence of linguistic change in progress rather than as examples of synchronic variation. However, all cases presented so far share two characteristics. The two scribes only rarely introduce new words or meanings but usually just shift the balance of words already extant in their exemplar; this shift, furthermore, always happens in favor of the more modern of the two terms. Second, the two versions contain many lexical changes that are too isolated to be seen as part of a pattern and that cannot be interpreted as modernizations on the basis of the dictionary evidence. Thus H replaces *recels* 'incense' by *stor* in Matthew 2:11 (the two words are last attested in 1483 and 1387, respectively) and *an . . . an* by *an . . . se oþer* in Matthew 20:21. For want of a better expression we may call this form of replacement *variation*. Such variation may sometimes be found in one and the same verse or within one chapter, as illustrated by the two following examples. In Matthew 10:26 *nan þing dygle . . . nan dihle þing* in Corpus and Royal appears as *nan þing dihle . . . nan þing ge-hyð* [= *ge-hydd*] in Hatton. The OED (s.v. *dighel*) and the MED (s.v. *diȝel*) last attest *diegol* in *Layamon's Brut* (?a. 1225/c. 1275) and in *The Owl and the Nightingale* (c. 1250). The participial adjective *ge-hydd* is thus clearly the more modern word, but elsewhere in the Hatton MS the two words are copied unchanged. Likewise, Corpus and Royal render the Latin *innuere* by *biecnian* in Luke 1:22 and 1:62; Hatton retains the first, but replaces the second by *cweðan*, influenced perhaps by the phrase in the previous verse (Luke 1:61 *dixerunt*/Luke 1:62 *innuebant*: *ða cwædon*/*ða bicnodon* in Corpus, *ða cwæðen*/*ða cwæðen* in Hatton). What may be deliberate or at least conscious variation on a small scale may simply be inconsistency on a larger one: throughout the four gospels, Corpus has thirteen instances of *gifta* 'wedding', of which Hatton replaces one (Matthew 22:2) by *brydgifta.*[19]

IV: Misunderstanding

Do we find cases where the Royal or Hatton scribes clearly misunderstood their exemplar? At first sight this might seem improbable, because when in doubt they could always go back to the Vulgate text to verify what exactly they were supposed to copy. However, a scribe who had little Old English may have had even less Latin, and it is by no means certain that the Vulgate was consulted when Royal and Hatton were copied. Moreover, the concept of *literatim* transcription allows for the possibility of a scribe copying something he understood badly or not at all. So far I have found one clear example of lexical *misunderstanding*, an example, moreover, which also throws some light on the processes discussed above. It is for this reason that I want to present it in some detail.

Luke 1:6 and 1:7 read as follows in the Vulgate version:

> erant autem iusti ambo ante deum incedentes in omnibus mandatis et iustificationibus domini sine quaerella / et non erat illis filius eo quod esset elisabeth sterilis et ambo processissent in diebus suis

> And they [Zacharias and Elisabeth] were both righteous before God, walking in all the commandments and ordinances of the Lord blameless. / And they had no child, because that Elisabeth was barren, and they both were now well stricken in years.[20]

In the Corpus manuscript this is translated as follows (my emphasis):

> Soðlice hig wæron *butu* riht-wise beforan gode. gangende on eallum his bebodum 7 rihtwisnessum *butan* wrohte. / 7 his næfdon nan bearn. forðam ðe. elizabeth wæs unberende. 7 hy on heora dagum *butu* forð-eodon.

This text, first of all, contains two instances of *butu* 'both', both rendering the Latin *ambo*. In Royal these two instances of *butu* are replaced by the Scandinavian loanword *bāðe*: a clear instance, it would seem, of what I have called lexical modernization. In Hatton, however, only the second *bāðe* is retained, while the first appears in the form of the Old English variant *ba twa*. Thus while Royal here evidences consistent modernization, Hatton somewhat mystifyingly shows variation. Things become even more puzzling when we consider the rendering of the Latin *sine quaerella* 'without blame' in Luke 1:6. Here Corpus, together with the other early manuscripts, has the correct *butan wrohte*, Royal the variant *buton wrohte*, but the Hatton scribe writes *ba twa wrohte*. Two explanations suggest themselves. The less likely one is that in trying to understand what he was copying (aural transcription), the scribe misinterpreted *wrohte* as a metathesized form of the verb *wyrcan/werchen* and thus replaced the prepositional phrase 'without blame' with the sentence 'both worked'. This reading is possible from the point of view of morphology, because in Hatton verbs in the preterite plural may end in either *-en* or *-e* (see *betahten* in Luke 1:2, but *þohte* in 1:1), but it seems highly unlikely for semantic reasons. The other explanation is that the scribe did not understand what he was copying (*literatim* transcription), and that he repeated the *ba twa* from earlier on in the same verse either through sheer carelessness or because he did not realize the difference between the pronoun *butu* and the preposition *butan/buton*.

V: Conclusion

In this paper I have studied instances of lexical modernization, variation, and misunderstanding in the Royal and Hatton manuscripts of the West Saxon Gospels. Though still tentative in parts, this examination has thrown light on several interesting aspects of the transmission of Old English and of Old English texts. It is certain that a full study of the lexis of the two manuscripts (now in progress) will further our knowledge in two, possibly three, areas. First, it will give us better insight into what happened in the process of post-Anglo-Saxon copying of Old English manuscripts; second, it will advance our knowledge of lexical change during the transition from Old English to Middle English; and third, it may even allow us to date the two manuscripts in question with more precision. Now that the *Linguistic Atlas of Late Middle English* (LALME) has been published,[21] work is under way to compile its companion, namely a *Linguistic Atlas of Early Middle English* (LAEME). A detailed examination of Royal and Hatton will contribute towards that project and will thus provide an ideal link between the study of Old English and Middle English.[22]

UNIVERSITÄT ZÜRICH

NOTES

1. Another notable example is provided by the glosses in many Old English manuscripts and by Worcester Cathedral F. 174 (Ker 398), all by the 13th-century scribe known as the "tremulous hand of Worcester"; see Christine Franzen, *The Tremulous Hand of Worcester: A Study of Old English in the Thirteenth Century* (Oxford, 1991).

2. F. F. Bruce, *The English Bible: A History of Translations* (London, 1963; first pub. 1961), p. 9.

3. Ker, *Catalogue*, pp. xlvii and xlix; quoted after Hans Käsmann, *Studien zum kirchlichen Wortschatz des Mittelenglischen 1100–1350: Ein Beitrag zum Problem der Sprachmischung*, Buchreihe der Anglia 9 (Tübingen, 1961), p. 4.

4. From Roy Liuzza, "Scribal Habit: The Evidence of the Hatton Gospels," an (as yet) unpublished paper given at Kalamazoo in 1991. I would like to thank Liuzza for helpful comments, for supplying me with the typescript of his paper, and for thus drawing my attention to Benskin and Laing (see n. 13 below), where the terms *literatim* and *aural* transcription are introduced and discussed. In his own paper Liuzza mainly discusses matters of phonology and spelling and only pays passing attention to the lexicon, which is the main concern of my study. A revised version of Liuzza's paper will be published

in *Rewriting Old English in the Twelfth Century*, ed. Mary Swan and Elaine Treharne (Cambridge, 1998 or 1999).

On scribal practice at the end of the late Old English period see also Gero Bauer, "Medieval English Scribal Practice: Some Questions and Some Assumptions," in *Linguistics across Historical and Geographical Boundaries*, vol. 1, ed. Dieter Kastovsky and Aleksander Szwedek, Trends in Linguistics Studies and Monographs 32 (Berlin, 1986), pp. 199–210.

5. It will be remembered that Walter W. Skeat as editor of *The Four Gospels in Anglo-Saxon, Northumbrian, and Old Mercian Versions*, 4 vols. (Cambridge, 1871–87; rpt. in 2 vols. Darmstadt, 1970) prints the texts of Corpus and Hatton in full and only gives variant readings from the other manuscripts (from Cambridge, Bodley, and Cotton below the Corpus text, from Royal below the Hatton text). It is for this reason that the readings from Hatton (and Royal) are here compared with those from Corpus rather than Bodley, their direct antecedent. Liuzza's edition has since been published as *The Old English Version of the Gospels*, vol. 1: *Text and Introduction*, EETS 304 (Oxford, 1994).

The Cambridge MS has been partially edited by M. Grünberg in *The West Saxon Gospels: A Study of the Gospel of St. Matthew with Text of the Four Gospels* (Amsterdam, 1967).

6. Regarding morphology, it is worth noting that the Hatton scribe quite radically modernized the inflectional morphology of the text by replacing the full vowels of the Old English suffixes by *e* (and *-um* by *-en*). The Hatton manuscript thus provides a textbook-illustration of the weakening of inflectional endings, which Samuel Moore in "Earliest Morphological Changes in Middle English," *Language*, 4 (1928), 238–66, called the defining characteristic of Middle English.

7. A few remarks concerning lexical changes are to be found in Grünberg, pp. 320–37, esp. 320–24, and in Liuzza, "Scribal Habit."

8. According to Franzen, pp. 166–67, the 13th-century Worcester scribe known as "the tremulous hand" may have glossed certain words in the Old English texts before him because they were obsolescent and he wanted to clarify their sense.

9. My search for the Latin lemmata was facilitated by Bonifatius Fischer's concordance, *Novae Concordantiae Bibliorum Sacrorum Iuxta Vulgatam Versionem Critice Editam*, 5 vols. (Stuttgart-Bad Cannstatt, 1977), that for the Old English translation equivalents by Mattie Anstice Harris' *A Glossary of the West Saxon Gospels: Latin-West Saxon and West Saxon-Latin*, Yale Studies in English 6 (Boston, 1899).

10. At Luke 1:14, C and R render *gaudium et exultatio* by *gefēa 7 bliss*, but H only retains *bliss*. This one example of *bliss* 'exultatio' in C and R is not included in the table.

11. *Rigare* is found only twice (at Luke 7:38 and 7:44); in all other cases the Latin word is *lavare*.

12. The table does not include *galli cantus* at Mark 13:35, which is rendered as *hancred* in C, R, and H.

13. In this case the word would belong to the scribe's "passive repertoire," which "comprises those forms which are not part of the active repertoire, but which are nevertheless familiar in everyday usage as the forms of other writers, and which the scribe does not balk at reproducing," Michael Benskin and Margaret Laing, "Translations and *Mischsprachen* in Middle English Manuscripts," in *So Meny People Longages and Tonges: Philological Essays in Scots and Mediaeval English Presented to Angus McIntosh*, ed. Michael Benskin and M. L. Samuels (Edinburgh, 1981), pp. 55–106, p. 59.

14. René Derolez discusses related problems in connection with the 11th-century Aldhelm glosses in "Good and Bad Old English," in *The History and the Dialects of English: Festschrift for Eduard Kolb*, ed. Andreas Fischer, Anglistische Forschungen 203 (Heidelberg, 1989), pp. 91–102.

15. The dates given below for Middle English texts are taken from *The Oxford English Dictionary* (OED), ed. J. A. Simpson and E. S. C. Weiner, 2nd ed. (Oxford, 1989), and the *Middle English Dictionary* (MED), ed. Hans Kurath, Sherman M. Kuhn, and Robert E. Lewis (Ann Arbor, 1952–).

16. For a more detailed presentation of the replacement of *ǣ* by *lagu* see Andreas Fischer, "Lexical Change in Late Old English: From *ǣ* to *lagu*," in *History and Dialects of English*, ed. Fischer, pp. 103–14. The total number of occurrences given here is somewhat higher than in Fischer (1989), where the count does not include the compound adjective *legisperitus* (*ægleaw* in C and R, *lagugleaw* or *laguwis* in H).

Occasional discrepancies among the counts for the three manuscripts (as here: 48 in C, 46 in R and H) are due to the fact that in the process of copying, words are sometimes added or omitted.

17. For a discussion of the Old English equivalents of *prudens* and *sapiens* see Elmar Seebold, "Die ae. Entsprechungen von lat. *SAPIENS* und *PRUDENS*: Eine Untersuchung über die mundartliche Gliederung der ae. Literatur," *Anglia*, 92 (1974), 291–333.

18. John R. Clark Hall, ed., *A Concise Anglo-Saxon Dictionary*, 4th ed. (Cambridge, 1960).

19. For details see Andreas Fischer, *Engagement, Wedding and Marriage in Old English*, Anglistische Forschungen 176 (Heidelberg, 1986), pp. 37–38.

20. The English translation is from the Authorized Version.

21. *Linguistic Atlas of Late Middle English*, ed. Angus McIntosh, M. L. Samuels, and Michael Benskin, 4 vols. (Aberdeen, 1986).

22. Two relevant papers have been published since the completion of this contribution: Andreas Fischer, "The Vocabulary of Very Late Old English," *Studies in Language and Literature. 'Doubt Wisely': Papers in Honour of E. G. Stanley*, ed. M. J. Toswell and E. M. Tyler (London and New York, 1996), pp. 29–41; and Saara Navanlinna, "Lexical Variation in the Old English Gospel Manuscripts and a Note on Continuation," *To Explain the Present: Studies in the Changing English Language in Honour of Matti Rissanen*, ed. Terttu Nevalainen and Leena Kahlas-Tarkka, Mémoires de la Société Néophilologique de Helsinki 52 (Helsinki, 1997), pp. 135–48.

FRANCISCUS JUNIUS AND THE VERSIFICATION OF *JUDITH*

FRANCISCI JUNII IN MEMORIAM: 1591–1991

PETER J. LUCAS

I

Franciscus Junius (1591–1677), or François du Jon, the Dutch scholar who was much interested in Old English and Germanic philology, Anglo-Saxon antiquities, and English historical lexicography, came to England in 1621 as librarian to the collector and patron Thomas Howard, Earl of Arundel (1604–46), and as tutor to his son. He stayed with the Howards for 30 years or so, living in England until about 1641, when they went to the Netherlands and he went with them. His interest in Germanic and Anglo-Saxon Studies began in earnest c. 1645. In 1651 he went to live with his widowed sister in the Netherlands, visiting Oxford several times in the ensuing years. In 1674 he returned to England to reside in Oxford, where he died three years later, bequeathing his books to the university. Junius was a laborious and exemplary student. He rose at 4 A.M. all year and worked until 1 P.M. (nine hours); then he engaged in "walking or running," and then worked again from 3 P.M. until 8 P.M. (five hours). By any reckoning, fourteen hours a day is a good work rate.[1]

There is still a considerable amount to show for Junius' labors. Considering that he was 54 or so years old when he took up Germanic and Anglo-Saxon Studies his achievement was remarkable, and his contribution to the preservation and transmission of Anglo-Saxon texts is an important one. In particular, a number of his transcripts of Old English manuscripts survive, some of which are extremely important for recovering the text of manuscripts subsequently damaged or destroyed by the 1731 Cotton Library fire.[2] The prose dialogue *Adrian and Ritheus* survives in two transcripts by Junius, both from London, BL Cotton Julius A.ii (Oxford, Bodleian Library, Junius 45 [SC 5157] and 61 [SC 5172]).[3] Junius also collated some Laws from BL Harley 55 (BL Harley 307,[4] fols. 38v–40r and 56r–70v), and transcribed a document from the same manuscript (BL Harley 6841, fol. 129), as well as the coronation oath from BL Cotton Vitellius A.vii, fol. 7 (lost in the 1731 fire): Bodleian Library, Junius 60 (SC 5171). His interest in glosses emerges from those he transcribed from Antwerp, Plantin-Moretus Museum 47 and BL Cotton Vespasian D.vi (Bodleian Library, Junius 71 [SC 5182]) and from BL Cotton Cleopatra A.iii and Otho E.i, pp. 205–21 (lost in the 1731 fire): Bodleian Library, Junius 77 (SC 5188). The largest body of transcripts, however, relates to Alfredian translations. He transcribed the Alfredian version of Augustine's *Soliloquies* from BL Cotton Vitellius A.xv, art. 1 (Bodleian Library, Junius 70 [SC 5181]). He collated three manuscripts, BL Cotton Tiberius B.xi (Junius' exemplar) and Otho B.ii, and Bodleian Library, Hatton 20 (SC 4113), of the Alfredian version of Gregory's *Pastoral Care* (Bodleian Library, Junius 53 [SC 5165]), which includes the *Metrical Preface* and the *Metrical Epilogue* (copied from Hatton 20), and copied the text (part of cap. xxxiii) that was missing on fol. 42 in Hatton 20.[5] Junius' transcription of the Alfredian version of Boethius' *De Consolatione Philosophiae* from BL Cotton Otho A.vi, collated with Bodleian Library, Bodley 180 (SC 2079) (Bodleian Library, Junius 12 [SC 5124]), includes the *Meters of Boethius* in verse.[6] But the most important transcription of verse made by Junius is probably the one he made of *Judith* from BL Cotton Vitellius A.xv, art. 2, the *Beowulf*-manuscript (Bodleian Library, Junius 105 [SC 5216]), and it is on this transcription that I shall focus in this paper. My concern is specifically with verse, and I have chosen to concentrate on *Judith* because it is well known, offers few metrical problems, and because it has the special interest of being preserved in the *Beowulf*-manuscript. It is also of greater interest than the transcripts of the *Meters of Boethius* as well as the rather briefer *Metrical Preface* and *Metrical Epilogue* to the *Pastoral Care* in that Junius seems to have adjusted his method of indicating the versification as he proceeded.

Most comments on Junius as a copyist are complimentary. In his edition of the Alfredian version of Gregory's *Pastoral Care*, for example, Sweet reports that "the words and letters of the original are given with great accuracy."[7] Dobbie finds that

> the errors . . . do not bulk very large, and the Junius transcript may therefore be regarded as a dependable source for the missing letters in the text of *Judith*—a more dependable authority, in view of its early date and its generally greater accuracy, than either of the Thorkelin transcripts of *Beowulf*.[8]

However, with regard to the presentation of the text Junius did more than merely transcribe it: as Dobbie puts it, "Junius supplied capital letters at the beginnings of the major divisions of the text and often at the beginnings of sentences, as well as in most proper names."[9] This statement applies to *Judith*, but it could equally well apply to the prose texts Junius transcribed. In other words, Junius was to some extent editing the text as he transcribed it. He was apparently thinking in terms of modern sentences and paragraphs. But "he also added a rather inconsistent punctuation, not in the modern manner but roughly imitative of the pointing in the Cædmonian poems of Junius MS 11."[10] Something much the same as what Dobbie calls "a rather inconsistent punctuation" in *Judith* occurs also in the *Meters of Boethius*, though Krapp is less complimentary about it: "Junius has attempted to introduce metrical pointing at the ends of half-lines, which has not [*sic*] counterpart in C[otton Otho A.vi], but this pointing is neither consistently carried out, nor very accurate where it does occur. . . ."[11] Evidently Junius' editorial thinking was not entirely modern; it also included the somewhat *recherché* aim of marking the versification of the text in an authentic Anglo-Saxon manner. Determining the extent to which Junius was successful (or not) in carrying out this aim is one of the purposes of this paper.

II

In Anglo-Saxon manuscripts Old English poetry is written out like prose. When it was read, it would normally have been read aloud, and so punctuation that aided this process is sometimes found.[12] One means of providing such aid was to use punctuation to mark off verses from each other. The philosophy presumably underlying this usage was succinctly expressed by Isidore of Seville, and repeated in a ninth-century commentary on Donatus: "Totus . . . uersus 'periodus' est."[13] A verse was interpreted as equivalent to the rhetorical unit known as a *period*: "Periodus . . . non longior esse debet quam ut uno spiritu proferatur."[14] In a number of Anglo-Saxon manuscripts, of which perhaps the most notable is Bodleian Library, Junius 11, containing the so-called "Cædmonian" biblical poems, *Genesis*, *Exodus*, and *Daniel*, the point is used in this way as a metrical punctuation. The usage has classical antecedents.[15] In an analysis of this metrical pointing in *Exodus* I found that it was 98 percent accurate.[16] In an earlier analysis John Lawrence found a degree of accuracy of nearly 96 percent for the whole of *Genesis*, *Exodus*, and *Daniel*.[17] Since Junius edited this manuscript for publication it may have been a model or authority for his own usage in his transcripts.[18]

III

I follow the versification of *Judith* in Dobbie's edition, except in the following instances:

89–90 sigor ond soðne geleafan, þæt ic mid þys sweorde mote geheawan
þysne morðres bryttan; geunne me minra gesynta

Dobbie and other editors print *geheawan* at the beginning of line 90, where it has to be an unstressed infinitive, one moreover that offends against Stanley's "rule" that an unstressed infinitive should never have the prefix *ge-*.[19] These difficulties are removed by the present arrangement, first proposed by Bliss.[20]

130 ond hit þa swa heolfrig hyre on hond ageaf

Dobbie and other editors print *hyre* as part of the *b*-verse. But this arrangement poses problems. The pronoun *hyre* is a particle in verse grammar, and by Kuhn's Law of Particles (*Satzpartikelgesetz*),[21] if (as here) it does not occur in the first metrical dip of the verse clause, it should receive a metrical stress. Since the line has *h*-alliteration, a stressed *hyre* would participate in the alliteration, thereby giving double alliteration in the *b*-verse, one, moreover, that will not scan regularly.[22] With *hyre* in the *a*-verse, however, there is no problem and the verse scans (with *hyre* stressed) normally as Type 3B1d (and the *b*-verse as Type 2B1a).[23]

The only other place where the versification might be considered problematical is

287 mid niðum neah geðrungen, þe we sculon nyde losian

where *nyde* has been supplied editorially (other editors supply *nu*) to provide alliteration and make the sense more complete.[24]

IV

The unique Anglo-Saxon text of *Judith* is preserved in the *Beowulf*-manuscript.[25] The text shows a sporadic pointing: vis-à-vis the other texts, the "fewest" points proportionately in the manuscript.[26] According to Malone, referring to both *Beowulf* and *Judith*, "the pointing is chiefly metrical" (p. 29). Malone notes 22 points in *Judith* (p. 31). Not all of these points, however, are strictly punctuation. Four occur immediately before or immediately after a section number, one after **X** on fol. 202r, one before and one after **XI** on fol. 205r, and one after **XII** on fol. 207v. That leaves eighteen points noted in the text of *Judith* by Malone.

According to my own observations, verified by inspection of the manuscript itself in the British Library,[27] there are fourteen points in the text of *Judith*, and one end-of-section marker (on fol. 207v), as indicated in Table 1 below. Malone's claim that there were three more

Table 1
Incidence of Points in the Text of *Judith* in the *Beowulf*-manuscript

Folio	Line	Line in Poem	Word after Which Point Occurs	Remarks
202r	18	14b	gesohte	At end of Sectional Division presumably numbered IX, 5mm. before **X**, the number of the next Sectional Division.
202v	6	21a	dryht*en*	
203r	8	40b	iudithðe	
203v	7	59a	besmitan	
	9	60b	gestyrde	
	18	67b	druncen	
204r	12	82b	a cwæð	
204v	1	90b	ge | synta	Second element of word begins page.
205r	12	121b	leas	At end of Sectional Division X, 2 cm. before point preceding **XI**, the number of the next Sectional Division.
205v	20	153b	leng	Last word on the page.
206v	13	190b	sende	
207v	11	235b	mihton	What looks like a point at the end of Sectional Division XI is in fact :~ with the upper point and the tilde bleached (as in *þe* in the previous line = 1st word in 235b).
209r	8	306b	g*e*lyste	
	12	312a	wiðer trod	
	21	322b	wæron	Last word on the page, added below last full line (= line 20).

points, one each on fols. 202v, 207v, and 208r, is misleading or ill-founded. On fol. 207v he has apparently counted the colon in the end-of-section marker as two points (cf. *Nowell Codex*, p. 30). On fol. 208r, at the end of line 16, there is a mark after *træf* (268a), but it is not a point by the scribe and is at the wrong height vis-à-vis the letters on the line to be one. On fol. 202v, at the end of line 9, there is a small hole in the parchment after *feor* (*feorran* 24b) that in a photograph might be mistaken for a point. All fifteen punctuation marks occur at the end of a verse, and their basic purpose may well be metrical, though the end-of-section marker and two of the points also mark the end of a sectional division. Why so few metrical divisions are indicated it is idle to speculate.[28] It should perhaps be noted that some points may have been lost at the end of manuscript lines as a result of the 1731 fire, especially on fol. 208v, but such losses could hardly amount to many.

As is well known, the last six (hypermetric) lines of *Judith* (344–49) were copied c. 1600 by someone whom I have elsewhere called "the rationalizer," at the bottom of fol. 209v.[29] These lines are pointed rather more heavily than the text written by the Anglo-Saxon scribe. Timmer noted seven points,[30] but Malone found nine (p. 31), and this finding of Malone's I am happy to confirm; the position of the points is indicated in Table 2. The fact that five of these points correctly mark metrical divisions suggests that copyists before Junius were interested in adding their perceptions of versification to their transcriptions.

V

In his transcription of *Judith* Junius wrote the poem out like prose, as in his original (though not with the same lineation), and he used two punctuation marks, the single point and the semicolon.[31] Nearly all of these (including all the semicolons) are Junius' additions to the text he was transcribing; they are editorial. According to Junius' own observation, "Unico puncto denotabant Anglo-Saxones sensum imperfectum: at perfectum sensum concludebant tribus punctis triangulari forma . . ." ['The Anglo-Saxons indicate incomplete sense with

Table 2
Points in Lines Copied c. 1600 at Bottom of Folio 209v

Line in Poem	Word after Which Point Occurs	Whether Marks a Metrical Division
344b	ahte	
345a	ælmihtigan	✓
345b	huru	
	tweode	✓
346a	þæs	
	lange	
	gyrnde	✓
347a	aldre	✓
348a	grundas	✓

a single point, but they terminate a unit where the sense is complete with three points arranged together in the shape of a triangle']. [32] It may have been this distinction that Junius was trying to capture authentically by his use of the point and semicolon. However, he apparently did not make the same distinction between the *sensus* and the *sententia* characteristic of much medieval practice. [33] Junius' punctuation seems to have had two functions: (1) to mark off the Old English verses from each other, and (2) to indicate modern sentence or paragraph divisions. All 33 semicolons mark both Old English verse divisions and modern sentence divisions. Some of the 33 do more. Six mark the beginning or end of a passage of direct speech (94a, 158b, 176b, 198b, 284b, 289a), and two more mark a paragraph division (27b, 170b). Four mark the end of sectional divisions (14b, 121b, 235b, 349b). The use of the point, however, is more purely metrical.

Judith has 696 verses, i.e., 348 *a*-verses and 348 *b*-verses. Of these, 68 *a*-verses and 67 *b*-verses are hypermetric, [34] nearly twenty percent of the total, a high proportion. [35] Potentially, therefore, there is scope for 663 points to mark verse divisions, excluding those marked by a semicolon. In fact there are 411 points, of which 390 are correctly placed at verse divisions. The degree of accuracy attained in the proportion of verse divisions that Junius attempted to so mark, including those marked by the semicolon, is 423 out of 444, or 95 percent, a very creditable performance indeed. But, since the proportion of actual verse divisions marked by Junius' punctuation is 423 out of 696, or 61 percent, consideration is necessary as to why Junius' "strike-rate" is apparently so comparatively disappointing. Two factors are of particular note in this respect.

First, from Table 3 it is evident that the distribution of Junius' pointing is uneven: the frequency increases in the first third of the poem to peak in sectional division XI, where 80 percent of the verse divisions are correctly marked and where Junius attempted to mark 83 percent of the verse divisions (190 points/semicolons to 228 verses; see Table 3, where points [181] and semicolons [9] are listed separately). Evidently, to begin with, as far as the pointing is concerned, Junius was thinking more in terms of modern sentence divisions than he was of Old English verse divisions. Before line 80 the pointing is sporadic: there are fourteen points and eight semicolons in 156 verses,

Table 3
Distribution of Junius' Metrical Pointing

MS Sectional Division No.	Line Nos.	No. of Lines	No. of Verses	No. of Points	No. of Points Placed Correctly	No. of Semicolons	Percentage of Verse Divisions Correctly Marked
[IX]	1–14	14	27	3	3	3	22%
X	15–121	107	213	58	56	13	32%
XI	122–235	114	228	181	174	9	80%
XII	236–349	114	228	169	157	8	72%
Total		349	696	411	390	33	61%

a strike-rate of only fourteen percent. Only five of the points occur at verse divisions which are not modern sentence divisions (8a, 35a, 40a, 60a, 63b), though two of these (40a, 60a) are modern clause divisions. So seventeen out of 22 verse divisions marked by the point or semicolon are also modern sentence divisions, some 77 percent. However, from the early occurrence of purely metrical pointing at verse 8a there can be no doubt that the separation of verses from each other was part of Junius' intention from the start. From line 80 onwards to the end of sectional division X (line 121) the metrical pointing is fairly regular, with sporadic omissions, the longest of which is from verse 103b to verse 106b inclusive, so that a strike-rate of 63 percent is achieved (53 verses correctly marked out of 84). The overall strike-rate from line 80 to the end of the poem is 74 percent (400 points/semicolons to 540 verses).

Even a strike-rate of three out of four, or four out of five, is not as high as might be expected from the 95 percent accuracy rating found for Junius' attempts at verse divisions, and this observation brings us to the second factor relevant to Junius' apparently comparatively disappointing strike-rate, a factor that, as far as I know, has hitherto escaped observation. Another early method of marking verse divisions was to use an extended space, larger than that between words, where a verse division did not coincide with a manuscript line division.[36] This method is found in Latin inscriptions from the period of the Roman Republic (510–30 B.C.), and it was used in Latin texts at least up to the sixth century A.D.[37] Sometimes it was used in conjunction with the point. Presumably Junius observed the extended space as a means of marking verse divisions in Old English vernacular manuscripts, such as Hatton 20.[38] Certainly he employed this method of verse division in his transcript of *Judith*. When the first 79 lines are analyzed taking into account both the extended spaces[39] and the points and semicolons, a different picture emerges. Of 156 verses, 126 are correctly marked off, some 81 percent. In addition there are fourteen erroneously placed extended spaces, so that the proportion of verses that Junius apparently intended to mark off rises to 90 percent (140 extended spaces, point/semicolons to 156 verses). When sectional division X is analyzed in this way, instead of the 32 percent strike-rate observed for points and semicolons alone we find 187 verses marked off correctly out of 213, some 88 percent. In addition there are eleven erroneously placed extended spaces and two erroneously placed points, so that the proportion of verses that Junius apparently intended to mark off rises to 94 percent (200 [i.e., 129 + 58 + 13] extended spaces, points/semicolons to 213 verses). For sectional division XI the figures are 209 verses marked off correctly out of 228, some 92 percent. When four erroneously placed extended spaces are taken into account, the proportion of verses that Junius apparently intended to mark off rises to 96 percent (220 [i.e., 30 + 181 + 9] extended spaces, points/semicolons to 228 verses). For sectional division XII the figures are 209 verses marked off correctly out of 228, some 92 percent. When three erroneously placed extended spaces are taken into account, the proportion of verses that Junius apparently intended to mark off rises to 98 percent (224 [i.e., 47 + 169 + 8] extended spaces, points/semicolons to 228 verses). These figures are set out in Table 4. From this table it would appear that Junius set out to mark verse divisions from the start, even though he changed his predominant method of doing so at line 80, and that he became increasingly confident of doing so. It would also appear that his success rate may have improved as he went along, but this impression is probably misleading (see further below, section VI).

From the sporadic pointing of metrical divisions in the text of *Judith* in the *Beowulf*-manuscript, Junius had little to go on. He does, however, reproduce all the verse divisions indicated by the Anglo-Saxon scribe. At the end of sectional divisions he used the semicolon (14b, 121b, 235b). At the end of three verses before line 80 he used an extended space (40b, 60b, 67b). Otherwise he used a point. With regard to the points put in by "the rationalizer," who c. 1600 copied lines 344–49 at the bottom of fol. 209v (above, p. 375), Junius wisely did not follow him slavishly. The rationalizer marked five verse divisions correctly and placed four points where there is no verse division.

Table 4
Distribution of Verse Divisions Marked

MS Sectional Division No.	No. of Verses	No. of Points	No. of Points Placed Correctly	No. of Semicolons	No. of Extended Spaces	No. of Extended Spaces Correctly Placed	Percentage of Verse Divisions Correctly Marked	No. of Attempts to Mark Verse Divisions as Percentage of Total No. of Verses
[IX]	27	3	3	3	18	14	74%	89%
X	213	58	56	13	129	118	88%	94%
XI	228	181	174	9	30	26	92%	96%
XII	228	169	157	8	47	44	92%	98%
Total	696	411	390	33	224	202	90%	96%

Junius follows the rationalizer in four out of five of his correct placements, omitting to mark the end of verse 345b (*tweode*), and takes over one of his placements that do not mark a verse division (*ahte* 344b); cf. below, p. 386. Junius' confidence in his own ability to indicate versification was evidently sufficiently high to discount guidance offered by a predecessor, even though both probably had the same aim of marking verse divisions.

In his printed edition of 1698, Edward Thwaites followed Junius' transcript,[40] as his reproduction of Junius' points and semicolons (for which Thwaites used a triple period),[41] including those wrongly placed, confirms. Of the 411 points Thwaites omitted just five (35a, 63b, 114b, 128b, 159a). Of the 33 semicolons Thwaites reproduced 31, while the other two are reduced to points (176b, 284b). What Thwaites completely failed to reproduce, however, are the extended spaces which Junius also used to separate verses. While Junius evidently knew he was transcribing verse, Thwaites may have thought he was printing prose.[42]

VI

Out of 668 attempts to mark verse divisions, whether by point, extended space, or semicolon, some 43 (6.4 percent) are wrongly placed. There are also 42 verses which Junius omitted to mark out of a total of 696, again some six percent. The distribution of these errors and omissions is set out in Table 5. Although, at first glance, it may appear that there is an observable trend towards a diminishing degree of error as the transcription of the poem progresses, this impression is probably misleading. What is of more significance is the distribution of errors in relation to the proportion of verses that are hypermetric. The lowest number of errors and omissions is found where the proportion of hypermetric verses is at its lowest (XI), and the highest number of errors and omissions is found where the proportion of hypermetric verses is at its highest (IX), and similarly in between. This correspondence suggests that there is a connection between errors and omissions on the one hand and metrical features on the other.

Table 5
Distribution of Errors and Omissions

MS Sectional Division No.	No. of Verses	No. of Errors	Percentage of Errors in Relation to Verse Divisions Marked	No. of Omissions	Percentage of Omissions in Relation to Total No. of Verses	No. of Hypermetric Verses	Percentage of Hypermetric Verses
[IX]	27	4	17%	4	15%	23	85%
X	213	13	6.5%	17	8%	73	34%
XI	228	11	5%	10	4%	2	1%
XII	228	15	6.7%	11	5%	38	17%
Total	696	43	6.4%	42	6%	135	20%

Such a connection is confirmed by a detailed examination of the incidence of the errors and omissions (see Table 6). For convenience I shall take first the errors where a point or extended space occurs within a verse as well as at the end (Table 6, rows F and G). All except one of these instances occur in a hypermetric verse, either where two divisions have been indicated in one verse (339a, 89b, 99b, 344b) or where three divisions have been indicated in two verses (9a, 58a, 273a, 287a, 341a, 346a, 347a). The one exception occurs in a group of verses following a heavy verse where four divisions are indicated in three verses (224a). Evidently Junius had difficulty with some of these longer verses. The same difficulty is reflected in the errors where a point or extended space has been incorrectly placed for marking the end of a verse (Table 6, rows D and E). Many occur in hypermetric verses (19a, 31a, 2b, 4b, 18b, 33b, 54b, 66b), including some where too many divisions have been indicated (8b, 57b, 272b, 340b, 345b, 346b).

Table 6
Analysis of Errors and Omissions

A. No. of appropriate positions		696
B. No. of *a*-verses not marked by a point or extended space	18	
C. No. of *b*-verses not marked by a point or extended space	24	
D. No. of points or extended spaces incorrectly placed for marking the end of an *a*-verse	7	
E. No. of points or extended spaces incorrectly placed for marking the end of a *b*-verse	22	
F. No. of points or extended spaces incorrectly placed within an *a*-verse as well as at the end	11	
G. No. of points or extended spaces incorrectly placed within a *b*-verse as well as at the end	3	
Total no. of errors	43	
H. Total no. of correct placements (ignoring rows F and G)		625

Some occur in a normal verse which is followed by a hypermetric verse (87b), and on one of these occasions too many verse divisions have been indicated (286b). Some occur in a group of verses beginning with a heavy verse where too many divisions have been indicated (223a, 223b). Two more occur in verses (166b, 316b) that are followed by heavy verses, one of them an exceptionally long sub-type (1A2c) not found in *Beowulf*. As well as with some longer verses, Junius had difficulty with some shorter verses. Three of the verses where a point or extended space has been incorrectly placed for marking the end of a verse are light verses (215a, 229a, 336b), and two are followed by a light verse (225b, and at one remove 142a). Altogether these verses of longer or shorter duration than the average account for some 81 percent (25 out of 31) of these errors (Table 6, rows D and E). Of the remainder, most are verses with a weak onset (Types 3B or 2C), verses which Junius may occasionally have had difficulty in distinguishing from light verses of Types a and d (137a, 52b, 53b, 184b, 323b).

All the omissions, where a verse-division is not indicated by a point or extended space, may be considered together (Table 6, rows B and C). A considerable proportion of these omissions affect light verses (15a, 28a, 50a, 75a, 126a, 131a, 139a, 140a, 229a, 242a, 248a, 249a, 314a, 47b, 48b, 73b, 231b, 242b, 248b); there is also one defective verse where only the last word survives (1b). Some affect normal verses which are followed by a light verse (326a, 126b, 142b, 241b, 270b). Taken together, these light (or defectively short) verses account for some 60 percent (25 out of 42) of the omissions. Here is confirmation that Junius had difficulty with some shorter verses. A further six omissions affect hypermetric verses (10a, 5b, 10b, 55b, 58b, 289b). Of the remainder, several are verses with a weak onset (43a, 49a, 50b, 51b, 110b, 123b, 188b).

Some notion of how a cluster of errors could arise may be seen from the following example. The verses are set out as in a modern edition (Dobbie's) with Junius' points or extended spaces superimposed as it were within square backets. The scansion is indicated to either side as appropriate.

1D*2	strælas stede[.]hearde styrmdon [.] hlude	2A1a
2A2	grame [ ] guðfrecan [ ] garas sendon [ ]	2A1a
		(223–24)

Both *a*-verses, 223a and 224a, are heavy verses with three rather than the usual two stressed elements. In the first Junius has indicated a verse division too soon, in the middle of what we now know to be a compound. Following on, Junius has indicated too many verse divisions. Nevertheless, his sense of Old English verse rhythm and alliteration is not entirely defective. In his verse pattern "hearde styrmdon hlude grame / guðfrecan garas sendon," the alliteration is satisfactory and only the second *a*-verse, *guðfrecan*, will not scan regularly (because it has only three syllables). *Strælas stede*, however, has been left as a single half-line. Even when he was wrong (as we now know), Junius' method had its commendable aspects, and these should be borne in mind as we come to evaluate his understanding of the poem's meter and his contribution to its editorial versification.

VII

In any assessment of Junius' contribution to the versification of the poem, the first point to be made is that 90 percent of the verse divisions as now identified by modern scholarship are accurately indicated by him (see Table 4). Few would disagree that for a seventeenth-century antiquary Junius' achievement in this regard is impressive. As we have seen from the discussion of errors and omissions, Junius had difficulty with some longer (usually hypermetric) and shorter (light) verses. Nevertheless, his success rate in indicating verse divisions in hypermetric verses and light verses was 85 percent in both cases (115 out of 135 hypermetric verses, and 139 out of 164 light verses), so the difficulty he experienced was relatively infrequent.

Some of Junius' omissions may be the result of sheer honesty; if he did not know where the verse divisions came he omitted to indicate them. This feature of his work is suggested by his treatment of lines 248–49, "ond wið þæs bealofullan burgeteldes / werigferhðe hwearfum þringan [ ].” For the editors’ *werigferhðe* the manuscript has *weras ferhðe*. Without Grein’s (or some other more drastic) emendation the lines will not make sense. Junius may therefore have decided that where something was wrong, he could not indicate the verse divisions with sufficient confidence.

As is evident above from examination of a cluster of errors in lines 223–24, Junius’ sense of the rhythm of Old English verse and of alliteration had much to commend it, and it is ironic that his errors are in some ways even more revealing of his scholarly virtues than statistics demonstrating the degree of accuracy he achieved. To illustrate this point further, lines 345b–47a may be cited:

a1b(1D1)[43]	to ðam ælmihtigan [.] huru æt þam ende [.] ne tweode	a1d(1A*1a)
+1A*1b(2A1a)	þæs leanes [.] þe heo lange gyrnde [;]	
	Ðæs sy ðam leofan [.] drihtne	a1c(2A1a)
1A*1a(2A1a)	wuldor [.] to widan aldre [.]	

Here Junius has indicated six verses instead of four. Some of them scan with no problem at all: *drihtne wuldor* 2A1a in particular, and as light verses *huru æt þam ende* a1, and *Ðæs sy ðam leofan* a1. Another scans as +1A*1a, *ne tweode þæs leanes*, anacrusis being perfectly acceptable in Type 1A*1, or, alternatively, it too could be a light verse, a1. Another, *to widan aldre*, will scan +2A1a, with anacrusis in Type 2A1, an anomaly that occurs rarely in Old English verse, but there is a certain instance in *Judith*: *aweccan dorste* 258b. The most problematical verse is *þe heo lange gyrnde*, which will only scan with disyllabic anacrusis in a verse that strictly should not show anacrusis at all: ++2A1a. Alternatively, the verse could be treated as a single hypermetric verse. Of none of these verses as indicated by Junius can it be said that they will not scan at all. When we come to arrange the verses in pairs linked by alliteration, while the result is not acceptable in the light of modern scholarship, it is a fair attempt:

a1b(1D1)	to ðam ælmihtigan	huru æt þam ende	a1d	(1)
a1d	ne tweode þæs leanes	þe heo lange gyrnde	++2A1a	(2)

a1c	Ðæs sy ðam leofan		(3)
2A1a	drihtne wuldor to widan aldre	+2A1a	(4)

Alliteration is satisfactory in lines (1) and (2), line (3) has to be taken as a single half-line, but in line (4) the alliteration falls on the second rather than the required first stressed element. In line (1) Type a1 should not occur in the *b*-verse.

Evidently Junius had a good sense of Old English verse rhythm, good enough in fact to indicate the versification correctly even on two occasions when the alliterating element was missing in the manuscript (201b, 287b). Indeed, in the latter instance the editors of *Sweet's Reader* would have done well to heed Junius' guidance.[44] Junius seems to have relied on this sense of rhythm more than on alliteration in indicating the versification. Where he made mistakes, it was mainly a matter of choosing the wrong pattern rather than arbitrarily imposing a non-existent one. Junius also seems to have had a good sense of the components of Old English verse in syntactical terms; even his erroneous verse divisions tend to avoid serious breaks in phrasing. All in all, Junius' contribution to the versification was remarkable: 90 percent accuracy with errors that reveal his intelligence and instinctive feel for Old English poetry. I hope that now, more than four hundred years after his birth, this paper will have gone some way to rehabilitate his reputation in this regard and to disprove Krapp's verdict of inconsistency and inaccuracy. On the contrary, Junius' efforts at versification deserve to be complimented. He was a careful scholar.

UNIVERSITY COLLEGE, DUBLIN

Appendix 1

THE SCANSION OF *JUDITH*: A SUMMARY

1.1 The distribution of the main types of normal verse is shown here in the three columns at the right: column (1) gives the number of *a*-verses with double alliteration, column (2) the number of *a*-verses with single alliteration, and column (3) the number of *b*-verses.

	(1)	(2)	(3)
Type a1		19	
Type d1		15	13
Type d2		26	13
Type d3		10	5
Type d4		2	1
Type d5		1	7
Type 1*A*1		1	2
Type 1*A**1			1
Type 1*D*1		17	6
Type 2*A*1		13	12
Type 1A1	10	2	15
Type 1A2	2		
Type 1A*1	32	5	38
Type 1A*2	4		
Type 1A*3			1

	(1)	(2)	(3)
Type 1D1	3	5	7
Type 1D2	1		
Type 1D3	1		
Type 1D5	4		1
Type 1D*1	2		
Type 1D*2	6		
Type 1D*3	4		
Type 2A1	10	21	56
Type 2A2	4		
Type 2A3	6	1	2
Type 2B1		3	12
Type 2B2			1
Type 2C1	3	1	18
Type 2C2		1	3
Type 2E1		1	1
Type 3B1	7	23	46
Type 3B*1		2	11
Type 3E1	2	2	3
Type 3E2	2	6	5
Defective			1
Hypermetric	64	4	67
Total	167	181	348

1.2 The distribution of the main types of hypermetric verse is shown here in columns as above.

	(1)	(2)	(3)
Type a(1A)			6
Type a(1A*)			20
Type a(1D)		1	
Type a(2A)		3	40
Type a(3E)			1
Type 1A(1A)	1		
Type 1A(1A*)	3		
Type 1A(1D)	1		
Type 1A(2A)	1		
Type 1A(3E)	1		
Type 1A*(1A)	1		
Type 1A*(1A*)	6		
Type 1A*(2A)	18		
Type 1A*(3A)	1		
Type 2A(1A)	1		
Type 2A(1A*)	2		
Type 2A(1D)	9		
Type 2A(2A)	16		
Type 3A(1A)	2		
Type 3A(2A)	1		
Total	64	4	67

APPENDIX 2

INDEX TO THE SCANSION OF *JUDITH*

1		def.
2	1A*1b(2A1a)	a1c(2A1a)
3	1A*3b(2A1a)	a1d(2A1a)
4	1A*1a(2A1a)	a1e(2A1a)
5	+2A1(2A1a)	a1c(1A1a)
6	2A3(1A*1a)	a1d(1A1a)
7	1A1b(1D1)	a1e(2A1a)
8	3A2(2A1a)	a1c(2A1a)
9	2A1(1D1)	a1d(2A1a)
10	1A*1a(3A1)	a1b(2A1a)
11	2A1(1D1)	a1d(2A1a)
12	2A1(2A1a)	a1c(2A1a)
13	3B1b	1A1b
14	1D*3	1A*1a
15	a1d	2A1a
16	1A*1a(1A1a)	a1c(1A1a)
17	2A1(1D1)	a1c(2A1a)
18	1A1b(1A*1a)	a1c(1A*1a)
19	2A1(1D1)	a1b(2A1a)
20	2A1(1D1)	a1c(1A*1a)
21	2A1(2A1a)	a1b(2A1a)
22	2A3a	d2a
23	a1b	1A*1a
24	3B1c	1A*1a
25	d2b	1A*1a
26	1A*2a	1A*1a
27	1*D*1	3B1c
28	d1b	3B1b
29	2A3a	1A*1a
30	2A3(2A1a)	a1d(2A1a)
31	a1e(2A1a)	a1e(1A*1a)
32	+2A1(1A*1a)	a1c(2A1a)
33	2A1(1D1)	a1b(2A1a)
34	3A1(1A1a)	a1b(1A*1a)
35	3B1a	2A1a
36	d2b	1A*1a
37	1A*1a	2C1a
38	2*A*1	3B*1d
39	3E2	2A1a
40	d2b	d1b
41	1D*2	d2b
42	1*D*1	1A*1a
43	3B1a	2B1a
44	3B1b	1A*1a
45	2A1a	3E1
46	2*A*1	d2b
47	2A3b	d3c
48	1A1a	d1b
49	3B1b	2A1a
50	d1a	3B1b
51	2A1a	2C1b
52	2A1a	3B1c
53	2A1a	2C1b
54	1A*1a(1A*1a)	a1c(1A*1a)
55	1A*1a(2A1a)	a1c(2A1a)
56	1A1b(2A1a)	a1c(2A1a)
57	+1A1b(1A1a)	a1c(1A*1a)
58	2A1(2A1a)	a1c(2A1a)
59	+1A*1b(1A*1a)	a1d(2A1a)
60	+2A1(2A1a)	a1d(1A*1a)
61	2A1(2A1a)	a1d(2A1a)
62	2A3(2A1a)	
63	1A*1a(2A1a)	a1e(1A1a)
64	1A*1b(2A1a)	a1d(1A*1a)

65	+2A1(1D1)	a1d(2A1a)
66	2A3(2a1a)	a1d(2A1a)
67	1A*1b(2A1a)	a1c(1A*1a)
68	+1A*1b(2A1a)	a1d(2A1a)
69	d3b	2A1a
70	1A1b	2A1a
71	1D1	d3c
72	2A2	1A*1a
73	2A1a	d1b
74	2a1a	1A*1a
75	a1d	2A1a
76	1A*1a	d1b
77	1A*1a	d5c
78	3E1	2A1a
79	2A1a	3B*1b
80	2A1a	3B1c
81	2C1a	2A1a
82	1*D*1	2B1b
83	3B1b	3B1a
84	1D1	2A1a
85	2A1a	1D1
86	3E1	1A*1b
87	1A*1a	2C1a
88	1A*1a(1A*1a)	a1c(2A1a)
89	1A1a(1A*1a)	a1d(1A*1c)
90	a1b(2A1a)	a1c(1A1c)
91	2A3(2A1a)	a1c(2A1a)
92	1A*1a(2A1a)	a1c(2A1a)
93	2A3(2A1a)	a1d(1A*1a)
94	1A*1a(2A1a)	a1c(2A1a)
95	1A*1a(1A*1a)	a1c(1A*1a)
96	1*D*1	3B1e
97	+1A*1b(1A*1a)	a1d(1A*1a)
98	3A1(1A1a)	a1e(2A1a)
99	1A*1a(2A1a)	a1c(1A*1a)
100	2*A*1	d1c
101	1A*1a	2A1a
102	d1c	2A1a
103	1A1a	d5b
104	d3b	2A1a
105	1*D*1	2B1b
106	3B1b	3B1c
107	1A*2a	2B1b
108	1D*1	d1b
109	1D5	2A1a
110	3B1b	3B1c
111	1A1b	3B1b
112	1A*1a	3E2
113	3B1b	3B1c
114	1A*1a	2A1a
115	1A*1a	1A*1a
116	1A*1a	d5a
117	d2b	3B1c
118	1A*1a	2C1b
119	d3b	3B1b
120	1A*1a	3B1b
121	3b1b	3E2
122	a1d	3E1
123	1A*1a	2C1c
124	2A1a	3B*1c
125	3B1b	1A*1a
126	d2a	1A*1a
127	d1b	d1c
128	2A3b	3B1b
129	1A*1a	1A1a
130	3B1d	2B1a
131	1*D*1	1A1a
132	2A1(2A1a)	a1c(2A1a)
133	3b1a	2*A*1
134	a1d	2*A*1
135	3E2	1A1b
136	d2b	2C1a

137	3b1b	2A1a
138	1*D*1	d2b
139	2*A*1	1D1
140	d2b	2C1a
141	d3b	2A1a
142	1D1	2A1a
143	d1b	3B1b
144	2*A*1	2E1a
145	3E2	2B1c
146	1D5	2C2b
147	1A1a	3B1b
148	3E2	2A1a
149	3B1c	3B1c
150	d2b	1A1a
151	3B1b	2B1b
152	d2b	3B1b
153	3E2	3B1c
154	1A*1a	2C1b
155	2A1a	3B1b
156	2C1a	d5c
157	2A1a	2C1a
158	a1b	3b1b
159	a1c	1*D*1
160	a1d	3B1b
161	3B1b	1A1b
162	d5b	1D1
163	1D3	1A*1a
164	1A*1a	1A*1a
165	3B1c	2*A*1
166	1A*1a	3E1
167	1A2c	1A1a
168	a1d	3B1b
169	1A1a	d2b
170	d2b	1A1a
171	3b1b	1A*1a
172	d1b	2*A*1
173	d2a	1A*1a
174	a1c	1A*1a
175	d2a	3B*1d
176	a1c	+1A*1a
177	a1d	3E2
178	2A1a	d1b
179	1D*2	2A1a
180	2*A*1	1*D*1
181	3B1b	1A*1a
182	2A1a	3B1b
183	2A1a	3B1c
184	2A1a	3B1c
185	2A1a	3B*1b
186	2C1a	3B*1b
187	d2b	2A1a
188	1*D*1	3B1b
189	1A*1b	3b1b
190	2A1b	2A1a
191	2A1a	3B1b
192	1A1a	d3a
193	2A1a	3B*1a
194	1D*3	2A1a
195	1D*2	1A1b
196	+1A*1a	2C1b
197	1A1a	3B1c
198	2A1a	3B1a
199	3B1b	1A*1a
200	1A*1a	d2b
201	1A*1b	d2b
202	a1d	1A1b
203	1A1b	3B1c
204	3B1b	2A1a
205	2A1a	3B*1b
206	1A1a	3B1b
207	3E2	2A1a
208	d3c	2A1a

209	1A*1a	2B1b
210	1D5	1A1
211	2A1	1D5
212	2A1	d2b
213	1A*1a	1A*1a
214	2A1a	3B1b
215	1D1	2A1a
216	3E1	3B1b
217	d3b	1A*1a
218	1D1	d1b
219	d3b	2C1a
220	d2b	d2b
221	2C1b	2A1a
222	2A1	d3a
223	1D*2	2A1a
224	2A2	2A1a
225	3B*1a	1A1b
226	1D1	2A1a
227	d2b	2A1
228	d1b	1A1
229	1D1	2A1a
230	1A*1a	3E2
231	1A*1a	d1b
232	1D1	2A1
233	1D1	1A*1a
234	d2a	1A*1a
235	2A1a	2C1d
236	d2b	d5b
237	1D*2	2A1a
238	a1c	2C1b
239	d2a	2A1
240	d4b	2A1a
241	1D1	3B1a
242	d1a	2A1
243	2A1a	d5b
244	d2b	2A3a
245	1D1	2A1
246	1D*3	3B*1b
247	3E2	1A*1a
248	d1c	1A1
249	2A1	2A1a
250	2A1	d1c
251	d1b	2A1a
252	a1e	2C1a
253	1D1	2A1a
254	3B1b	3B1b
255	3B1b	1A*1a
256	1A*1a	d2b
257	1A*1a	3B1b
258	a1c	+2A1a
259	d1c	d5c
260	3B1b	1A*1a
261	2A1a	1D1
262	1D1	2A1a
263	1D*2	2A1a
264	d4b	2A1a
265	1D*1	3E2
266	d2b	1A1a
267	1A1a	2A1a
268	3B1d	1A*1a
269	2A1	2C1b
270	d1c	2A1a
271	d2a	1D1
272	+2A1(1D1)	a1d(1A*1a)
273	1A*1a(2A1a)	a1d(1A*1a)
274	d2b	2B1a
275	2B1b	2B2-
276	d2b	d4d
277	2A3a	2B1c
278	a1d	2A1a
279	d3a	2A1a
280	1A*1a	3B*1b

281	1A*1a	2C2c
282	1A1a	2C2b
283	2B1b	d1b
284	d1b	2A1a
285	a1c	3B*1b
286	1A*1a	3B1c
287	+2A1(1A1a)	a1d(2A1a)
288	1A1a(1A*1a)	a1b(1A*1a)
289	+2A1(2A1a)	a1b(2A1a)
290	1A*1b(1A*1a)	a1d(2A1a)
291	2C2a	2B1b
292	3E2	3B1b
293	3B1a	1A*1a
294	d2b	1A*1a
295	1A*1a	d2b
296	1A*1a	1A1b
297	2A2	3B1b
298	1D1	1A*1a
299	1A*1a	3B1b
300	1A*1a	1D1
301	d2b	2A1a
302	1D2	2A3a
303	3B*1a	2A1a
304	2A3a	2A1a
305	1A*1a	1D1
306	2E1b	1A*1a
307	1_A_1	2B1b
308	2B1a	1_A_*1
309	1_D_1	2_A_1
310	2A1a	2A1a
311	1A*1a	d2b
312	1A*2a	1A*3
313	3E1	1A1b
314	1_D_1	d1b
315	d2b	1_D_1
316	2A2	2A1a
317	1A2a	2A1a
318	2A1a	d2b
319	d3b	1A1b
320	2_A_1	1_D_1
321	1A*1a	2C1b
322	a1d	2A1a
323	2A1a	3B1b
324	2A1a	3B1b
325	1D5	1A*1a
326	3B1c	1_D_1
327	1A*2	2A1a
328	2A3a	1A*1a
329	2A1a	2C1b
330	3B1a	1_D_1
331	d3c	1A*1a
332	1A*1b	d3a
333	d1a	2A1a
334	1D1	3B1b
335	d1b	2A1a
336	1D*2	2_A_1
337	1A1a(3E1)	a1c(2A1a)
338	+2A1(2A1a)	a1d(2A1a)
339	2A3(2A1a)	a1b(2A1a)
340	1A*1a(2A1a)	a1d(2A1a)
341	+2A1(1D1)	a1c(2A1a)
342	2A1(2A1a)	a1c(3E1)
343	1A*1a(2A1a)	a1c(1A*1a)
344	1A*3a(2A1a)	a1e(1A*1a)
345	a1b(1D1)	a1d(1A*1a)
346	+1A*1b(2A1a)	a1c(2A1a)
347	1A*1a(2A1a)	a1c(1A1a)
348	1A*1a(2A1a)	a1c(2A1a)
349	a1a(2A1a)	a1b(2A1a)

APPENDIX 3

NOTES ON PARTICULAR ASPECTS

1. There is one instance of what appears to be Type 1*A**1, a type not found in *Beowulf*, and, as far as I know, unique. It is *heafodgerimes* (308b). No doubt this verse is modelled on one such as *dogorgerimes* (*Beowulf* 2728a) in which the second *o* in *dogor-* may be underscored to indicate that it is metrically insignificant;[45] however, no such underscoring of the *o* in *heafod-* is permissible. Either the *Judith*-poet is guilty of faulty composition or, more probably, he has deliberately invented a special kind of verse to emphasize the sense. The verse occurs in a passage stating that most *heafodgerimes* 'of the number of heads' of the Assyrian army fell in the dust in the battle following the discovery of Holofernes' headless body. In this way the fall of the Assyrians mirrors that of their leader.

2. One normal sub-type not found in *Beowulf* occurs:

1A2c	*men on ðære medobyrig*	(167a)

Two hypermetric sub-types not listed by Bliss, *Metre*, pp. 130–33, occur:

a1c(1A1c)	*geunne me minra gesynta*	(90b)
a1d(1A*1c)	*þæt ic mid þys sweorde mote geheawan*	(89b)

3. There are two instances in the *b*-verse of heavy verses that should occur only in the *a*-verse with compulsory double alliteration:

1A*3	*wælscel oninnan*	(312b)
1D5	*sang hildeleoð*	(211b)

In 312b *oninnan*, a preposition, is printed as one word.[46] On *wælscel* see Dobbie's note. *Sang hildeleoð* is an instance of misuse of convertibility, where a light verse of Type d has been inappropriately subjected to the process of conversion from *a*-verse use to *b*-verse use.[47]

4. *Judith* shows a low incidence of Types D (34 out of 560 = six percent) and E (22 out of 560 = four percent). For comparative figures from other poems

see Lucas, "*Genesis B* as Old English Verse," § 31. There are no instances of Types 1D4, 1D6, 1D*4–6, 2E2, 3E3, 3E*1–3. This limitation in the variety of verse types is also shown by the hypermetric verses. All of these are based on a pattern beginning with Type A or a light a-type.

5. *Alliteration.* Although *Judith* is often considered a relatively late poem, other late poems avoid alliteration of *g* = /j/ with *g* = /g/.[48] There is, however, some evidence that the *Judith*-poet knew both systems, one utilizing alliteration of the two *g*'s and the other avoiding it. The first system is reflected by alliteration of the two *g*'s in lines 9, 13, 22, 123, 238, 256. As for the second system, in line 149 double alliteration in the *b*-verse is avoided by following it, and so is triple alliteration in verse 2a. This evidence is perhaps sufficient to suggest that *Judith* was composed during a transitional phase, while the traditional system was still practiced but the new one was already known.

Alliteration of *sn-*/*st-* in line 55 is apparently irregular but may be explained by epenthesis of *t* in the *sn*-forms.[49] Double alliteration in Types 1A and 1A* occurs in 86 percent and 88 percent of instances respectively, which is quite high: for comparable figures from other poems see Lucas, "*Genesis B* as Old English Verse," § 22.

6. There is an instance of the numeral *an* unstressed in verse 324b, *anes monðes fyrst*. As a numeral *an* should be a stressword. However, sometimes in such phrases the sense of numerical contrast (with two or more) was weak and the word functions more or less as an indefinite article.[50] Here *anes* should be treated as a particle that is proclitic on *monðes* and therefore unstressed.

7. There is a high incidence of anacrusis in the hypermetric verses; fourteen out of 68 such *a*-verses show this feature, some 21 percent.[51] As a proportion of the number of hypermetric *a*-verses with double alliteration (64), in all of which anacrusis is theoretically permissible, the percentage figure is slightly higher: 22 percent, against fourteen percent for the whole of Old English poetry (excluding *Genesis B*) including *Judith*.[52]

8. Adherence to the laws of verse grammar observed and formulated by Kuhn is fair.[53] There are three breaches of the Law of Particles, *mihte* (49a), *mote* (89b), *leton* (221a), but only one breach of the Law of Clause Openings, *Wið þæs fæstengeates* (162a).

NOTES

1. For some account of Junius and his career see Philippus H. Breuker, "On the Course of Franciscus Junius' Germanic Studies, with Special Reference to Frisian," in *Aspects of Old Frisian Philology*, ed. Rolf H. Bremmer, Jr., Geart van der Meer, and Oebele Vries, Amsterdamer Beiträge zur Älteren Germanistik 31, 32 (Amsterdam, 1990), pp. 42–68, esp. 46–49. Cf. also M. Sue Hetherington, *The Beginnings of Old English Lexicography* (Spicewood, TX, 1980), pp. 222–36; for a brief notice see the DNB (1975), s.n. Junius, Francis. See also Johan Kerling, "Franciscus Junius, 17th-Century Lexicography and Middle English," in *LEXeter '83 Proceedings: Papers from the International Conference on Lexicography at Exeter. . .* , ed. R. R. K. Hartmann, Lexicographica, ser. maior 1 (Tübingen, 1984), pp. 92–100. Kerling adduces evidence for Junius' year of birth being 1591 rather than 1589 (p. 93), confirmed by Breuker, p. 46.

2. For a listing of Junius' transcripts of Old English material see Ker, *Catalogue*, pp. 508–09; to this should be added Bodleian Library, Junius 61 (SC 5172), one of the transcripts of *Adrian and Ritheus*. Some of Junius' transcripts, including that of *Judith* (no. 20), are reproduced in *Old English Verse Texts from Many Sources: A Comprehensive Collection*, ed. Fred C. Robinson and Eric G. Stanley, EEMF 23 (1990). There is a list of Junius' manuscripts in the *A Summary Catalogue of Western Manuscripts in the Bodleian Library at Oxford*, vol. 2, pt. 2 (Oxford, 1937), pp. 962–90.

3. Cf. *The Prose Solomon and Saturn and Adrian and Ritheus*, ed. James E. Cross and Thomas D. Hill (Toronto, 1982), pp. 15–16.

4. A copy of *Archaionomia sive De Priscis Anglorum Legibus Libri*, ed. William Lambarde, rev. Abraham Wheloc (Cambridge: R. Daniel, 1644).

5. See the facsimile edition by N. R. Ker, *The Pastoral Care*, EEMF 6 (1956). For Junius' copy of the *Metrical Preface* see Robinson and Stanley, eds., no. 6.1.5. Junius' copy of the *Metrical Epilogue* occurs in Bodleian Library, Junius 53, pp. 256–57, but is not reproduced in Robinson and Stanley, eds. Dobbie's statement that "the metrical epilogue does not appear in J[unius 53] at all" is incorrect: *Beowulf and Judith*, ed. Elliot Van Kirk Dobbie, ASPR 4 (1953), p. cxiii. See now Peter J. Lucas, "The *Metrical Epilogue* to the Alfredian *Pastoral Care*: A Postscript from Junius," ASE, 24 (1995), 43–50.

6. Robinson and Stanley, eds., no. 5.

7. *King Alfred's West-Saxon Version of Gregory's Pastoral Care*, ed. Henry Sweet, EETS OS 45 (1871; rpt. New York, 1978), p. xix.

8. Dobbie, ed., p. xxiv.

9. Ibid., p. xxiii.

10. Ibid.

11. George Philip Krapp, *The Paris Psalter and the Meters of Boethius*, ASPR 5 (1932), p. xliv.

12. For punctuation in ancient Latin manuscripts see Rudolf W. Müller, *Rhetorische und syntaktische Interpunktion* (Tübingen, 1964). For a survey of research on ancient punctuation see Jeannette Moreau-Maréchal, "Recherches sur la Ponctuation," *Scriptorium*, 22 (1968), 56–66. For discussion of pointing in Old English poetical manuscripts see Katherine O'Brien O'Keeffe, *Visible Song: Transitional Literacy in Old English Verse* (Cambridge, 1990), and my review in *The Review of English Studies*, NS 44 (1993), 401–03.

13. Isidore of Seville, *Etymologiae* I.20 (PL 82, 96), cited in Martin Hubert, "Corpus Stigmatologicum Minus," *Archivum Latinitatis Medii Aevi*, 37 (1970), 5–169, p. 71; also "Index," 39 (1974), 55–84. For the 9th-century *Commentum Einsidlense in Donati Artem Maiorem* see Hubert, p. 81, or Henricus Keil, *Grammatici Latini*, vols. 1–8 (Leipzig, 1855–1923), vol. 8, p. 231.

14. Diomedis in *Ars Grammatica*, II, cited in Hubert, p. 37, repeated by Isidore, *Etymologiae* II.18, cited in Hubert, p. 71.

15. E. O. Wingo, *Latin Punctuation in the Classical Age*, Janua Linguarum, ser. pract. 133 (The Hague, 1972), Appendix 2.3.1, pp. 158–63.

16. *Exodus*, ed. Peter J. Lucas (London, 1977; rev. ed., 1994), p. 22.

17. John Lawrence, *Chapters on Alliterative Verse* (London, 1893), pp. 15–16.

18. Franciscus Junius F.F., *Cædmonis Monachi Paraphrasis Poetica Genesios ac Praecipuarum Sacrae Paginae Historiarum*... (Amsterdam: C. Cunrad, 1655). See now

also the facsimile edition of this work, ed. Peter J. Lucas, Early Studies in Germanic Philology 3 (Amsterdam, 1997). Junius may have inherited the practice from earlier antiquaries: cf. the remarks above, p. 375.

19. Eric G. Stanley, "Verbal Stress in Old English Verse," *Anglia*, 93 (1975), 307–34, pp. 322–23.

20. Alan J. Bliss, "Single Half-Lines in Old English Poetry," *Notes and Queries*, 216 (1971), 442–49, p. 447, n. 30. See also Lucas, "Some Aspects of *Genesis B* as Old English Verse," *Proceedings of the Royal Irish Academy*, 88C (1988), 143–78, p. 157, n. 53.

21. Hans Kuhn, "Wortstellung und -betonung im Altgermanischen," in Paul Braune's *Beiträge zur Geschichte der deutschen Sprache und Literatur*, 57 (1933), 1–109, rpt., *Kleine Schriften*, vol. 1 (Berlin, 1969), pp. 18–103 (where the original page numbers are also indicated). For discussion see Lucas, "Some Aspects of the Interaction Between Verse Grammar and Metre in Old English Poetry," *Studia Neophilologica*, 59 (1987), 145–75, and "On the Role of Some Adverbs in Old English Verse Grammar," in *Papers from the 5th International Conference on English Historical Linguistics*, ed. Sylvia Adamson et al. (Amsterdam, 1990), pp. 293–312.

22. In favor of Dobbie's arrangement it could be argued that in *hyre on hond ageaf* the pronoun *hyre* is effectively dative of possession and so belongs in the *b*-verse with *hond*, the word for what is possessed. But in Old English verse even possessive adjectives are sometimes separated from the nouns they describe by a verse division: see Lucas, "Interaction," § 40 and n. 114. For a pronoun to be so displaced therefore seems the less remarkable, and similar instances occur at *Genesis A* lines 1455 and 2649 and *Christ and Satan* 458. I have benefited from discussing *Judith* 130 with Hal Momma (Toronto, now New York), but I am solely responsible for the view expressed.

23. I follow the metrical notation of Alan J. Bliss, *The Metre of Beowulf* (Oxford, 1967), except as indicated in my "Some Aspects of *Genesis B*," § 3. For an early discussion of the meter of *Judith* see Karl Luick, "Über den Versbau des angelsächsischen Gedichtes *Judith*," *Beiträge zur Geschichte der deutschen Sprache und Literatur*, 11 (1886), 470–92.

24. See Dobbie, ed., note to *Judith*, lines 287–88*a*.

25. For a facsimile see *The Nowell Codex*, ed. Kemp Malone, EEMF 12 (1963).

26. Ibid., p. 32.

27. I am grateful to the staff of the Dept. of Manuscripts for granting me this facility.

28. For some remarks on why medieval punctuation often appears to be sporadically marked see Malcolm B. Parkes, "Punctuation, or Pause and Effect," in *Medieval Eloquence*, ed. James J. Murphy (Berkeley, 1978), pp. 127–42, esp. 138–39. For discussion of the pointing in the *Beowulf*-manuscript see O'Keeffe, pp. 172–79.

29. Lucas, "The Place of *Judith* in the *Beowulf*-manuscript," *Review of English Studies*, NS 41 (1990), 463–78, p. 472.

30. *Judith*, ed. Benno J. Timmer (London, 1961; rpt. Exeter, 1978), p. 34. Timmer omitted notice of the points after *þæs* and *lange* in verse 346a.

31. For the earliest use of the term *semicolon* (Hodges, 1644) see the OED, s.v. Earlier the mark was known as a comma-colon or subdistinction. See also Anthony G. Petti, *English Literary Hands from Chaucer to Dryden* (London, 1977), p. 26, 6.vi, and Astley C. Partridge, *Orthography in Shakespeare and Elizabethan Drama* (London, 1964), p. 190.

32. Franciscus Junius F.F., *Observationes in Willerami Abbatis Francicam Paraphrasin Cantici Canticorum* (Amsterdam: C. Cunrad, 1655), p. [xvi].

33. Parkes, pp. 130–33.

34. These hypermetric verses are scanned in Bliss, *Metre*, Appendix E, pp. 162–63. For his line numbers 289ff. read the number minus 1. For the scansion of verse 8a read 3A2(2A1a). With Bliss' own later reading of 89b–90a these verses scan a1d(1A*1c) and a1b(2A1a), respectively. I scan 90b a1c(1A1c) with a stress on *me* rather than the possessive adjective *minra*. Dobbie's reading of 287b scans a1d(2A1a) and that of 349a (without the emendation proposed by John C. Pope, *Rhythm of Beowulf* [New Haven, 1942], p. 130, n. 16) scans a1a(2A1a). As a result of the modifications I have adopted (see n. 23 above) to the application of Bliss' method of scansion, I scan 31a a1e(2A1a), thus avoiding the only potential instance of disyllabic anacrusis in the poem, and one of only three found in hypermetric verses by Bliss in the whole of Old English poetry; *oferdrencte* is a particle in the first metrical dip of the verse clause and so, by Kuhn's Law of Particles, should not be stressed—see also Lucas, "Interaction," §§ 9–10. Bliss'

scansion of verse 96b as hypermetric need not be accepted. Since the *a*-verse is normal, it is preferable to assume syncope in *seceð* and scan *þe hyne him to helpe seceð* as 3B1e. Such syncope was standard in West Saxon (Alistair Campbell, *Old English Grammar* [Oxford, 1959], § 347; E. Sievers rev. K. Brunner, *Altenglische Grammatik* [Tübingen, 1965], § 358, Anm. 4). For *Judith* as a West Saxon poem see Franz Wenisch, "*Judith*—eine westsächsische Dichtung?" *Anglia*, 100 (1982), 273–300. Consequently there are no instances in *Judith* of a normal verse and a hypermetric verse being combined in one line.

35. Exceeded only by *The Dream of the Rood* (20.5 percent) and by *Maxims I*, a poem notorious for its metrical peculiarities.

36. Wingo, Appendix 2.3.a, pp. 147–49.

37. Müller, 1.3, pp. 22–27.

38. In the *Metrical Preface* and *Metrical Epilogue* to the *Pastoral Care*, reproduced in Ker, *Pastoral Care*, EEMF 6, fols. 2v and 98r–v (also in Robinson and Stanley, eds., nos. 6.1.4 and 6.2.2, respectively). Both extended spaces and points are used—with moderate accuracy. This manuscript (Hatton 20, dating from 890–97) is probably the one where the practice may be observed most clearly. But it can also be observed elsewhere, albeit sporadically, as in CCCC 41, p. 484, line 3 (Robinson and Stanley, no. 8.3, *Metrical Epilogue* 8a) and CCCC 326, p. 6, line 3 (Robinson and Stanley, 9.2, *Aldhelm* 14b). The practice is not common, and indeed it seems to have been missed by modern scholars. Junius' acuity in noticing it is all the more remarkable. For another method of indicating the versification, one that may have been contemporary with the scribe or added somewhat later, see D. S. McGovern, "Unnoticed Punctuation in the Exeter Book," *Medium Ævum*, 52 (1983), 90–99.

39. Some verse divisions coincide with a line division in the transcript. I have included these (nineteen here) in the figure for extended spaces. There is perhaps room for disagreement in some cases as to when a space is an extended space, but most are obvious, so any variations among the conclusions of different observers are likely to be minor.

40. Edward Thwaites, *Heptateuchus, Liber Job, et Evangelium Nicodemi, Anglo-Saxonice. Historiae Judith Fragmentum* (Oxford, 1698). On Thwaites see Michael Murphy, "Edward Thwaites, Pioneer Teacher of Old English," *Durham University Journal*, 73 (1980–81), 153–59. Thwaites used Junius' typeface for the printing of his

book, as noted by Talbot Baines Reid, *A History of the Old English Letter Foundries*, rev. A. F. Johnson (London, 1952), p. 145.

41. For this terminology see L. C. Hector, *The Handwriting of English Documents* (London, 1966), p. 47, and Petti, p. 26, 6.i. Cf. above, n. 32, and the quotation to which it refers on pp. 375–76.

42. Cf. M. Murphy, pp. 156–57. In his journal for 20 March 1824 (Bodleian Library, Eng. hist. C.145, pp. 162–63), Sir Frederic Madden noted that Thwaites printed *Judith* as prose even though it is verse. However, Madden also noted that in Junius' transcript "the divisions are marked by a point at the end of each verse" (23 March 1824, p. 181). Presumably he was not satisfied with Thwaites' reproducing these points in his printed text but thought the poem should be printed in verse lines. For some comments on early 19th-century attempts at prosody cf. Eric G. Stanley, "The Scholarly Recovery of the Significance of Anglo-Saxon Records in Prose and Verse . . . ," ASE, 9 (1981), 223–62, esp. pp. 251–53, rpt. in *A Collection of Papers with Emphasis on Old English Literature*, Publications of the Dictionary of Old English 3 (Toronto, 1987), pp. 3–48, where the original page numbers are indicated. On Madden's journal see Alan Bell, "The Journal of Sir Frederic Madden, 1852," *The Library*, ser. 5, 29 (1974), 405–21.

43. Sweet and other editors add *a* 'ever' to the beginning of this verse by way of emendation so that it conforms to verse 7a and scans 1A1b(1D1).

44. Sweet's *Anglo-Saxon Reader*, rev. Dorothy Whitelock (Oxford, 1967), lines 287–88 on p. 146, and earlier editions. Cf. Luick, "Über den Versbau," p. 471, I.A.12.

45. Bliss, *Metre*, § 75.

46. Cf. Lucas, "Interaction," § 21.

47. Ibid., § 47.

48. See Lucas, "Some Aspects of the Historical Development of English Consonant Phonemes," *Transactions of the Philological Society*, 89 (1991), 36–63, § 1.3.1.

49. Cf. Karl Luick, *Historische Grammatik der Englischen Sprache* (Leipzig; rpt. Oxford, 1964), § 650, and *The Salisbury Psalter*, ed. Celia Sisam and Kenneth Sisam, EETS OS 242 (1959), p. 32, n. 2.

50. Matti Rissanen, *The Uses of "One" in Old and Early Middle English* (Helsinki, 1967), pp. 22–26. Cf. also Lucas, "*Genesis B* as Old English Verse," § 21(a).

51. The hypermetric verses are 5a, 32a, 57a, 59a, 60a, 65a, 68a, 97a, 272a, 287a, 289a, 338a, 341a, 346a. According to Bliss, 31a shows disyllabic anacrusis, but this feature is removed by the modifications to his method of scansion referred to in n. 23 above; cf. also n. 34 above.

52. Cf. Lucas, "*Genesis B* as Old English Verse," § 28.

53. Cf. Lucas, "Interaction," § 3.

The Preservation and Transmission of Ælfric's Saints' Lives: Reader-Reception and Reader-Response in the Early Middle Ages

Joyce Hill

I

In 1986 Allen Frantzen anticipated his *Desire for Origins*[1] by publishing, in company with Charles Venegoni, a combative essay which castigated Anglo-Saxon scholars for their "pursuit of pure origins" and pleaded for the appropriate use of "the methodologies that contemporary criticism makes available."[2] One of the approaches that they singled out as the most broadly useful for Anglo-Saxonists was reception criticism, which they defined for our purposes as the process of "studying the development of a text and its use, through several centuries, and examining the ways in which texts were conditioned to accommodate the worlds in which they functioned" (p. 152). When he came to develop his views in *Desire for Origins*, Frantzen focused his attention on how Anglo-Saxon texts have been read since the sixteenth century, when our interpretation of them—and hence our interpretation of Anglo-Saxon England itself—has been shaped and reshaped by a series of often undeclared and sometimes even unrecognized programmatic concerns. Frantzen argues that since scholarship is in fact always interested rather than disinterested and is conditioned by its own cultural context, it is necessary to analyze how these contexts have changed and developed over time in order to appreciate that what we think we understand as a stable, objectifiable text is in reality something that is quite fluid, since it is a text which is "rewritten" by its various readers in successive generations in ways determined by prevailing ideologies. Thus, the history of scholarship achieves prominence as an object of study for the literary critic; its analysis in *Desire for Origins* leads Frantzen to the deconstructionist position that it is not Anglo-Saxon England which has caused Anglo-Saxon Studies, as is generally assumed, but rather that "'Anglo-Saxon studies' [are] the cause of 'Anglo-Saxon England'" (p. 111).

In establishing his case, Frantzen draws upon the work of many modern literary theorists, but he is chiefly influenced by *Rezeptionsästhetik* as developed by Hans Robert Jauss since his provocative inaugural lecture at the University of Konstanz in April 1967.[3] Jauss, in common with others, appreciates that texts are "eventful" rather than fixed and so argues forcefully for the study of reader-reception across the centuries. But he argues with equal force that *Rezeptionsästhetik* must also concern itself with the reception of a work "in the historical moment of its appearance,"[4] when it is just as much an "event" and just as unstable from the point of view of reader-reception as it is in its later "eventful" life. Frantzen acknowledges this strand in Jauss' theory but in *Desire for Origins* does not systematically examine its value for Anglo-Saxon textual study. It is, however, particularly applicable, not least because (unlike the study of subsequent reader-reception and reader-response) examination of contemporary or near-contemporary reception and response is concerned directly with Old English texts. Whereas we can study how interpretations of Anglo-Saxon texts are "constructed" by reading what is written *about* them and noting how they are presented in the sixteenth, nineteenth, or twentieth centuries, in studying Anglo-Saxon reader-reception we are obliged to examine what readers (users) *do* to the texts in transmitting them. As Jauss has observed, a "literary event" continues to have an effect only if there are readers who "appropriate the past work or authors who want to imitate, outdo, or refute it."[5] For Anglo-Saxon England, as for any manuscript culture, this "appropriation" is often literal, as works are recontextualized and often rewritten, in being augmented, abbreviated, excerpted, or plundered for use in composite compositions. The history of a text's transmission thus provides clues to contemporary or near-contemporary reader-reception, and it is with this purpose in mind that I wish to analyze the transmission of Ælfric's hagiographies, developing my earlier survey of the *Lives of Saints* collection by comparing and contrasting the manuscript evidence for reader-reception and reader-response to its hagiographies with the manuscript evidence for reader-reception and reader-response to the hagiographies that were first issued in *Catholic Homilies I* and *II*.[6]

In identifying reader-reception and reader-response, it is an advantage for comparative analysis to have texts that are of the same genre but which were initially incorporated in collections which were put together for different purposes. In the case of the *Catholic Homilies* there is some distinction to be made between the First and Second Series, but we can nevertheless generalize to the extent of saying that the collection as a whole was written with the secular church in mind and that the items were composed, in the main, as preaching texts.[7] The hagiographies of the *Catholic Homilies*, as Ælfric later explained in the Old English preface to the *Lives of Saints*, were those "þe angel-cynn mid freols-dagu*m* wurþað."[8] The *Lives of Saints*, by contrast, was commissioned by Æthelweard and Æthelmær, Ælfric's secular patrons who, like Ælfric, were vigorous supporters of the monastic Benedictine Reform. Although they were laymen, they clearly wanted their own copy of monastic material, and so Ælfric produced a vernacular version of the monastic legendary with which he was familiar, which included those saints "þe mynster-menn mid heora þenungu*m* betwux him wurðiað," but which omitted the more generally venerated saints, who were already in the *Catholic Homilies*.[9] The functional difference between the two collections is also evident stylistically, in that the *Lives of Saints* is mainly composed as a collection for reading, whereas the *Catholic Homilies* is characterized by the voice of the preacher projected as if addressing a lay congregation. A further and equally important distinction is that Ælfric continued working on the *Catholic Homilies* but did not work subsequently on the *Lives of Saints*;[10] the former was generated by his own concern for the standards of the secular church, which continued to preoccupy him, while the latter was a private commission that was finished with once it was completed. The *Catholic Homilies* and the *Lives of Saints* were thus two quite distinct literary "events" "in the historical moment of [their] appearance."[11] Investigation of Anglo-Saxon readers' responses to their hagiographical items, as witnessed by the manuscript transmission, will thus have the added dimension provided by contrast and comparison, since it will be possible to see not only how individual items were responded to but also whether Ælfric's different starting points influenced subsequent reading and use; or, to put it another way, how much the initial "event" (which was certainly programmatic in each case, and "worldly" in Said's terms[12]) influenced the subsequent "eventfulness" of the texts when they were still within the medieval culture of the tenth to twelfth centuries. It should be noted that Ælfric himself, fully aware of the literal appropriation that could take place as texts were transmitted, attempted to control this particular form of eventfulness, for he made a plea for correct copying in the Old English prefaces to each series of *Catholic Homilies* and the *Lives of Saints*, and he stipulated that neither collection should be augmented by or mingled with the work of others.[13] But the appropriation common to a manuscript culture prevailed almost immediately.[14] It tells us most directly something about the interests and standards of subsequent users of Ælfric's work, but since the analysis depends on the perception of continuity and change, it also provides comparisons and contrasts that further our understanding of Ælfric's intellectual and political position within the larger Anglo-Saxon church.[15]

II

In order to be consistent with my analysis in "The Dissemination of Ælfric's Lives of Saints: A Preliminary Survey," with which the material from the *Catholic Homilies* will here be compared, I continue to use Zettel's list of what is to be considered a hagiography.[16] In the tables below I also follow my previous practice of identifying the manuscript at the head of each column by its number in Ker's *Catalogue* and the position of each item in its manuscript by Ker article number.[17] The manuscripts in the tables are:

15 CUL Gg.3.28 s. x/xi

18 CUL Ii.1.33 s. xii^{2}

41 CCCC 178 + 162, pp. 139–60 s. xi^{1}

43 CCCC 188 s. xi^{1}

48 CCCC 198 s. xi^{1}, xi^{2}

56 CCCC 302 s. xi/xii

57 CCCC 303 s. xii^{1}

63 CCCC 367, pt. II, fols. 3–6, 11–29 s. xii

81 Cambridge, Queens' College (Horne) 75 + Bloomington, Lilly Library, Poole 10 s. xi^{in}[18]

117 Gloucester Cathedral 35 s. xi^{1}–xi^{2}

118 The Hague, Koninklijke Bibliotheek 133. D. 22 (21) s. xi^{1}

138 London, BL Cotton Caligula A.xiv, fols. 93–130 s. xi^{med}

144 BL Cotton Cleopatra B.xiii, fols. 1–58 s. xi$^{3rd\ quarter}$

154 BL Cotton Faustina A.x (Part B) s. xii^{1}

162 BL Cotton Julius E.vii s. xi^{in}

177 BL Cotton Otho B.x, fols. 1–28, 31–50, 52, 53, 54(?), 57, 59, 60, 67 + Oxford, Bodleian Library, Rawlinson Q. e. 20 (15606) s. xi^{1}

209 BL Cotton Vespasian D.xiv, fols. 4–169 s. xii^{med}

220 BL Cotton Vitellius C.v s. x/xi, xi^{1}

222 BL Cotton Vitellius D.xvii, fols. 4–92 s. xi^{med}

235 BL Harley 2110, fols. 4*, 5* s. xi

257 BL Royal 7 C.xii, fols. 4–218 s. x^{ex}

260 BL Royal 8 C.vii, fols. 1, 2 s. xi^{in}

283 London, Lambeth Palace 489 s. xi$^{3rd\ quarter}$

309 Bodleian Library, Bodley 340 + 342 s. xi^{in}–xi^{med}

310 Bodley 343 s. xii^{2}

331 Bodleian Library, Hatton 113, 114 s. xi$^{3rd\ quarter}$

332 Hatton 115 s. xi^{2}, xii^{med}

333 Hatton 116 s. xii^{1}

CF Copenhagen, Rigsarkivet, Aftagne pergamentfragmenter 637–64, 669–71, 674–98. [No Ker number.][19]

Of these, Ker 18, 81, 138, 162, 177, 222, and 260 are collections that are or appear to have been wholly or predominantly hagiographic. It is possible that Ker 117 should also be added to this group.[20] The rest are less specialized; most of them combine homilies with some saints' lives in a manner suitable for secular use, but it is noteworthy that few of them draw upon the *Lives of Saints* collection for their hagiographic element. There are other manuscripts that transmit material originating in the *Catholic Homilies* and Cotton Julius E.vii (which Skeat edited as *Ælfric's Lives of Saints*), but it is material that falls outside the scope of this paper.[21]

Some hagiographies are elements in multi-part texts which are not wholly hagiographic, but in cases where the material for a saint's day was originally divided up, or was potentially divisible by subject (as with Clement in *Catholic Homilies I*), distinctions of subject are noted and the transmission of each element is recorded. If this is not done, we lose some of our evidence for the reception of and response to these texts because, as the tables will show, there are instances where hagiographic and non-hagiographic subjects circulated initially under one liturgical rubric, yet divergent transmission shows that subsequent users responded to generic distinctions by exploiting the items in different ways.

The distribution tables for the *Catholic Homilies* arrange the manuscripts according to the Clemoes, Pope, and Godden sigla, which are given at the head of each column in addition to the Ker *Catalogue* number; the order of these manuscripts reflects the successive stages in the development of the First Series.[22] The few manuscripts at the end of the *Catholic Homilies* tables are listed in order of date, or in numerical order where date cannot be distinguished. For the *Lives of Saints* I follow the manuscript order as established for the master-table in "The Dissemination of Ælfric's Lives of Saints," where the reasons for the arrangement are given in detail.[23] In brief, the first seven manuscripts are those listed above as actually or apparently wholly or predominantly hagiographic; the next four are collections of homilies with some saints' lives, which nevertheless make very limited use of the hagiographies originating in the *Lives of Saints*; the last five are also general collections but, in using material represented in the *sanctorale* part of Cotton Julius E.vii, they draw upon the non-hagiographical items only (although the collections themselves may well include saints' lives, as the tables for the *Catholic Homilies* show). In each group the manuscripts are arranged by date or by Ker *Catalogue* number where the dates cannot be distinguished. The roman numerals at the extreme left are the numbers in Skeat's edition. The line numbers of Skeat's edition are given in parentheses where it is necessary to observe divisions in items that are continuously lineated. It is important to remember that Cotton Julius E.vii, as the best extant manuscript of the *Lives of Saints*, is augmented, contrary to Ælfric's wishes, by four anonymous saints' lives (not in the table), so that it is already a partly rewritten context, as it may also be by the inclusion of some non-hagiographical items by Ælfric.[24] The earliest manuscripts of the *Catholic Homilies*, however, take us very close indeed to the Ælfrician original.

Throughout the tables the following symbols are used:

( )	lost or imperfect owing to external circumstances, but where Ker was nevertheless able to assign article numbers bearing some relationship to the original makeup of the manuscript
*	unequivocal evidence for existence but no useful article number, owing to loss of most of the manuscript
-	extract, either free-standing or because apparently copied from an incomplete exemplar
+	whole text combined with other material
-+	extract combined with other material.

Readers should consult Ker's *Catalogue* for further information about those instances where the symbol ( ) or * is used. In cases where + or - or -+ is used, explanations are given following the tables, since this is often directly relevant to the present discussion. These explanations will take the texts in order, beginning with the table for *Catholic Homilies I*.

Table 1

Catholic Homilies I (The page numbers and major textual divisions are those of Thorpe.)

		A 257	B 310	C 57	D 309	E 48	G 209	H 220	K 15	L 18	O 56	P 332	Q 43	S 333	T 331	X^c 154	f^a 63	f^d 117	f^i 177	f^k 222	118	235	CF
Assump.John Bapt.	pp. 58–76	4			3	3		(6)	6	11	8		4		35					(3)		*	
Peter & Paul																							
Gosp.	pp. 364–70	} 26	44	20	51	41	(10)	(38)	} 28				27	3	65								
Passio	pp. 370–84		45	21+	52	42		39		9			28	4	66			*		(1)			*
Laurence	pp. 416–36	29	14	24		53		(43)	31	24			(31)	6						(23)	*		*
Assump.BVM	pp. 436–54	30	55				16+ 18	47	(32)				(32)	7	68		*			(35)			
Bartholomew	pp. 454–76	(31)	15			(65)		50	33	14			33	8	69		*			(6)			
Ded.Eccles.S.Michaelis																							
Narr.	pp. 502–10	} 34	} 74	} 29		} 55		53	} 36				} 37	} 11	} 73					(19)			
Gosp.	pp. 510–18						22	54									*						
Clement																							
Passio	pp. 556–66	} 37		} 32	} 72			} 58	} 39	33-			} 41	} 14						(24)			*
O.T.	pp. 566–76						36-																
Andrew																							
Gosp.	pp. 576–86	} 38	30	} 33	78			59	} 40				} 42	} 15									
Passio	pp. 586–98				79			60		10										(22)			

Table 2

Catholic Homilies II (The page numbers and major textual divisions are those of Godden, with Thorpe page numbers in parentheses.)

		A 257	B 310	C 57	D 309	E 48	G 209	H 220	K 15	L 18	O 56	P 332	Q 43	S 333	T 331	X^c 154	f^a 63	f^d 117	f^i 177	f^k 222	118	235	CF
Gregory	pp. 72–80 (116–32)				11	11			52	25					59	[*+-]				(18)			
Cuthbert	pp. 81–91 (132–54)				12	12			53														
Benedict	pp. 92–109 (154–88)				13	13			(54)	(5)										(16)			
Philip	pp. 169–71 (294–98)				}30	}30			61	12					60					(4)			
James (the Less)	pp. 171–73 (298–304)								62	13					61					5			
Inv.of Cross	pp. 174–76 (302–06)				31	31			63						62				(14)	20			
Alex.,Event.,Theo.	pp. 176–79 (308–12)				32	32			64						63				(15)	21			
[In Letania Maiore Feria Tertia]																							
Fursey	pp. 190–98 (332–48)				37		37		66			8											
[Alia Visio]																							
Drihthelm	pp. 199–203 (348–56)				38		38		67	43-		9											
Effic. of Mass	pp. 204–05 (356–58)				39		39		68			10											
James	pp. 241–47 (412–24)		59		}57	58			75	15										(2)			
7 Sleepers	pp. 247–48 (424–26)						12		76														
Matthew																							
Gosp.	pp. 272–74 (468–72)						21		}82								}*			}15			
Passio	pp. 275–79 (472–80)		17							16													
Simon & Jude	pp. 280–87 (480–98)								83	17										(7)			
Martin																							
Dep.	pp. 288–95 (498–514)					}56			}84											}17			
Ob.	pp. 295–97 (516–18)																						

Table 3
Lives of Saints (Skeat, vol. I)

		162	81	260	177	222	138	18	48	117	63	310	41	283	332	57	333
II	Eugenia	5			(9)												
III	Basil	6			(3)	(43)											
IV	Julian and Basilissa	7			(5)												
V	Sebastian	8			(6)	(13)			60								
VI	Maur	9			(4)												
VII	Agnes (1–295) Alia Sentantia (296–429) [Constance & Gallicanus, Terrentianus & John & Paul]	10 11		*	(7) (8)	(47) (48)											
VIII	Agatha	12		*		(49)											
IX	Lucy	13				(50)											
X	Chair of St. Peter	14				(51)		6				22					
XI	Forty Soldiers	15															
XIV	George	18			(22)	(30)		26									
XV	Mark (1–103) Item alia (104–226) [Four Evangelists]	19 20				8 9		} 19	} 59								
XIX	Alban (1–154) Item alia (155–258) [Absolom and Ahitophel]	24 25				(52) (53)		27 28						6-+	20	70	

Table 4
Lives of Saints (Skeat, vol. II)

		162	81	260	177	222	138	18	48	117	63	310	41	283	332	57	333
XX	Æthelthryth	26			(23)	(54)		4									
XXI	Swithun (1–463, 496–98)	27			(20)					(1)							
	Item alia (464–95) [Macarius]	28											8+				20+
XXII	Apollinaris	29	*			(26)											
XXIV	Abdon and Sennes (1–80)	32	*			(27)		} 37									
	Item alia (81–191) [Christ's letter to Abgarus]	33	*			(28)											
XXVI	Oswold	37				(31)		31									
XXVII	Holy Cross	38				(37)		39			(7)						
XXVIII	Theban Legion (Maurice)	39				(33)											
XXIX	Dionysius	40				(34)		32									
XXXI	Martin	42					(1)					18-					
XXXII	Edmund	43			(21)	(42)		29-				31					
XXXIV	Cecilia	45				(25)											
XXXV	Chrysanthus and Daria	46															
XXXVI	Thomas	47				(32)	2	18-									

Peter and Paul: Passio (CH I)

The additional material in CCCC 303 (Ker 57, art. 21) is a short prayer apparently intended for reading at the end of a homily for an apostle or for apostles. It also occurs in CCCC 419 + 412, pp. 1, 2 (Ker 68, art. 16), where it is a separate item.

Assumption of the Blessed Virgin Mary (CH I)

The version of the Assumption in Cotton Vespasian D.xiv (Ker 209) is a composite, made up of *Catholic Homilies I*, Thorpe, pp. 436–38, line 22 (Ker, art. 16) + *Catholic Homilies II*, Godden, pp. 255–59, line 126 (i.e., the complete homily except for the final lines; Ker, art. 17) + *Catholic Homilies II*, Thorpe, p. 448, line 23–p. 454, line 9 (i.e., taking to its conclusion the homily used in the first part; Ker, art. 18). It is printed by Warner from this manuscript as three successive items, although there is no break in the manuscript between the first two of these.[25] The subjects are respectively: the Assumption of the Virgin (on which Ælfric tried to avoid saying a great deal, since he was uneasy about the material), a homily on Martha and Mary (which Ælfric provided for the Feast of the Assumption in the Second Series as a means of avoiding the liturgical subject), and the story of the confrontation between Julian the Apostate and Bishop Basilius (which illustrates the Virgin's effective intervention and which formed a coda to the First Series homily).[26]

Clement: Passio (CH I)

The passion of Clement in CUL Ii.1.33 (Ker 18, art. 33) is an abbreviated text, which omits the brief account of Dionysius' mission to the Franks (Thorpe, p. 558, line 31–p. 560, line 15) and the final part of the text (Thorpe, p. 566, line 28–p. 576, line 14), which consists of a sequence of Old Testament stories and some concluding comments on divine salvation using the apostles John and Paul as named examples. This rewritten version thus "rationalizes" the text by removing everything not directly concerned with Clement in order to produce a firmly focused hagiography.[27]

Clement: Old Testament material (CH I)
Cotton Vespasian D.xiv (Ker 209, art. 36) also shows a reader/user response to the change of subject in Ælfric's text, but here, by contrast with CUL Ii.1.33, this is signalled by the opposite effect of selecting the Old Testament part and not Clement's hagiography. The Old Testament material is slightly abbreviated, however, in summarizing Thorpe, p. 570, line 4–p. 572, line 19 to a mere five lines in Warner's edition of this manuscript.[28]

Gregory (CH II)
The extracts from Gregory in Cotton Faustina A.x, Part B (Ker 154, art. 4) are quite different from all other adaptations in the tables, since they are five part-sentences written in the margin and marked for insertion at various points in Æthelwold's account of the revival of monasticism in England.[29]

Drihthelm (CH II)
The copy of Drihthelm's vision in CUL Ii.1.33 (Ker 18, art. 43) replaces Godden, p. 199, lines 1–7, with a more abrupt *incipit* and it provides a similarly abrupt *explicit* in place of Ælfric's supplementary example from Gregory's *Dialogues* and the concluding exhortation (Godden, p. 203, lines 111–37).[30] Thus, as with Clement in the same manuscript, the reader/user's response at some stage in the transmission has been to exclude material which was evidently seen as extraneous to the hagiography as narrowly defined. It is noteworthy that this ruthlessness occurs in a hagiographical manuscript, and it is entirely consistent that this same kind of editing is to be seen in its copies of Edmund and Thomas from the *Lives of Saints*.[31]

James the brother of John (CH II)
In Cotton Vespasian D.xiv (MS G: Ker 209) the Seven Sleepers (art. 12) is preceded, as in Bodley 340 + 342 (MS D: Ker 309) and CUL Gg.3.28 (MS K: Ker 15), with a James narrative (art. 11), but uniquely in Vespasian D.xiv it is an anonymous version, derived from BHL 4057.[32]

For some of its Second Series items Vespasian D.xiv draws on the same manuscript tradition as Bodley 340 + 342 (MS D: Ker 309), CCCC 198 (MS E: Ker 48), and CCCC 162 (MS F: Ker 38), deriving from a source shared with Bodley 343 (MS B: Ker 310).[33] CCCC 162 has no saints' lives (and is thus not in the tables above), but Bodley 340 + 342 has Ælfric's James narrative and the Seven Sleepers as a continuous item, and CCCC 198 and Bodley 343 have Ælfric's James without the Seven Sleepers.[34] It is therefore just possible that the compiler or his predecessor had access to Ælfric's James and that the use of the anonymous text instead was a deliberate choice. Equally, it might simply be an instance, in this manuscript or its immediate exemplar, of making good a defect by using whatever James narrative was at hand. This would not be counter to Godden's case for the Vespasian manuscript being generally in the tradition of the DEF and B manuscripts for its Second Series material. The feast days are 25 July for James and 27 July for the Seven Sleepers. When compilers chose to provide for only one of these, the natural choice was James, as the tables show. Ælfric's version provides an account of James' confrontation with Hermogenes, a brief summary of his preaching to the Jews, his capture, the healing of the cripple, the conversion of Josias, and the martyrdom of James and Josias together. The anonymous version omits the Hermogenes episode and greatly elaborates on the preaching to the Jews, which is a list-like sequence of brief teachings from the patriarchs and prophets. To the extent that the anonymous text includes a convenient collection of major prophetic teachings, it could be said to be more suitable than Ælfric's narrative for a manuscript which Godden has described as "A collection of homilies and other religious pieces, not in the form of a homiliary but perhaps selected for their doctrinal interest."[35]

Alban: Item alia (LS)

The *item alia* with St. Alban is the Old Testament narrative of Absalom and Ahitophel used as an exemplum in a homily against thieves and traitors. According to Humphrey Wanley, it was entitled "De iniustis" in Vitellius D.xvii (Ker 222), which shows a response to it as a moral piece, even though in that manuscript (which is a collection of homilies for saints' days) it had what was presumably its original position relative to Alban.[36] It was suitable for independent use in more general contexts, as in Hatton 115 (Ker 332, art. 20) and CCCC 303 (Ker 57, art. 70), and it was also plundered, as in Lambeth Palace 489 (Ker 283, art. 6), where Skeat lines 248–54 form part of a complex composite homily rubricated for the dedication of a church.

Swithun: Item alia (LS)

The *item alia* with Swithun is the story of Macarius and the sorcerers. In CCCC 178 + 162 (Ker 41, art. 8) and Hatton 116 (Ker 333, art. 20) it is combined with Ælfric's homily "On Auguries" and material about Saul and the Witch of Endor to produce a distinctly non-hagiographical text.[37]

Martin (LS)

As far as we can tell, Martin is the only hagiography from the *Lives of Saints* to be adapted (apart from the editing out of prefatory material from Edmund and Thomas, which are otherwise transmitted intact). Ælfric wrote two versions, the shorter one for *Catholic Homilies II* and a much longer reading text for the monastically-oriented *Lives of Saints*.[38] The unique abbreviation of the *Lives of Saints* version in Bodley 343 (Ker 310, art. 18) reduces it to a manageable preaching length consistent with the other items in the manuscript. In its adapted form it performs the function of Ælfric's "secular" (*Catholic Homilies*) narrative and was adapted in this way for use in a mixed collection presumably because no shorter version was available. Here, as with other examples noted so far, the reader-response is functional rather than personal, but this is to be expected, given the utilitarian nature of the texts and the cultural circumstances in which they were transmitted.

Edmund (LS)

The copy of Edmund in CUL Ii.1.33 (Ker 18, art. 29) is without its prefatory non-rhythmical opening statement in which Ælfric explains how he came to know the story, but the text is otherwise complete.

Here, then, as with Clement, Drihthelm, and Thomas, this predominantly hagiographical manuscript presents a text which has been edited so that only the hagiography proper remains.

Thomas (LS)
In parallel with Edmund, the copy of Thomas in CUL Ii.1.33 (Ker 18, art. 18) is without its prefatory material. In this case it is a Latin note explaining why Thomas was not included in the *Catholic Homilies* (where he would have been expected as an apostle), and how his inclusion in the *Lives of Saints* is in response to pressure from Æthelweard.

Hagiographies do not figure much in Ælfric's corpus outside the two main collections. The passion of Vincent was printed by Skeat in an appendix to his edition of the *Lives of Saints*, although it has no connection with the Julius E.vii texts but occurs uniquely in CUL Ii.1.33 (Ker 18, art. 23) which, as we have seen, is chiefly a passional, drawing on both the *Catholic Homilies* and the *Lives of Saints* and presenting edited texts that sharpen the hagiographic focus. Originally the passion of Vincent was probably part of a larger two-part homily, consisting of the *passio* preceded by a short exposition of John 12:24–26, but the gospel exposition now survives only as a separate item in Bodley 343 (Ker 310, art. 61), a much more general collection than CUL Ii.1.33, which mixes homilies and saints' lives drawn mainly from the *Catholic Homilies*.[39] Susan Irvine has suggested that the Vincent homily as a whole was commissioned by the Abingdon monks, who claimed to have some of the saint's relics, although it may have initially been composed for preaching to a mixed congregation that included laity and secular clergy as well as the monks.[40] Even so, the over-riding context was monastic. The existence of the gospel exposition as a separate item in a general collection, by contrast with the *passio*'s survival in a hagiographical one, suggests that readers responded to the generic difference and contextualized accordingly although, as Irvine suggests (p. 122), it may have been Ælfric rather than subsequent readers who realized that the gospel exegesis could be used in the less specialized context of the Common of Saints.

The only other miscellaneous item that needs to be commented on here is additional material on Alexander, Eventius, and Theodolus, which occurs only in an extra gathering at the beginning of Hatton 114 (Ker 331, art. 84), with a clear indication that it was to be joined to the briefer Alexander, Eventius, and Theodolus item as we know it from *Catholic Homilies II* (art. 63 in the same manuscript).[41] This unique survival, then, tells us something about Ælfric's desire for completeness and reminds us that many of Ælfric's works had an "eventful" life at the hands of the author himself, but it happens not to contribute to our perception of the reception of his work; the fluidity of texts in a manuscript culture is here signalled by evidence of authorial rewriting rather than the literal rewriting of subsequent readers.

III

The tables confirm that it is indeed necessary to note the transmission pattern of all elements in a multi-part item. The different transmission of non-hagiographical items, which is evident even in these tables, is particularly marked when we trace the transmission of all the material printed by Skeat as the *Lives of Saints*, for then the true hagiographies are seen to have a much more restricted dissemination than other items, such as the Nativity (Skeat I), Ash Wednesday (Skeat XII), the Prayer of Moses/Mid-lent Sunday (Skeat XIII), Memory of the Saints (Skeat XVI), "On Auguries" (Skeat XVII) and the Old Testament pieces (Skeat XVIII and XXV).[42] Furthermore, these contrast with the true hagiographies in being much more liable to adaptation. The converse of this, as we have seen, is that when new hagiographical collections were created by selective rearrangements of mainly Ælfrician items in circulation, care was often taken to include only the directly hagiographical material and to omit the rest, as in the case of Peter and Paul, Michael, and Andrew in Cotton Vitellius D.xvii (Ker 222)[43] and Peter and Paul, Clement, Andrew, Drihthelm, Matthew, Edmund, Thomas, and Vincent in CUL Ii.1.33 (Ker 18).

Another general observation is that, although hagiographies originating in the *Catholic Homilies* were incorporated into the new hagiographic collections, along with those from the *Lives of Saints*, they were otherwise more widely disseminated than those of the *Lives of Saints*, to a degree comparable with the exegetical homilies. We must, of course, allow for the fact that the evidence may be distorted by loss of manuscripts, but it seems likely that the dissemination was influenced by the distinctive nature of the initial literary "events."[44] Ælfric's principal source for all the hagiographies in the *Catholic Homilies* and the *Lives of Saints* was his version of the monastic Cotton-Corpus legendary, supplemented by material on English saints, which inevitably had to be drawn from elsewhere.[45] But, given this monastic starting point, Ælfric had to make a selection for the *Catholic Homilies* that would be responsive to the needs and expectations of the secular congregation. The same considerations were not applicable for the *Lives of Saints*. Zettel has shown that Ælfric's choice of saints for the secular-oriented *Catholic Homilies* was based on importance and popularity,[46] and if such a choice is sensitively made, it is likely to be perpetuated in transmission: what was considered to be more generally useful or interesting at the start may well be considered to be so by later users; what was conceived of as more specialized may continue to be transmitted in more specialized contexts. I have argued in "The Dissemination of Ælfric's Lives of Saints" that the hagiographies originating in the *Lives of Saints*, which are a vernacular reflection of monastic interests, continued to be associated mainly with the monastic milieu, where there was a greater need of saints' lives than in the secular church. Compilers of subsequent specialized collections were obliged to draw on the *Catholic Homilies* to fill the major gaps caused by Ælfric's avoidance of repetition when producing the *Lives of Saints*, but there was little movement of hagiographical material in the other direction, that is to say, from the *Lives of Saints* to mixed collections suitable for the secular church. This suggests that Ælfric's own response to his traditions was an intelligent one, and that, as we might expect from such a self-aware writer, he was fully alert to the differing worldly contexts of his large collections.

Analysis of this kind depends on the assemblage of "facts" (which of course for the Middle Ages necessarily include elements of reasonable conjecture). Frantzen is uneasy about such approaches, believing that the marshalling of "facts" has become a self-fulfilling methodology that stands in place of meaning. But as McGann has recently reminded us, "'facts' are not mere data, objects, or monads; they are heuristic isolates which bring into focus some more or less complex network of human events and relations."[47] As such, they contribute directly to our understanding of the sociology of the text and in the present case allow us to glimpse something of the eventful life of certain Anglo-Saxon works at a time relatively close to their production. Ælfric, as we have seen, attempted to control that eventfulness by insisting that the authorially determined context should be perpetuated. He lost the battle then, but he has in a sense won it now, for modern scholarship, properly interested in Ælfric's *œuvre* and rightly concerned to understand *him*, has given priority, both in editing and analysis, to Ælfric's original collections. Thus, for any single item in them, the reading context for the modern scholar who consults the printed edition is as close as possible to the one determined by Ælfric. That context did not last long in medieval times, however, and if we are to understand Ælfric's intellectual relationship to the rest of the Anglo-Saxon church, as well as the extent of his influence and the resistance to it, we need to direct our attention to the subsequent treatment of his work.[48] Yet this investigation cannot be carried out unless it deals in hard-won textual facts and unless it is based on a well-founded understanding of Ælfric's starting points, since it is by his relationship to past traditions and contemporary concerns that Ælfric defines his position in the reformist Anglo-Saxon present. Only under these circumstances can we hope to understand Ælfric and thus the responses of those readers whose needs and interests shaped the manuscript traditions. As Holub has expressed it, in summarizing Jauss' *Rezeptionsästhetik*, "the text is grasped in its becoming rather than as a fixed entity."[49]

UNIVERSITY OF LEEDS

NOTES

1. Allen J. Frantzen, *Desire for Origins: New Language, Old English, and Teaching the Tradition* (New Brunswick, 1990).

2. Allen J. Frantzen and Charles L. Venegoni, "The Desire for Origins: An Archaeology of Anglo-Saxon Studies," *Style*, 20 (1986), 142–56, at p. 152.

3. In this article I refer particularly to Hans Robert Jauss, *Toward an Aesthetic of Reception*, tr. Timothy Bahti, introd. Paul de Man (Minneapolis, 1982), and within this esp. to ch. 1, which is a retranslation of "Literary History as a Challenge to Literary Theory," *New Literary History*, 2 (1970), 7–37. But see also Hans Robert Jauss, *Aesthetic Experience and Literary Hermeneutics*, tr. Michael Shaw, introd. Wład Godzich (Minneapolis, 1982).

4. Jauss, *Toward an Aesthetic of Reception*, p. 22 (Thesis 2). For the concept of the "eventful" text see pp. 32–36 (Thesis 5).

5. Ibid., p. 22.

6. Joyce Hill, "The Dissemination of Ælfric's Lives of Saints: A Preliminary Survey," in *Holy Men and Holy Women: Old English Prose Saints' Lives and Their Contexts*, ed. Paul E. Szarmach (Albany, 1996), pp. 235–59.

7. For an analysis of the differences between the two series, see Malcolm R. Godden, "The Development of Ælfric's Second Series of *Catholic Homilies*," *English Studies*, 54 (1973), 209–16. The editions used in this present paper are: *The Homilies of the Anglo-Saxon Church*, ed. Benjamin Thorpe, 2 vols. (London, 1844–46); *Ælfric's Catholic Homilies: The Second Series. Text*, ed. M. Godden, EETS SS 5 (1979). Volume I of Thorpe's edition is used for *Catholic Homilies I* and Godden's edition for *Catholic Homilies II*, with the addition that, in the tables for *Catholic Homilies II*, Thorpe's page numbers are given in parenthesis.

8. *Ælfric's Lives of Saints*, ed. Walter W. Skeat, 2 vols. in 4 pts., EETS OS 76, 82, 94, 114 (London, 1881–1900), rpt. as 2 vols. (London, 1966), vol. I, p. 4.

9. *Ælfric's Lives of Saints*, vol. I, p. 4; Stanley B. Greenfield and Daniel G. Calder, *A New Critical History of Old English Literature* (New York, 1986), p. 76, argue that the

Catholic Homilies and the *Lives of Saints* may be considered together because "they were viewed by Ælfric as something of a continuum." This is true, however, only to the extent that the content of the *Lives of Saints* (completed c. 992–1002) was affected by the content of *Catholic Homilies I* and *II*; in all other respects Ælfric seems to have viewed them as being quite distinct. For the dates of Ælfric's work see Peter A. M. Clemoes, "The Chronology of Ælfric's Works," in *The Anglo-Saxons: Studies in Some Aspects of Their History and Culture, Presented to Bruce Dickins*, ed. Clemoes (London, 1959), pp. 212–47 [rpt. OEN *Subsidia* 5 (1980)]. The modern redating of Sigeric's period of office from 989–95 to 990–94 does not invalidate Clemoes' date of c. 989 for *Catholic Homilies I* because, as Clemoes points out, the copy which was sent to Sigeric with a prefatory letter was not the earliest copy of the text (p. 243, n. 2). The redating of Sigeric's archiepiscopacy does, however, mean that Godden's date of 995 for *Catholic Homilies II* is no longer tenable (see *Ælfric's Catholic Homilies*, pp. xci–xciii). Clemoes' proposed date for the Second Series is 992. On Sigeric's dates see Michael Lapidge, "Ælfric's *Sanctorale*," in *Holy Men and Holy Women*, ed. Szarmach, p. 126, nn. 9 and 13.

10. See Clemoes, "Chronology," esp. pp. 227–38. Further, as Clemoes notes, p. 235, there is no evidence that Ælfric ever organized a *sanctorale* set of homilies mixing material from the *Lives of Saints* and the *Catholic Homilies*. The manuscripts of such collections must therefore depend on reader-response. It should be noted that Ælfric's expanded *Temporale Homilies* for the Proper of the Season develop *Catholic Homilies I* and *II* using, among other things, non-hagiographical material that survives in Cotton Julius E.vii, the best extant manuscript of the *Lives of Saints*, but these items were not necessarily part of Ælfric's original *Lives of Saints* collection, so that their use in the development of the secular-oriented *Temporale Homilies* cannot be taken as evidence of Ælfric drawing upon the *Lives of Saints* as such. On these non-hagiographical items in Julius E.vii, see my "Dissemination of Ælfric's Lives of Saints."

11. See n. 4 above.

12. Edward W. Said, *The World, The Text, and the Critic* (Boston, 1983; London, 1984), p. 35.

13. *The Homilies of the Anglo-Saxon Church*, ed. Thorpe, I, p. 8; *Ælfric's Catholic Homilies*, ed. Godden, pp. 2, 345; *Ælfric's Lives of Saints*, ed. Skeat, I, p. 6.

14. For examples see my study of "Ælfric, Authorial Identity and the Changing Text," in *The Editing of Old English*, ed. D. G. Scragg and Paul E. Szarmach (Cambridge, 1994), pp. 177–89.

15. By "political" in this context I refer particularly to the ecclesiastical politics of the 10th-century reform, although this was inseparable from the power politics of the secular world. See, for example, Barbara Yorke, "Aethelmaer: The Foundation of the Abbey at Cerne and the Politics of the Tenth Century," in *The Cerne Abbey Millennium Lectures*, ed. Katherine Barker (Cerne Abbas, 1988), pp. 15–26, and her "Æthelwold and the Politics of the Tenth Century," in *Bishop Æthelwold: His Career and Influence*, ed. Yorke (Woodbridge, 1988), pp. 65–88. Ælfric also positions himself "politically" in relation to the reform in his dependence on patristic writers and their Carolingian intermediaries, an aspect of the "worldliness" of his writings that can only be elucidated by source study. On this, see my studies of "Ælfric and Smaragdus," ASE, 21 (1992), 203–37, "Reform and Resistance: Preaching Styles in Late Anglo-Saxon England," in *De l'homélie au sermon: histoire de la prédication médiévale*, ed. Jacqueline Hamesse and Xavier Hermand (Louvain-la-Neuve, 1993), pp. 15–46, and Godden's study of Ælfric's maneuverings in relation to sources in "Ælfric's Saints' Lives and the Problem of Miracles," *Leeds Studies in English*, NS 16 (1985), 83–100. Source study is thus an essential part of reception criticism, showing how, to quote Jauss, a work "does not present itself as something absolutely new in an information vacuum, but predisposes its audience to a very specific kind of reception by announcements, overt and covert signals, familiar characteristics, or implicit allusions" (*Toward an Aesthetic of Reception*, p. 23). It should not therefore be seen, following Frantzen, as a sterile, methodologically-bound regression to "pure origins" but as part of the exploration of the continuous dialogue among past, present, and future, in which the author himself is seen to participate in the act of "rewriting" the traditions by which he is defined.

16. Patrick H. Zettel, "Ælfric's Hagiographic Sources and the Latin Legendary preserved in B.L. MS Cotton Nero E. i. + CCCC MS 9 and Other Manuscripts," D.Phil. Diss., Oxford 1979, p. 42.

17. Ker, *Catalogue*. The details in the following list are taken from Ker. For further comments on many of the manuscripts referred to here see Clemoes, "Chronology"; *The Homilies of Ælfric: A Supplementary Collection*, 2 vols., ed. John C. Pope, EETS OS 259, 260 (1967–68); *Ælfric's Catholic Homilies*, ed. Godden; D. G. Scragg, "The Corpus of Vernacular Homilies and Prose Saints' Lives before Ælfric," ASE, 8 (1979), 223–77.

18. The details given in the tables under Ker 81 bring together information from Ker's *Catalogue*, pp. 127–28, Ker's "A Supplement to *Catalogue of Manuscripts Containing Anglo-Saxon*," ASE, 5 (1976), 121–31, p. 123, and Rowland L. Collins and Peter A. M. Clemoes, "The Common Origin of Ælfric Fragments at New Haven, Oxford, Cambridge,

and Bloomington," in *Old English Studies in Honour of John C. Pope*, ed. Robert B. Burlin and Edward B. Irving, Jr. (Toronto, 1974), pp. 285–326.

19. *Fifty-Six Ælfric Fragments: The Newly-Found Copenhagen Fragments of Ælfric's "Catholic Homilies." With Facsimiles*, ed. Else Fausbøll, Publications of the Dept. of English, Univ. of Copenhagen, 14 (Copenhagen, 1986). The fragments were discovered in 1980.

20. Four of the five items testified to by the Gloucester fragments are *sanctorale* pieces. Since the other item, an imperfect extract from the Benedictine Rule, was probably added later, it is an open question whether this group of fragments is really a witness to a single manuscript consisting mainly of saints' lives.

21. A full table for the *Catholic Homilies* is given by Ker, *Catalogue*, pp. 512–15, and for the *Lives of Saints* (as known from Julius E.vii) by Hill, "Dissemination of Ælfric's Lives of Saints," pp. 246–47. Ker's tables are unhelpful, however, in not always distinguishing among the elements that appear under one over-all rubric, so that they disguise the extent to which readers' (users') responses to subject governed adaptation and transmission.

22. For a note on the sigla see *Ælfric's Catholic Homilies*, ed. Godden, pp. xiii–xiv. As Godden observes, the sigla are also generally appropriate for the Second Series.

23. In *Holy Men and Holy Women*, ed. Szarmach, pp. 243–45.

24. The anonymous saints' lives are: the Seven Sleepers (Skeat XXIII), Mary of Egypt (Skeat XXIIIB), Eustace (Skeat XXX), and Euphrosyne (Skeat XXXIII). For Ælfric's non-hagiographical items, the content of Julius E.vii as a whole, and the problems caused by Skeat's method of editing it see my "Dissemination of Ælfric's Lives of Saints."

25. *Early English Homilies from the Twelfth Century MS. Vesp. D. XIV*, ed. Rubie D.-N. Warner, EETS OS 125 (1917), pp. 41–52.

26. On Ælfric's attitude to Marian apocrypha see Mary Clayton, *The Cult of the Virgin Mary in Anglo-Saxon England* (Cambridge, 1990), pp. 258–66, 272–74. Thus Ælfric's homily for the Nativity of the Virgin (Homily III in *Angelsächsischen Homilien und Heiligenleben*, ed. Bruno Assmann, Bibliothek der angelsächsischen Prosa, 3 [Kassel 1889]), despite the rubric, is not a hagiography and so is not considered in the present essay.

27. It is probable that this edited version of Clement was the one used also in Cotton Vitellius D.xvii (Ker 222): see n. 43 below.

28. *Early English Homilies*, ed. Warner, pp. 106–09.

29. The brief additions from Ælfric's homily are given in full by Ker, *Catalogue*, p. 195. The most recent edition of the main text is in *Councils and Synods, with Other Documents Relating to the English Church I, 871–1204*, ed. D. Whitelock, M. Brett, and C. N. L. Brooke, *Part I, 871–1066* (Oxford, 1981), pp. 142–54 (edited by Whitelock, who was responsible for *Part I*). For Æthelwold's authorship, see Whitelock, "The Authorship of the Account of King Edgar's Establishment of Monasteries," in *Philological Essays: Studies in Old and Middle English Literature in Honour of Herbert Dean Meritt*, ed. J. L. Rosier (The Hague, 1970), pp. 125–36.

30. The wording of the *incipit* and *explicit* are given in Ker, *Catalogue*, p. 26, and as textual variants by Godden, *Ælfric's Catholic Homilies*, pp. 199 and 203, respectively.

31. Discussed below, pp. 419–20.

32. As noted by Ker, *Catalogue*, pp. 272–73. This text is edited by Warner, *Early English Homilies*, pp. 21–25.

33. *Ælfric's Catholic Homilies*, ed. Godden, p. xli.

34. However, Ker observes (*Catalogue*, p. 80) that the text of Ælfric's James in CCCC 198 has a number of variant readings peculiar to this copy. For details see *Ælfric's Catholic Homilies*, ed. Godden, pp. 241–47.

35. *Ælfric's Catholic Homilies*, ed. Godden, pp. xl–xli. See also Rima Handley, "British Museum Cotton Vespasian D. xiv," *Notes and Queries*, NS 21 (1974), 243–50.

36. Because the manuscript was so badly damaged in the Cotton fire of 1731, we are obliged for most items to rely on the account in Humphrey Wanley's *Librorum Veterum Septentrionalium*, in vol. 2 of George Hickes, *Linguarum Veterum Septentrionalium Thesaurus* (Oxford, 1705). For more detailed discussion of the transmission of the Alban and Absolom and Ahitophel material, see my "Dissemination of Ælfric's Lives of Saints," p. 239.

37. In listing what is not hagiographic in Skeat's *Lives of Saints*, Zettel makes no reference to the *item alia* with Swithun, but he excludes it from the hagiographic canon in its "extended" form, by which he means those versions where the entire Macarius story is combined with "On Auguries" and material about Saul and the Witch of Endor: "Ælfric's Hagiographic Sources," p. 42. The combination of Macarius with other material is discussed by Pope, vol. 2, pp. 786–89, and by Audrey L. Meaney, "Ælfric's Use of his Sources in His Homily on Auguries," *English Studies*, 66 (1985), 477–95. In the table Swithun is shown as Skeat lines 1–463 and 496–98. This is because Skeat's lines 496–98, which are a formal homiletic conclusion, come at the end of the Swithun narrative in Julius E.vii but were marked by an 11th-century corrector for transposition to the end of the Macarius narrative, and Skeat here, as elsewhere, followed the corrector: see Geoffrey Needham, "Additions and Alterations in Cotton MS. Julius E VII," *Review of English Studies*, NS 9 (1958), 160–64, p. 162, n. 3.

38. For comment on this unusual duplication see n. 46 below.

39. The gospel is published in *Twelfth-Century Homilies in MS Bodley 343*, ed. A. O. Belfour, EETS OS 137 (1909), pp. 74–76 (Homily 8), and as the second part of a reconstructed original by Susan Irvine, ed., *Old English Homilies from MS Bodley 343*, EETS OS 302 (Oxford, 1993), pp. 111–15. For the argument that the gospel and *passio* originally formed one homily, see Clemoes, "Chronology," p. 236.

40. Susan E. Irvine, "Bones of Contention: The Context of Ælfric's Homily on St. Vincent," ASE, 19 (1990), 117–32. See also *Old English Homilies from MS Bodley 343*, ed. Irvine, pp. 77–98.

41. The extra material in Hatton 114 is edited and discussed by Pope, vol. 2, pp. 734–48 (Homily XXIII).

42. On these texts see Hill, "Dissemination of Ælfric's Lives of Saints."

43. We can be sure that the gospels for these saints were omitted, even though the manuscript was badly burnt in the Cotton fire: see Ker, *Catalogue*, pp. 292–98, arts. 1, 19, and 22. From the information in Humphrey Wanley and in Ker's *Catalogue*, p. 295, art. 24, it would also appear that Vitellius D.xvii, in common with CUL Ii.1.33 (Ker 18), omitted the Old Testament material from the Clement narrative, since the missing folios for the end of the Clement and the beginning of Cecilia would not have had room for it. However, there is direct evidence that the manuscript included both the gospel and *passio* for Matthew: *Catalogue*, p. 294, art. 15.

44. Part of this distinction is, of course, the stylistic difference, as noted above, p. 407; another is the likelihood that, because of the differing purpose and Ælfric's consequent development of the *Catholic Homilies*, there were more copies of these texts in circulation than there were of the *Lives of Saints*.

45. Zettel, "Ælfric's Hagiographic Sources" and "Saints' Lives in Old English: Latin Manuscripts and Vernacular Accounts: Ælfric," *Peritia*, 1 (1982), 17–37. The legendary was apparently compiled in northern France or Flanders in the late 9th century but survives uniquely in English manuscripts, of which the earliest (the Cotton-Corpus legendary) was written at Worcester in the third quarter of the 11th century. It is now broken up and preserved as Cotton Nero E.i pts. 1 and 2, and CCCC 9. For its original constitution see Ker, "Membra Disiecta, Second Series," *British Museum Quarterly*, 14 (1939–40), 79–86, pp. 82–83. For further details see Peter Jackson and Michael Lapidge, "The Contents of the Cotton-Corpus Legendary," in *Holy Men and Holy Women*, ed. Szarmach, pp. 131–46.

46. "Ælfric's Hagiographic Sources," pp. 74–82. Zettel's ranking is based on the evidence of calendars. Martin comes high on the list and so it is not surprising that he was included in the *Catholic Homilies*. In general the saints in the *Lives of Saints* collection are from farther down the rank order, and predictably they include some who are of special significance for monks. It was presumably for this reason that Ælfric included a much more detailed account of Martin in the *Lives of Saints*, even though it was contrary to his general principle of avoiding repetition.

47. Jerome J. McGann, "Introduction: A Point of Reference," in *Historical Studies and Literary Criticism* (Madison, 1985), pp. 3–21, at 12.

48. For the view that this is a direction for future editorial activity (not, of course, confined to Ælfric), see Malcolm Godden, "Old English," in *Editing Medieval Texts*, ed. A. G. Rigg (New York, 1977), pp. 9–33, esp. 29, and my article "Reform and Resistance," esp. pp. 45–46. Some studies of the subsequent treatment of Ælfric's work have already been made, for example, Paul E. Szarmach, "Three Versions of the Jonah Story: An Investigation of Narrative Technique in Old English Homilies," ASE, 1 (1972), 183–92, and Malcolm Godden, "Old English Composite Homilies from Winchester," ASE, 1 (1975), 57–65. But there are many texts and manuscripts still to be studied.

49. Robert C. Holub, *Reception Theory: A Critical Introduction* (London, 1984), p. 149.

ÆLFRIC'S *DE INITIO CREATURAE* AND LONDON, BL COTTON VESPASIAN A.XXII: OMISSION, ADDITION, RETENTION, AND INNOVATION

ROBERT MCCOLL MILLAR AND ALEX NICHOLLS

Ælfric's *De Initio Creaturae* homily survives in thirteen manuscripts covering a period of roughly two hundred years.[1] The earliest version is found in London, BL Royal 7 C.xii (fols. 4r–9r), a copy of the First Series of *Catholic Homilies* that dates from the end of the tenth century and has direct associations with Ælfric himself.[2] The latest is preserved in BL Cotton Vespasian A.xxii (fols. 54r–56r)[3] and may be dated from the beginning of the thirteenth century.[4] This present essay examines the relationship between the Royal and Vespasian versions of Ælfric's text in order to develop a context for this particular piece as well as to explore some aspects of the late transmission of Old English in general.

De Initio Creaturae is one of four vernacular pieces found in the Vespasian collection. The other three are, in order: a homily given the heading *An Bispel* ("A Parable") in Morris' edition,[5] a short exposition on St. Paul's words "Invite vos arma Dei,"[6] and the opening pericope exposition from Ælfric's homily for the Fourth Sunday after Pentecost, from the First Series of *Catholic Homilies*.[7] The two non-Ælfrician texts in this group have no parallel in extant Old English, nor are they found elsewhere in Middle English. The second homily shares similar themes with *De Initio Creaturae* and echoes its description of God's might, although here it seems to be following the original version, not the one in this manuscript.[8] These four pieces all show an interest in divine punishment and salvation and emphasize the need for obedience to God. They may well have been deliberately written down as an organized group.[9]

All four homilies share similar linguistic features and may, with some confidence, be considered the work of one man, acting both as writer and adapter. The English pieces are written consecutively in one early Gothic hand, occupying fols. 54r–59v.[10] However, the Vespasian copy of these texts appears to be incomplete. Space had been left at the beginning of each homily for a large initial capital, but only *De Initio Creaturae* was actually furnished with one (a red two-line, pointed *u*). The subsequent three have blank spaces. Furthermore, there is evidence that the fourth piece—the pericope exposition from Ælfric's Fourth Sunday after Pentecost homily—was originally intended to include much more of the text. In *De Initio Creaturae* there is a description of the nine ranks of angels in heaven followed by an additional remark, "for wan hi beoð þuss icwéðe me scel sigge an oðre stowe,"[11] but no such explanation is found in the other pieces as preserved in the Vespasian manuscript. However, in the full text of the homily for the Fourth Sunday after Pentecost there is a lengthy discourse on the nine ranks of angels suitable to this comment.[12] The obvious conclusion is that this passage was intended for inclusion in the Vespasian homilies at the time of the copying of *De Initio Creaturae* but was never completed. The last piece was originally followed by four blank folios (60r–61v), and this would have provided more than enough room for the whole of the Fourth Sunday after Pentecost text.

The problem here is whether it is valid to see the reviser and copyist of the Vespasian homilies as two distinct people. Mary Richards has suggested that they were, even assigning specific orthographical developments to a "reviser" and a "scribe."[13] Yet it seems unlikely that such fine divisions can be discerned confidently. The script and language of the Vespasian homilies are clearly close in date, and the group as a whole looks like a personal collection rather than a copied exemplar. The presence of glosses and corrections in the main hand may also suggest an autotype manuscript. In this context, it seems most likely that the adaptations of the *Catholic Homilies* pieces, as well as the two non-Ælfrician texts, represent the work of the Vespasian copyist himself.

Aside from the vernacular pieces, the codex is entirely in Latin, mostly consisting of chronicles, benefactions, and lists of properties, many of which show a connection with Rochester. There is no other homiletic material present.

Each homily begins on a fresh page and there are gaps at the end of all four, some of which have been filled with Latin in a later Secretary hand. After the last piece the Secretary hand continues on three folios, and fol. 61v is blank.[14] Fols. 54r–61v are all ruled in two columns with the Old English written above the top line.[15] It looks, therefore, as if the vernacular texts were written *en bloc* (with gaps), as part of one eight-sheet quire,[16] and then included in the larger, Latin codex. At a later stage, Latin was added in some of the gaps in the quire. The Vespasian scribe has a rather clumsy and cramped hand and makes a number of simple copying errors: for instance, *hi* is copied as *li*,[17] *god* as *go*,[18] *of* twice as *os*,[19] and *wolcnum* as *folce*,[20] although here there is an additional gloss above the line *vel wlcne* to clear up the mistake.[21] There are also two examples of *homeoteleuton*, where the scribe's eye has skipped from the first occurrence of a phrase to the second, thus missing out lines of text.[22] Furthermore, a number of letter forms are highly irregular and poorly written.[23] From this evidence it may be proposed that the Vespasian scribe was not a particularly accurate or well-practiced copyist.[24] This is consistent with the view that the collection of homilies preserved here represents a selection written down for personal use (perhaps in the pulpit), rather than a careful copy of an exemplar.[25] The Vespasian copyist had some scribal training, as the spaces left for large initial capitals would seem to indicate, but the rather shoddy and incomplete copy preserved in this manuscript is much more convincing as a private booklet than a poor-quality copy of a complete exemplar.

The version of *De Initio Creaturae* preserved in Cotton Vespasian A.xxii represents an almost unique case, in that it is one of the latest copies of an originally Old English text extant.[26] It was probably written down at roughly the same time that the *Ormulum* was being composed[27] and not much before the earliest text of the *Ancrene Wisse* was copied.[28] This makes it unusually late. That the homily was of enduring interest is not in doubt—it presents a concise and useful biblical history of the world from Creation to Doomsday—but that a copyist in the thirteenth century should have turned to such an old text is still surprising. It would appear, therefore, that the Vespasian scribe had a particular interest in Old English materials and that despite having some difficulties with his text he saw it as of quite contemporary significance.

Treatment of the Text

The Vespasian copy of *De Initio Creaturae* is radically different from that preserved in the Royal manuscript. It is approximately fifteen percent shorter (c. 3,080 words compared with c. 3,525) and there are major omissions when it is compared with the original. These seem to be primarily in order to simplify the text.[29] Thus, much of Ælfric's exegesis is missing as well as some of the biblical detail found in the Royal version. The Vespasian text leaves out both minor details such as Ælfric's brief comment on the Trinity, "þas þry hadas syndon an ælmihtig god; Se geworhte heofonas 7 eorðan 7 ealle gesceafta"[30] or the details of Shem, Arphaxad, and Salah's ages,[31] and also larger passages of exegesis such as the lengthy explanation of the typological significance of the "dead skins" in which the fallen Adam and Eve were clothed and of God's endowment to Man's soul.[32]

Sometimes the Vespasian text abridges or paraphrases when compared with Royal, thus:

> ne næfre se yfela ræd ne com of godes geþance. ac com of ðæs deofles. swa swa we ær cwædon; Nu þencð mænig man 7 smeað hwanon deoful come; þonne wite he þæt god gesceop to mæran engle þone þe nu is deoful. ac god ne sceop hine na to deofle. ac þa ða he wæs mid ealle fordón 7 forscyld god þurh ða miclan upahefednysse 7 wiðerweardnysse þa wearð he to deofle awend. se ðe ær wæs mære engel geworht[33]

is rendered in a single line, "ne yfel tó þence. né tó donne."[34] It appears that the Vespasian copy of *De Initio Creaturae* aimed to simplify Ælfric's text and as a result much of its intellectual vigor is lost. Whether this reflects confusion on the part of the copyist as to the meaning of Ælfric's exegesis or a deliberate attempt to excise extraneous detail from what is essentially a useful summary of the biblical history of the world is unclear. However, it is beyond doubt that the Vespasian text concentrates the narrative of the homily at the expense of its analysis.

There are also examples of simplification of syntax in the Vespasian copy. For instance, some of the rhetorical devices of the Royal text are absent in the later version. A typical example is the omission of some characteristically Ælfrician *repetitio*: where Royal reads "he is ęnde buton ælcere geendunge. for ðon þe he bið æfre ungeendod," Vespasian omits the second clause.[35]

Finally, the conclusion of the homily is quite different in the Vespasian copy when compared with that in Royal. Ælfric's text closes with an account of Doomsday and an earnest exhortation to righteousness,

> 7 he þonne þa manfullan deofle betæcð Into ðam ecan fyre helle susle; þa rihtwisan he læt mid him into heofonan rice. on ðam hi rixiað á on ecnysse; men ða leofestan. smeagað þysne cwyde. 7 mid micelre gymene forbugað unrihtwisnesse. 7 geearniað mid godum. weorcum. þæt ece lif mid gode se ðe á on ecnysse rixað. amen.[36]

The Vespasian version makes the same point in a devastatingly laconic fashion: "and elc ʒéélt efter his ʒearnunge."[37]

Although the Vespasian homily is shorter than its distant ancestor in the Royal manuscript, that is not to say that it is simply an edited version of the earlier text. The opening twenty lines in the Vespasian manuscript are not found in any other version and may be considered an addition at this stage:

> Vre hlaford almihtiʒ god wile and ús hót. þat we híne lufie. and óf him smáʒe and spece. naht him tó níede ac hús to freme and to fultúme. fór him seíʒt alle hiscéfte. Bonorum meorum non diges. hlaford to mine góde

> ne beníedeð þe. Ac alswó sanctus augustinus cweð. Gif non mán ne þoht óf Góde. non ne spece of him. Gif non óf him ne spece non híne ne lufede. Gif non híne ne lufede. non to him ne cóme. ne delende nére óf his éadinésse. nóf hís merhðe. Hit is wel swete of him tó spécene. þenche ȝíe ælc word of him swete. alswá án hunitíar felle upe ȝíure híerte. Héo is hefone liht. and eorðe brihtnesse. loftes leom. and all hiscefte ȝímston. anglene blisse. and mancénne hiht and hope. richtwisen strenhcþe. and niédfulle fróuér. Heo his ælra þínga angin. and hordfruma and ænde.[38]

The new opening includes a glossed quotation from the fifteenth Psalm[39] and a translation from Augustine, perhaps based ultimately upon his 117th sermon.[40] The Vespasian homily is not furnished with a heading, so it is possible that the scribe had an imperfect copy before him, one which would have required a new opening (this may also explain the abridged conclusion). However, it is equally likely that the copyist deliberately adapted the Old English homily for his own use by inserting a new beginning and a compressed conclusion.

Another series of additions can been seen as consistent with the apparent overall aim of the Vespasian text to simplify its material, in this case not by omission but by expanded explanation. For instance, in the Royal manuscript Ælfric lists nine ranks of angels primarily by their Latin names: "þæt synt englas. 7 heahenglas. trhoni. [*sic*] dominationes. principatus. potestates. uirtutes. cherubim seraphim."[41] The Vespasian text rather laboriously glosses each term: "þat beoð. angeli. bóden. archangeli. hahboden. Troni þrimsetles. Dominationes. hlafordscipe Principatus alderscipen. Potestates. anwealda gastes. Uirtutes. mihti gastes. Cherubim. ȝefildnesse of ywítte. Seraphim birninde oðer anhelend. for wan hi beoð þuss icwéðe me scel sigge an oðre stowe."[42] Interestingly, the promise to explain these ranks further is never fulfilled within this text or the group of homilies preserved in the Vespasian manuscript as a whole.[43]

The late copy also includes several explanatory glosses in what looks to be the main hand. Thus *wisdom* is glossed with *se sune* and *wile* with *ali gast*.[44] These glosses equating God's Wisdom and Will with the Second and Third Persons of the Trinity are somewhat unnecessary, as the passage immediately following reiterates the point.[45] Consequently, there is a sense here of discomfort with typology, perhaps reflecting a rather literal mind on the part of the copyist.[46]

Lexis

In addition to the numerous large-scale differences between the Royal and Vespasian versions of *De Initio Creaturae*, there are a number of interesting lexical variants. The most significant of these show the Vespasian copyist replacing Old English vocabulary with synonyms (or near synonyms) more in tune with the increasing influence of High Medieval culture at the time. There seem to be two degrees of modernization here: in some cases the copyist simply provides modernizing glosses, in others the obsolete word is actually replaced or omitted.

A typical example of the first grade of modernizations may be seen where *ǣ* 'law' is given the gloss *vel laga*.[47] The last recorded occurrence of *ǣ* is from around the beginning of the thirteenth century in the Lambeth Palace 487 version of Ælfric's homily for Pentecost.[48] There is evidence from Old English that the Norse loan-word *lagu* (ON *lög*) steadily overtook native *ǣ* as the natural word for *law* from the late tenth century onwards,[49] and by the time of the Vespasian copy of *De Initio Creaturae ǣ* seems to have been obsolete. The modernizing gloss *vel laga* clearly reflects this shift.

A second example is somewhat more complex. In the Vespasian text *werod* 'host' is glossed four times with *hād* 'rank'[50] and twice with *hēap* 'crowd, troop'.[51] There is little recorded evidence for the use of *werod* after the first part of the thirteenth century, and it does not survive much beyond 1300 (it seems last to be found in the *Cursor Mundi*[52]), so it is possible that the Vespasian copyist would already have felt a need for modernizing glosses here. Alternatively, it has been suggested that these glosses represent an attempt to improve sense, showing a concern on the part of the Vespasian copyist that *werod* 'host' is less appropriate a description of the ranks of angels than *hād* 'order'.[53] However, since Ælfric had no qualms about using *werod* for the ranks of angels in the original homily, it seems somewhat less likely that the Vespasian copyist would have seen this as a semantic problem than one of obsolescence.

There is also an interesting example of what appears to be a grammatical gloss: the verb *ȝenuman* is glossed *vel á*, presumably indicating that the word could also be spelt *ȝenaman*.[54] This would seem to demonstrate that the Vespasian copyist was aware of the inherited system of Old English grammar (at least with respect to the class IV strong verb *geniman*) and recognized that the more usual spelling of the third-person preterite indicative plural would be in <a>. As is shown below with respect to the language of the Vespasian *De Initio Creaturae*, it seems that the copyist felt a loyalty to certain Old English conventions, even when they went against his own natural idiolect.[55]

The second grade of modernizations in the text take the form of replacements of words already obsolete or on the verge of obsolescence at the time of the writing of the Vespasian text. A good example of this is the adjective *wlitig* 'beautiful'. On two occasions it is omitted in the Vespasian copy,[56] while in a third it is replaced by a paraphrase.[57] According to the MED and OED^2, the adjective is last recorded in *Saint Katherine* dating from around 1225, or probably not long after the time when our text was being written down.[58] A similar example may be seen with the systematic replacement of the Germanic noun *neorxnawang* 'paradise' with the late Latin loan-word *paradīs*.[59] *Neorxnawang* is last recorded in the Bodley Homilies (Oxford, Bodleian Library, Bodley 343) dated approximately 1175 or some 30 years before the Vespasian copy.

There are a couple of other interesting replacements. The Germanic noun *ofermēttu* 'pride' is rejected in the Vespasian version in favor of the French loan-word *prȳt-prȳte*.[60] Again, existing evidence suggests that *ofermēttu* died out before 1200—it has its last recorded occurrence in the Bodley Homilies.[61] Furthermore, in the latter half of the homily *mǣgð* 'kin, family' is omitted on one occasion[62] and replaced twice by *cyn*[63] and once by *mægiecynn*.[64] Since *mǣgð* is last recorded in the *Ormulum*, which is usually dated around 1200, it seems likely that the Vespasian copyist would have felt that the noun was approaching obsolescence and was thus unsuitable for inclusion in his text.[65]

None of these substitutions is found in any other copy of *De Initio Creaturae*; thus, they may be assigned with relative confidence to the Vespasian copyist as his own modernizations of Old English vocabulary.[66]

In addition to these specific changes there are a number of what may be called typically Middle English (or perhaps very late Old English) changes in the Vespasian text, when compared with that in Royal. For instance, the present indicative plural realization of *beon-wesan* as *sind-sindon* is never found; instead there is a systematic use of *beoð*.[67] Two other similar examples are the Vespasian text's replacement of forms of *syllan*, in the sense 'to give', with forms of *gifan*[68] and *geond*, in the sense 'throughout', with *ofer*.[69]

An examination of the textual relationship between the the earliest and latest copies of Ælfric's *De Initio Creaturae* reveals how free a rendering the Vespasian version is.[70] It may be noted that Bodley 343, a codex dating from perhaps 30 years before Vespasian A.xxii, follows the text far more closely, although this too was written at a considerable remove from the original. There is no clear path of transmission for the Vespasian version[71] and it must therefore be seen as standing alone as one man's own adaptation of what would probably have seemed a very old homily.

LANGUAGE[72]

It really need not be said that the language of Ælfric's original *De Initio Creaturae* was "classical" late West Saxon Old English. This, it can be argued, is the *Grundlage* of the Vespasian text. Given the considerable period of time between the original composition and the Vespasian scribe's writing, there could be a number of differing dialectal traditions underlying the final version, but there can be little doubt that the dialect of the Vespasian scribe himself was from the southeast of England, something supported by the manuscript's connections with Rochester.[73]

PHONOLOGY

It was once the belief among philologists that "man schrieb wie man sprach."[74] One of the main problems—and joys—of modern phonological analysis is the fact that these two separate activities are no longer perceived as intrinsically linked. That, with the exception of the small (but important) evidence derived from semi-literate sources where, we might imagine, a more "phonetic" attitude is applied to orthography, it has to be assumed that—in a linguistic system where no actual standard spelling system exists—there will be a number of influences working upon a writer, often of a conflicting nature, not least the tradition of orthography he inherits from the manuscript he is copying.

For the purposes of this paper the Royal text of *De Initio Creaturae* has been accepted as a control, in the double sense that it probably represents the text as Ælfric envisaged it and because late West Saxon Old English is a fairly stable orthographical-phonological system.[75]

There are a number of points that could be made about the general sense of flux apparent in the Vespasian text, but perhaps the most pressing question concerning the relationship between phonology and orthography can be seen in the treatment of the reflexes of Old English [ɑ:].

As is well known, this phoneme altered over a number of centuries from its original phonetic realization of [ɑ:] to [ǭ], in a rough progression from southeast to northwest, eventually including all of the area to the south of the Humber-Ribble line.[76] Given the fact that by the time at which the Vespasian text was written we can assume that this "sound-change" was in the process of being carried out, the actual orthographic situation at "ground level" is complex.

It has to be stated from the beginning that the great majority of examples of this phoneme retain the historical spelling.[77] But there are a few examples where the expected developed spelling <o> is found in the main body of the text, for instance, Vespasian reads "forgang þu *ones* treowes westm"[78] compared with "forgang ðu *anes* treowes wæstm" in CUL Gg.3.28.[79]

More interesting, perhaps, is the example "Ac *alswo* sanctus augustinus cweð,"[80] in one of the passages which is an addition to Ælfric's original *De Initio Creaturae*. It might be argued from this that where the text of Vespasian has no immediate antecedent—as far as we can tell—the scribe is less under the influence of an inherited spelling system, and perhaps writes in a manner more akin to his own phonetic system. The situation is not quite as clear-cut as this, however. In the same passage the scribe produces the spelling "al*swa*."[81]

It seems more likely that, in general, the Vespasian scribe prefers to use the system which he has inherited when—and if—he can understand it. Something as simple as the change from <a> to <o> would provide a perfect opportunity for this.[82] Indeed, there is some evidence of similar phenomena from other texts of approximately the same date and slightly later, although without Anglo-Saxon antecedents, such as Laȝamon's *Brut* or the Nero text of the *Ancrene Wisse*.[83]

But although this tension is inherent in any attempt to write in a manner not immediately representing the standards of the time, it can be seen that—far more often than not—the Vespasian scribe is "correct" in his use of <a> as against <o>. In more complex matters this is not, and cannot be, the case.

MORPHOLOGY

The ending <-um> is one of the most distinctive pieces of morphology in Old English, with a highly defined and restricted functional purpose; yet in the witnesses immediately following the late Old English period it appears to be among the first functional markers to be jettisoned by the language.[84]

There are a number of occasions in *De Initio Creaturae* where the original endings-system has been retained intact: for example, "mid mistlic*um* leahtr*um*."[85] This is also seen even where the case-syntax interface is quite complex: for example, "ȝelifd his word*um*."[86] Indeed, on occasion the Vespasian text is closer in this respect to Ælfric's "original" than are earlier versions of the homily: thus, where Vespasian has "on syx dag*um*"[87] in agreement with CUL Gg.3.28,[88] Bodley 343 reads "on syx daȝ*æs*."[89] But this kind of example is much outweighed by others where Vespasian no longer contains the original morphological realization, the most "organic" of which being the apparent substitution of the various <-n> endings for <-um>.

This alternation is principally associated with the situation where <-en> in Vespasian is matched by <-um> in the earliest versions: for example, "beoð engl*en* ʒelice"[90] compared with CUL Gg.3.28 "ge beoð engl*um* gelice."[91] There are also some where "accusative case" explanations might be inferred: for example, Vespasian reads "he forʒiaf . . . halt*en* and lam*en* richte gang"[92] compared with the Royal version, "he forgeaf . . . healt*um* 7 lam*um* rihtne gang."[93]

This development can, perhaps, be seen as a rationalization of the paradigmatic system, as may also be the case with the realization of <-an> for original <-um>: for example, Vespasian has "wod*an* h[e] ʒeaf ʒewitt"[94] compared with Royal "wod*um* he sealde gewyt."[95] But the fact that there is considerable confusion between these endings and others—both <-en> and <-an> are used where <-on> is realized in the earliest extant versions of the homily—would tend to suggest that the <-n> endings can only really be seen as a marker of "oblique case," and an overloaded and untrustworthy one at that.

On a far more radical level there are also a number of examples of an apparent replacement of <-um> by <-e>, thus practically neutralizing the original case-orientation of the phraseology. On some occasions this may have taken place because the "case" nature of the expression has been concentrated in only part of the phrase. This is particularly true where personal pronouns are involved, giving more *Kraft* to the functional intention of the phrase:[96] for example, Vespasian has "þa becom godes grama ofer ha*m* all*e*"[97] where Royal reads "ofer hi*m* eallu*m*."[98] However, more common are those examples where <-e> has been substituted for all <-m> endings in a phrase. This can be seen where Vespasian reads "buton elc*e* eorðlic*e* feder*e*"[99] compared with Royal "buton ælc*um* eorðlic*um* fæder."[100]

This process is carried through even where its application appears to affect the semantic appropriateness of the phrase: thus, Vespasian has "he hi ledde ofer se mid drei*e* fot*e*"[101] where Royal reads "mid dri*um* fot*um*."[102] Unless we accept that there has been a change in the conception of number on this occasion,[103] it has to be assumed that it is actually the traditionally unmutated vowel in *fote* which is causing the problem, not the lack of traditionally full endings.[104]

A final example needs to be commented upon—one which shows the level to which these endings were understood or differentiated between at this time: Vespasian has "se eorðe his awirigd on þin*e* weorc*um*"[105] where CUL Gg.3.28 reads "seo eorðe þe is awyrige on þinum weorc*e*."[106] It is interesting to note that whereas earlier versions of this homily have realized the final outcome of the shift from <-um> to <-e>, Vespasian appears, strangely, to have switched the <-e> and <-um> endings of the original around. It seems unlikely that a change in number has taken place[107]—although this could never be ruled out—so another explanation is required.

As the evidence discussed above suggests, the <-um> endings, when they occur, are merely ossified remnants of the original Old English system which—of course—the Vespasian scribe will respect, but may not comprehend fully. The fact that he is willing to switch endings around leads to the conclusion that, to him, <-um> was little more than one of a number of variant endings, all of which had basically the same semantic and syntactic purpose.

It seems, therefore, that the Vespasian scribe does find the language of his exemplar difficult, although, to a certain extent, comprehensible. Yet he cannot understand the full extent of differentiation originally felt between the various endings. Thus a tension is built up between his "gut reaction" to represent his original as closely as possible and his understanding of the manner in which his own idiolect should be analyzed.

"SIMPLE DEMONSTRATIVE" PRONOUNS[108]

Of the three linguistic categories discussed here, it is probably true to say that it is the "simple demonstrative" pronouns, the descendants of Old English *se*, *sēo*, *þæt*,[109] which have survived best in an uncompromised form. Yet there are signs of the tension that will lead eventually to the complete breakdown of the system.

This tendency appears to be at its most developed with the *þe* form which was used in the late Northumbrian glosses as an equivalent to, and substitute for, Old English *se*.[110] Even at that time it was spreading into areas normally associated with other, more "case"- and "gender"-sensitive forms to the extent that, by the early Middle English period, it can, perhaps, be seen as the undeclined form which it eventually became. This initial equation did not take place in the southeast of England in the early Middle English period, however, since the <s-> forms were retained for longer there.[111] But bearing this in mind, the *þe* form does seem to be spreading its functional purpose within the Vespasian text.

Arguably, the most obvious environment for the employment of this "new" form is where the Royal text has *þā*: for example, Vespasian reads "michte . . . *þe* oðre . . . don"[112] where Royal has "mihton . . . *þa* oðre . . . don."[113] Since, as we have seen, OE [ɑ:] is developing towards redundancy as a phoneme within the system of Vespasian, it could be argued that the Vespasian scribe understood the *þe* and *þa* forms merely as variants of each other,[114] even if this questions the formal integrity of the paradigm.

Rather more common in the Vespasian text is the apparent development of Old English *þæm* to *þe*: thus, Vespasian "he geð of *þe* fader and of *þe* sune ʒelice"[115] compares with Royal "he gæð of *þam* fader 7 of *ðan* suna gelice."[116] If these examples were to be found in "hiatus position" (i.e., followed by either a vowel or <h>), it might be sufficient to suggest that the nasal consonant at the end of the demonstrative had been "swallowed,"[117] but since this particular formal environment never occurs, it would be dangerous to assume this.[118] We might have to accept that—on this occasion—*þe* should be seen as an "undeclined" form in an environment where it was deemed no longer necessary to represent all "case" and "gender" relationships.[119]

This may also be seen in an example where *ðæs* in CUL Gg.3.28 corresponds to *þe* in Vespasian: thus CUL Gg.3.28 "þurh *ðæs* deofles lare"[120] and Vespasian "þurh *þe* deofles lare."[121] Although other explanations might be put forward—not least that there has been a partial reinterpretation of the possessive nature of the phrase[122]—because of the lack of further evidence it can only be said that, again, the syntax and grammar of the phrase no longer demand the use of the full-blown Old English system of function-marking. This is also to be seen in the way in which—probably for semantic purposes—Vespasian *þe* appears to be a substitute for Old English *þæt*:[123] for example, Vespasian reads "þa nam *þe* iudeisce folc micel anda"[124] where Royal has "*þæt* iudeisce folc."[125]

The main problem with this kind of usage is not the fact that it is realized but that it occurs alongside the original system which is still apparently functioning. Although this phenomenon is not uncommon in early Middle English literature, it might be argued that it is particularly striking here, given the length of tradition associated with *De Initio Creaturae.*

There is probably no complete explanation for this confusion, but it might be assumed that, again, this points to a conflict between the desire to retain as much as possible of the original formal position and the need for clarity of expression.

It is too much, perhaps, to assume that the Vespasian scribe no longer understood his original model in linguistic terms, but it does seem as if it is just on the edge of his understanding, as almost typical "mistakes," such as <*se*> for <*seo*>, suggest.[126] Some of the traditional system's elements must have become stereotypical expressions, essentially redundant.

Conclusions

The copy of Ælfric's *De Initio Creaturae* preserved in Cotton Vespasian A.xxii represents a radical departure not only from the "original" as found in Royal 7 C.xii, but also from any other extant copy. It seems to stand apart from the traditional transmission of the text and may well represent a personal adaptation of the homily. That the scribe of the Vespasian texts seems to be ill-practiced in copying and glosses his own work may also indicate that this represents a private copy. With the three other vernacular homilies, *De Initio Creaturae* may have been part of a private, devotional booklet (perhaps also designed for public use) later incorporated in the Vespasian codex. Clearly, the copyist had an interest in Old English materials, but to what extent he recognized a formal difference between the text he copied and that which he wrote down must remain uncertain. From some aspects of script, lexis, and language it may be proposed that the copyist was an old man with experience of Old English towards the end of its currency, but this is impossible to prove.

The linguistic comparison between the earliest known copy of *De Initio Creaturae* and the Vespasian text is also ambivalent. There can be little doubt that the Vespasian scribe does at times reproduce an earlier version of the language than his own, but some of his usage is undoubtedly contemporary with the composition—this is particularly the case with some of the more complex syntactical and grammatical constructions.[127]

The many differences between the Royal and Vespasian versions of this homily would seem to show the late copyist having a number of difficulties with his material, but he clearly understood his exemplar well enough to edit, augment, and adapt it with some skill and thus continue the tradition of Ælfric's *De Initio Creaturae* into the early Middle English period.[128]

UNIVERSITY OF ABERDEEN
UNIVERSITY OF TORONTO

NOTES

1. See Ker, *Catalogue*, pp. 512–13. Ker dated the earliest copy (London, BL Royal 7 C.xii) "s.x^{ex}," *Catalogue*, p. 324, and the latest (London, BL Cotton Vespasian A.xxii) "s.xiii^{i}," p. 511. The presence in the latter of a "spikey" <e> and a Tironian sign sometimes dented at the top and with a long descender clearly curving to the left are signs of a hand best dated from s.xii^{med}; however, the use of heavy letter strokes, strong differentiation between light and shade, and examples of "biting" (see, for instance, "boden," 54rb, line 4) suggest a more developed Gothic hand. The balance of palæographical evidence points to a date perhaps around 1200. The Vespasian hand does not appear to be a bookscript and this may explain some of these irregularities, but it is also possible that the copyist was an old man whose ingrained writing habits were a feature of his later script. Our thanks go to Dr. David Dumville for his comments on this problem. Ker assigned the manuscript to Rochester: *Medieval Libraries of Great Britain: A List of Surviving Books* (London, 1941; 2nd ed., 1964), p. 161.

2. The standard edition of the text is found in *The Homilies of the Anglo-Saxon Church: The First Part, Containing the Sermones Catholici, or Homilies of Ælfric*, ed. B. Thorpe, 2 vols. (London, 1843–46), I, pp. 8–29, although this is based upon CUL Gg.3.28 (fols. 3r–7r). P. A. M. Clemoes edited *De Initio Creaturae* from the Royal manuscript as part of his "Ælfric's *Catholic Homilies* First Series. The Text and Manuscript Tradition," Diss. Cambridge Univ. 1955–56, pp. 9–32, and this is the text used here. References are given to both Thorpe and the manuscript. The Royal copy of the homily lacks two folios between 5v and 6r, amounting to 50 manuscript lines of text. This missing text is quoted here from CUL Gg.3.28. This manuscript is available in facsimile: *Ælfric's First Series of Catholic Homilies (British Museum Royal 7 C.XII, fols. 4–218)*, ed. N. E. Eliason and P. A. M. Clemoes, EEMF 13 (1966). For details of Ælfric's relationship with the codex see pp. 28–35. In this present paper the Royal manuscript is given the siglum R.

3. A later hand has altered in pencil the numbering of folios by two: hence fols. 54 to 61 become fols. "52" to "59."

4. *Old English Homilies: First Series*, ed. Richard Morris, 2 vols., EETS OS 29, 34 (1867–68: rpt. as one vol. 1969), XXIV (pp. 216–31). The Vespasian text has been re-edited for this essay and some corrections have been made; however, for ease of reference all examples given are to Morris' edition.

5. Folios 56v–58r: Morris, XXV (pp. 230–41). This text is perhaps based in part on Anselm's treatise *De Similitudine inter Deum et Quemlibet Regem Suos Judicantem* (PL 159, 626): see J. E. Wells, *A Manual of Writings in Middle English* (New Haven, 1916), p. 285.

6. Fol. 58v: Morris, XXVI (pp. 240–43). 'Put on the armor of God'. The quotation is from Ephesians 6:11.

7. Fol. 59v: Morris, XXVII (pp. 242–45). See Thorpe I, p. 338, lines 9–15 (passage abridged), Clemoes, "Ælfric's *Catholic Homilies*," p. 347, line 1–p. 348, line 2.

8. The second Vespasian homily reads:

Þes king is ure hlaford almihti god þe is king ofer alle kingen. and hlaford ofer alle hlaforden. Strang he his and michti. for he ʒesceop alle þing of nahte. and na þing ne máʒi áʒenes his wille. ne him wiðstande. for þan him seígd se

> witíȝe. Qui celorum contines tronos et cetera. þat is. hlaford of mihte þe alste hefenen þrimsettles. and tó neowelnesse þe under eorðe is belocést. in. pon. þe dunan þu awiðhst eorðe belucst mid þina hand (Morris, p. 233, lines 9–16),

and this has a closer parallel in a passage from the *Catholic Homilies* text of *De Initio Creaturae*,

> He is ealra cyninga cyning. 7 ealra hlaforda hlaford. He hylt mid his mihte heofonas. 7 eorðan. 7 ealle gesceafta butan geswynce 7 he besceawað. þa niwelnessa þe under þissere eorðan synd; he awyhð ealle duna mid anre handa (Thorpe I, p. 8, line 27–p. 10, line 1 [R, 4r, lines 5–10])

than the corresponding passage in the Vespasian version,

> heo is alra kingene king. and alra hlaforden hlaford. he hált mid his mihte hefene and eorðe. and alle ȝescefte buton ȝeswince (Morris, p. 219, lines 1–3).

The first two passages share the image of God weighing the hills of the earth with his hand, a detail omitted in the Vespasian version.

9. For a more detailed, thematic description of the group as a whole see Mary P. Richards, "MS Cotton Vespasian A. XXII: The Vespasian Homilies," *Manuscripta*, 22 (1978), 97–103, at pp. 98–100.

10. There was originally one blank folio after the third piece (59r).

11. Morris, p. 219, lines 13–14.

12. See Thorpe I, p. 342, line 26, to p. 344, line 11.

13. Richards, "MS Cotton Vespasian A. XXII," pp. 97–98.

14. Folio 62rv is also blank, but this clearly belongs with the following quire; unlike the preceding eight leaves it is not ruled in two columns and it has visible pricking in the outer margins. It is immediately followed by eight cut pages, but shares its size and design with the next extant page and seems to belong with it. When the manuscript was renumbered the peculiar place of p. 62 was recognized, as it was classed as number "59*."

15. The number of lines per page varies markedly from 28 to 38 lines.

16. This organization is confirmed by the configuration of sheets of vellum within this quire—it is made up of four sheets stitched together with the flesh sides facing each other. Thus the final sequence in the quire is: hair, flesh, flesh, hair, hair, flesh, flesh, etc.

17. Morris, p. 219, line 27.

18. Ibid., p. 221, line 36.

19. Ibid., p. 223, line 24, and p. 227, line 7.

20. Ibid., p. 225, line 30.

21. Another possible miscopy can be seen at Morris, p. 223, line 16, where the original has *heofenan rice* (CUL Gg.3.28, fol. 4v, line 20) and Vespasian reads *hefe rice.*

22. In the first example the error is on *understanden ymbe god* (Thorpe I, p. 10, lines 3–5 [R, fol. 4r, lines 13–16] at Morris, p. 219, line 4), in the second on *ealle gesceafta* (Thorpe I, p. 14, lines 27–29 [CUL Gg.3.28, fol. 4r, lines 23–24] at Morris, p. 223, lines 3–4).

23. For instance, ð in "cweð" (Vespasian A.xxii, 54ra, line 8) and "beoð" (54rb, line 10) or ʒ in "forʒeaf ʒetocnisse" (56ra, lines 13–14).

24. E. G. Stanley has pointed out a further corrupt spelling at Morris, p. 229, line 9, *ʒetocnisse* compared with Royal *getincnysse* (fol. 8v, line 1), Thorpe *getingnysse* (I, p. 26, lines 12–13); see E. G. Stanley, "The Treatment of Late, Badly Transmitted and Spurious Old English in a Dictionary of That Language," in *Problems of Old English Lexicography*, ed. A. Bammesberger (Regensburg, 1985), pp. 331–67, at 349.

25. It has been suggested that due to the lack of rubrics and variety of their subject matters the Vespasian homilies represented a series of lessons aimed at "an unlettered, unsophisticated audience," perhaps young theological students: see Mary P. Richards, "Innovations in Ælfrician Homiletic Manuscripts at Rochester," *Annuale Mediaevale*, 19 (1979), 13–26, at pp. 23–24. First-person asides support the proposition that at least two of these homilies were intended for oral delivery: see, for instance, at Morris, p. 219, lines 13–14, and p. 237, lines 32–34. However, the remaining two pieces are far too short to have had a public function. The exact use for which these homilies were designed is

difficult to establish. The selection and treatment of the texts seems to show an individual's interest rather than an attempt at assembling preaching materials; but it is possible that they represent a stock of materials collected for later adaptation to the pulpit.

26. There are two other very late manuscripts that also contain versions of originally Old English prose homiletic texts: Cambridge, Trinity College B.14.52 (s.xii/xiii) and London, Lambeth Palace 487 (s.xii/xiii). The Trinity College manuscript includes some adaptations of Old English homilies alongside early Middle English rhyming verse and appears to be written in a Southeast Midlands dialect. The Lambeth Palace collection contains fifteen homilies and three rhyming, devotional pieces and probably originated in the West Midlands. Two of the Lambeth Homilies are versions of Ælfrician pieces from the First Series of *Catholic Homilies* (Palm Sunday and Pentecost). Morris edited both collections: the Lambeth Homilies in *Old English Homilies: First Series*, pp. 2–159, and the Trinity Homilies in *Old English Homilies: Second Series*, EETS OS 53 (1873; rpt. 1973).

27. *Ormulum*, ed. R. M. White and R. Holt (Oxford, 1878). From the palæography of its unique witness—Oxford, Bodleian Library, Junius 1—the *Ormulum* is normally dated around 1200: see Ker, *Catalogue*, p. xix, and *Early Middle English Texts*, ed. B. Dickins and R. M. Wilson (London, 1951), p. 81.

28. See, for instance, the CCCC 402 version: *Ancrene Wisse*, ed. J. R. R. Tolkien, EETS OS 249 (1962). This manuscript is dated from the first half of the 13th century: see Tolkien, p. xv. The text itself is usually dated about 1230: see *Seinte Katherine*, ed. S. R. T. O. d'Ardenne and E. J. Dobson, EETS SS 7 (1981), p. xxxviii.

29. The full set of significant omissions and paraphrases is as follows:

Thorpe I	Manuscript	at Morris
p. 8, lines 26–27	R, fol. 4r, lines 4–5	p. 217, line 32
p. 8, line 29–p. 10, line 1	R, fol. 4r, lines 8–12	p. 219, line 3
p. 10, lines 10–12	R, fol. 4r, lines 22–24	p. 219, line 8
p. 12, lines 16–23	R, fol. 5r, line 19–5v, line 2	p. 221, lines 11–12
p. 14, lines 4–9	CUL Gg.3.28, fol. 4r, lines 7–11	p. 221, lines 26–28
p. 14, lines 16–17	CUL Gg.3.28, fol. 4r, lines 15–16	p. 221, line 34

Thorpe I	Manuscript	at Morris
p. 14, lines 22–25	CUL Gg.3.28, fol. 4r, lines 19–21	p. 223, line 2
p. 14, lines 27–29	CUL Gg.3.28, fol. 4r, lines 23–24	p. 223, line 4
p. 14, line 31–p. 16, line 10	CUL Gg.3.28, fol. 4r, line 26–4v, line 6	p. 223, lines 5–6
p. 16, lines 16–17	CUL Gg.3.28, fol. 4v, lines 10–11	p. 223, line 12
p. 16, lines 19–26	CUL Gg.3.28, fol. 4v, lines 12–18	p. 223, line 14
p. 18, line 21–p. 20, line 6	CUL Gg.3.28, fol. 5r, lines 9–24	p. 225, line 2
p. 20, lines 12–20	R, fol. 6r, lines 13–22	p. 225, line 6
p. 22, lines 14–15	R, fol. 7r, lines 5–6	p. 225, line 33
p. 22, lines 23–24	R, fol. 7r, lines 13–14	p. 227, line 3
p. 22, line 35–p. 24, line 2	R, fol. 7v, lines 1–3	p. 227, line 10
p. 24, lines 7–10	R, fol. 7v, lines 9–11	p. 227, lines 14–15
p. 24, lines 33–35	R, fol. 8r, lines 10–13	p. 227, line 35
p. 26, lines 29–32	R, fol. 8v, lines 19–22	p. 229, line 24
p. 28, line 3	R, fol. 9r, line 3	p. 229, line 29
p. 28, line 15	R, fol. 9r, line 16	p. 231, line 4
p. 28, lines 17–23	R, fol. 9r, lines 18–24	p. 231, line 5

30. Thorpe I, p. 10, lines 10–12 (R, fol. 4r, lines 22–24) at Morris, p. 219, line 8; tr.: 'These three ranks are one Almighty God, who made the heavens, and the earth, and all creatures'.

31. Thorpe I, p. 24, lines 7–10 (R, fol. 7v, lines 9–11) at Morris, p. 227, lines 14–15.

32. Thorpe I, p. 18, line 21–p. 20, line 6 (CUL Gg.3.28, fol. 5r, lines 9–24) at Morris, p. 225, line 2.

33. Thorpe I, p. 12, lines 16–23 (R, fol. 5r, line 19–5v, line 2); tr.: 'For the evil counsel never came from God's conception, but came from the devil's, as we said

before. Now many a man will think and inquire, from where did the the devil come? then let him know that God created him who is now the devil as a great angel, but God did not create him as the devil. Yet when he was entirely corrupted and guilty towards God through his great arrogance and enmity, then he became changed to the devil, he who was formerly created a great angel'.

34. Morris, p. 221, lines 11–12; tr.: 'Neither to think nor to act wrongly'.

35. Thorpe I, p. 8, lines 26–27 (R, fol. 4r, lines 4–5); Morris, p. 217, line 32; tr.: 'He is end without any ending, because he is always unended'. The Vespasian copyist sometimes adds to the rhetorical structure of the original by alteration: for instance, where Royal reads "⁊ let hi habban agenne cyre. swa hi heora scyppend lufedon ⁊ filidon" (Thorpe I, p. 10, lines 19–20: R, fol. 4v, lines 7–8), Vespasian has "and lét hi hi habban áȝen chíre. to chíesen ȝíef y wolden hare sceappinde lufie" (Morris, p. 219, lines 19–21) with an emphatic repetition of *chíre-chiesen*.

36. Thorpe I, p. 28, lines 17–23 (R, fol. 9r, lines 18–24); tr.: 'And then he will deliver the wicked to the devil, into the eternal fire of hell-torment; the righteous he will lead with him into the kingdom of heaven, in which they shall rule always in eternity. Most beloved men, consider this discourse, and with great care avoid unrighteousness, and earn with good works the eternal life with God, He who rules always in eternity. Amen'.

37. Morris, p. 231, line 5; tr.: 'Each be rewarded according to his deserts'.

38. Morris, p. 217, lines 19–31; tr.: 'Our Lord Almighty desires and commands us that we love him and think and speak of him, not at all for his need, but as a support and help for ourselves; for all creatures may say to him, Bonorum meorum non diges—Lord, you have no need of my goods. But as Saint Augustine says, "If no man thought of God, none would speak of him. If none spoke of him, none loved him. If none loved him, none would come to him, nor would be sharing his happiness or his glory." It is most sweet to speak of him. You should think that each word concerning him is sweet, as if a honey-drop fell upon your hearts. He is heaven's light and earth's brightness, the sky's radiance, and jewel of all creation; the angels' joy, and the comfort and hope of mankind; the strength of the righteous and solace of the needy. He is the beginning of all things, and both beginning and end'.

39. Morris, p. 217, lines 21–22; tr.: 'You have no need of my goods'. The quotation is from Psalms 15:2; *Bibla Sacra*, ed. R. Weber (Stuttgart, 1969; rpt. 1984), "bonorum meorum non eges."

40. Morris, p. 217, lines 23–26. Cf. PL 38, 663, sect. 5, although this does not look like the immediate source. There is no better source to be found in Caesarius of Arles; cf. *Sancti Caesarii Arelatensis Sermones*, ed. G. Morin, 2 vols., CCSL 103–04 (Turnhout, 1953).

41. Thorpe I, p. 10, lines 12–14 (R, fol. 4r, line 25–4v, line 2). M. Förster noted that the source of this passage was Gregory the Great, perhaps Homily XXXIV, 7–10 (PL 76, 1249–52); "Ueber die Quellen von Ælfrics Exegetischen Homiliae Catholicae," *Anglia*, 16 (1894), 1–61, at p. 57.

42. Morris, p. 219, lines 9–14; tr.: 'That is *angeli* [messengers], *archangeli* [archangels], *throni* [thrones], *dominationes* [lordships], *principatus* [sovereignties], *potestates* [spirits of powers], *virtutes* [mighty spirits], *cherubim* [fulness of understanding], *seraphim* [burning or inflaming]. Wherefore they are named in this way shall be told by me in another place'. Similar glossing is found in another, much earlier copy of *De Initio Creaturae* preserved in London, BL Cotton Vitellius C.v (s.x, xi):

> þa synd þuss genamode. Angeli. þæt synd godes (...) Archangeli. healice bodan. Virtutes. mihta. Potestates. anwealdu. Prin(c)ipatus. ealdorscypas. Dominationes. hlafordscypas. Throni. synd þrymsetla (.C)herubin. 7 Seraphin. Cherubin is gecweden on englisc. gefyllednyss gewittes oððe (wis)domes. 7 Seraphin synd gereht byrnende oððe onælede (5v, lines 19–23).

There is no evidence that these two versions share a distinct line of transmission.

43. The orders of angels are mentioned again in the second Vespasian homily (Morris, XXV, p. 239, line 18), but there is no further explanation. See p. 432 above.

44. Morris, p. 219, lines 5–6.

45. Ibid., lines 6–8.

46. Other explanatory and qualifying additions may be seen at Morris, p. 219, lines 18–19, 32, and p. 223, lines 7–8, 10.

47. Ibid., p. 227, line 21.

48. Morris, *Old English Homilies: First Series*, pp. 86–101. See the MED and OED, *Supplement* (Oxford, 1972), ed. R. W. Burchfield; 2nd ed., ed. J. A. Simpson and E. S. C. Weiner, 20 vols. (Oxford, 1989).

49. For instance, in Ælfric's early work *ǣ* is used for all forms of law; in his middle period works there is a semantic distinction between *ǣ* (which he uses for canonical Law) and *lagu* (secular law); however, in his later work *lagu* comes to be used almost exclusively. See M. R. Godden, "Ælfric's Changing Vocabulary," *English Studies,* 61 (1980), 206–23, at pp. 214–17.

50. Morris, p. 219, lines 9, 15, and p. 221, lines 5, 13.

51. Ibid., p. 221, lines 2 and 5. Furthermore, on two occasions *hēap* is added to *werod* in the body of the text (Morris, p. 219, lines 9 and 15) and on two others *werod* is actually replaced by *hēap* (Morris, p. 219, lines 21 and 26). In the first two a gloss *oðer had* is also included, but in the others *hēap* stands alone. Stanley proposed that *hapes* (Morris, p. 219, line 15) probably represents a "very bad spelling" for *hadas*, "The Treatment of Late . . . Old English," p. 348. However, there seems no good semantic reason for taking this as a scribal error. The text has *hapes* at Morris, p. 219, lines 9 and 21, *hape* at p. 219, line 26, and *heapes* as a gloss at p. 221, line 5. It is true that the MED lists the Vespasian text as including the only occurrence of *hēp* meaning a 'rank of angels', but it is found in Old English (cf. in Ælfric: Thorpe I, p. 342, line 22) and should not be seen as that unusual.

52. *Cursor Mundi*, ed. R. Morris, 5 vols., EETS OS 57, 59, 62, 66, 68 (1874–78). This group of texts is usually dated from the last quarter of the 13th century: see, for instance, Dickins and Wilson, *Early Middle English Texts*, p. 114.

53. Cf. Stanley, "The Treatment of Late . . . Old English," p. 348.

54. Morris, p. 229, line 25.

55. This again suggests the possibility that the Vespasian copyist was an old man whose idiolect had its roots in language at the end of the currency of Old English.

56. Thorpe I, p. 10, lines 16 and 21 (R, 4v, lines 4 and 10) at Morris, p. 219, lines 16 and 22.

57. The phrase *to wlitegum engla gecynde* (Thorpe I, p. 12, line 14; R, 5r, line 17) is replaced by *to meren anglen* (Morris, p. 221, line 10), and this seems to be a simplification based upon both a misunderstanding of the complex grammar of the original and a distrust of the adjective *wlitig*, as seen elsewhere.

58. The text is dated from "the first quarter of the thirteenth century": *Seinte Katherine*, ed. d'Ardenne and Dobson, p. xxxviii.

59. Thorpe I, p. 12, lines 32, 34, 35–36 (R, fol. 5v, lines 13, 14, 16–17), Thorpe I, p. 16, line 34 (CUL Gg.3.28, fol. 4v, line 24), Thorpe I, p. 18, line 13 (CUL Gg.3.28, fol. 5r, line 4) at Morris, p. 221, lines 20, 21, 23, and p. 223, lines 20, 32.

60. Thorpe I, p. 12, lines 4–5 (R, fol. 5r, line 7) at Morris, p. 221, line 2. The spelling *préde* is actually used in the Vespasian homily and this would seem to show both Kentish and late influence. See A. Campbell, *Old English Grammar* (Oxford, 1959), § 567, n. 4. For further background information concerning this interesting loan-word see W. Hofstetter, "Der Erstbeleg von AE. *Pryte/Pryde*," *Anglia*, 97 (1979), 172–75.

61. See *Twelfth-Century Homilies in MS. Bodley 343*, ed. A. O. Belfour, EETS OS 137 (1909; rpt. 1962). Ker dated the manuscript "s.xii^{2}"; *Catalogue*, p. 368.

62. Thorpe I, p. 24, line 6 (R, fol. 7v, line 8) at Morris, p. 227, line 14.

63. Thorpe I, p. 24, lines 16 and 19 (R, fol. 7v, lines 17 and 21) at Morris, p. 227, lines 20 and 23.

64. Thorpe I, p. 24, line 5 (R, fol. 7v, line 6) at Morris, p. 227, line 12. Unlike the other synonyms used by the Vespasian copyist, *mægiecynn* has no recorded occurrence in Old English but is exclusively found in Middle English.

65. Stanley noted a further modernizing replacement: *ȝefestnéde* for *getrymde* (Thorpe I, p. 12, line 7 [R, fol. 5r, line 10] at Morris, p. 221, line 4). Again Old English *getrymman* was becoming obsolete at the time of the Vespasian copy and was consequently replaced. See Stanley, "The Treatment of Late . . . Old English," pp. 346–47.

66. However, Bodley 343 shares the omission of *wlitig* at Morris, p. 219, line 16 (cf. Bodley 343, 1r, line 18).

67. Thorpe I, p. 10, lines 12, 14, 15 (R, fol. 4r, line 25, 4v, lines 2 and 3), Thorpe I, p. 12, line 34 (R, fol. 5v, line 15), Thorpe I, p. 26, lines 5 and 6 (R, fol. 8r, lines 18 and 19) at Morris, p. 219, lines 9, 14, 16, p. 221, line 21, and p. 229, lines 2, 3. Since *beoð* is used for the present indicative in the Vespasian homily, where Royal has *sind-sindon*, *weorðan* is used to express a future sense, where Royal used *beon*: thus where Royal has *byst* (Thorpe I, p. 14, line 1 [R, fol. 5v, line 18]), Vespasian reads *wurst* (Morris, p. 221, line 24). However, these features are not exclusive to the Vespasian version of *De Initio Creaturae*; the use of *beoð* rather than *sind-sindon* is also found in Bodley 343 and other late copies.

68. Thorpe I, p. 18, line 9 (CUL Gg.3.28, fol. 5r, line 2), Thorpe I, p. 22, line 22 (R, fol. 7r, line 12), Thorpe I p. 26, line 14 (R, fol. 8v, line 2) at Morris, p. 223, line 29, p. 227, line 2, and p. 229, line 10.

69. Thorpe I, p. 22, line 26 (R, fol. 7r, line 16), Thorpe I, p. 24, line 3 (R, fol. 7v, line 4), Thorpe I, p. 28, line 7 (R, fol. 9r, line 7) at Morris, p. 227, lines 4, 11, and p. 229, line 33; omitted: Morris, p. 229, line 32 (Thorpe I, p. 28, line 6 [R, fol. 9r, line 5]). The Old English *ge-* prefix is also regularly dropped: *brohte* (Morris, p. 221, line 20); *hyrsumnesse* (p. 221, line 29); *wircan* (p. 221, line 35); *hersamnisse* (p. 223, line 15); *ęteð* (p. 223, line 24); *ęat* (p. 223, line 29); *æt* (p. 223, line 30); *halden* (p. 225, line 13); *timbringe* (p. 227, line 4); *sceafte* (p. 231, line 1); and past participle *ʒéarcod* (p. 221, line 1). However, *ʒeworhta* (Morris, p. 225, line 1) corresponds to *worhte* in earlier copies (i.e., CUL Gg.3.28, fol. 5r, line 8).

70. Since the homily lacks a heading in Vespasian A.xxii and has a new opening, it is possible that the copyist did not know that the piece was originally by Ælfric, or indeed part of the *Catholic Homilies* set. This might help explain the freedom of his handling of the text.

71. However, P. A. M. Clemoes has suggested a relationship with Oxford, Bodleian Library, Bodley 342 (s.xi^{in}–xi^{med}), another Rochester manuscript: "Ælfric's *Catholic Homilies*," p. xcix. Clemoes noted that Bodley 342 shared variant *heofonlican-hefonlice* with the Vespasian text (Morris, p. 227, line 20) compared with the usual reading *healican-healice* (Thorpe I, p. 24, line 15 [R, 7v, line 17]) and cited this as evidence for a common line of transmission (see the stemma diagram, p. xcvi). Although he could find no textual evidence for a similar relationship between Bodley 342 and the Vespasian version of the Fourth Sunday after Pentecost homily, he proposed a connection on the grounds of the relationship between the two versions of *De Initio*

Creaturae (pp. ci–cii). Given the considerable differences between the Bodley 342 and Vespasian versions of these texts, such connections are, at best, tenuous. Clearly the Vespasian text is directly linked to Ælfric's original, but by which path of dissemination is not clear. For a full account of the homiletic manuscripts produced in the Rochester scriptorium see Mary P. Richards, *Texts and Their Traditions in the Medieval Library of Rochester Cathedral Priory*, Transactions of the American Philosophical Society 78.3 (Philadelphia, 1988).

72. Since this section's analytical precepts differ somewhat from those to be found in the above, we have thought it better to arrange the citations in the following manner: citations from Morris, then citations from either R or CUL Gg.3.28, then from any other manuscript of the homily cited. In notes, reference is therefore made first to Morris, then to the manuscripts, and finally to Thorpe.

73. See Richards, "MS Cotton Vespasian A. XXII," pp. 97–98.

74. 'One wrote as one spoke'. See K. Luick, *Historische Grammatik der englischen Sprache* (Leipzig, 1921–40), § 27. This assumption has recently been discussed in considerable depth: see E. G. Stanley, "Karl Luick's 'Man schrieb wie man sprach' and English Historical Philology," in *Luick Revisited*, ed. D. Kastovsky and G. Bauer in collaboration with J. Fisiak (Tübingen, 1988), pp. 311–34.

75. For a discussion of the "standard" form of Old English see H. Gneuss, "The Origin of Standard Old English and Æthelwold's School at Winchester," ASE, 1 (1972), 63–83. With particular reference to the Winchester School see W. Hofstetter, *Winchester und der spätaltenglische Sprachgebrauch* (Munich, 1987), "Winchester and the Standardization of Old English Vocabulary," ASE, 17 (1988), 139–61.

76. See R. Jordan, *Handbook of Middle English Grammar: Phonology*, 3rd ed., ed. and tr. E. J. Cook, Janua Linguarum, Series Practica 218 (Paris, 1974), § 44.

77. As Pope has pointed out in connection with other Ælfric homilies, "Among the various manuscripts there is indeed some deviation, but what is remarkable is the degree to which, in the course of the eleventh century, the conventions of spelling remained constant. Even manuscripts of the twelfth century, thanks in part to the conservatism of the scribes, show fewer departures from the earlier standard than might be expected"; *Homilies of Ælfric: A Supplementary Collection*, ed. J. C. Pope, 2 vols., EETS OS 259, 260 (1967–68), vol. I, p. 177.

78. Morris, p. 221, line 28.

79. Fol. 4r, line 11: Thorpe I, p. 14, lines 9–10.

80. Morris, p. 217, lines 4–5.

81. Ibid., line 9.

82. It should be noted that the two Vespasian homilies not related to Ælfric also include this alternation between <a> and <o> for OE [ɑ:]. For example, where <a> has been retained: "and to mine *fa* ȝebuȝon" (*An Bispel*, Morris, p. 233, line 3), "Þer for sede se *hali* iob" (*Induite Uos Armatura Dei*, Morris, p. 243, lines 4–5); and where <o> is employed: "Æer þanne we mid ure friende toðe mete *go*" (*An Bispel*, Morris, p. 231, line 28), "s[t]range bieð þes *ifo*" (*Induite Uos Armatura Dei*, Morris, p. 243, lines 13–14). This might suggest that this "sound-change" is actually in the process of taking place, and that [ɑ̄] and [ǭ] are free phonemic variants. However, if these pieces have a history in whole or part before the present manuscript, it seems most likely that it is the scribe who is unconsciously changing some of the forms to suit his own pronunciation.

83. See E. G. Stanley, "The Date of Laȝamon's *Brut*," *Notes and Queries*, 213 (1968), 85–88, "Laȝamon's Antiquarian Sentiments," *Medium Ævum*, 29 (1969), 161–72, "Karl Luick's 'Man schrieb wie man sprach,'" pp. 327–28; G. Jack, "Archaizing in the Nero Version of the *Ancrene Wisse,*" *Neuphilologische Mitteilungen*, 80 (1979), 325–26.

84. For the situation in Old English see A. Campbell, chs. 11 and 12, and B. Mitchell, *Old English Syntax*, 2 vols. (Oxford, 1985), §§ 1345–79. For a discussion of the breakdown in the distinction and differentiation between cases, and the rise of a complementary extension (particularly in the case of the "dative") in the use of prepositions in the early Middle English period, see T. F. Mustanoja, *A Middle English Syntax*, vol. 1 (Helsinki, 1960), pp. 94–96.

85. Morris, p. 225, line 8; this is consistent with earlier copies, cf. "mid mys-lic*um* leahtr*um*" (R, fol. 6r, lines 24–25) and Thorpe I, p. 20, lines 22–23.

86. Morris, p. 227, line 28; see also "gelyfde his word*um*" (R, fol. 8r, line 2) and Thorpe I, p. 25, line 26.

87. Morris, p. 223, line 25.

88. Fol. 4r, lines 24–25: Thorpe I, p. 14, lines 29–30.

89. Fol. 2r, line 7.

90. Morris, p. 223, line 25.

91. Fol. 4v, line 28: Thorpe I, p. 18, line 5.

92. Morris, p. 229, lines 7–8.

93. Fol. 8r, lines 23–25: Thorpe I, p. 26, lines 10–11.

94. Morris, p. 229, line 10.

95. Fol. 8v, line 2: Thorpe I, p. 26, lines 13–14. These last two examples may be seen as part of what Jones calls the "GIVE" phrase, where either indirect or direct object analyses could be inferred from the evidence presented (see C. Jones, "Determiners and Case-Marking in Middle English: A Localist Approach," *Lingua*, 59 (1983), 331–43, in particular at pp. 337–40).

96. As can be seen by the fact that these pronouns are the ones which have survived with ostensibly "dative case" markings into Modern English.

97. Morris, p. 219, line 28.

98. Fol. 4v, lines 19–20: Thorpe I, p. 10, line 29.

99. Morris, p. 227, line 32.

100. Fol. 8r, line 7: Thorpe I, p. 24, lines 30–31. Note the fact that, on this occasion, Vespasian has added a non-historical, but nonetheless functionally useful, <-e> to *f-der*. For this noun's Old English paradigm see Campbell, § 629.

101. Morris, p. 227, lines 20–21.

102. Fol. 7v, line 18: Thorpe I, p. 24, line 17.

103. It does seem unlikely that the Children of Israel should have a single collective foot.

104. See Campbell, § 620, for the paradigm of this noun.

105. Morris, p. 223, lines 34–35.

106. Fol. 5r, line 6: Thorpe I, p. 18, lines 15–16.

107. Morris suggests as much (p. 222), but this goes against the idea that it was a single act of disobedience which caused the Fall of Man.

108. See R. M. Millar, "Ambiguity in Function: Old English 'þæt' and the Demonstrative Systems of Laȝamon's 'Brut'," *Neuphilologische Mitteilungen*, 95 (1994), 415–32, "Ambiguity in Ending and Form: 'Reinterpretation' in the Demonstrative Systems of Laȝamon's 'Brut,'" *Neuphilologische Mitteilungen*, 96 (1995), 145–68, and "Paradigm Fissure: 'Ambiguity' in the Simple Demonstrative Paradigm in the Late Old English and Early Middle English Periods" (forthcoming), for a consideration of the forms discussed below in the early Middle English period.

109. See Campbell, § 708.

110. For a diagrammatic consideration and analysis of the spread of this form over a wide historical and dialectal area see C. Jones, "Grammatical Gender in Late Old English and Early Middle English," B.Litt. Diss. Glasgow Univ. 1964, pp. 28, 101, 165–66, "The Functional Motivation of Linguistic Change," *English Studies*, 48 (1967), 97–111, at p. 110, "The Grammatical Category of Gender in Early Middle English," *English Studies*, 48 (1967), 289–305, at pp. 292, 294, and *Grammatical Gender in English 950–1250* (New York, 1988), p. 25. See U. Lindelöf, "Die Sprache des Rituals von Durham," Diss. Helsingfors (Helsinki) Univ. 1890 for a discussion of this phenomenon in late Northumbrian Old English.

111. N. von Glahn, "Zur Geschichte des grammatischen Geschlects im Mittelenglischen," *Anglistische Forschungen*, 53 (1918) describes the situation in Vespasian (pp. 56–58) as well as elsewhere in texts from the southeast of England in the period (pp. 48, 60–98). <S> forms are still realized in texts from Kent as late as the 14th-century *Ayenbite of Inwyt*, although they are confined to relative collocations such as *ze þet* and *zy þet* (see P. Gradon, *Dan Michel's Ayenbite of Inwyt*, vol. 2, *Introduction,*

Notes and Glossary, EETS OS 278 [1979], p. 80, n. 1). See M. L. Samuels, *Linguistic Evolution with Special Reference to English* (Cambridge, 1972), pp. 86–87, for one possible explanation for this retention.

112. Morris, p. 221, line 9.

113. Fol. 5r, lines 15–16: Thorpe I, p. 12, lines 12–13.

114. See Jones, "Grammatical Category," p. 298, n. 25.

115. Morris, p. 219, line 8.

116. Fol. 4r, lines 21–22: Thorpe I, p. 10, lines 9–10.

117. The fact that this "ending environment" is under attack at this time can be seen in the variation between Royal *þ-m*—variant forms of Old English *þæm*—and Vespasian *þ-ne*—variant forms of Old English *þone*. This can be seen clearly with the examples "binnon *þane* arce" (Morris, p. 225, line 25), "binnan *þæm* arce" (R, 6v, line 20: Thorpe I, p. 22, lines 1–2). It is true that all dictionaries of Old English say that *binnan* triggered both "dative" and "accusative" case-usage, so that we may have here merely a difference in personal realization patterns. But the evidence of A. di Paolo Healey and R. L. Venezky, *A Microfiche Concordance to Old English* (Toronto, 1980, rpt. with corrections 1985) suggests that what "accusative" usage there is, is far less common than "dative" usage.

118. Even if external evidence does tend to suggest that it is in just such environments that this particular ending began to break down. See D. Minkova, "Early Middle English Metre Elision and Schwa Deletion," in *English Historical Linguistics: Studies in Development*, ed. N. F. Blake and C. Jones, CECTAL [Centre for English Cultural Traditions and Language] Conference Papers Series, 3 (Sheffield, 1984), pp. 56–66.

119. This has always been the theory to which most authorities have subscribed, to the extent that it is often assumed without being discussed. Of course it is true that the *the* form will eventually become the sole form, undeclined in all environments, but in the period when the inherited demonstratival systems were beginning to break down this development was seriously retarded in certain functional environments—particularly where the semantic environment demanded more "case-heavy" realizations. It is one of the sad truths of historical morphological studies that it is actually easier

to analyze forms which are no longer current in the language than those which have survived. As an interesting side-note, *þā* forms are also used where we would expect *þ-n*: for example, "of *þā* cynn" (Morris, p. 227, line 17) compared with "of *þam* cynne" (R, 7v, line 13: Thorpe I, p. 24, line 10). It is possible that this particular problem has been caused merely by the omission of a nasal marker (von Glahn, pp. 48–50, discussed just such a development), but if it is to be seen as a genuine development it points further to the conclusion that here *þā* and *þe* are, in practice, variants.

120. Fol. 5r, line 1: Thorpe I, p. 18, line 8.

121. Morris, p. 223, line 30.

122. The opposing view, that *þe* in possessive contexts represents merely the substitution of an undeclined form for a declined is upheld by many authorities on the subject, among them O. Diehn, "Die Pronomina im Frühmittelenglischen," in *Kieler Studien zur englischen Philologie*, vol. 1 (Heidelberg, 1901), p. 65, and O. Seidler, "Die Flexion des englischen einfachen Demonstrativpronomens in der Übergangzeit 1000–1200," Diss. Jena Univ. 1901, pp. 14–18.

123. The semantic development of *that* over the historical continuum is something of a problematic area, mainly because a great deal of evidence from the late Old and early Middle English period has been judged by modern writers on the subject by modern semantic standards. See Millar, "Ambiguity in Function," pp. 421–25, for a discussion of this problem.

124. Morris, p. 229, line 17.

125. Fol. 8v, lines 9–10: Thorpe I, p. 26, line 21.

126. For instance, Vespasian "*se* eorðe" (Morris, p. 223, line 34) corresponds to "*seo* eorðe" in CUL Gg.3.28 (5r, line 6: Thorpe I, p. 18, lines 15–16). For examples of this confusion in the *Peterborough Chronicle* (such as *seo wurðfulle Æþelred* [675]), see C. Clark, *The Peterborough Chronicle 1070–1154*, 2nd ed. (Oxford, 1970), pp. lix–lxi. For further discussion see Diehn, p. 65, Seidler, p. 10, Jones, "Grammatical Gender," p. 151, Jones, "Determiners and Case-Marking," p. 330, and R. M. Millar, "Some Patterns in the Non-Historical Demonstrative Usage of the *Peterborough Chronicle* Annals 1070–1127," *Notes and Queries*, 242 (1997), 161–64. See von Glahn,

p. 48, for a discussion of this problematic realization in the Middle Kentish version of the West Saxon Gospels.

127. The scribe has been described as "Anglo-Norman" (Richards, "MS Cotton Vespasian A. XXII," p. 97). However, while the date and provenance of the manuscript might support this proposition, the presence of *wyn* and the striking absence of any Anglo-Norman features in the orthography of the four homilies is surprising if the scribe was not English.

128. We should like to thank Prof. Malcolm Godden for reading this essay prior to publication.

INDEX

Note: A range of page numbers followed by "passim" indicates an entire chapter. Page numbers in *italics* refer to figures.